387.709

DOYLE, NEVILLE

FROM SEA-EAGLE TO FLAMINGO

8/91 £14-95

Please renew/return this item by the last date shown.

So that your telephone call is charged at local rate, please call the numbers as set out below:

	From Area codes 01923 or 0208:	From the rest of Herts:
Renewals:	01923 471373	01438 737373
Enquiries:	01923 471333	01438 737333
Minicom:	01923 471599	01438 737599

L32b

FROM SEA-EAGLE TO FLAMINGO

Channel Island Airlines 1923–1939

Neville Doyle

Published in 1991 by
The Self Publishing Association Ltd
Lloyds Bank Chambers,
Upton-upon-Severn, Worcs
A MEMBER OF

in conjunction with
NEVILLE DOYLE
Rugby, Warks.

British Library Cataloguing in Publication Data
Doyle, Neville
   From sea-eagle to flamingo.
   1. Great Britain. Civil aviation, to 1984
   I. Title
   387.70941

ISBN 1 85421 103 X

Front cover: From "The Graphic" of 20.10.1923 by permission of the British Library
Back cover: The D.H. "Flamingo" (R.A.F. Museum)

Designed and Produced by The Self Publishing Association Ltd
Printed and Bound in Great Britain by Devonshire Press Ltd, Torquay.

CONTENTS

Page

To the airmen who pioneered the air-routes
to the Channel Islands

ACKNOWLEDGEMENTS

I owe my interest in Channel Islands aviation to the enthusiastic help given on my visit to Jersey by the late Jack Beuzeval, the photographic staff of the Jersey Evening Post, Alastair Layzell, the others. Subsequently, J. Edouard Slade, Diploma of the University of Rennes F.R.G.S. ARAeS. etc., and pioneer historian of Jersey aviation, volunteered his assistance and has since proved a prodigious source of valued information. In Guernsey Roger Sweet has been an unfailing ally, and on Alderney Jim Wallin has kept me in touch.

My thanks, also, to Colin Bailey and Paul Soens, the late Lord Balfour of Inchrye, Captain Cecil Bebb, Mrs Colin Bragg (the former Wilma Le Cocq), A. Bridle (Guernsey Airport Director), Mrs. Emily Diddams, Miss Betty Ewens (D.H. Museum), D. Gorin (Dinard Airport Commandant), Leslie Harrington, O.B.E., John Herbert, M.B.E., Frank Hotton, Miss Brenda Jacob, David Judd, John King, Mrs. Phyllis Mackenzie, Senator the Rev. Peter Manton, Nigel Overton (Southampton Museum), Arthur Robert, Tony Richardson (Southampton Library), Leslie Strachan, Carel Toms, John Tustin, R.A.R. Wilson, V.R.D. (British Airways archives), and Mrs. Joan Whitby (of the Thurgood family).

I am most grateful to British Aerospace, The Pearson Group, Michelin Tyre Plc., Southampton Corporation, Ward, Lock Ltd., and the librarians, archivists and staff of The British Library, Exeter Central Library, Guille-Allès Library, Portsmouth Central Library, The Public Record Office, The Royal Aeronautical Society, The R.A.F. Museum, Rugby Library, The Science Museum Library, The Société Jersiaise, *The Southern Evening Echo*, The States of Jersey Library, and the West Sussex Record Office.

For permission to use material from their publications I thank the editors of the *Guernsey Evening Press*, the *Jersey Evening Post*, *Aeroplane Monthly*, *Flight International*, *The Journal of Croydon Airport Society*, and Group Captain J.W. Tritton, Clerk to the *Guild of Air Pilots and Navigators*.

And last but not least I would like to thank my hard-working research assistant, my wife Pat.

Neville Doyle,
C.Eng. MIMechE, ARAeS.

FOREWORD

The origins of this book date back to the many hours of my youth idled away on the edge of our local aerodrome hopefully awaiting the arrival of some unusual aircraft as a relief from the monotonous ups and downs of the Club Avro. From time to time perhaps a Hillman's Dragon or a Midland and Scottish Fox Moth might put in an appearance, but there were others; some carried the signal red and green of Railway Air Services, others wore the black and white of the "West Coast", and there were names like Olley, Crilly, Northern & Scottish, and K.L.M., whose sturdy Fokker tri-motors were black and blue. On very rare occasions, one of the stately strut-encumbered biplanes of the Imperial Airways might be spotted bravely defying the law of gravity.

At the age of 16 I left school and, as a temporary measure so I thought, joined Blackpool & West Coast Air Services, Ltd. at Speke Airport, near Liverpool. Our offices consisted of two garden sheds joined end-to-end by some flimsy connection like two coaches of a corridor train, with the manager occupying the inner section and his trio of minions the outer. The manager was Mr Clifton Smith, formerly the secretary of the Guernsey Aero Club, and a nicer "boss" would be very hard to find. We weighed the passengers, filled in the load-sheets, checked the fuel, loaded the mail, freight and newspapers, made out the radio messages, and dispatched the plane. In between we answered the 'phone, took bookings, laboriously typed out letters, and generally made ourselves useful. Our first plane left at 8 am and our last one landed at about 8 pm so we took early and late turns, and one of us covered the Sunday services. Our "terminal building" was an old red sandstone farm-house, and "control" was in a large attic affair in the roof. Here sat Captain Andrews with a fearsome scowl of concentration on his face as he prodded away with two fingers at the defenceless teleprinter. A rough road led to another farm on the opposite side of the field and red Verey lights had to be fired if the butcher's boy on his delivery bike was caught mid-field by unexpected aircraft.

My job turned out to be a temporary measure after all because "West Coast" stopped operating in 1937 and, like Mr Smith, I had to leave. However, undeterred I soon bounced back this time as the Speke representative of Irish Sea Airways, who were planning a Croydon-Dublin service, via Liverpool. This service never got off the ground so my duties were correspondingly light and I was able to do a fair amount of work on an old Avro Avian, for which efforts I was promised a few flying lessons if the hoped for c. of a. was ever obtained. In addition to the occasional D.H.86 of our Croydon-Bristol-Dublin service diverted to Speke because of bad weather at Baldonnel, (with a plane-load of disgruntled passengers who thought they were in Ireland), I looked after any Olley machine, passing through, or coming for a day's joy-riding, but I was rather concerned one day by the arrival of an Olley Rapide to collect a foreign seaman who had contracted leprosy. Neither the pilot nor his operator looked too happy about it, but as the departure was planned for some time like 4 am Captain Andrews very kindly offered to see it off for me, which offer I gladly accepted.

Early in 1939, I was lured by the then very handsome sum of £2 per week to join Isle of Man Air Services, Ltd., and take over their very large contract for army co-operation flying which covered the North-West of England. This work had developed into a big business and was a godsend to the struggling firms of the day. Flying took place by day and by night with one or more aircraft on fixed courses at fixed heights flying to and fro for the benefit of our anti-aircraft defences. At night they often flew without lights and if more than one aircraft was on the same course they flew at different heights, or so it was intended. The main problem was to find planes and pilots and every Saturday night in the summer of 1939 aircraft left Croydon to go on course 200 miles to the north-west with other aircraft and flew until 2 am before returning direct to Croydon. At one stage, to avoid disappointing our customers, usually a regiment of the T.A. with guns or searchlights, I allowed an 'A' licence pilot to fly for us in a very small aircraft with an engine more suitable for a motor-bike, and there were no complaints from the army, but my misdeeds were reported to the Air Ministry. Many were the adventures of the army co-op pilots, but the outbreak of the war called a halt, and as one pilot and part-owner of his machine said: "Just as we were beginning to earn a bit of money they have to start a . . . war!" (He was shot down 18.8.1940)

Waiting for R.A.F. air-crew standards to drop to my level I sidled into industry and by the summer of 1940 I was working in South-East London at Woolwich Arsenal, just in time for the big raid of September 7th and the "Blitz". In 1941 I was accepted for flying duties as a "special observer" to operate the radar in a night-fighter, but it was eighteen months before I could extricate myself from the Ministry of Supply, by which time I had been remustered to "navigator" under the arrangements being made for our four-engined bombers. Almost at once I was sent for an overdue medical and much to my disgust they decided I was "unsuitable for high altitudes". Not wishing to be on the groundstaff I took my discharge and by a mild subterfuge managed to enlist in the Royal Navy as an ordinary seaman. My further adventures have little to do with aviation although when commissioned into the R.N.V.R., I did eventually perform the duties of navigator, but with an Admiralty-pattern sextant! I left the Navy in 1947 and returned to industry spending the last thirty years or so on steam turbine design.

Despite, or perhaps because of, my lack of contact with aviation in the post-war years I have never lost interest in the pre-war years, and especially the numerous small civil air-lines that came and went during that time. When I "shut up shop" in September, 1939 I kept a few souvenirs; the last issue of Bradshaw's International Air Guide, some company brochures, photographs, a small plastic notice from a crashed Rapide, and so on. Over the years, in a small way, I added to this collection, but as so little was written about the internal air-lines I decided, about twelve years ago, to compile my own history. Cheerfully I set out to read every copy of "Flight" and "The Aeroplane" from 1919 to 1939, and all the other magazines and books of, or dealing with, that period. Eventually I was reading local newspapers to fill in the gaps, either in London at the British Newspaper Library or on the spot, with visits to the local aerodromes, or their sites and this, in 1983, took me to Jersey. Here everything went so well; the Jersey papers of the pre-war days gave the local air-lines excellent coverage, the *Jersey Evening Post* invited me to see all their old photographic plates of aircraft, and enlarged and printed those I asked for whilst I waited. I was taken to the Channel T.V. Studios and given a private showing of their documentary on pre-war Jersey Airways, and I was introduced to people who had worked on the beach landing ground for Jersey Airways. I was so pleased with my week in Jersey that on the way home I decided to concentrate all my efforts on the Channel Islands and, hopefully, produce at least one part of my project complete in itself. Naturally my Jersey trip was followed by equally enjoyable excursions to Guernsey and Alderney, and the English airports used by Channel Islands air-lines, as well as the French airports of Le Bourget (Paris), Dinard and Rennes. The book is now finished and whatever its defects I think I can claim that it has been very thoroughly researched, and the development of the Channel Islands air-lines shown against the background of contemporary events on the other side of the Channel with which, in many ways, they were involved.

It is hoped that this book will be of interest to the general reader, especially in the Channel Islands, as well as to students of air transport history. It is not a highly technical work but, for completeness, a description of all aircraft in regular use is given in Appendix 1, whilst the aerodromes are described in Appendix 2.

Despite the considerable advantages of the 24 hour clock, particularly for time-tables, it is still not normal practice for the average person, and its use has been sparing. In fact, during the period of this book there was so little flying outside normal "office hours" that, in many cases, a.m. and p.m. have been omitted as unnecessary.

Monetary transactions are expressed in terms of pounds, shillings and pence, the legal tender of the brief age chronicled by this record of aviation history. The triple division of currency units will still be remembered by the older generation, together with such expressions as "penny a mile", or "fifty bob", but for the younger generation the following notes explain the system:- The pound (£) was divided into 20 shillings (s) and each shilling into 12 pence (d), usually written thus:- Four pounds, ten shillings and sixpence or £4. 10. 6d. In this notation the max. no. of shillings was 19 and the max. no. of pence was 11, but values were sometimes given in just shillings and pence so that £4. 10. 6d. became ninety shillings and sixpence, written 90/6d. As there were 20 shillings to the pound two shillings were equal to 0.10 of a pound or ten new pence, hence:-

Conversion Table Old shillings to new pence

/-	np	/-	np
1	5	6	30
2	10	7	35
3	15	8	40
4	20	9	45
5	25	10	50

or shillings x 5 equals new pence

12 old pence equalled 5 new pence therefore one old penny was equal to 0.4167 of a new penny, or half a new penny, approx.

To convert today's pound to its September, 1939 value divide by a factor of 25 (approximately)

In the years before 1914 anyone "indulging in aviation" was probably regarded as somewhat eccentric, but even amongst these Noel Pemberton Billing stood out. He was said to be "flamboyantly eccentric". A brilliant, but erratic character, every willing to try new ideas, and pursue them until the next flight of fancy sent him off in another direction. This lack of concentration and singleness of purpose prevented his achieving any notable success in his many enterprises. During 1903 he was building man-carrying kites, and by 1905 designing a petrol engine to power them.

Later he built aircraft, and in 1908 founded a magazine called *Aerocraft*, but in 1909 he turned to other things, and it was 1913 before he was back in aviation with the opening of a factory on the site of an old coal wharf near the Itchen ferry at Woolston, Southampton. On 27.6.14. Pemberton-Billing, Ltd. was registered with a capital of £20,000, and set out to build "Supermarines" or "aeroplanes essentially designed for the navigation of the sea", with the motto "Not an aeroplane which floats, but a seaworthy boat which flies". By the outbreak of war the P.B.7 was under construction; a flying-boat with jettisonable wings, the hull being able to proceed independently as a motor-boat with the engine power transferred to a ship's screw in the stern, but it was never completed, and the prototype P.B.9 single-seater scout rushed out in six days and ten hours. It went to the R.N.A.S. as did twenty P.B.25's in 1916, but no Pemberton Billing design was selected for large-scale production and they were obliged to build aircraft to other people's designs, including the A.D. flying-boat for the Air Department of the Admiralty. (See Appendix 1A) This was a two-seater biplane with a 150/200 h.p. engine driving a pusher propeller. However, Pemberton Billing joined the R.N.V.R. at the beginning of the war and by 1916 was a Squadron-Commander in the R.N.A.S., but he resigned his commission and stood for Parliament as its first independent "Air Member" to campaign against incompetence in the procurement of aircraft. To divest himself of all pecuniary interest in aircraft production he sold out to his colleague, Hubert Scott-Paine, who renamed the enterprise the Supermarine Aviation Works Ltd. Pemberton Billing failed to win Mile End, but was successful at his second attempt and represented East Hertfordshire.

An advertisement from a Southampton Docks Magazine of September, 1923.

(From the Scrap-book of Mr. George Cozens now in the Southampton Library)

Burly, red-headed Hubert Scott-Paine was a forceful character of great energy, and a keen businessman with a flair for publicity. Born in Shoreham in 1891, he had learned to fly in 1910. Although the service career of the A.D. flying-boat had been in no way remarkable, ten were bought back by Supermarine in 1919 and converted to civilian use as the Supermarine Channel (See Appendix 1A) with a 160 hp engine and accommodation for three passengers. The ending of the war and the immediate cancellation of orders brought major problems, to the rapidly-swollen aircraft industry. By October 1918, British air power was the strongest in the world, with 27,906 officers, 263,842 other ranks, 22,171 aircraft, 37,702 engines, and a commensurate aircraft industry. Demand ceased overnight, and there was no market for civilian machines. Huge stocks of unwanted aircraft were stored in depots around the country, and civil aviation was not even legal until May 1, 1919, when flights were restricted to Britain, although flying, in Service type aircraft, had been permitted at Easter – within three miles of the airfield! Flights between Hounslow and Le Bourget were allowed in the week of the Peace Celebrations (July 14 – 20), and regular flying between England and France was permitted from August 25, 1919.

There were few doubts about the future prospects of aviation, but could the manufacturers survive until this golden future arrived? Some were optimistic, especially if their designs resembled contemporary ideas of civil aircraft, and some were planning air routes. Others, as a stop-gap, fell back on joy-riding and taxi services, mainly to make money, but hopefully to encourage the public to accept flying as a normal mode of transport. In this joy-riding they were joined by a multitude of ex-service pilots in war-surplus machines. The Avro 504K was one of the best joy-riding aircraft and the makers formed the Avro Transport Company to fly them, and its numerous variants, from bases in different parts of the country, inaugurating, in the process, Britain's first regular passenger air service on May 26, 1919 which was between Manchester and Blackpool. It ran every weekday until September 30 using Avros modified by the removal of the dual-controls to provide seating for two passengers, and called at Southport. Early in 1919 the Air Ministry had laid down suggested air routes over Britain using existing aerodromes, and although a purely academic exercise some disappointment was expressed in Blackpool at not being on one of these "air routes". It is quite possible that Avro's John Lord offered to inaugurate a Manchester-Blackpool service and put Blackpool on the "air route" map as part of their successful bid for the sole rights to joy-riding from Blackpool's sandy shore in the face of strong competition from Sopwith. It is noticeable that Avro made no other attempts to start regular services if the short-lived daily positioning flight between Swansea and Llanwrtydd Wells and the twelve newspaper flights from Windermere to Douglas Bay flown by Howard Pixton in an Avro seaplane are discounted. Various "regular air services" are claimed to have been operated about this time. but most were just positioning flights for joy-riding, or trips to local towns or places of interest during a week or so of joy-riding. In one or two cases a firm with a number of aircraft to move from one aerodrome to another offered seats to the public.

The Avro Transport Company operated along the South Coast from their "stations" at Brighton and Paignton, but there were plenty of "free-lance" pilots offering flights from a wide variety of sites, such as Ensbury

Park, Bournemouth, where Mr Etches, of the Bournemouth Aviation Company offered "Joy Rides in Avro and F.E. Machines . . . Flying Kit Provided . . ." for a mere 10/6d. or £1. 1s. 0d, whilst at week-ends there were "Joy Rides in Handley Page Bombers" at £2. 2s. 0d. for a 15 minute flight. Mr Etches made a charge for admission to his aerodrome and the Handley Page was a major attraction, supplemented by "stunts" performed by Avro and F.E. pilots. Between June 6 and August 18 a Handley Page 0/400 flew down to Bournemouth from Cricklewood every Friday, and returned from Ensbury Park at 11 am every Monday morning. With typical Handley Page canniness seats were offered to and from London at £5. 5s. 0d. a time, and this positioning flight for the week-end's joy-riding has been described as a "regular air service" although it was never intended as a serious competitor to the L.S.W.R.! Another aircraft manufacturer began joy-riding at Bournemouth on July 19 with: ". . . Sea flights from moorings off Bournemouth Pier. The Super Marine Aviation Works Company will send their latest four-seater Channel type flying boat, No 1710 (later G-EAEE), holding the Air Ministry's latest air worthiness certificate, which will be in (the) charge of Commander Bird, O.B.E., late R.N., assisted by Captain Horsey, late R.A.F. . . ." (49) Frequent flights were promised at £2. 2s. 0d., and by July 23 two flying-boats were at Bournemouth: ". . . A seaplane lies on either side of the Pier and passengers are conveyed to it in a small boat" (50) There were plans to extend operations to the Isle of Wight and other coastal towns, but Supermarine's main objective was to run services across the Channel, and even farther. On July 31 James Bird, the director of Supermarine handling air transport, wrote to the Controller-General of Civil Aviation: ". . . We understand . . . that the Ministry are making temporary arrangements with Holland for flying between Great Britain and Holland . . . very much obliged if you would advise us as to what these arrangements are . . . also . . . if you could give us any indication as to when it is likely that Civilian flying will be permitted between the English and the French coasts as we have already received numerous enquiries from passengers for the Channel Islands, Havre, Cherbourg, etc. . . ." (51)

At the end of July an Avro 504L seaplane of the Avro Transport Co. appeared at Ryde, and gave what the *I.O.W. Times* called "delightful flits over the Solent", followed by similar "flits" from other Isle of Wight resorts, to conclude at Cowes, where Supermarine joined in during "Regatta

Week" to allow people the opportunity of watching the racing from 1,000ft. On August 14 Supermarine started what they claimed was the "First Flying Boat Passenger Service in the World" from the slipway at Woolston with flights at two or three guineas to Bournemouth, Totland Bay, Cowes, Ryde, Southsea, and any other coastal town "until further notice". Machines could be hired by the hour, and there was an official inauguration on August 18 by the Mayors of Southampton and Winchester from the Royal Pier at Southampton. Evidently the "passenger service" was not intended to mean a regular air-line, but just a hire service, although the Bournemouth machine returned to Woolston every evening and from August 15 seats had been offered to Southampton in the evening and to Bournemouth in the morning at £4. 4s. 0d. single, £7. 7s. 0d. return, which could be regarded as a regular air service, of sorts. The first foreign civilian pilot to arrive after the war was Mr Etienne Poulet who landed his Caudron biplane at Hounslow on July 14, and the first commercial flight to France took place on July 15, when Jerry Shaw of Air Transport & Travel, Ltd. flew Colonel Pilkington, of the famous glass firm, from Hounslow to Le Bourget in a D.H.9. A.T. & T. had the honour of inaugurating the world's first international daily passenger service on August 25, when Bill Lawford made his well-known flight to Paris in a D.H.4a with his equally well-known cargo of one Press representative, (George Stevenson-Preece), several brace of grouse, and some tins of Devonshire cream. Handley Page followed on September 2 with an alternate day service to Paris, and on September 23 with a similar service to Brussels. During this period Commander Bird was pressing the Air Ministry to open Southampton as "the first Air Port in the World" for international flying-boat services, and to obtain approval from the French for the use of Le Havre as a Customs Sea Aerodrome. Writing from the French Ministry of War in Paris on September 22 General Duval said: ". . . I willingly give my consent to the landing of the British Seaplanes at Havre . . . This Port is the only one in the Channel which is suitable for this work, the only difficulty being that British Seaplanes will not find either shelter or fuel there . . ." (51) However, before the details of either "Sea Customs Aerodrome" could be settled there was a railway strike in which the cross-Channel steamers joined.

It began on September 27, and was thought to be a great opportunity for the struggling air transport concerns to show their worth, Avro's going so far as to employ sandwich-board men to carry placards through the streets of London saying "RAILWAY CRISIS – GO BY AIR – AVRO AEROPLANES ARE AT YOUR SERVICE". In the evening Commander Basil Hobbs, D.S.O., D.S.C., destroyer of the Zeppelin L43, flew a Channel loaded with copies of the *Football Echo* from Woolston to Bournemouth for delivery by a fleet of cars to the surrounding districts, and all the other companies with aircraft available were busy with newspapers, passengers, and urgent freight. On October 5 two Avro seaplanes left Southampton for the Channel Islands with copies of *Lloyd's Weekly News*, and although Alan Storey reached Jersey safely in G-EACC, Evans in G-EAFG came down off Alderney in fog and was wrecked on the breakwater of Braye harbour. The B.A.T. Company and the North Sea Aerial Navigation Company both started passenger air services (from London to Birmingham and Leeds to London, respectively), but the Air Ministry chartered their aircraft, with others, to operate a mail service for the G.P.O., which resulted in aircraft ranging from Avro 504's to Blackburn Kangaroos flying between Hounslow and Birmingham, Bristol, Manchester, Newcastle, and Glasgow at charges ranging from £20 to £70 per hour carrying ridiculously small amounts of mail (1 lb. ½oz. min. to 17 lb. 8½oz. max.) at an extra fee of 2/- per oz. On September 28 Supermarine started a passenger service between Southampton and Le Havre when, just after 5 pm, two Channels, piloted by Hobbs and Biard, each with two passengers and luggage, left Woolston and successfully reached Le Havre although separated by a storm on the way. Thereafter a daily service, at £25 return, was kept up until the end of the strike on October 5. It only ran for eight days, but has been put forward as the world's first international flying-boat service, and it has been suggested that some official encouragement should have been given to keep it going. In fact, even with the fare reduced by a subsidy it is doubtful whether any but the most enthusiastic and hardy would have chosen this mode of transport, especially during the winter, to judge by Henri Biard's own account. (52) The passenger accommodation was a cockpit for one in the bow, a cockpit for two behind this, and then the pilot's cockpit just forward of the wings and engine.

On September 30 there were two passengers for the crossing, one a naval officer, and the other, thought by Henri Biard to be a Swedish millionaire, was Albert Loewenstein, a Belgian, and more than likely a multi-millionaire. He was destined to become one of the so-called

"Mysteries of Flying" when he disappeared from his own private Fokker F.VII over the Channel in July, 1928. In addition to gale force winds it was bitterly cold, and in all the odd nooks and corners of the flying-boat hail was building up into lumps of ice. Hubert Scott-Paine ran out with a small bottle of rum which he thrust into Loewenstein's pocket "in case he felt cold"! They took off with the hail hitting them like "machine-gun bullets . . . icicles grew on our gloves and coats . . ." and after about half-an-hour the cold was deadly. Henri's hands and feet were numb, and the Belgian, in the cockpit immediately in front, in a similar state or worse, took a hearty swig from the bottle of rum, and then tried to hand it back to the pilot without looking behind him. The bottle tilted and all the rum ran out, which was bad enough, but caught by the slip-stream it was blown straight into Henri's face and eyes and they were literally flying blind. The Belgian was quiet for a while, but the hail: ". . . which was lashing at us . . . almost to draw blood . . ." became too much for him, and he produced a gold-handled umbrella which he attempted to open over his head! Had he succeeded it would have blown straight back into the propeller, with disastrous consequences, and Henri had no choice but to lean over and hit him on the head with the empty rum bottle. This kept him quiet for the rest of the trip, which took over five hours, and very sportingly, on their arrival the battered Belgian took Henri into the nearest hotel and bought him a drink. Nothing was said about the poor naval officer sitting in the bow, perhaps considered to be inured to the elements or, more than likely, had brought his own bottle of rum.

After the strike the Channels continued to fly from Woolston and Bournemouth, but demand gradually petered out with the onset of winter. There was no resumption the following year and joy-riding, in general, was left to a few hardy individuals, some of whom survived until 1939. By March, 1920 the proposals for a sea-drome at Southampton had been accepted by all concerned, but no attempt was made to initiate cross-Channel services from there, although the two companies flying from London to Paris were joined by a third on May 15, 1920, when Instone, a shipping company which had been using aircraft for its own convenience, began to accept passengers. Supermarine may have realised that the Channel flying-boat was not really suitable for all-the-year-round service in British waters and they now had a more rugged machine on the drawing-board. This was the Commercial Amphibian G-EAVE with a similar arrangement and wing span to the Channel but power increased to 350 hp and an all-up weight of 5,700 lbs. The two passengers had the comfort of a glazed cabin, but the life of this machine was brief, although a tractor development called the Seal II, renamed the Seagull in its production form, was accepted by the Fleet Air Arm and the Mark III version with almost the same max. weight, but both wings of equal 46' span to give a wing area of 593 sq. ft. had a 492 hp Napier Lion engine. From a later development, the Mark V, would evolve the famous Walrus of World War Two. (See Appendix 1A)

Financially, the situation was bleak and early in 1920 Supermarine had to borrow £20,000 from Lloyd's Bank. The arrival of the third company on the cross-Channel services from London had not helped matters and the heavy French subsidies to their air-lines made life difficult for the British. In March, 1920, during a debate on the Air Estimates, Winston Churchill uttered the oft-repeated words: ". . . Civil aviation must fly by itself; the Government cannot possibly hold it up in the air . . ." Churchill was both Air Minister and War Minister at the same time, but the Advisory Committee on Civil Aviation, in its Report of June, 1920 did recommend a subsidy, for certain approved routes, such as London to Brussels and Paris, and another approved route, such as England to Scandinavia:" . . . on which the possibilities of a service employing flying boats, of 'amphibian' machines, or a mixed service of sea and land aircraft, can be demonstrated." Trenchard, who was a member of this Committee opposed subsidies, and issued his own Minority Report. C. G. Grey, of *The Aeroplane* was also against subsidies, but the Committee could only make recommendations and had no power to put them into effect. By December, 1920 Air Transport & Travel was in serious trouble and had gone into liquidation, a fourth company, Air Post of Banks had come and gone, Instone's were just running "on demand" and Handley Page were making one or two trips per week. By the end of February, 1921 all of the British companies had ceased to operate, leaving the field free to the subsidised French. The prospect of the miserly sum voted for civil aviation being used to provide aerodromes, radio, and meteorological services for the French did bring about a change of heart, and just too late to avert the closing down of the Handley Page and Instone operations the Government managed to find £60,000 for direct assistance to British companies operating on approved routes during the financial year 1921—22.

19

Compared with this £60,000 it was proposed in the Air Estimates of 1921—22 to spend £670,000 on R.A.F. aerodromes in Egypt, and Churchill wanted to spend £17,000,000 on service aviation and only £1,000,000 on civil aviation. There was a considerable outcry in the Press, and *The Times* complained bitterly about 17 million going on Air Marshal and Air Vice-Marshals, "on the air-chaplains, air-doctors, air-matrons, air-cadet schools (with the professors of English), on the barracks and stores, on the bill-posting and accountancy and on all the other appurtenances" against only one million on the civil side. Handley Page and Instone were soon revived and their services resumed on March 19 and 21 respectively. They were joined in 1922 by the Daimler Airway, owned by B.S.A., who had taken over the assets of The Aircraft Manufacturing Co. Ltd., the parent company of Air Transport & Travel, although the Daimler Airway was a completely new company with new aircraft and not a reincarnation of A.T. & T.

It is not necessary to follow the various changes in the subsidy payments to the three London-based companies from "Temporary Scheme" to "Permanent" followed by "Revised Permanent", but in June, 1922 the Air Ministry issued a "Communiqué" (as its official announcements were still being called), and this gave details of a cross-Channel seaplane undertaking which, said *The Aeroplane*, had been for some time past the subject of vague rumour. The scheme was to be operated by a company in the process of formation, and would run services between Cherbourg and Southampton, and Le Havre and Southampton, the main object being, (a) to shorten the cross-Atlantic journey to London by picking up passengers at Cherbourg and bringing them to Southampton, and (b) to speed up the London – Paris service via Southampton and Le Havre by carrying passengers and mail by seaplane instead of by boat. Subsequently, it was proposed to operate a passenger and mail service between Southampton and the Channel Isles. These services were to be carried out by aircraft designed and built by the Supermarine Aviation Works, Ltd.

Why anyone would choose to fly from Woolston to Le Havre with two long rail journeys at each end, instead of flying direct from London to Paris was not explained. Both the British and French railways involved, the L.S.W.R. and the Etat, were said to be willing to co-operate in the matter of through bookings and connections, although it has been said of the Etat that they had difficulty enough in connecting with the Southampton – Le

Havre boats which were run by the L.S.W.R. This rather mild concession on the part of the railways, probably under pressure from the new Director-General of Civil Aviation, the ebullient Sir Sefton Brancker, was carried to rather absurd lengths by C.G. Grey of *The Aeroplane* who said that the proposal of Supermarine and the L.S.W.R. to run "joint air-lines" was "One of the most important steps in the history of civil aviation"!

The British Marine Air Navigation Co. Ltd. was registered as a private company on March 23, 1923 with a nominal capital of £15,000 in £1 shares. The objects were to adopt agreements: "(1) with the Supermarine Aviation Works Ltd. (a) for them to supply three 'Sea Eagle' type Amphibian Flying Boats complete with engines, certain machine spares, seagoing tenders, and pontoons for embarking and disembarking, on similar terms as are already agreed between the Air Council and the said company, for the granting of a subsidy under the Civil Aviation Scheme, (b) that all aircraft shall be supplied to the company by or through them providing same are charged at fair and reasonable market prices and (c) that they shall be appointed consulting aeronautical engineers at a suitable remuneration to be settled by the Board and: (2) with the Asiatic Petroleum Co. Ltd. for them to have the exclusive supply of all petrol and lubricating oils to the company providing same are charged at fair and reasonable market prices, and subject to the engine-makers approving of the brand of fuel and oil; and the Asiatic Co. will procure Shell-Mex Ltd. to make supplies under the above terms; to establish, maintain, and operate an air-service of seaworthy flying-boats and flying-boat 'Amphibian' aircraft between Southampton, Le Havre, Cherbourg, and the Channel Islands, and lines of aerial, land and sea conveyances and craft, in such place or position, and between such places as may be selected by the company and on such terms as may be thought fit . . ." (3) The Supermarine Aviation Works and Asiatic Petroleum held 5,000 shares each.

The Supermarine Sea Eagle (See Appendix 1A) was designed specifically for the new air service on the basic Channel/Seagull plan of single-engined biplane. The two wings had a span of 46', the all-up weight was 6,050 lbs. and the horse-power of the pusher Eagle IX was 360 compared with the Channel's 160 h.p. The hull was much more robust, with a bow like a ship's life-boat, and the six passengers were enclosed in a cabin. Despite its max. speed of only 93 mph it was designed by R.J.

Mitchell, and from the same stable would emerge the Schneider Trophy winners S.5 and S.6 of 1927, 1929, and 1931, as well as the Spitfire! Of the three Sea Eagles built the first was G-EBFK which received its c. of a. on July 11, 1923 just in time for the King's Cup of that year.

Supermarine "Sea Eagle" G-EBFK at Woolston
(From the Royal Aeronautical Society Library)

As the King's Cup is a handicap the amphibian, presumably, had as much chance of winning as any of the others, and Henri Biard set off from Hendon with a spare wheel, a mechanic, and four passengers on board. At Birmingham, to reduce weight, they decided to discard the spare wheel which, when the mechanic managed to heave it over the side, narrowly missed decapitating the Lord Mayor, but succeeded in knocking his top hat for six! At Newcastle, left standing in the sun, the "unusual heat" caused one of the tyres to burst, which was unfortunate as they had just jettisoned the spare. There was nothing else for it but to let the air out of the good tyre and take-off on two "flats", but at Glasgow, the next control, they were disqualified because, in this condition, the aircraft was deemed to be unsafe.

On August 5 Sir Sefton Brancker was taken on a tour of the Woolston works and given a two hour flight in 'FK. On August 8 the air-minded Lord Apsley, M.P. for Southampton was taken from Cowes to Sea View in the Sea Eagle, and on August 11 the Air Ministry announced that the subsidy for the Cherbourg and Channel Islands service would be £10,000 annually, with the company guaranteeing a minimum of 60,000 miles in the year, and that the Air Ministry would pay 50% of the cost of the aircraft up to £21,000. *The Southern Daily Echo* of the 13th reported that the Cherbourg and Channel Islands service would start in three week's time, but it was the intention of Hubert Scott-Paine, and his half-brother, Victor Paine, to attempt a more ambitious scheme – England to India! *The Guernsey Evening Press* of the same date said: ". . . The advent of the air services between England and the Channel Islands has been heralded for months, and the recent re-establishment of the wireless station of Fort George under the auspices of the Air Ministry, with its daily communications to and from Croydon, gave concrete evidence that the long-talked of service between the Islands and Southampton was on the way to becoming an actual fact . . . On the 14th inst. Major-General Sir W.S. Brancker is taking one of the first three machines to Cherbourg . . ."

The Air Ministry's Annual Report gave the starting date of the Southampton – Guernsey service as August 12, 1923, presumably a misprint for the 14th when 'FK was chartered to take Sir Sefton Brancker, Lt.-Col. Shelmerdine, and others, to a light aeroplane and glider meeting at Vauville. The pilot was Henri Biard, Supermarine's chief test pilot, and one of those veterans who had learned to fly before the war at Hendon. His "ticket" was No. 218, dated 4.6.1912, and he became an instructor. During the war he was in the R.F.C. still instructing, but spent some time on anti-U-boat patrols. In 1923 he was famous as the Schneider Trophy pilot who had won the 1922 race at Naples with the Supermarine Sea Lion. His father was French master at Charterhouse, but retired to Jersey where Henri had received part of his education at Victoria College. Because of the weather forecast they did not leave Woolston (Appendix 2A) until about 10 am, and after fifty minutes flying they emerged from the fog over Cherbourg to receive an enthusiastic welcome from officials and fellow aviators before motoring to Vauville, a few miles from Cherbourg on the west coast of the peninsula opposite Alderney. At the end of the afternoon Sir Sefton and his party were taken to the beach to board the Sea Eagle which had been flown down from Cherbourg to alight on the sea and taxi ashore. Some twenty minutes after take-off they arrived at St Peter Port and moored to a buoy off the Great Western berth. (See Appendix 2B) The following day the party flew to Jersey for lunch at Government House and then returned to Woolston.

THE NEWEST AIR-SERVICE.
Southampton to the Channel Islands
The New Air Station at Woolston
Pictured for "The Sphere"

One of the Seaplanes Getting Up Speed

The Average Time from Woolston to Guernsey is 1½ Hours

The British Marine Air Navigation Co., Ltd., is responsible for the operation of the new Cross-Channel Flying-Boat Services. The services, which are subsidised by the Air Ministry, are run on strictly Air Ministry lines. A regular service of one flying boat per day between the Southampton Marine Airport and St. Peter's Port, Guernsey, is being maintained. The boat leaves Southampton at 11 a.m. daily, and arrives at St. Peter's Port at 12.30 p.m., whence it returns at 3 p.m. The boat away from Southampton connects with the 8.30 train from Waterloo, so that a passenger leaving Waterloo at 8.30 in the morning, weather permitting, may lunch in Guernsey at 1 o'clock. Passengers leaving Guernsey at 3 o'clock are able to connect at Southampton with the 6.22 train and be in London at 8.20.

Passengers Embarking at Woolston in a Flying Boat

Weighing Intending Passengers Before Starting

The flying boats used are cabin cruisers of the "Sea Eagle" type. They were built especially for this service by Messrs. The Supermarine Aviation Works, Ltd., who are famous as the pioneers of flying-boat construction, and whose boat it was that brought back the Schneider Cup from Italy in 1922. The cabins of the "Sea Eagle" flying boats are luxuriously fitted with seating accommodation for six passengers. The airport premises, which have been newly built for the purpose, are the result of experience gained at Croydon, combined with the special features necessary for a marine service. There is a permanent Customs officer.

Seaplane Leaving Southampton Station for Channel Islands

Special Sphere pictures

Receiving the Latest Air Reports at Woolston

After the passengers have embarked on dry land, the flying boats, which are amphibious, run down a slipway and take to the water. On departure and arrival each machine is attended by a fast motor-launch, which returns to port as soon as the flying boat leaves the water. In addition to the clerical staff of the airport, there are telephonists, the launching crew, in charge of the airport bo'sun, and the staff of the ground engineer, who are men trained in the maintenance of aircraft and aero engines. The pilots used on such a service are essentially first-class sea navigators. Inset is a portrait of Captain Garwood (manager).

"The Sphere", 20 October, 1923. (From the Illustrated London News Picture Library)

If this was the start of the service it was certainly not a regular, nor a daily one, as yet, and would be restricted to the Channel Islands. In fact, the B.M.A.N. Co. would never again fly to Cherbourg, nor reach Le Havre, so the original purpose of the airline was never fulfilled, and the Channel Islands, which had been added, almost as an afterthought, became the sole route to be operated. The French were blamed for this state of affairs, but Cherbourg being one of the main bases of the French Navy it was not unreasonable of them to make it a prohibited area. As for Le Havre, it is hardly mentioned again. Whether it was not considered a suitable port-of-call on its own, without a previous call at Cherbourg, or whether there were other reasons against it, is not known.

The first fare-paying passenger appeared on August 24 when H.E. Cook of the Sport & General Press Agency left Woolston at 2.15 pm and reached St Peter Port at 4.30. He intended to take pictures of water sports, his speciality, such as ". . . swimming, surf-riding, and water-gambols"! On this flight Henri Biard was accompanied by F.J. Bailey, who was to become one of the regular pilots on the route. Flight-Lieut Bailey had joined the R.N.A.S. in 1914 at the age of 17 or thereabouts, and served until 1919. In 1916 he had suffered the unusual experience of being shot down by a submarine and was a P.O.W. until 1918. He joined B.M.A.N. Co. with about 1,000 hours flying to his credit. On their return they brought back Mrs Fletcher and her son, who had been staying at the Royal Hotel, although Mr Fletcher preferred to travel by the boat. The Royal, on the sea-front near the harbour, became a very convenient rendezvous for flying-boat crew and passengers. The next "commercial flight" to be reported, took place on August 31, and in the afternoon 'FK made a local flight from Guernsey with Mr Cook, the photographer and a party including Mr and Mrs Adams of the Royal. On September 1 the Sea Eagle made the first commercial flight to Jersey, (See Appendix 2C) taking Mr Wilkinson, the Colman's mustard representative, who had been unable to book a berth on the steamer, and on the return three people in Jersey took the opportunity of a flight to the mainland for £3. 18. 0. There was another trip to Guernsey on September 3 and the passengers on the return included H. E. Cook and Advocate H. H. Randell, who kept a log of his journey: ". . . Left Guernsey 6.25 pm – Passed Casquets 6.43 – Sighted England 7.10 – The Needles 7.36 – Calshot 7.47 – Landed Woolston 7.53 . . . Speaking was conducted with difficulty as the roar of the engine resembled that of a train in a tunnel . . ." (22)

By September 4 "about a dozen round trips" had been made to the Channel Islands, and the time taken "1¾ hours on the tick". According to Hubert Scott-Paine, the most authoritative source, the trips were being conducted in order to settle comparatively minor matters, such as timetable, costs, and so on, and he did not intend to commence a public passenger-carrying service until everything had been perfected down to the last detail. However, the *Guernsey Evening Press* said that the present series of flights were "being made to accustom pilots to this port". Another reason put forward for the delayed start was the lack of facilities at Woolston for the Customs and Immigration, and although it is true that the terminal was still under construction, all the flights so far must have been dealt with by these officials. The *Southern Daily Echo* of September 4 described the new terminal as: "A V-shaped block facing a concrete slipway . . . There is an imposing entrance to the port. At the near end . . . is the enquiry and booking office. Above are the handsomely-appointed main and general offices, which adjoin the passenger's waiting room, buffet, and kitchen. Other important apartments on the top floor are the pilot's rest room, the marine superintendent's office, the wireless and telephone . . . room, and the duty office, where a duty officer will have complete charge of operations . . . from a flagstaff above visual signals can be made to the machines. Wireless . . . in each machine . . . in touch with Guernsey and Woolston . . . The ground floor offices include the airport engineer's office, and the airport bosun's office . . . There are also a private room for the port doctor, passport and customs rooms, and a baggage and bonded stores . . ." Captain V. Garwood was in charge and the words MARINE AIRPORT were painted on the roof. The first commercial mechandise passed through the Customs on September 5 when a consignment of cooked hams "from a well-known Bath firm" was placed aboard the Sea Eagle at 10.55 am to reach Guernsey 1¾ hours later.

It was announced in *The Aeroplane* and certain London papers that: "On Tuesday of this week (Sept. 25) the B.M.A.N. Co. Ltd. started a regular daily service between Southampton and Guernsey. Machines leave Southampton daily at 11.15 hrs. and leave Guernsey at 15.30 hrs. The fare is £3. 18. 0 single". The 11.15 departure connected with the 8.30 from Waterloo, and the return with the 6.22 to Waterloo. *The Guernsey Evening Press* of September 27 disagreed: ". . . Contradicting the statement in some of the London papers we are able to state that the daily air service . . . has not yet begun. For instance, the Sea Eagle arrived yesterday, but will not be crossing to-day or tomorrow . . ." The Sea Eagle that "arrived yesterday", incidentally, took five passengers back to the mainland including Mrs Boyd, her son, and Master Boyd's tortoise, which: ". . . is now able to claim to the world, and any hare running, that it covered 120 miles in 80 minutes . . ." With only one aircraft, (G-EBFK), some delays were to be expected and interruptions due to bad weather, or even rough water outside the harbour at St Peter Port (much less sheltered than the Solent), and if there were no passengers booked either way it would have been reasonable to cancel the trip on economy grounds. However, the second and third Sea Eagles became available on October 2 and this eased the situation, although the B.M.A.N. Co. may have taken second place in Supermarine's order of priorities at the end of September because of the Schneider Trophy races at Cowes. Henri Biard was flying the Super-marine Sea Lion III but he could not beat the Americans in their Curtiss C.R. One Sea Eagle set out for Guernsey on October 2 with Frank Bailey at the controls and, as it gave a demonstration flight before leaving, it may have been 'GR on test. It carried 90 lbs. of newspapers (*Daily Sketch*) with photographs of the big fight – Carpentier v Beckett. The photographers must have acted quickly because Beckett was knocked out in 15 seconds, to the disgust of British fans, this being the second time in four years that George Carpentier had K.O'd Beckett in the first round. "He was too quick for me" poor Joe had said, almost in tears. On the return flight with one passenger they ran into a severe northerly gale and were forced to put back into St Peter Port there to remain until the afternoon of the 4th. The *Southern Daily Echo* of the 5th confirmed that: ". . . a daily service, weather permitting, is now in operation . . ." and gave the times, also that 30 lbs. of luggage could go free, but any excess would cost 4d. per lb.

'GS set out for its maiden flight to Guernsey on October 13, flown by Henri Biard, and 'GR, flown by Bailey, went in company. They were due to take part in an official inauguration; ". . . my friend, Mr Howard Martin, who had recently been operating a service of flying-boats between Southampton and Guernsey, decided to take advantage of a trade exhibition in Guernsey to hold a formal inaugural ceremony, and invited a large party, including myself (Mr A.E. Turner, chairman of de Havillands) . . . Unfortunately, one of the boats reported engine trouble on the journey

27

from Southampton, and this and other causes delayed the inaugural ceremony to a later hour than that originally contemplated . . ." (53) The distinction of inaugurating the daily flying boat service between Southampton and Guernsey belongs to: ". . . Miss Edith Carey, Guernsey's historian, and Mrs W.W. Watkins, wife of the Senior Constable of St Peter Port" said the *Guernsey Star*, when from a small boat ". . . These two ladies each broke a bottle of champagne over the flying boat's bows . . ." This unusual double christening resulted in G-EBGS receiving the name *Sarnia* which, for the benefit of a small minority of mainlanders, is another name for Guernsey. It may have been the intention to christen both flying-boats but the lateness of the hour brought a hurried change of plan, and some sources claim that 'GR was named *Sea Eagle*, perhaps without ceremony, but if so it was a very confusing name as, of course, *Sarnia* was a Sea Eagle, also. Fortunately the naming of aircraft was very much a public relations exercise, usually forgotten after a few weeks, except in certain notable cases when the names seemed to catch on, as with the old *Heracles* of Croydon fame, or the *Cloud of Iona*. The normal practice of air and ground personnel was to use the last two letters of the aircraft's registration, and considering some of the names chosen this was just as well. Pilots were spared the embarrassment of having to announce over the air "This is the Spirit of Stoke-on-Trent calling", or of being asked "Can you hear me, Sir Isaac Newton?", or even "Hallo, Eurydice!" Imperial Airways had a dreadful selection ranging from *Amalthea* to *Euterpe*, and heaven knows what sort of ribald comment these would have extracted from other pilots in the vicinity all tuned to the same frequency. Pilots, generally, being more renowned for their sense of humour than their love of classical mythology. To avoid confusion it will be assumed that 'GR was unnamed so that any reference to Sea Eagle means any one of the three. Late in the day, *Sarnia* and her sister set out for Woolston in deteriorating weather, and because of the doubts about 'GR's engine, Bailey carried a mechanic named Linsdale, but no passengers, while *Sarnia* carried a mechanic and three passengers, two journalists and A.E. Turner. Somewhere between Alderney and the Casquets, in what was now a howling gale, 'GR's engine failed and Bailey was forced to alight near to a dangerous group of rocks. The sea was rough, but they were in the lee of the rocks, although the sea-anchor could not prevent them from drifting away from their shelter into the surrounding heavy seas. It was too dangerous for

Biard to attempt a landing so he flew to Alderney and managed to get down into the harbour at Braye.

An exciting gale incident during an aerial trip from Guernsey to England
(From "The Graphic" 20.10.23. By permission of the British Library)

There he was told they had no boat strong enough to go out to the Casquets in such weather so Henri decided to return to Guernsey for help. ". . . On learning that no boat was available . . . our mechanic, a cheery young man with a perpetual smile, came through the cabin and announced as though it were the most amusing joke in the world: ". . . "E says (pointing with his thumb to the pilot) 'e's going back to Guernsey – but we'll never get there'! The significance of this remark lay in the fact that the harbour was too small to enable us to get up sufficient speed to rise from the water, so that it was necessary for us to proceed outside and get up a speed of some 60 miles an hour on the rough water . . ." (53) According to Henri Biard: ". . . I chose my time for trying to rise from Alderney harbour . . . But a wave about fifteen feet high ran at the 'Sarnia' just as we were taking off, sent her bouncing forty feet up into the air before she had enough flying speed to climb; she bumped down on the crest of the next wave and then bounced up again, with a feeling as though every stick in her was broken by the concussion. It was a bit of luck that she did not go nose under and sink like a stone . . . When we had got into the air . . . I looked round to see what damage had been done. We had smashed off one wingtip float, and all the undersurface of the plane had gone along with it. The ribs were naked and splintered, several of them broken, and some of the tailplane had gone entirely . . ." (52) In the cabin it was a complete shambles with all passengers in a heap on the floor. One was flung straight into a large basket of grapes he was taking home for his wife, and Mr Turner was violently sick to add to the hilarity of the situation. They landed at St Peter Port with the mechanic out on the wing to make sure the sound float hit the water first, and the dishevelled passengers made their way to the Royal Hotel. Henri Biard claimed that one journalist wrote a marvellous account of their return from Alderney although unconscious the whole time! Hour after hour 'GR drifted in and out of groups of jagged rocks, being battered and smashed out of shape by huge waves, and there was nothing they could do except fire Verey lights at intervals. To their great relief, when they were in the vicinity of Les Etacs the Alderney motor launch Lita arrived on the scene commanded by a well known Alderney character, Captain Nick Allen and carrying local pilot Dave Ingrouille. In a risky and difficult operation, during which the punt capsized, a line was secured to the flying-boat and, against a very strong tide, she was towed into Longis Bay and left at anchor to await a tide suitable for a tow round to Braye harbour. For certain, this timely arrival saved the flying-boat and the lives of the two men, but the loss of all the equipment from the punt was somewhat embarrassing because the punt had been "borrowed" from a visiting cargo barge! From Guernsey the S.R. cargo boat had left for

Southampton with the intention of giving assistance, but failed to make contact. On Monday, October 15 'GR managed to fly to Guernsey and, after an engine overhaul, returned to Woolston on the 17th. 'GS was completely out-of-action and remained on the careening hard at St Peter Port until she was shipped to Southampton at the end of the month and the newly-inaugurated service was only kept going by G-EBFK.

An account of a less eventful trip appeared in *The Lady* on October 25 when Ethel Hargrove, F.R.G.S. described her first flight: ". . . A short stroll brought us to a steep flight of stone steps, and after a few minutes wait an ancient Guernsey marine arrived in a stout, flat-bottomed boat, into which we embarked . . . We were soon alongside the seaplane, and its ballast was thrown into our boat . . . we deposited ourselves aboard the plane, ascending by cut steel steps. Once there we stepped down a light staircase into a small cabin. I had the seat of honour, a cushioned easy-chair. Then we started, a rush of speed at eighty miles an hour through the calm harbour waters into the stormy waves beyond. A few jolts of bump-like nature and then, suddenly, we rose, a bird-like easy motion . . ." Throughout November Captain Bailey made frequent trips to Guernsey, and a daily service was obviously intended if not quite achieved. On November 9 Henri Biard took one of the Sea Eagles up to Croydon in the evening, but found it enveloped in fog. He tried Brooklands only to find more fog, and in the end he came down in a small field near Guildford. The following morning he went to continue his flight to Croydon, where he was expected, but found the wind had changed and it was impossible to take off. The next day, Sunday, the wind was from a convenient direction so he was able to return to Woolston. On the 22nd the flying-boat left Woolston at 8.10 and crossed at "a great altitude" to reach Guernsey at 10 and "many people watched its graceful descent into the Pool". On the 30th two flying-boats crossed to Guernsey, 'GR and *Sarnia* making her first cross-Channel flight since the day of her christening. From the end of November the service was reduced to "on demand" which, in December, was minimal. Although a quiet month for flying much was happening behind the scenes, and on December 3 an agreement was signed for the merger of the four cross-Channel air-lines:- Handley Page, Instone, Daimler and B.M.A.N. Co. It had become obvious that the subsidies, or "hand-to mouth doles" as Sir Samuel Hoare called them, were useless for long-term development, and a small committee of businessmen, under Sir Herbert Hambling, deputy-chairman of Barclay's Bank, had been formed to examine the problem. As is well-known, the Hambling Committee recommended that a single company be formed with a capital of one million pounds and Government nominees on the Board, to take over and expand the existing services. The Government was to guarantee a subsidy of not less than a million pounds, spread over ten years, and the public was to raise a corresponding million. The terms of the agreement were published on December 28 and provided for: ". . . a Heavier-than-Air Air Transport Company to be called the Imperial Air Transport Co. Ltd . . ." The subsidy was £137,000 for the first four years, and then dwindled annually; £112,000, £100,000, £86,000, £70,000, £52,000, to £32,000 in the tenth year, but these figures were subject to various conditions, including the flying of an average annual 1,000,000 miles. Of interest to the B.M.A.N. Co. was the requirement that the new company should continue to operate: ". . . an efficient air service . . . between the following places, that is to say: London and Paris, London and Brussels, London and Amsterdam, and Southampton and the Channel Islands, or such other places approved by the President (of the Air Council) as . . . may be commercially desirable, provided always that the air service to be operated by the company, under the provisions of this clause, between Southampton and the Channel Isles, or alternative places respectively, shall be operated by sea-going marine aircraft . . ." (54) There was no great rush to take up shares, and it was obvious that the City did not have a very high opinion of civil aviation as a profitable activity. However, the agreement did not come into force until April 1, 1924, and in the interval the name was shortened to Imperial Airways, Ltd.

Bailey and Biard made a few Sea Eagle sorties to Guernsey during January but there was little demand and much bad weather. On the 10th Henri Biard left St Peter Port harbour but the water was too rough and he had to turn back. It was the 14th before he was able to make the return flight to Woolston. Britain's first Socialist Government took office on January 22, 1924 under Ramsey MacDonald and Lord Thomson replaced Hoare as Air Minister, but with no noticeable effect on civil aviation. There was an increase in flying-boat activity in February when bad weather kept the Sea Eagle storm-bound in St Peter Port for almost a week, but a strike by dockers brought considerable business in the second half of the month. Although the times of the service had been given in the early days as 11.15 am from Woolston and 3.30 pm from Guernsey they were not taken too seriously and actual departures from Woolston ranged from 8 am to 10 am whilst those from Guernsey were generally between 12 noon and 2 pm. On February 14 Hubert Scott-Paine sailed from Southampton to Cherbourg in the *Berengaria* on his way to the Mediterranean where he was going to look at possible flying-boat routes. Scott-Paine became a director of Imperial Airways, together with one man from each of the other companies, and with his departure from Supermarine the management was taken over by the capable Commander Bird.

In St Peter Port an office was opened opposite St Julian's weigh-bridge at No. 1, Glategny Esplanade manned from 9 am to 6 pm by G.F. Drury-Hudson. He was expecting a new launch, the *Laura*, to arrive soon, and this would take the passengers to and from the flying-boats and was fitted with large tanks for aviation spirit and a semi-rotary pump for refuelling. The Sea Eagles used 77 gallons on the round trip, and the distance from Woolston to St Peter Port was 102 miles, but deviations in flight meant that the aircraft usually covered about 115 miles. He was inaugurating cheap week-end trips straight away at £2. 15s single, £5 return, compared with the ordinary fares of £3. 18s. 0d. single, £7. 16s. 0d. return, and these would be available Fridays to Mondays (including Sunday). The return to be made on one of these days also, but an ordinary day could be used if the weather was too bad on the Monday, indicating that a daily service was in operation. Mr Drury-Hudson kept the Press well-informed and put them into the habit of referring to the Sea Eagles as 'GR or 'GS. A new pilot, Captain J.H. Horsey, brought the Sea Eagle into Guernsey on February 22. John Horsey had learned to fly in the R.N.A.S. during the war, and his experience included five hours sitting on a float some 45 miles off the Lizard. He had flown one of the Channels at Bournemouth for Supermarine in 1919, and on August 14 of that year had managed to overturn it to give his two passengers an unexpected ducking. The passengers survived and the Channel was towed ashore. In June, 1920 he went to the R.A.F. at Felixstowe as a flying-boat instructor, and started his own business in 1923, but this venture failed and he joined the B.M.A.N. Co. At the Fort George wireless station Mr Finch, formerly of the Croydon wireless station, was in charge, and contact with the flying-boats maintained. In addition to their 200 ft. of trailing aerial the Sea-

Eagles had telescopic masts for use when afloat. Because of the strike the Sea-Eagles were carrying newspapers and on Saturday, the 23rd: "two flying vessels came over with newspapers and returned to Southampton in the afternoon" and on the Sunday the Sea Eagle took 54 boxes of flowers and two packages of beans belonging to E. Roussel of Vale, and C.R. Falla of Câstel: ". . . the first consignment (of produce) to leave by air . . .".

March began in a blustery fashion and on the 2nd Horsey's machine was nearly swamped as he tried to take-off outside St Peter's harbour. He returned to the Pool and left at 10.17 on the morrow. 'GR arrived soon afterwards but had to be taken off the service. She was hoisted up on to No. 2 berth on the 5th, and a new engine fitted on the 8th. Rolls Royce Eagle IX engines cost about £1,000 and had a life of 3,000 hours. Following tests 'GR left for Woolston at 4.14 pm on the 10th. There were three arrivals and departures on the 12th, probably to collect gear and personnel connected with the engine change, and Captain Bailey arrived in the last machine at 6.45 pm with: ". . . exhausts gleaming like twin lighthouses as he dashed in a circle round Bellegreve Bay . . ." (22) On Saturday, 15th, two members of the *Guernsey Evening Press* took advantage of the cheap week-end fares to the mainland (by this time available from Southampton to Guernsey, also).

They arrived at the office near the weigh-bridge at 8 am, were weighed (not on the weigh-bridge, presumably), and given their £5 tickets in duplicate. The pink slips were then handed to Tom, the boatman, who, from the bottom of the slipway took them out to 'GR in about 60 seconds: "We left the boat, ascended the two steps of the flying-boat and, descending to the cabin, found a delightful little room . . . within were reposeful armchairs . . . Pilot Horsey gave a little turn to the great shining propeller . . . to a gentle purr we found ourselves gliding through the water, circling the harbour . . . then the purr became a hum – the hum became a roar. We passed the Spur in two seconds. The speed increased second by second. The whipped spray hit the bottom like rifle-shots, then suddenly the sea-feeling ceased . . . an immediate sense of rock-like stability . . . In half a minute we were looking at the sea from the hurricane deck of the *Majestic*, ten seconds later from the top of the Doyle Monument, and then, with a toccata of sound, the great flying-boat swung her head to the North", and so on in vein until they reached Woolston at ten o'clock. On Saturday, the 22nd, Captain Bailey in 'GS left Guernsey at 3.15 pm but ran into thick fog and landed off Calshot. He taxied the rest of the way into Woolston but still managed to complete the whole trip in 86 minutes. The final days of March were foggy, and the service much curtailed, so that the British Marine Air Navigation Co. Ltd. faded away in the mists of March, 1924, the last flight, as the first, of this Woolston-Guernsey service passing unrecorded. At midnight on March 31, 1924 the company ceased to exist and its place was taken by Imperial Airways Ltd.

In settlement the owners of B.M.A.N. Co. received £21,500, one third in cash and two thirds in fully paid up £1 shares in Imperial Airways. Of the available subsidy of £10,000 they received a total of £4,024, which may have born the same relationship to £10,000 as the actual miles flown bore to the required minimum of 60,000. If so, B.M.A.N. Co. flew about 24,000 miles, or 209 journeys of 115 miles making 104 round trips at an average of 15 per month.

There are Press reports of Sea Eagle arrivals and/or departures on 6 days in January, 16 days in February, and 16 days in March. Some may have been overlooked, and there was much bad weather, but it seems that a daily service was attempted from the end of January encouraged, perhaps, by strikes affecting other forms of transport.

Notes

In 1924 the White Star liner *Majestic* (ex *Bismarck*) at 56,551 tons was the largest liner on the transatlantic service. Her bridge was about 100 feet above the water-line. The Cunard liner *Berengaria* (Ex *Imperator*) was slightly smaller at 52,000 tons.

The original monument to Lieut-General Sir John Doyle was 100 feet high and stood on a point some 300 feet above sea-level.

At its formation the board of Imperial Airways consisted of two businessmen, two Government nominees, and one nominee from each of the four companies involved. The businessmen were Sir Eric Geddes, chairman of the Dunlop Rubber Co. Ltd, and Sir George Beharrell, deputy chairman of the same company.

The Government nominees were Sir Robert Hambling, of Hambling Committee fame, deputy chairman of Barclay's Bank, and Major J.W. Hills, Financial Secretary to the Treasury in Bonar Law's Government. The four air-line men were (1) Hubert Scott-Paine of B.M.A.N. Co, (2) Sir Samuel Instone, chairman of S. Instone & Co. Ltd., a Cardiff-based firm of ship-owners, ship-brokers, and coal merchants who had started the Instone Air Line. Originally named Einstein, Sam and his two brothers, Albert and Theodore, considered Instone to be more suitable for a British shipping line. (3) Lieut.-Col. Barrett-Lennard from Handley Page, where he had been installed as general manager by the Bank of Scotland when the Handley Page finances were in a bad way, and (4) Col Frank Searle from Daimler. Trained as a locomotive engineer he had moved into road transport and became chief motor engineer to the L.G.O.C., but joined B.S.A./Daimler in 1911. After serving in the Tank Corps during the war he returned to become managing director of the Daimler Airway, where he startled everyone with his ideas on the intensive utilisation of aircraft.

Sir Eric Geddes was invited to be chairman because, said Sir Samuel Hoare: "It was essential to have . . . a recognised expert on transport questions. Eric Geddes, formerly General Manager of the North Eastern Railway and afterwards the very successful Inspector-General of Military Transport in France, seemed to me the man best fitted for the post . . . he knew nothing of aviation . . ." (58)

Sir Eric was not universally admired: ". . . one of the energetic and domineering personalities which Lloyd George brought forward . . ." thought Major-General Sir Frederick Sykes (38) "A machine to be feared rather than a human being to be loved and followed." wrote C.G. Grey. (56) Eric Campbell Geddes, born Agra in 1875, was the son of Acland Geddes, a civil engineer who had founded a firm of public works contractors after many years with Indian railways. He was the eldest son, and attended many excellent schools, usually with the same result; if not actually expelled he was invited to leave at the end of term. Obviously of a robust disposition and rebellious spirit he decided, at the age of 17, to go to America to make his fortune, and early in 1893 he sailed for New York. After 2½ years trying his hand at various jobs including logging, labouring, bar-tending and salesmanship he ended up in hospital and his mother sent him his fare home. However: ". . . the British Isles were too small for Eric's volcanic energy" (59), and a job was found for him out in India, clearing jungles and building light railways, and becoming, in good time, the traffic superintendent of the Rohilkund and Kumaon Railway. Because of his wife's poor health he returned to Britain and joined the staff of the North Eastern Railway, of which, by 1914, he was the general manager designate. In May, 1915 he went to the new Ministry of Munitions, taking with him from the N.E.R. a brilliant statistical expert called George Beharrel, and with two other assistants achieved considerable success in stepping up the production of armaments and shells, to the great relief of Lloyd George who was Minister of Munitions. When Lloyd George became Secretary of State for War, Eric, now Major-General Sir Eric Geddes, was sent to France, with George Beharrel and his colleagues, to sort out the transport situation and the badly tangled lines of communication to the Front. Once again, his drive and energy, backed by his "troupe" of experts, succeeded, and there was no problem too great for him, so it seemed, because Lloyd George, now Prime Minister, sent him to the Admiralty and created him a vice-admiral whilst remaining a major-general! By 1917 he was First Lord of the Admiralty, but resigned in January, 1919 and became the Minister of Transport in the following August. The economic situation was bleak and a Committee on National Expenditure was formed to investigate ways and means of reducing Government spending. Sir Eric was appointed chairman with George Beharrell as financial adviser, and when the severe economies proposed in the Committee's Report were put into effect, this drastic measure was called the Geddes Axe. Probably Sir Eric was not happy in this particular role, and, as a practical man, somewhat out of his depth in matters of economics and high finance, since he resigned from the Government and from Parliament before his Committee's proposals were approved and implemented by the Cabinet. Therefore he helped to forge, but did not wield, his infamous "axe". In May, 1922 he was elected to the board of the

Dunlop Rubber Company, and six months later became chairman. Once again he was joined by his right-hand man, George Beharrel, and when invited to be chairman of Imperial Airways he accepted, somewhat reluctantly: ". . . but only on condition he brought Sir George Beharrel, the chartered accountant upon whom he always depended for financial advice . . ." (58)

Major George Woods Humphery, formerly of Handley Page and Daimler, was made the general manager. He had started in marine engineering and, as an apprentice, spent some time in the drawing-office with a certain J.C.W. Reith, who, many years later, as Sir John Reith, would replace Geddes at the head of Imperial Airways. Woods Humphery: ". . . was a professional. He knew all about flying, was an economist, a business man and a politician, able to take on a government, or conduct foreign negotiations. Strong and severe, he was not so much liked as respected, and what he said, went." (60) Although formed at Government behest, Imperial Airways was a public limited company, and the directors were responsible to the share-holders, with the normal obligation of trying to earn a reasonable dividend. However, provided they kept to the terms of the agreement, the company would receive an annual subsidy for at least ten years. The first pilots included:- Bailey, Barnard, Brackley, Dismore, Hinchliffe, Horsey, Johnson, Jones, McIntosh, Olley, Powell, Rogers, Robertson, Robins, Robinson, Walters, Wilcockson, Wolley Dod, and Youell, names that are still remembered in the annals of civil aviation, and of these Franklyn Barnard became the chief pilot, and Major Brackley, air superintendent. Thirteen aircraft were taken over:- three Handley Page W8b's from Handley Page Transport, four D.H.34's and one Vickers Vimy from Instone, three D.H.34's from Daimler, and the two Sea Eagles, G-EBGR and G-EBGS from the B.M.A.N. Co. The registration of the prototype Sea Eagle, G-EBFK, was cancelled on 21.5.24, and probably it did not exist in a usable state on 1.4.24 the date of the take-over. It was last reported on the Guernsey service in October, 1923, and may have been used to provide spares to keep the other two machines flying.

The Imperial Airways' *Pilot's Handbook and General Instructions* of 1924 gave the times for the routes:- London - Paris - Basle - Zurich, London - Ostend - Brussels - Cologne, London - Amsterdam, with a connection to Berlin and Malmo, Amsterdam - Cologne, and Cologne - Paris. The inland extension of the Daimler Airway route from London to Manchester was discontinued, and the existence of a Southampton – Guernsey service was not even mentioned. It said that: ". . . the activities of the Imperial Airways are, for the coming season, devoted mainly towards affording communication between London and many of the principal cities of Western Europe. Important as this function is, the Company appreciates the ultimate utility of the air as a means of transit between different portions of the British Empire . . ." Obviously, they intended to live up to their title, and the implication was that Southampton and Guernsey were not the different portions of the British Empire that they had in mind. When, full of enthusiasm for flying-boat services, and somewhat obsessed with the idea of saving time on the transatlantic journey of passengers and mail, the British Marine Air Navigation Co. had been formed, with Cherbourg as its main objective, no steps had been taken, apparently, to ensure that Cherbourg was available. Perhaps the impulsive Brancker had hoped to sweep aside any French objections with his usual bonhomie, but, if so, the French naval authorities refused to be bonhomied, and Cherbourg remained a prohibited area. For some reason, interest in the London-Paris route, via Le Havre, about which there had been so much hysteria, seemed to evaporate and, faute de mieux, Guernsey became the sole target of the new air-line. Imperial Airways now inherited this compromise and, by the terms of their agreement, were obliged to keep it in being unless they could offer an acceptable alternative flying-boat service. Nevertheless, haphazard as the planning may have been, the intentions were good, and if, in any way, the survival of the Supermarine Aviation Works was assisted by the formation of the B.M.A.N. Co. then many a fighter pilot in 1940 had reason to be grateful.

Some of the more enterprising citizens of Plymouth also had developed a keen interest in the saving of time on the transatlantic mail routes, and in 1923 they had arranged two demonstration flights, one to London on April 27, and the other to Manchester on May 9, in which Lt.-Col. Henderson in the Surrey Flying Service's D.H.9, G-EBEP, carried dummy mail, supposedly picked up from an American liner by the steam pinnace which brought the parcel into Plymouth Harbour, from whence it was rushed out to Chelson Meadow, the local race-course being used as an aerodrome. These flights inspired the Air Ministry to carry out a full-scale experiment using two D.H.9c's and two D.H.50's of the de Havilland Aircraft Co's hire department between September 15 and October 19, 1923 during which 22 flights were made from the Plymouth polo ground at Roborough to Alexandra Park, Manchester, and 14 flights on to Belfast (Aldergrove). However, the official report pointed out that British mail-carrying steamers did not call at Plymouth, but the slower American ships that did could take as long as eight or nine days on the crossing, in which case the "problematic saving of a few hours after its sea transit might not seem an appreciable advantage", especially as two or three days could often be saved by arranging for the letter to go by a fast British liner due to leave about the same time as the American ship. Whilst this was perfectly true the Plymouth interests had hoped that the introduction of an air-mail service might have induced the Cunard and White Star shipping lines to call at Plymouth.

1924

A regular air service was inaugurated as a result of the Plymouth experiments but this was between Liverpool and Belfast! Northern Air Lines, run by D. M. Greig and E. Higgs (well-known as tennis players at that time), in conjunction with de Havillands, made its first flight on April 30, 1924 using D.H.50, G-EBFP and attempted a daily service (Sundays excepted) which lasted until June 2, when it was suspended. Due to bad weather there were no flights on eleven days in May. From May 2 mail was carried from Belfast (Malone) to Liverpool at an extra fee of ½d. per 2 oz. as well as passengers but in the opposite direction there was only room for the regular load of newspapers. The machines landed at Aintree, but took off empty for Southport sands where they collected the newspapers and then had a sufficient length of run to get off the ground. The D.H.50's used were landplanes, but no attempt was made to fly the long direct route over water; they followed the coast to the Mull of Galloway and then crossed to Donaghadee.

On the Southampton-Guernsey route the Imperial Airways' time-table showed considerable optimism with two return trips every weekday and one on Sundays. Departures from Woolston were to be at 7 am and 2 pm on weekdays, 9 am on Sundays, and from St Peter Port at 10 am and 5 pm weekdays, 5 pm Sundays. One hour 50 mins. was allowed for the flight, and the fares were £3 single, and £5. 10s. 0d. return, with 30 lbs. of luggage free, and 4d. per lb. for excess. Unfortunately, on the appointed day, appropriately April 1, not one Imperial Airways' machine left the ground – all the pilots were on strike! Technically it was not a strike but a refusal to join. The new management offered them £100 a year plus flying pay based on mileage, but the pilots wanted £450 a year plus flying pay based on time. By April 25 agreement had been reached on terms and the sole point at issue was the question of who was to manage the company. This problem was solved by making Major H. G. Brackley ("Brackles") air superintendent and representative of the pilots in dealings with the board and the "strike" ended on May 2. In anticipation Captain Horsey made a trip to Guernsey in 'GR on May 1 with Drury-Hudson and a travel correspondent, and the regular service started on May 4 when Horsey made two return trips, although it was a Sunday. Bailey and Horsey did one trip each on the 5th, and on the 6th Frank Bailey made his first "double-crossing" in one day for Imperial Airways. This "brisk communication" was maintained for a while but did not last. On May 14 Bailey left St Peter Port in 'GS at 5.47 pm with Finch of the radio station and ran into fog mid-Channel. It was too thick to climb over so he landed on the sea and set course for the Needles. Atmospherics prevented them from making contact with a shore station until they were abeam of the Beaulieu River. At the end of the month the new launch *Laura* was off-loaded at St Peter Port, and with tanks for 250 gallons of aviation spirit the old chore of refuelling from cans was eliminated.

Talking to Rotarians in June the Guernsey Postmaster spoke of the air service and said: ". . . There is a scheduled time-table, but temporarily only, there is considerable irregularity in running . . . I understand that shortly sufficient machines will be available to ensure reasonable regularity . . ." (22) Presumably 'GR was out-of-action as it was last reported on the service about May 9.

According to a schoolboy's log 'GS left eight minutes early on June 17, thus:-

"Left 1.52, passed Netley 1.54, over *Mauritania* 1.58, Calshot 2 pm, Needles 2.10, over mailboat *Alberta* 2.23, France sighted 3 pm, Alderney lighthouse 3.6, over wrecked *Buchanness* 3.9, over Humps 3.21, Herm and Jethou 3.24, landed 3.30 . . ."

Supermarine "Sea Eagle" G-EBGS of Imperial Airways at the Woolston Marine Air Port   ('*The British Airways Archive and Museum Collection*')

'GR was back in service by June 19, and when Captain Horsey was flying it to Guernsey on the 24th he ran into thick fog and was forced to stop at Alderney until the weather cleared.

In the House of Commons on July 3 Lord Apsley was told that valuable experience was being gained on the Southampton – Guernsey route: ". . . The preliminary negotiations which had been opened with the French . . . had not been brought to a conclusion because, in view of the experimental nature of the employment of this type of aircraft on regular air transport services, it had been considered necessary to confine operations, in the first instance, to the Southampton – Guernsey service . . ." Lord Apsley complained that these experiments had been going on for over a year; and he thought the matter should be expedited before the holiday season was over. Making it very clear that it was not an Air Ministry responsibility Mr Leach, Under Secretary of State for Air, said he hoped that Imperial Airways would carry out the Noble Lord's suggestion. In other words, the Air Ministry was not pressing the French for landing facilities because Imperial Airways regarded their flying-boat operations as experimental only. The afternoon departure times in August and September were advanced one hour to leave Woolston at 1 pm and St Peter Port at four, but departures were infrequent, and when the *Guernsey Star* printed the new time-table they added, rather sarcastically: ". . . Must be these noiseless (and invisible) machines for we have no recollection of seeing or hearing a flying-boat for over a fortnight. The explanation, apparently, is that the one and only machine has gone bust and the Imperial Airways are so busy with the Continental service that they have no time to patch up the engine . . . But what about that wonderful . . . (Supermarine Swan) . . . inspected by the Prince of Wales on his recent visit to Southampton? We were informed that this machine was . . . for the Southampton – Guernsey service . . ." (See Appendix 1A) Mr Drury-Hudson who was not amused and evidently no diplomat, wrote a most abusive letter in reply, including such remarks as: ". . . Guernsey after all, is but a very small place (so small that one misses it altogether when flying if not careful) with only a very small percentage of the population able to pay the fare . . ."

There were no flying-boat operations at all during September or October and on October 25 the *Guernsey Star*, quoting the *Southern Daily Echo*, said: ". . . The machine at present employed experiences some difficulty in taking-off owing to the roughness of the water outside Guernsey Harbour," and then asked ". . . Is that really the reason why the service has been, well – temporarily discontinued! . . ." From the beginning of October the time-table gave the service as once daily leaving Woolston at 10 and St Peter Port at 2, but flying was not resumed until November 3 by which date the Woolston departure had been put back to 11.15. G-EBGR now had the 450 hp Napier engine and the extra power meant a shorter take-off run which was very useful in a big sea or heavy swell, meanwhile 'GS was away for modification. Mr V.W. Garwood was still in charge at Woolston, and Mr Finch, responsible for wireless communication. Throughout November and December 'GR carried on single-handed and made a number of crossings despite the weather. On December 3 Frank Bailey left Woolston dead on time at 11.15 in poor visibility, but failed to pick up Alderney. He retraced his steps to Cap de la Hague and set out once more but again "missed" Alderney and again had to turn back but when he reached the French coast for the second time he followed it all the way down to Carteret before striking off for Guernsey to arrive at one minute past two. On December 9 John Horsey brought over Mr Finch of the radio station, Mr Hodges of the *Guernsey Press*, and Captain F.L. Barnard, the chief pilot of Imperial Airways, who wanted some experience of the flying-boat operations, and Captain Horsey: ". . . afforded him a wonderful coup-d'oeil of the approach to the Island as he wheeled his seaplane over and above the town before making a descent over the roofs of the Pollett into the Pool . . ." (22) The first recorded visit to Jersey of a Sea Eagle in the colours of Imperial Airways took place on December 12 when Colonel Blandy of the Air Ministry and his wife left Woolston at 10.45 with Captain Bailey and flew direct to St Helier. On December 22 Captain Bailey, Captain Barnard, and Mr Sinclair of the Air Ministry went for a 26 minute flight round Guernsey, but coming down forgot to wind in the trailing aerial. The weight hit the water and rebounded into the propeller, which was badly split, and this put the Sea Eagle completely out-of-action.

During 1924 73 passengers arrived in Guernsey by air, and at the end of the year 'GS was still being fitted with a new engine, and a larger top wing to increase lift. Imperial Airways lost three of their D.H.34's: one by fire at Ostend, one in an accident at Purley, and one was withdrawn, but three new aircraft joined the fleet, a Vickers Vulcan, a Handley Page W8f, and a D.H.50. In addition, a Bristol Type 75 was loaned by the Air Ministry for the Cologne route.

1925

The time-table for January, 1925 remained unaltered at 11.15 ex Woolston and 2 pm ex St Peter Port and 'GR made the trip on January 5 to be followed by about half-a-dozen more that month. February was nothing but reports of "Heavy Seas" and "Gales" and little was heard of the flying-boats until 'GR crossed to Guernsey and Jersey on the 21st. It reappeared on the 22nd, but more "Gales" and "Heavy Seas" followed and on March 5 came the surprise announcement that the service would close down at the end of the month due to the expiration of the lease to the Marine Airport, which was the property of the Supermarine Company. In a long rambling statement Scott-Paine said: ". . . the Marine Airport will have to be moved from its present base at the end of March. During the past nine months experiments have been carried out from which we are able to make definite improvements to the machines . . . Orders for some of these experiments to be incorporated in the old machines have been placed . . .

the most important of which has been completed and is now awaiting trial
. . . A speeded-up service was tried during the summer months whereby a
double return journey per machine per day was made . . . Improvements
were also made regarding fuelling, mooring, handling of machines, and
inspection of engines and machines with a view to a more rapid turn-round
. . ." (50) Drury-Hudson returned to the mainland, and Lord Apsley, in
reply to his question, heard that: ". . . further experience of seaplane
services was needed before more ambitious schemes were undertaken, . . .
the Channel Islands service was being stopped to reorganize in the light of
last year's experiments . . ." The speaker was Sir Phillip Sassoon, who
had replaced W. Leach as Under Secretary of State for Air when the
Conservatives were returned in the election of October, 1924.

And so the spring and summer of 1925 passed with the Guernsey service
suspended. Elsewhere within the British Isles the only air-line activity
was a resumption by Northern Air Lines of its Belfast service, with the
other terminal now at Stranraer, but this only lasted from March 17 until
the latter end of May. When asked, at the beginning of August, what
services were being flown by Imperial Airways, Sir Samuel Hoare (back in
Office as Secretary of State for Air) had replied: " . . . the Southampton-
Guernsey and the Amsterdam-Berlin have been discontinued . . . the former
will shortly be resumed . . ." During September "signs of life" were
observed at the Imperial Airways' office at St Peter Port, and *The
Aeroplane* reported: ". . . that the marine branch of Imperial Airways,
Ltd., which may be remembered as having run an almost annual service
between Southampton and Guernsey, is shortly to spring into life once
more. The two "Sea Eagles", which during their hibernation have grown
another 100 hp, are now equipped with Napier "Lions". These machines,
one hears, leap off the ground . . ." By the end of October 'GS was ready for
service, John Horsey was flying on the Paris route, V.W. Garwood was
representing Imperials in Amsterdam, and, instead of Drury-Hudson, a
station engineer, Mr A. Browne, was at St Peter Port assisted by young
apprentice Frank Hotton. Frank Bailey was the sole flying-boat pilot and
was also the manager of the new Imperial Airways marine airport at
Durham Wharf, south of the floating bridge between Thorneycroft's and
Messrs Dixon Bros and Hutchinson, Ltd. (See Appendix 2B), although Mr
G.H. Miles was the manager of the marine branch of Imperial Airways.
On November 11 Captain Bailey set out for Guernsey in the revitalised

'GS, but strong winds and snow forced him to return, and it was December 10 before the *Guernsey Evening Press* was able to announce that: ". . . the weather was sufficiently fine yesterday to allow a seaplane to cross from Southampton . . ." According to the Guernsey States' local statistics for 1925 three passengers arrived in Guernsey by air! Imperial Airways received three new machines, one D.H.50a, one Vickers Vulcan, and one Handley Page W9, but one Vulcan and one Vimy were withdrawn. An Avro Andover was operated on loan from the Air Ministry.

1926

During 1926 Imperial Airways would fly from Croydon to Paris-Basle-Zurich, to Ostende-Amsterdam, and to Brussels-Cologne, and at the beginning of the year details were published of a new agreement with the Air Ministry.

Instead of the minimum annual mileage of 1,000,000 to qualify for the subsidy a new composite minimum of 425,000,000 horse-power miles was substituted, and every mile performed by a marine aircraft was to count as a mile and a half. This was to encourage the use of more highly-powered aircraft, and to take into account the high cost of operation of the marine types used so far. Nevertheless, the revived Southampton-Guernsey service, details of which appeared in *Airways* for January, 1926, was to be one return trip per week only; the flying-boat to leave Woolston at 10 am, and St Peter Port at 1 pm every Wednesday. With the extra 100 hp the time of flight was reduced by ten minutes to one hour forty minutes. It was February 24 before Captain Bailey arrived at St Peter Port in 'GS, and the *Guernsey Star* was optimistic: ". . . With the advent of finer weather we can look forward to a regular air service between this island and the mainland . . ."

By March the regular service seemed to be in "full swing", if such a description can be applied to a weekly appearance, and the March issue of *Airways* gave an account of a return trip by the editor, T. Stanhope Sprigg, a well-known writer on aviation: "his three passengers comfortably ensconced in armchairs inside the glass-sided cabin, Captain Bailey, attired in a wondrous flying suit of his own design that would have graced equally well a diver or a dustman, and of which he was inordinately proud, climbed into the little cockpit above the cabin and the skylight was closed down. A motor-boat took us in tow until, well-out in mid-stream, our escort departed and, emulating her example, we taxied away downstream, the foam curving gaily past our bows . . . it was only as, abeam of the mighty *Majestic*, we soared up into the air . . . We sped down Southampton Water, flew low over Calshot Castle . . . To the left stretched the Isle of Wight . . . a gaunt grey cliff towering up from a foam-splashed coast – the Needles . . . The little white cottages of the coast-guards, on the cliff above . . . the glint of the sun on a glass showed that our passing was observed and would be reported to Southampton . . . We were flying by compass now, and I remembered the pilot's earlier remark that he could find his way across by the smell of his exhaust from the last day's trip . . . The Casquets set in a blue, sunlit sea, . . . A great flight of sea birds rose . . . as we passed high above the lighthouse, and in a few minutes Guernsey was ahead . . . Alderney, grim, dark, and deserted was passed on our left . . ." For the return they were joined at the last moment by a very large person, and as they were clambering aboard the v.l.p. mentioned that he weighed 18 stone: ". . . – The pilot wilted visibly, and then, after a rapid calculation on the back of an envelope, groaned in awed tones to the mechanic 'Throw out 16 bags of ballast' . . ." The flying-boats reported their positions by radio, of course, as recalled by Mr George Cozens who used to live in Scholing. He watched them take-off from the garden, and then he listened in on his radio to hear the message "Passing Hythe", followed by "Crossing the coast at Beaulieu", and then "Passing the Needles". On its return the flying-boat would pin-point these landmarks in reverse order, and when he heard "Approaching Hythe" young George just had time to jump on his bike and ride down to the floating bridge to watch the Sea Eagle securing to its buoy. Instead of the brown hull and silver wings of the B.M.A.N. Co. the Imperial Airways' Sea Eagles were painted blue and white.

There was a special flight to Jersey on May 17 when Captain Bailey in 'GS collected the parents and sister of Miss Ena Single, one of the chorus of "Wildflower" at His Majesty's Theatre. She had been injured in a car smash on the Great West Road opposite the Maclean's toothpaste factory, and the S.O.S. broadcast from London 2L0 and other stations was heard in Jersey. A car took them from Woolston to Gosport, where another Imperial Airways' machine was waiting to carry them on to London. Happily, all this effort was not in vain, and Miss Single recovered, returned to the stage, and, in due course, played a leading part with Ivor Novello. About the same time there was a special flight to Cherbourg in: "A THRILLING RACE by aeroplane and flying-boat to overtake the *Olympic* . . . A consulting engineer, sailing for America, left London before important plans which he had to take with him were ready and these were later despatched from London by car with just sufficient time to catch the liner at Southampton. But the car broke down and another one was hired and driven to Croydon Aerodrome where a fast aeroplane was waiting. On arrival at Southampton, the plans were transferred from the 'plane to a flying-boat, which, travelling at 100 miles an hour, reached Cherbourg just before the liner's departure . . ." (67).

On Tuesday, May 25, the *Jersey Evening Post* reported that the seaplane would leave Southampton for Jersey at 10 am the following morning, and return via Guernsey – "'Phone 167 for seats". Messrs S. Tolcher and J. Boleat appear to have taken up this offer and the next day soon after 12.30 pm Captain Bailey and his Sea Eagle duly arrived at St Helier with two passengers ". . . a lady and a gentleman . . ." The flying-boat departed at 2.10 pm for Guernsey, where lunch had been arranged, with the same "lady and gentleman", evidently on a pleasant excursion, and the two Jerseymen. Before passing Corbière it was noticed that the water in the radiator was boiling and when the passengers returned to the plane after lunch Captain Bailey had to tell them that the journey could not be completed. A new radiator was needed. The Imperial Airways' agents in Jersey were the Jersey General Engineering Co.

According to the *Jersey Morning News*, ". . . The seaplane has only room for four passengers or 750 lbs. of goods . . . the passenger finds a compact cabin with two wicker chairs and a comfortable double seat forward . . . the windows are sliding, and can be opened in flight . . . the pilot sits amidships . . . a wheel similar to a car . . . One of the most interesting gadgets is the Vickers Stabiliser for use in fog, which is gyroscopic, and shows the least variation from the horizontal by a series of small red and green electric lamps . . . the pilot closes the hatch . . . Once in the Bay the engine is stopped and the plane automatically swings into the wind . . . With a steady hum the engine restarts . . . half-an-hour finds you alongside the quay at Guernsey where a special filling station has been installed . . ." The weekly service continued at the same times until the end of July, and details were given in *The International Aerial Time Table* published by Lep Transport. The editor of *Flight* commented: ". . . The book is depressing because out of a total of 32 pages of aerial time-tables, fares, etc. but two are occupied by Imperial Airways . . . With all our resources, with all our 'million pound monopoly company' with the best aeroplanes in the world we can only manage four insignificant air lines . . . but the Southampton – Guernsey, our only seaplane service, is the Cinderella of Imperial Airways with one service per week in each direction, both made on Wednesdays and judging from the time-table, so planned as to allow one machine to maintain the service . . . What possible use such a service could be is not very clear. If there is sufficient traffic . . . to make it worthwhile operating a service then it should be a daily one. If there is not sufficient traffic, then a weekly service is merely a farce and can have no possible value except that of complying with the letter of the agreement between the company and the Government for the purpose of earning (or rather obtaining) the subsidy . . ." At the beginning of June 'GR was out-of-action in St Peter Port and on June 4 it was shipped to Southampton on board the S.S. *Fratton*. On June 9 the Supermarine Swan made its first flight with seats for ten passengers. This machine had been spoken of as a candidate for the Guernsey route ever since its appearance in 1924 and now, at long last, it had flown in a form suitable for the service. Henri Biard had taken it up on a test flight with F. J. Bailey, and another representative of Imperial Airways, a man from the Press, and eight young ladies from the Supermarine Works! It received its c. of a. for passenger carrying on June 30, and made its maiden flight to Guernsey the same day. The Supermarine Swan (See Appendix 1A), by this time, had been fitted with two 450 hp Napier Lion engines and was much larger than the Sea Eagle, having a wing span of 69 feet, and an all-up weight of 13,710 lbs. Its cruising speed was 87 mph and its bluff bow made it rather ugly, but it was, nevertheless, the "father and mother" of the Supermarine Southampton which gave excellent service in the R.A.F.

It was flown to Guernsey by Frank Bailey with four passengers and: ". . . At 12.35 . . . the splendid new . . . Swan . . . swooped down over the Castle wall and alighted majestically on the water opposite the Spur, piloted unerringly by Captain Bailey . . . Southampton to Guernsey in 91 minutes. It left again at 2.55 with two passengers . . .

A NEW ADVENTURE FOR THE FLYING PUBLIC.

From England to the Channel Islands by a New Supermarine Flying-boat

SKIMMING LIGHTLY OVER THE SURFACE OF SOUTHAMPTON WATER—THE NEW TWIN-ENGINED SWAN, THE LATEST THING IN AERIAL LOCOMOTION, COMPARED WITH A LITTLE YAWL.

SEATED IN A COMFORTABLE WICKER ARMCHAIR, THE PASSENGER HAS A PLEASANT JOURNEY ACROSS THE CHANNEL.

A MECHANIC ATTENDING TO ONE OF THE TWO NAPIER-LION ENGINES WHICH PROPEL THE FLYING-BOAT AT NINETY MILES PER HOUR

THE BIGGEST FLYING-BOAT YET CONSTRUCTED IN ENGLAND IN FULL FLIGHT TO THE CHANNEL ISLANDS

Last week a new service by air to the Channel Islands and Cherbourg was inaugurated by the Imperial Airways. A passenger to Jersey and Guernsey can now leave Southampton Water in the comfortable saloon shown here, and in one hour and ten minutes the big flying-boat is alighting in Guernsey harbour. The new craft is known technically as a Supermarine Napier Swan flying-boat, and is propelled by two 450-h.p. Napier-Lion engines. There are at present two flying-boats on the new service, which connects Southampton with both the Channel Islands and Cherbourg, where passengers from the big Transatlantic liners can connect with the flying-boat service. A view given above shows the interior of the comfortable cabin. This is in the lower, or boat portion of the main structure. From its port-holes one can view the shining waters below. The interior "walls," it will be noticed, are padded to lessen the vibration of the huge engines. Above the saloon is a superstructure whence the pilot controls the flight of the Supermarine.

The Sphere, 10 July 1926

(From the Illustrated London News Picture Library)

The appointments are exquisite. The passengers obtain access to the nose of the aircraft this leading to a commodious passenger saloon padded luxuriously, and in which there are ten cosy armchairs. An ample porthole is provided for each chair . . ." (22). It was presumed by *The Aeroplane* that the padded sides were to guard against shocks on the water and not in the air, although sound-proofing a more obvious reason. Advertisements in the *Guernsey Evening Press* at regular intervals proclaimed that: ". . . The luxurious new Swan 12-seater will leave Guernsey every Wednesday at 2 pm to arrive Southampton at 3.40 pm – Sole Guernsey agent: Messrs R. G. Davies & Co. 12, Smith Street . . ." In the other direction the flying-boat was leaving Woolston at 11 am, and on July 31 it was chartered by Mr R. Mond (Major Brackley's wife's uncle) of the well-known chemical family for a week-end trip to Dinard, via Guernsey with a party of ten. Another flying boat was in action over the August Bank Holiday week with Mr Leslie Hamilton flying the *Daily Mail* from Southampton to Jersey every morning in his Vickers Viking, G-EBED, but the Swan made the Guernsey trip on three Wednesdays out of four in August, and on two, at least, in September, and after fog had prevented the flight on September 2 it was decreed that, in future, if the weather was unfavourable on the Wednesday the flying-boat would leave on Thursday, and, if still the same, on Friday.

The last report of the Swan on the service during 1926 was on September 29, and the following week it was the Sea Eagle again. The Winter time-table showed the flying boat leaving Woolston at 11.30 am every Tuesday, and St Peter Port at 9.15 am every Wednesday to connect with the 11.14 restaurant car for Waterloo (12.49) which allowed a good half-day in London before a return on the 9.30 boat train. A waiting room was being prepared at No. 7, The Pollett, where luggage could be left, and on the day of the flight passengers were asked to be at the waiting room by 9 am. Every Tuesday there were flights round Guernsey, Herm and Jethou at 3 pm for £1. 5s. 0d. Throughout October and November the Sea Eagles made regular appearances, but on December 1 Bailey in 'GS had engine trouble and had to make a forced landing off the Needles, to be towed back to Southampton by a motor boat. In the House of Commons the same old question was being asked, this time by Colonel Day, who wanted to know what steps were being taken with the French regarding the extension of the Channel Islands service to Cherbourg. The Secretary of State for Air gave the same old answer which was that this was primarily a matter for Imperial Airways. Occasional flights were undertaken to Cherbourg, and the question whether the special permission required could be dispensed with, was under discussion. "Is it not a fact" said Col. Day "that it would save a day coming from America to England, or vice versa, if this service were established . . ." Sir Samuel Hoare agreed that considerable time would be saved in the transport of American mails. *Flight* claimed that negotiations were in progress to save about one day, and both passengers and mails from the Atlantic liners would be transferred to Querqueville (about two miles west of Cherbourg), and thence by flying-boat to Southampton. Imperial Airways said nothing, but on the drawing-board at Short's Rochester works new flying-boats for their eastern Mediterranean service were taking shape, and it may be assumed that they were not too interested in "pushing" the French for landing facilities at Cherbourg.

When the Imperial Airways' staff at St Peter Port went down to the harbour on the morning of December 15 to prepare 'GS for the regular Wednesday flight to Woolston they were horrified to find she had sunk at her moorings. When lifted on to the Castle Emplacement they discovered that about two feet of the wing had been smashed. Obviously the Sea Eagle had been struck by a vessel during the night, and a reward of £10 was offered for for the identity of the culprit. However, there was no service for a week or so afterwards and the reason given was that one of the boat moorings in the harbour was too near the Imperial Airways' mooring, which might mean that a possible cause of the sinking was fouling by a ship at an adjacent buoy.

The engine was shipped back to England, but 'GS was never repaired, and the service had to rely on 'GR, the sole survivor, and the problematic Swan. 67 passengers arrived in Guernsey by air during 1926. On the European routes of Imperial Airways two new types of aircraft appeared, the Handley Page W10, and the Armstrong-Whitworth Argosy, but more significant was the D.H. Hercules for the Middle East. A Cairo to Baghdad service, mainly for mail and communications between the various Middle East squadrons, had been flown by the R.A.F. since 1921, and because of the absence of landmarks in this featureless area, and the dangers to be faced in the event of a forced landing, a furrow had been ploughed across the desert for the planes to follow, in what itself had been quite an adventure. Not a very great compliment to R.A.F. navigation, but much appreciated nevertheless. In 1925 Imperial Airways had agreed to operate the route for an annual subsidy of £93,600, and de Havillands designed the Hercules for this purpose. The winter time-table of January, 1927, in addition to the times of the Paris, Brussels, and Amsterdam services, gave the details of the forthcoming Cairo-Gaza-Baghdad-Basra service scheduled to leave Cairo on January 12 and 26, February 9 and 23, and March 9 and 23.

Imperial Airways' first Short "Calcutta", G-EBVG.
(From the Royal Aeronautical Society Library)

The new Short Calcutta flying-boat was described in *Flight* of 6.1.27, the general arrangement drawings were shown, and *Flight*, claiming to be "the champions of the seaplane as a factor in Empire communications . . . with very considerable satisfaction" . . . was . . . "able to place on record the fact that at last Imperial Airways appear to be seriously contemplating the organisation of seaplane routes. Hitherto the only route of this kind has been that between Southampton and the Channel Islands, and a service operated once a week over a route where, in the very nature of things, there cannot be much traffic, is scarcely in keeping with the spirit of British Empire aviation. The solitary flying-boat used on this route has been spending nearly the whole of its time "sitting" on the Itchen, a familiar landmark to those who regularly use the floating bridge . . . Doubtless this use of a flying-boat may have provided data as to weathering qualities, hull soakage, etc., but is scarcely the way to progress in Empire seaplane communications . . ." Nevertheless the *Guernsey Evening Press* carried its regular advertisement for the winter service leaving Woolston at 11.30 on Tuesdays and St Peter Port at 9.15 on Wednesdays. Intending passengers were asked to book the previous day, if possible, at R. G. Davies & Co., 12 Smith Street (2nd floor), and to be at the Pollett waiting room ten minutes before the time of flying. Captain Bailey, pilot and Woolston manager made his weekly flight, more often than not, and on January 11 he took his wife over to Guernsey, but she, having to be home the following evening "for certain", elected to return by boat, such was her faith in the Sea Eagle. Leaving St Peter Port some two hours behind schedule Captain Bailey still managed to beat the *Lorima* by about three hours! The last reported appearance of the Swan in Guernsey was in February, 1927 when it arrived on the 8th and left the following morning, and there were no more flying-boats until March 8 when a Sea Eagle put in an appearance. *Flight* of March 17 said: ". . . True, we have our weekly flight to the Channel Islands . . . but the less said of that the better . . . As long ago as 1919 or 1920 the Supermarine Aviation Works proved the feasibility of a Channel service, to which the travesty of a service since operated by Imperial Airways Ltd. has added no useful knowledge . . . Imperial Airways show that they have no faith in the seaplane service and have remained content with the Channel Islands joke for more than a year . . ."

The weekly flights continued through March until April 6 but later that month Imperial Airways were obliged to express their regret to the many intending passengers, both for trips round the Island and to England, for the suspension of the service over the Easter holidays. Owing to the Swan being laid-up the Sea Eagle is the only machine available. "During the normal rigourous inspection prior to leaving Southampton on April 12 a structural defect was discovered which necessitated the stripping of the whole machine . . ." (22). The Swan was never used again on the Guernsey service and, like the Sea Eagle, G-EBFK, it just faded away with the records now saying it was scrapped in 1927! It was not until the end of June that the weekly flights (weather and circumstances permitting) were restarted, and at the end of September the days were changed so that departures from Woolston were on Thursdays and from St Peter Port on Fridays. About the same time Captain Bailey left the Channel Islands route to fly seaplanes on the Nile, and Henri Biard took his place, although still employed by Supermarine. During 1927 only 43 passengers arrived in Guernsey by air.

1928

The first of the Short Calcutta flying-boats, G-EBVG, (See Appendix 1B) was launched at Rochester on Monday, February 13, 1928. It was an all-metal aircraft, with a stressed-skin hull, and fabric-covered wings of 93 feet span. There was accommodation for 15 passengers and a steward and the three Bristol Jupiter engines gave a cruising speed of nearly 100 mph. The max. all-up weight was 22,500 lbs. It made its first flight on February 21, followed by a series of test flights at Felixstowe. Meanwhile Henri Biard continued to fly the last of the Sea Eagles on the Guernsey run and at the beginning of March he took it on one of the rare visits to Cherbourg. A Mr and Mrs Mackie were due to arrive at Cherbourg from America on board the *Olympic* and to leave Southampton the same day for Madeira on the *Balmoral Castle*. Henri Biard flew from St Peter Port to Cherbourg and collected the two passengers in time to put them aboard the Union Castle liner at Southampton. "Instead of taking about six hours to cross we took only one hour and ten minutes" said Mr Mackie. Mr Bailey was back on the Guernsey service in March, and in May the advertisements, which appeared in Guernsey more often than the Sea Eagle announced that "ON AND AFTER JUNE 1 . . ." the flying boat would leave Woolston every Friday at 11.30, return from Guernsey at 4 pm the same day to arrive Southampton at 5.40, and connect with the 6.18 restaurant car express to Waterloo. Round the Island trips would be on Friday afternoons. There were few changes on the other Imperial Airways routes and the summer time-table for 1928 showed the old-established London-Paris-Basle-Zurich, and London-Ostend-Brussels-Cologne services, plus a new line from London to Paris, via Le Touquet. The Cairo-Gaza-Baghdad-Basra service was now running weekly.

On May 29 the new Calcutta 'VG left Calshot at 11 am and flew to Jersey with Sir Samuel and Lady Hoare on board, accompanied by Supermarine Southampton S-1231, passing over Alderney at about mid-day. After lunch at Government House, the Secretary of State for Air and

55

his wife were taken by car to see something of Jersey and returned to St Helier about 3.30 pm to board the flying-boat and continue on to the Cattewater, Plymouth. On July 27 the Calcutta set out from Southampton for Guernsey with Captain Bailey and Major Brackley and eleven others on board, but "the cliffs at the Needles were wreathed in low-lying clouds, and as the Calcutta hummed her way steadily into the Channel the visibility became worse . . . Captain Bailey could barely see 200 yards ahead. At 12.8 the wireless-operator, in his cabin abaft of the pilot's cockpit, received a message from Guernsey . . . Visibility 100 yards" (50) and the Calcutta was turned for home. If this was a regular service flight in place of the Sea Eagle then the passengers were the first on a British machine to enjoy the concession of smoking, and a steward serving drinks.

On August 1 the Calcutta caused a sensation by landing on the Thames at Westminster, and during the following three days it attracted widespread public interest, and was inspected by several hundred M.P.'s. The flight itself was something of an achievement and Hugh Short recalls how he often went with John Lankester Parker on first trial flights: ". . . My most interesting experience with him was when he landed the Calcutta flying-boat on the Thames. This was done at the request of Imperial Airways Ltd. and the landing on the Thames was made between Vauxhall and Lambeth Bridge. Only a most skilful pilot could achieve that feat of landing a big flying boat in such a restricted space . . . I doubt if a flying-boat will ever land there again . . ." (57) It was August 10 before the Calcutta finally reached Guernsey, again with Brackley and Bailey as pilots, and various important people were taken for a flight together with a representative of the local Press. "The Calcutta is imposing outwardly and luxurious inwardly . . . an armchair on land could have been scarcely less unsteady than seemed that super-flying-boat as she taxied out of harbour . . . The engines began to roar – and the cotton wool – hygienically encased in an envelope, with which each passenger is supplied, was hastily adjusted, and though the spray rushed past the port-holes no motion was felt . . ." (22) The latest advert in the Guernsey paper, after a false start due to the non-arrival, now gave the times of the new bi-weekly service in the luxury 15-seater Calcutta as Tuesdays and Fridays, departing Woolston at 11.30 and St Peter Port at 4.30 with the flying time still 1 hr. 40 min. as for the Sea Eagle. Fares remained at £3 single, £5. 10s. 0d. return and there were well-patronised flights around the island for £1, at convenient times.

After the maiden flight Captain Bailey was the regular pilot, and the Calcutta kept very much to schedule. On August 24 it brought Mr Webb from Imperial's London office to act as traffic manager for a while to try to obtain freight for the Calcutta's capacious hold. A new motor-boat was brought over on the *Fratton*, and on August 26 'VG was chartered at a cost of £450 to fly to Queenstown to pick up Mr Leeds, a millionaire's son, and his valet, arriving on the Liverpool bound *Scythia*. They were unable to reach Ireland in one day because of the weather and spent the night on the Cattewater at Plymouth to continue in the morning. Leaving Queenstown about noon with their two passengers they reached Cherbourg at 3.30 pm. The following day Frank Bailey flew the regular Tuesday service flight plus one round the island with 11 passengers (35 miles in 30 minutes) for which the price was now 25/- as it was for the Sea Eagle flights, and then on the Wednesday (29th) there was a special flight to Guernsey with Sir Eric Geddes and other directors. Because of the increased activity Captain Bailey was joined by his old comrade John Horsey, and newcomer Donald Drew, who was well-known at the time as the pilot of the plane from which Albert Loewenstein had fallen to his death. The *Daily News* of September 21 described a flight in the Calcutta under the heading: "FLIPPING TO GUERNSEY . . . after the exhilarating rush of the take-off the great machine 93' across the wings has swung up to 500 ft almost before you realise she has left the water, two revelations of her remarkable performance. Then smoothly down Southampton Water by Calshot and Hurst Castle and over the Needles . . . You are now climbing steadily . . . after sixty short minutes a tiny island materialises out of the haze and passes slowly beneath, red cliffs, green and brown fields with little coves edged with creamy sand. This little arcadia is Alderney. On the starboard side lie the Casquet rocks – miles of them – dreadful to ships but to flying-boats faintly useful as a landmark. An exhilarating swoop down a few minutes later and the Calcutta slips through the entrance of St Peter Port to the waiting motor-boat which lands the 15 passengers at the harbour steps." (71)

The second Calcutta, G-EBVH, had been delivered to Southampton on September 12, and two days later set off for Scotland on private charter to Sir Eric Geddes with a large party of family and friends. "Brackles" and Bailey were the pilots and they flew to Loch Ryan on the first day, via

Weymouth, Bridgewater, Anglesey, and the Isle of Man. The charter lasted four days and ended at Liverpool in time for their "Civic Week" of September 24-29, during which the Calcutta was to fly a demonstration service to Belfast.

Following an inaugural flight on September 22 the service commenced on the 24th and flew every day of the week except on the 28th when there was fog. The service was very popular with all 15 seats booked on every flight and it was decided to run for a second week, but fog caused cancellation on two days, and on October 4 after arriving in the Mersey a wing strut was damaged by the passenger tender. The service was abruptly terminated, but a new strut was fitted by October 6 and 'VH took off from the Mersey at 12.45 to return to Southampton via the Welsh coast, but an inlet valve failed in the centre engine and they stopped at Pembroke Dock. From the beginning of October the service was reduced to once weekly, leaving Woolston at 11.30 and St Peter Port at 1.50 every Wednesday with the adverts adding ". . . all metal flying boat – refreshments on board," but the Woolston departure was moved forward to 11.10 in November. During 1928 160 passengers travelled to Guernsey by air from Southampton.

Imperial Airways' second Short "Calcutta", G-EBVH on the Mersey in 1928.
(Photo. by Mr. T. Lloyd-Jones, M.A)

1929

On January 16, 1929 the second Calcutta, G-EBVH, took over the service, but on February 27 the *Guernsey Evening Press* informed its readers that the: ". . . air service has been suspended until further notice. To-day was to have been the final flight but the weather prevented a departure . . ." The last flight of Imperial Airways then, must have taken place on Wednesday, February 20, and like its predecessor, the B.M.A.N. Co., when the end came it just quietly disappeared – "Not a bugle sounded a farewell note."

Guernsey was inured to flying-boat services and faced the future philosophically with the hope that it would be resumed in the spring, but Imperial Airways had no such illusions, and both Calcuttas were soon on their way to the Mediterranean, to be joined by others. For the summer of 1929 the Imperial Airways' time-table was showing a through service from England to India: from Croydon to Basle, via Paris, by Armstrong-Whitworth Argosy, from Basle to Genoa by train (night sleeper), and from Genoa to Alexandria by Short Calcutta, calling at Rome, Naples, Corfu, Athens, Suda Bay, and Tobruk. From Alexandria a D.H. Hercules continued on to Karachi. An alternative flying-boat service was now in existence and by the terms of the agreement Imperial Airways was no longer obliged to persevere with the Channel Islands service.

Notes

The 4,362 ton steamship *Buchanness* of Swansea, owned by the Cornborough Shipping line Co. was sailing in ballast from Dunkirk to Barry when her tail shaft broke and she drifted helpless in a N.W. gale until wrecked on Nannel's Rock between Alderney and the Casquets about 1 am April 13th, 1924.

The *Alberta* was built by John Brown of Clydebank for the L.S.W.R.'s Southampton-Channel Islands service as a replacement for the *Stella* which foundered on the Black Rock off the Casquets on 30.3.1899 with the loss of 105 lives. The *Alberta* was in service from 1900 to 1929 when she was sold. 1,240 tons, two triple-expansion engines, speed 19½ knots. Bombed and sunk off Greece in 1941.

The *Lorima* was built by Denny Bros. of Dumbarton for the L.S.W.R.'s Southampton-Channel Islands service. 1,457 tons, 19½ knots, two sets of Parsons geared turbines. She was in service from 1919 to 1939 and was damaged on 23.9.35.

when she hit a rock off St Helier. She was named after the wife of the L.S.W.R.'s general manager, Sir Herbert Walker and the story is told of his horror at being handed a message: "*Lorima* on the rocks outside Jersey making water fast through a hole in her bottom". Lost off Dunkirk, 1940.

The Humps are a group of rocks to the north of Herm, the principal and most northerly being La Grande Amfroque which separates the Great from the Little Russel channel.

The first *Mauritania* of 1907-35 was the famous four-funnel quadruple screw turbine sister ship of the *Lusitania* and held the Blue Riband for 20 years. 31,938 tons, 790' x 88', 26 knots. Maiden voyage Liverpool to New York (16.11.07.) and returned at an average speed of 23.69 knots. Broken up Rosyth 1935. Built for Cunard by Swan, Hunter and Wigham Richardson, Wallsend-on-Tyne.

The *Olympic* 1911-1935 of 46,439 tons, 883' x 92' triple screw combined triple-expansion and turbine vessel of the White Star line was the sister ship of the*Titanic*. Maiden voyage Southampton-New York 14.6.11.

The Cunard line *Scythia* (1921-1957) of 19,730 tons, 624' x 73' twin screw turbine vessel of 16 knots was built by Vickers-Armstrong at Barrow-in-Furness. Maiden voyage Liverpool-New York. Single funnel.

The *Fratton* was one of the three fast cargo boats built for the S.R. by D. & W. Henderson mainly for perishable freight from the Channel Islands and French ports. She became an armed boarding vessel in 1940 and a barrage balloon vessel later. Lost 18.8.44.

Queenstown, Near Cork, was renamed Cobb in 1922.

The Pollett. A street in St Peter Port leading down to the harbour.

The *Balmoral Castle* of just over 13,000 tons was one of the older Union Castle liners on the Southampton – South Africa service. Launched in 1910 she was broken up in 1939.

At the beginning of 1929, as Imperial Airways carefully extricated themselves from the British Isles as a theatre of operations, the four big railways (L.N.E.R., L.M.S., G.W.R. and S.R.) were seeking powers to provide air services. The forerunner was "the Western Highlands and Islands Transport Service Bill, which, for the first time in history, gives the Minister of Transport, after consultation with the Secretary of State for Air, power to authorise the railway companies specified in the Bill to provide mail, cargo, and passenger services between the Highlands and the Islands by air, as well as by sea and land . . ." (61) and on January 25, 1929 the Bills "to empower" the four railways ". . . to provide air transport services, were read for the first time . . ." (62) From the end of the war the railways had sat back losing traffic to the rapidly developing motor-bus services, and then, when they woke up to the fact, had been compelled to buy their way into road transport at great expense. As Mr H.P. MacMillan, K.C. pointed out: ". . . They were authorised to engage in transport by sea. Last year, after prolonged enquiry . . . the right to engage in road transport . . . The Railways were taunted last year with being supine . . . allowed themselves to be left in the rear altogether with regard to road transport. They did not propose to be exposed to the same taunt with regard to the air . . ." (17) All four companies were duly empowered to engage in air transport, within certain boundaries, and the G.W.R. took immediate, if limited action, when the general manager said that now the Company had their powers: ". . . they should consider whether they could not be used. He was anxious that (the G.W.R.) should be first in the field . . ." (13), and he entrusted S.B. Collett (assistant secretary of the G.W.R.) to look into the position, talk to Imperial Airways, and start an office in Westminster.

There was interest elsewhere on the G.W.R. and in June, 1929 the superintendent of road services, Mr F.C. Coventry, forwarded the following letter to Sir Felix Pole:

". . . Dear Sir,

The G.W.R. pioneered road services, so why not air services? What a fine chance they have got! Plymouth – Bristol, or Penzance – Cardiff, Aberystwyth by hydroplane this summer.

I personally feel it would pay well. Again what about trips to Channel or Scilly Isles, or even France.

Yours truly,
H. L. Weltch
(Road Transport supervisor at Penzance)

ps. I've got one pilot certified . . ." (13)

A few weeks later, R.W. Nicholls, (office of the superintendent of the line) wrote to the general manager:

". . . the S.R. are about to institute a service between Southampton and the Channel Islands in connection with the Tour and Travel Association. It would seem to me that the G.W.R. have an interest in this matter and that they should have been consulted . . ." (13)

With the departure of Imperial Airways from the Channel Island routes the field was now wide open to all comers, and the first to appear was Captain Richard Taylor, of Orviss Ltd., a store well-known in Jersey, with a branch in France. In addition he ran a travel agency called the Tour and Travel Association which was now to have an Aviation Department and proposed to operate between Southampton and Jersey with a call at Guernsey. So far Guernsey had always been the terminus with only an occasional flight on to Jersey, but now St Helier would replace St Peter Port as the main Channel Islands base. Press announcements gave the starting date as May, 1929, but the only connection with the S.R. was their timing to meet convenient trains at Southampton, although they had written from an address at 32, Mitre House, 177 Regent Street, London to offer the S.R. 10% to act as agents. Activity was centred at Brooklands until they leased the former Imperial Airways' marine airport at Woolston, and Mr G.W. Higgs, who had just left the R.A.F. with considerable flying experience in war and peace, was appointed manager. ". . . Although Imperial Airways abandoned the service" he said ". . . I feel confident that it can be made to pay. I don't say that we shall make a fortune out of it, but I do think there is a real demand for a steady service between Southampton and the Channel Islands. As long as we can pay our overhead charges at the start we shall be satisfied . . ." (50) There was some talk of a fleet of flying-boats, but the service started with just one which was Supermarine Seagull N9605. (See Appendix 1A) This had been converted to a Mark IV during its R.A.F. service by the addition of Handley Page slots and twin tail fins and rudders but retained its Lion IIB engine and was modified for civilian use as G-AAIZ with accommodation for five passengers.

Bellingham's were the Jersey agents and Mr B.C. de Guerin acted for Tour & Travel in Guernsey, but no flying-boat appeared in May, nor in June, although Captain Taylor left Jersey on June 29 with the intention of meeting the Seagull in Guernsey and returning in it to Jersey. It was, he learned, held up awaiting its c. of a. Early in July Bellingham's received a letter which said:

> ". . . We have several machines on hand; the first of these left the Supermarine works on June 28. Before it can be used . . . it has to have a Certificate of Airworthiness . . . As a result of the wrecking of an Imperial Airways' machine last month the regulations have received several amendments, and the Air Ministry has been very cautious about the granting of new certificates without the machine being subjected to very drastic tests . . ." (6)

Bellingham's passed this news on to the local Press in all good faith and their consternation can be imagined when, in the following month, Imperial Airways asked the *Evening Post* to publish the fact that:

> ". . . no amendments have been made to Airworthiness Regulations as a result of the wrecking of the Imperial Airways' . . . machine recently in the Channel . . .!"

At long last the Seagull's c. of a. was signed on July 10, and a preliminary flight made the following day to survey the route and, at the same time, provide a special charter for Captain Grant of the R.A.F. Club, his French bride, and two others. The Seagull left Woolston at 2 pm decorated with streamers and a pair of old shoes and arrived St Peter Port about 4. Two hours later, with the wedding party increased to six people, 'IZ took off from Guernsey and reached Jersey at 6.45 pm.

The time-table was as follows:-

Waterloo	Southampton	Woolston	Guernsey	Guernsey	Jersey	
Dep.	Arr.	Dep.	Arr.	Dep.	Arr.	
8.30 am	10.57 am	11.30 am	12.45 pm	1 pm	1.25 pm	weekdays
9.35 am	11.50 am	12.15 pm	1.30 pm	1.45 pm	2.05 pm	Sundays

Jersey	Guernsey	Guernsey	Woolston	Southampton	Waterloo	
Dep.	Arr.	Dep.	Arr.	Dep.	Arr.	
5.45 pm	6.15 pm	6.30 pm	7.45 pm	8.23 pm	11.14 pm	weekdays
5.20 pm	5.50 pm	6.05 pm	7.20 pm	7.56 pm	9.36 pm	Sundays

The Supermarine "Seagull", G-AAIZ of the Tour and Travel Association in St. Helier harbour.

The fare between Southampton and Jersey or Guernsey was £3. 10s. 0d. single, £6. 10s. 0d. return, and included transport to and from Southampton West station. 30 lb. of luggage was allowed free and 5d. per lb. charged on excess. Between Jersey and Guernsey the fares were £1 single, £1. 15s. 0d. return. A regular service was maintained from July 13 to July 28, with flights on to St Malo on the 15th and 17th, and the normal routine was for the Seagull to land outside the harbour entrance at St Helier and taxi through to a buoy opposite the G.W.R. berth. There was no call at Guernsey when there was no traffic so arrivals at St Peter Port were less frequent. On July 28 the flying-boat arrived at St Helier with one passenger but had to stay there because of the weather. At 6.30 am on the 30th she was taxied out through the pier heads, but the pilot, J. Oliver, was not happy about the performance of the engine, and the Seagull was brought back into harbour, to be hoisted up onto Albert Pier the following day to receive attention. Before joining Tour and Travel Mr Oliver had been an instructor at Brooklands for many years dating back to the time of the Henderson School of Flying. They were able to resume the service on August 2 when they left for Woolston at 12.30 pm, but the bad weather returned and 'IZ was storm-bound in St Helier from August 6 until 5 pm on the 8th when she set off with four passengers. It was a period of spring tides with low water predicted for 4.28 pm and there was no wind. The pilot taxied out into the open sea and gave the engine full throttle, but the run was longer than normal in the flat calm and 'IZ ran straight over a rock lying just beneath the surface of the water at its lowest level, but undetected in the slack water. A large piece was torn out of the hull bottom and with water flooding in the Seagull was returned to harbour at the best possible speed. Once again she was hoisted on to the Albert Pier, but repairs could not be carried out locally and she was shipped to Southampton on August 17 on board the *Haslemere*. At this stage Mr Oliver seems to have retired from marine aviation and its tidal problems and returned to instructing but with the Lancashire Aero Club.

The Seagull was back in service on August 30 and arrived at St Helier at 11 with two passengers, and new pilot S.S. Kirsten, ex. R.A.F. It left at one with five passengers and returned in the evening with three more. Business appeared to be picking up. On the evening of September 2 Stanley Kirsten left Jersey for Woolston at 6.30 pm. with the one lady passenger but engine trouble forced him to reduce speed. It was getting dark and he came down on the water off Southsea about 10 pm. and taxied close inshore. Pilot and passenger continued by car while a mechanic was left on board the Seagull. This was the last scheduled flight of Tour & Travel. Although George Higgs took over the Aviation Department and G-AAIZ, the Seagull was never seen again in the Channel Islands and nothing more was heard of its operations. By the following year Higgs was working for the aviation department of Ford's European Division.

In the summer of 1929 Tour and Travel had been Britain's sole domestic air-line, this had now gone. As the Hon. Mrs Bruce was to say of her Croydon competitors: ". . . We always knew when they were on their way out . . . they would leave sad little notes . . . 'No milk to-day' . . ." (63), and so the Marine Airport at Woolston became vacant again. Locally the demise of T & T passed unnoticed in the excitement of the 11th Schneider Trophy Contest taking place over the Solent, and won by the Supermarine S6 N247 on September 7. Upstream of the floating bridge the Supermarine Aviation Works was now owned by Vickers (Aviation) Ltd., and at nearby Weston the two-seater Spartan biplane designed by Oliver Simmonds, a former Supermarine senior engineer, was in full production, whilst over at Cowes the new combination of Saunders-Roe, Ltd. was turning out their first aircraft, the Saro Cutty Sark. Moses Saunders, grandfather of S.E. Saunders, had started a boat-building business on the Thames at Streatley in 1830, later spreading across the river to Goring and South Stoke. In 1901 Sam Saunders expanded to West Cowes in partnership with others, but five years later he set up on his own at East Cowes and became S.E. Saunders, Ltd., building aircraft as well as boats. After the war they built flying-boats to their own design, and hulls for other firms. The name of A.V. Roe is now well-known, but the firm of A.V. Roe and Co. was only registered on 1.1.1910 with the aid of capital supplied by Sir Alliott's brother, Humphrey, and this was derived from another firm called Everard's which made elastic webbing, the essential ingredient of gent's trouser braces. A basement floor of their Mill in Manchester was used as a workshop, and John Lord, Everard's manager, soon became Sir Alliott's right-hand man. In 1928 Sir Alliott sold his stake in the Avro concern to J.D. Siddeley (Later Lord Kenilworth) and bought a controlling interest in S.E. Saunders, Ltd. because he wanted to build flying-boats, and he took John Lord with him, as well as Harry Broadsmith, another Avro stalwart. In 1929 the name of the firm was changed to Saunders-Roe Ltd., and their first machine was an amphibian monoplane with two engines which they called the Cutty Sark and took the registration, G-AAIP. (See Appendix 1C)

As the Twenties drew to a close momentous events were taking place on the other side of the Atlantic so that 1929 became, if not a year to remember, a year that few would forget. On Thursday, October 24 nearly 13,000,000 shares changed hands, and the slide in share prices continued in the following months and years until mid-1932. According to the more sensational papers Wall Street was littered with the bodies of suicides, and with a certain amount of grim humour it was said, in New York, that receptionists in multi-storey hotels were asking prospective guests whether the room was for sleeping or jumping. Will Rogers claimed that people had to queue for windows! But Professor Galbraith has produced statistics to show that the suicide rate at this time was not abnormal. (64)

The prototype Saro "Cutty Sark", G-AAIP
(From the Royal Aeronautical Society Library)

Towards the end of May, 1930 the *Jersey Morning News* said there was "every probability" of a Jersey – Southampton air service starting within a few weeks. Early in June this was confirmed by the *Evening Post* in an interview with Mr R. B. Mace: ". . . We have ordered a big all-metal flying-boat with amphibian gear and two Gipsy engines . . ." (Saro Cutty Sark G-AAIP), and delivery was imminent. Four passengers with luggage could be carried, or six passengers without luggage. They had rented Imperial Airways' offices at Woolston, and cars would take the passengers to Southampton railway station. His partner was Stanley Kirsten, who had flown the Seagull for Tour and Travel in the previous

67

year, and the aircraft would be based at Jersey and be available for private charter to places like Le Touquet and Deauville, or to collect passengers from Atlantic liners at Cherbourg.

G-AAIP was not quite "brand new", having first flown in July, 1929 as a flying-boat with two 105 hp Cirrus engines. After some demonstration flights it was fitted with an amphibian undercarriage and sold to a Mr Holden. It appears that at some stage the Cirrus engines were replaced by 120 hp Gipsy engines and following the renewal of its c. of a. on 12.6.1930 it was taken over by Kirsten and Mace. On Friday, 13th it made its first flight to Jersey, alighting in the harbour at St Helier just after 11 am. The following day it returned to Southampton, but on Sunday, 15th it was back in Jersey by 12.55 and at 2.30 it started to give joy-rides from the beach of St Aubin's Bay near the First Tower. When not on charters or scheduled trips to Woolston G-AAIP spent most of its time joy-riding, usually from West Park, the nearest point to St Helier, although on one or two occasions the venue was Millbrook or First Tower. Flying usually started at 10.30 or 11.30 and lasted until 2 with an afternoon session sometimes continuing until 7, 8, or 9 pm. On Sundays there was no joy-riding before noon "so that no possible offence will be given to church-goers", and there was no joyriding up to and from two hours each side of high tide.

The Saro "Cutty Sark" as an amphibian   (M.A.P., Lossiemouth)

The amphibian made its first visit to Guernsey on June 17, taking four passengers from Jersey, and returning with three. It reached St Peter Port at 1.15 pm and was cleared in and out by Messrs H.G. Benest & Co. the agents there for Kirsten and Mace. The next day it arrived at St Peter Port at 8.50 pm but when it tried to take-off outside the harbour 35 minutes later it was unable to do so, for some unspecified reason and returned to the Pool to await the morning. There were a couple of unscheduled flights to Woolston in June, but the regular service did not start until July 7, after a formal christening on July 3 following a tea-party at the Villa Millbrook, home of Lord and Lady Trent of Nottingham (and Boot's the Chemists), attended by various people of note. The guests of honour were His Excellency Major-General E.H. Willis, C.B., C.M.G., the Lieutenant-Governor, and his wife, and it was Mrs Willis who, on the sands opposite, broke the customary bottle of champagne over the bows of the aeroplane and named it *Silver Bat*. It was a perfect summer's day and short flights were then given (at no charge presumably) to the local dignitaries lead by H.E. the Lieut.-Governor and his wife.

The baptismal ceremony of the "Silver Bat" Saro Cutty Sark
(By permission of the British Library)

Scheduled flights were on Mondays and Fridays leaving Jersey at 10.30 and Woolston at 2.30 although there was considerable flexibility in this timing, and the first flight of July 7 was advertised to depart at 10.30 "and return at 6 pm". The journey was to take about 1½ hours and cost £3. 10s. 0d. single, £6. 10s. 0d. return. Large adverts in the local press kept the public well informed, as on July 8 when it was announced that ". . . Apart from the scheduled Monday and Friday return trips . . ." there would be ". . . joy-riding on the sands at West Park on every available day – weather and conditions permitting – from 11 am to 6 pm – Special trips can be made to any ports on the French coast on application to Bellingham's. R.B. Mace will be at Bellingham's office daily from 9.30 to 11.30 . . ." There was a special charter to Southampton on the 9th but after taking off at 11.30 they ran into fog and had to return to Jersey and wait until the afternoon. The second scheduled flight, on Friday 11th, left at 11.30 to suit the convenience of the passengers, and the *Silver Bat* is reported to have left Jersey again at 7 pm with more passengers for Southampton. On Monday, 14th, the advert said "Tomorrow the *Silver Bat* will be doing return trips to Granville – four seats – The machine can be booked for Dinard, St Malo, or Granville for £15 . . ." The advert of the 16th announced two trips to Granville on the following day, leaving at 10 and 11 and returning at 5 pm and 6 pm, with joy-riding in between. At the end of July the amphibian took part in the "Battle of Flowers" flying over the stadium several times, and on one occasion going in low to drop flowers on the spectators. The only Guernsey excursion during July was advertised for the morning of Saturday, the 19th, so that joy-riding could not start until 3.30. Joy-rides were now "Round the Island" for a £1, or "Short Trips" for 10/-.

A similar routine of Monday and Friday return trips to Woolston with joy-rides interspersed continued throughout August with occasional interruptions for special charters as on August 14 when the *Silver Bat* was flown to Reading and returned at 5.30 pm in time to take Dr Halliwell to Guernsey for 6.30 and on August 20 by a special trip to Woolston. At the end of August 'IP went to Cowes for a routine overhaul, and its return to Jersey was confidently expected, but on September 10 it left Cowes for Renfrew on charter, and, like its predecessor the Seagull, never returned to the Channel Islands. No explanation was offered, but it must be assumed that the profits so far were not sufficient to warrant a continuation through the bleak months of the winter with no support from joy-riding holiday-makers. In fact, Kirsten and Mace had been hoping to acquire a much larger amphibian called the Saro Cloud (See Appendix 1C) which was now being produced and they had written to Saunders-Roe in July to tell them about their activities and adding that: ". . . we have found your Cutty Sark to be the ideal type for such operations . . . So delighted are we with our experience of the Cutty Sark that we hope to take a very early delivery of the Flying Cloud in order to cope with the demand the Cutty Sark has set up . . ." (20) At the end of September S.D. Scott flew Sir Alliott Verdon Roe and John Lord to Jersey in the prototype Saro Cloud, G-ABCJ, to see the situation for themselves, and talk to Kirsten and Mace, and they concluded that the Channel Islands had distinct possibilities, but needed a sound commercial firm with sufficient capital to buy at least two Saro Clouds. Saunders-Roe were in no position to help, and although Stanley Kirsten tried very hard to find backers he had no success and had to give up. Nevertheless, some interest in aviation had been stimulated and in the June of that year a meeting of the committee of the local Chamber of Commerce had considered the idea of making a proper aerodrome on Jersey in place of the tidal beach of St Aubin's Bay, first used by Avro 536, G-EBOY, in 1927. Correspondence with the Air Ministry followed, and Sir Alan Cobham was invited over in his capacity of consultant, but his visit did not take place "for reasons not germane to this review" to quote the *J.E.P.* of 10.3.37.

By 1930 nearly 50 Simmonds Spartans had been manufactured at Weston, to be assembled and flown at Hamble, although the prototype was built in Oliver Simmonds' own home, which presented a few problems when the time came for it to be moved. In order to reduce costs various ingenious features had been incorporated, such as interchangeable components, including the four half-wings of symmetrical aerofoil section, but this section was criticized as being susceptible to spinning, (a "vicious stall" according to Harald Penrose), and the aeroplane was not a commercial success. Mr Simmonds (later Sir Oliver) approached the Whitehall Securities Corporation, a powerful financial group, and a new company was formed on 26.4.30 called the Spartan Aircraft Co. Ltd. to take over the business of Simmonds Aircraft Ltd. and Simmonds Interchangeable Wing Co. Ltd. Three directors of Metal Propellers, Ltd. (W.S.C.'s other aviation concern): chartered civil engineer K.S. Chambers, chartered accountant J. de C. Ballardie, and wartime fighter pilot Captain Balfour, M.C. (later Lord Balfour of Inchrye) joined Simmonds, and his associates Lt. Col L.A. Strange D.S.O., M.C., D.F.C. and W.D.L. Roberts to form the board of the new company. The two latter had invested considerable sums in the Simmonds enterprise and Strange was involved on the sales side whilst Roberts became works manager. Strange who was well-known in aviation circles learned to fly before the war and then served with distinction in the R.F.C. and R.A.F. until 1919. In 1928 and 1930 he had flown to Berlin to take part in the Deutscher Rundflug and enjoyed meeting some of his old adversaries including a Captain Goring "who has since been prominent in politics . . ." Roberts was comparatively unknown. He had taken his degree and become an associate member of the Institute of Civil Engineers in 1902, and from 1919 until 1927 he was Inspector-General of the Public Works Department of Egypt, followed by a period in the Sudan advising on engineering projects on the Upper Nile.

A new version of the machine was produced with a "Clark Y" wing section, and this was called the Spartan Arrow, with a three-seater version which made a useful joyriding machine. By this time "Moth" had become the synonym for any open two-seater sporting biplane, the original already having strong competition from Avro and Blackburn, but, the impact of the Spartan version was not so great as had been hoped. However, as the late Lord Balfour recalled "W.S.C. wanted a card of entry into the aeroplane construction world". Simmonds departed in 1931 to produce specialist items for the aircraft industry eventually employing over 10,000 people. In the same year he became an M.P. (for the Duddeston Division of Birmingham) and retained his seat until 1945. Sir Oliver spent his last years quietly in Guernsey and died in 1985.

In the time of "The Great Depression" between 1929 and 1931 the value of British exports dropped from 729 million pounds to 389 million, and by the end of 1930 there were over two million unemployed. Saunders Roe were now looking for capital, and Whitehall Securities took a very substantial holding with the result that the Spartan Aircraft Co. was transferred from Weston to East Cowes, alongside Saunders-Roe, and Sir Alliot, John Lord, and Harry Broadsmith joined the Spartan board. Here was evolved the Spartan Cruiser, based on the earlier Saro-Percival "Mailplane", and as a three-engined, low-wing monoplane designed to carry six passengers at 110 mph on 360 hp the prototype made its first flight in May, 1932. During 1930 the efforts of Kirsten and Mace had been joined on the domestic scene by a regular service between Croydon and Liverpool (Speke), calling at Birmingham (Castle Bromwich), and Manchester (Barton) flown by Imperial Airways, but as the three provincial cities concerned had each paid a large sum towards the cost, whereas the number of passengers carried was small, the service was not repeated in the summer of 1931. The only regular air service in Britain in 1931 was M.D.L. Scott's three-seater Puss Moth, G-AAXL flying between Skegness and Hunstanton for £1 return! This was the lowest point of the "Thirties", but 1932 saw a number of enterprises starting up, some to last longer than others.

Michael Scott expanded his operations at Skegness, now as Eastern Air Transport Ltd. Edward Hillman, well-known for his buses running east out of London after starting in 1928 with just one vehicle, leased Maylands aerodrome, near Romford, and began a regular service to Clacton, as well as joy-riding and taxi services, first with Puss Moths and later with Fox Moths. The D.H.Fox Moth was a single-engined biplane with an open cockpit for the pilot and a small cabin between the wings for three or four passengers, depending somewhat on the size of the passengers. The British Air Navigation Co. Ltd. (BANCO) was formed in February, 1932, mainly as a charter firm, but ran an experimental service between Bristol and Cardiff for one week in July, 1932 when C.D. Barnard in his Fokker FVIIa, G-EBTS, *The Spider* averaged about four return trips per day, and this was followed in September by a regular twice-daily service run by Norman Edgar using Fox Moth, G-ABYO. During 1931 the Cutty Sark, G-AAIP, formerly the *Silver Bat* had been taken on a sales tour of Europe, but early in 1932 it was sold to D. Campbell-Shaw who, with Flight-Lieut. Tommy Rose, formed Isle of Man Air Lines to run regular services between Liverpool and the Isle of Man. Joy-riding turned out to be their main activity until August 8 when 'IP hit an obstruction in Douglas Bay and immersed the four passengers up to their necks in salt water. A similar activity was being carried on at Blackpool by R.C.H. Monk who was flying the Cutty Sark, G-ABBC, on a Blackpool – Isle of Man service, but spending most of his time joy-riding from Blackpool beach. Another company called British Flying Boats, Ltd. bought Saro Cloud, G-ABXW and had it christened *Cloud of Iona* by Lady Hamilton, after which it carried out joy-riding and charter flights in Scotland, Northern Ireland, and the Isle of Man, and, for one week in August, ran a daily service between Greenock and Belfast. On June 27, 1932 the "Spithead Ferry" came into operation with four trips each way daily between Portsmouth and Ryde by the brand-new Westland Wessex G-ABVB, of Portsmouth, Southsea, and Isle of Wight Aviation, Ltd. This company had started life some years earlier at Apse aerodrome, near Shanklin, as Wight Aviation,

Ltd., but early in 1932 the board of A.G. Murray, L.M.J. Balfour, and J.H.A. Wells had been joined by old Etonian Flight-Lieut. Francis Luxmore, D.F.C., the nominal capital increased from £2,500 to £17,500, and the name changed to Portsmouth, Southsea, and I.O.W. Aviation, Ltd. 82 acres had been bought on the outskirts of Ryde and made into an aerodrome, and at the newly opened Portsmouth municipal airport P.S.I.O.W.A. had the sole right to joy-rides, air taxis, services to the Isle of Wight, the sale of petrol, and the provision of servicing and repairs. They rented the large hangar, provided airport management and control, and ran an Aero Club. Later in the year they started round the island trips calling at Ryde and Shanklin, and a regular service along the coast to Shoreham.

In Jersey the Chamber of Commerce was still pursuing the idea of an island aerodrome, and at their invitation, Lionel Balfour of P.S.I.O.W.A., with his wife, the former Lady Myrtle Jellicoe, flew to Jersey on October 17, 1932, and Mr Balfour was taken on a tour of possible sites. He selected one near St Peter's Barracks as most suitable and had supplied a full report by the end of that month. With commendable energy the Chamber of Commerce made a survey of the land on the site to establish its ownership and value, and, at the same time, the War Office was approached with a view to an exchange of land and buildings in the barracks area. P.S.I.O.W.A. were hoping to be appointed as consultants for the construction of the Jersey airport, should it come to pass, and they indicated their willingness to use it for a regular service to their base at Portsmouth. Unfortunately, although they were trying to get on to the Air Ministry's approved list, they had not been accepted and, when the time came at a later date for the selection of consultants they were not chosen because they did not have the recommendation of Mr Bertram, the Deputy Director of Civil Aviation.

Early in 1933 there was a visit by the then Col. The Master of Semphill, who confirmed the suitability of the site, and there were further meetings, but in the spring the Chamber of Commerce accepted the advice of the Attorney-General, Mr A.M. Coutanche (later Lord Coutanche) and handed over the results of their investigations to the States, as it was felt that the airport should be a States project, and not be left in private hands. In Britain, in 1933, there was increasing activity on the internal air-line scene, and, of the previous year's entrants, Eastern Air Services, Hillman's, BANCO, Norman Edgar's Western Airways,

British Amphibious Air Lines, and, of course, P.S.I.O.W.A. survived and, in most cases, expanded. One landmark was the introduction of the de Havilland Dragon, (See Appendix ID) an economical twin-engined biplane which could carry eight passengers at 110 mph on 13 gallons of fuel per hour. Edward Hillman bought six and started a Romford-Paris service in competition with Imperial Airways, whilst extending his local services to Margate and Broadstairs. Another bus operator, John Sword, started Midland and Scottish Air Ferries and instituted a regular service between Glasgow and Belfast, via Campbeltown. In the north of Scotland E.E. Fresson founded Highland Airways and opened a regular Inverness-Wick-Kirkwall service, and between Liverpool, Blackpool, and the Isle of Man, the Dragon and Fox Moths of Blackpool and West Coast Air Services were providing stiff competition for Mr Monk's Cutty Sark. At long last Great Western Railway Air Services inaugurated the Cardiff-Teignmouth-Plymouth route planned by S.B. Collett using a Westland Wessex on hire from Imperial Airways, and the Spartan Aircraft Company, to demonstrate the capabilities of their Spartan Cruiser founded their own airline on February 2, 1933 when Spartan Air Lines, Ltd. was registered with a capital of £10,000. Twice daily the Spartan Cruisers of the first air-line to be controlled by the Whitehall Securities Corporation flew to London from their home aerodrome at Somerton, Cowes, and as this comparatively unknown group was to have a major influence on the development of British airlines, including those to the Channel Islands, some account of its long history may not be out of place . . .

Its origin was in Yorkshire, in 1844. when Samuel Pearson, of Scholes, took a partnership in a Huddersfield firm of builders and contractors which, in 1856, became S. Pearson and Son when he brought his eldest son, George, into the business. The firm prospered, and George, who had married a Sarah Weetman Dickinson, moved to Bradford with the business. Before the move their eldest son, Weetman Dickinson Pearson, had been born on July 15, 1856, and he joined the firm at the age of sixteen. By the time he was twenty-one he was being entrusted with important contracts. In 1882 their tender for the Deptford storm outfall sewer was accepted, and in 1884 their headquarters was moved to London, with Weetman very much in charge. By 1898 their assets were nearly £1,000,000 and the only firm of similar standing in the contracting field was John Aird and Sons. Their contracts were world-wide and usually on a massive scale; they included Milford Haven Docks, Halifax Dock (Nova Scotia), Empress Dock (Southampton), the deepening of Alexandria Harbour, railway lines in Spain, the great tunnels – Hudson River, East River, and Blackwall, the Mexican Grand Canal, Vera Cruz Harbour, the Tehuantepec National Railway, and, in 1897, Dover Harbour. As Liberal M.P. for Colchester Weetman was obliged to convert S. Pearson and Son into a limited liability company in order to tender for the Dover Harbour contract. In 1901 he moved into oil. After a dubious start this became another saga of success as the Mexican Eagle Oil Company. He made a huge fortune and, contrary to to-day's cynical view of the 19th century capitalist, it was largely the result of hard work, absolute competence, a genius for costing and organization, and complete honesty and integrity. He was a most humane employer of labour British and foreign, and in 1917 he was created Viscount Cowdray of Cowdray, having been made a baronet in 1894. When made President of the Air Board he was regarded as: ". . . the greatest public works contractor of his day . . ." (18) The Air Board was the immediate fore-runner of the Air Ministry, which came into being as the result of the Act passed in November, 1917 to form the Royal Air Force. "Lloyd George, shaken by renewed public outcry over the air raids and anxious to placate what was considered to be the most influential part of the Press, offered the Air Ministry, not to Cowdray but to Northcliffe and the first Cowdray heard of the matter was an insolent letter of refusal published in *The Times* of 16th November, 1917. Cowdray, furious, at once resigned . . ." (18) Following the 1914-18 War opportunities for contracting were shrinking as Government departments expanded and in 1919 S. Pearson & Son (Contracting Dept.) Ltd. was formed to undertake work of that nature. Earlier, in 1907, the Whitehall Securities Corporation had been formed to take over all the interests outside contracting but between 1919 and 1922 some were hived off into separate groups such as the Whitehall Petroleum Corporation, the Whitehall Trust, and Whitehall Electric Investments.

After Lord Cowdray's death in 1927 his eldest son inherited the title but took no part in the business, and it was his second son, the Hon. Clive Pearson, who tried to follow in his father's footsteps. The connection with aviation began when they took over a firm called Metal Propellers Ltd., which made metal airscrews for aeroplanes and airships (including the ill-fated R-101), and it was decided that aviation had "a future". Sound advice on this subject was available from Captain Harold Balfour, M.C., who had joined Whitehall Securities in 1925, and was a most experienced airman having fought on the Western Front in various types of aircraft, including the famous Sopwith Camel, and had been an instructor at the legendary Smith-Barry School of Special Flying. As a dashing young man with a good war record he had found favour with the electors of Thanet and became their M.P., although remaining with Whitehall Securities. Two other members of W.S.C. who became prominent in their air-line interests were J. de C. Ballardie, who was an accountant, and W.D.L. Roberts, M. Inst. C.E. As we have seen, by the end of 1933 W.S.C. were in control of Saunders-Roe, Spartan Aircraft, and Spartan Air Lines.

Meanwhile, in Jersey, the question of the airport had been taken up by the States on March 23, 1933 and handed to a Joint Committee consisting of the Finance Committee and the Piers and Harbours Committee, and there were meetings with representatives of the Chamber of Commerce and their advisers, Balfour and Luxmore. The site was inspected and approved by Air Chief Marshal Sir Edward Ellington, an old friend of the Lieutenant-Governor, letters were exchanged with the Air Ministry, plans drawn and expropriation laws drafted, in case approval was forthcoming, but there was a certain amount of opposition to this "wild cat scheme" mainly on grounds of expense, and there was a suggestion that aerodromes would soon be obsolete with the development of the auto-giro. Air Ministry opinion was sought, and they, although admitting to being unable to predict the future, thought that normal aircraft would be in use for some time to come. On October 12 the St Peter's site was visited by the Special Committee of the States and J.L. Harrington of the Southern Railway with two of their consultants, Nigel Norman and Graham Dawbarn. Like the G.W.R., the Southern had obtained powers to run air services but, apart from buying shares in Imperial Airways, and making an agreement with them of mutual assistance, and to allow Imperial Airways to run any air service for them should they wish to exercise their powers, they had taken no further action, until, in April, 1933, they had heard of the G.W.R. plans to open a regular air-line. At the suggestion of Sir Herbert Walker (the S.R.'s general manager) the board had established a committee (under the chairmanship of Gerald Loder, later Lord Wakehurst), to consider what the company's attitude should be "towards aerial transport", and within a couple of months they had engaged Norman, Muntz, and Dawbarn to make a report on the influence of aviation development on the policy and business of the Southern Railway.

There was another meeting of the States Special Committee on December 1, 1933, but no major decisions were taken and "no spade had actually touched the soil of St Peter's" (6) when, to the surprise of many, a company calling itself Jersey Airways, Ltd. was registered by the Jersey Royal Court on December 9, 1933, with an office at No. 1, Mulcaster Street, and two directors, who announced their intention of initiating, forthwith, a regular daily air service between Jersey and Portsmouth! These two directors were W.L. Thurgood and L.T.H. Greig, and the idea had come to Mr Greig in the October of 1933 when he had visited Jersey with a friend. The friend was taken ill, and seeing "air travel advertised outside a travel agent's office, he enquired as to the possibility of getting his friend back to England . . . He was politely informed . . . £30 . . . a specially chartered machine . . ." (69) He decided there and then that Jersey should have an air service, and being convinced: " . . . that such a venture stood a good chance of proving successful . . . " he approached Mr Thurgood: ". . . and after a whole month of energetic persuasion he managed to obtain the latter's interest in the matter". Returning to Jersey Mr Greig then "pursued some very delicate negotiations with the Receiver-General, the official in charge of the beaches, and was rewarded by the atmosphere of mutual goodwill which soon prevailed . . ." (2)

Greig was fortunate in knowing Mr Thurgood, who was a man of considerable enterprise with practical experience of public transport. In 1925, at the age of twenty-two, Walter Thurgood had taken over the premises in Church Street, Ware, previously used as a saw-mill by the Pheonix Coach Works, for whom he had worked as a foreman, and set up his own coach-building business. Once established, he moved to larger premises in Park Road, and these became the headquarters of another of his concerns, the People's Motor Services, which he started in 1927 and registered as a private company on June 11, 1928. By 1929 his buses were plying regularly along the highways and by-ways of rural Hertfordshire and adjoining counties, in an area roughly bounded by a line joining Epping, Wormley, Hertford, Hitchin, Royston, and Bishop's Stortford. The most expensive journey, from Hertford to Baldock, cost 2/4d. and by a meandering route through numerous villages and small towns lasted over two hours. After the free-for-all of the Twenties the licensing of bus routes under the Road Traffic Act of 1930, and the passing of the London Passenger Transport Act, which came into force on 1 July 1933, brought considerable rationalisation to road transport, with the result that a number of companies disappeared as some or all of their routes were sold to others. Edward Hillman started his air-line, taxi, and joy-riding business before selling any of his bus routes and was evidently not short of capital, but it has been said that he did it out of frustration at the new regulations. John Sword had built up a large motor-bus system in south-west Scotland which he sold for about £200,000 to Scottish Motor Traction and when he started his air-line he was still the general manager of the Western Division of S.M.T. With the formation of the London Passenger Transport Board Walter Thurgood had no choice but to sell out, and on November 30, 1933 all his routes and nineteen of his buses were transferred to the new Board. Retaining his coach-building as a source of steady income, the proceeds of the sale were available to provide capital for other enterprises, but being a very prudent man, he needed a lot of persuasion to sink his hard-earned money into what seemed more of an adventure than a good solid business venture.

"At day-break on Friday, December 15th, 1933 Mr Thurgood took delivery of his first Dragon, G-ACMJ, at Stag Lane, and with Mr W.B. Caldwell as pilot, made a proving flight to Portsmouth and on to Jersey in wintry gales. The regular service commenced on Monday, December 18th, 1933 . . ." So reads the caption beneath a copy of Frank Wootton's painting of:

". . . the Dragon flying low above the sands of St Aubin's Bay, close to the town of St Helier, Jersey searching for rocks or rivulets which might hazard the very first landing. This picture illustrates the presentation certificate which is given to every member of the de Havilland Enterprise who 'joined the firm' in 1933. It is the custom of the Twenty-Year Club to depict a memorable event relating to the year in which members joined." (1)

Frank Wootton's painting
(By kind permission of British Aerospace)

THE YEAR OF THE DRAGON (1934)

After reporting the registration of Jersey Airways the *Jersey Evening Post* went on to say: ". . . The inaugural flight is to take place from Portsmouth on Monday, December 18th, when a passenger-carrying plane is scheduled to leave Portsmouth at 10 am and due in Jersey at 11.15 am, leaving Jersey on her return same day at 11.30 am, due to arrive at Portsmouth at 12.45. A daily service will be maintained throughout the winter months.

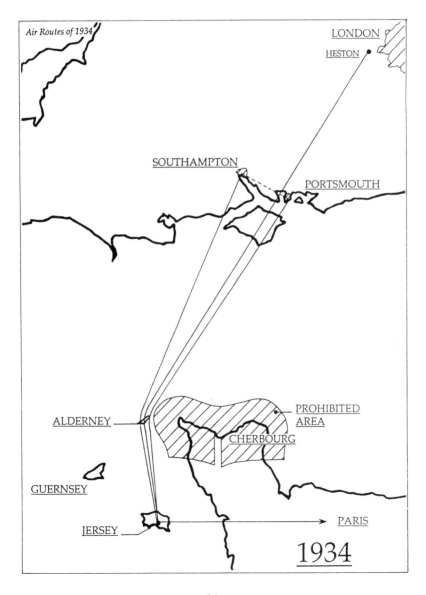

The approximate time of flight is one hour, the return fare has been fixed at 55/-, while the single fare is to be at 32/6 . . . Mr Caldwell will be No 1 pilot, and he comes with the highest of credentials and experience, gained whilst flying between the North of Scotland and the Orkneys and Shetland Islands . . . Messrs W.G. Bellingham (G. Le Benest), the passenger and shipping agents, of No 1 Mulcaster Street, will be the booking agents and . . . will maintain a 24-hour service, so that passengers may obtain the best of attention at any time during the day or night, while the freight and general business office of the Company will be established on the first floor of No 1, Mulcaster Street . . ."

The two directors were interviewed by the *Jersey Morning News* and much was made of the aircraft: ". . . which will be De Havilland 'Dragons' . . . the same type . . . as Mr and Mrs Mollison's *Seafarer*, in which they flew the Atlantic. (See Appendix 1D) Accommodation will be provided for eight passengers with light baggage, and plenty of window space provides a good view of the surrounding countryside for all. The pilot's view is almost entirely unobstructed, which makes for greater safety in landing. Many safety precautions include having all petrol pipes and tanks as far as possible away from the passengers' compartment. These 'Dragons' are equipped with two engines which give a range of 500 miles, which means that five crossings can be made without a stop. Even in the remote event of one engine failing, the machine can still fly at 1,000 feet with the other . . . Normal weight, when loaded, will be 4,000 pounds, and it is interesting to note that the Mollisons' plane . . . started on its Transatlantic flight with a load of 7,000 pounds . . . they will be checked out daily as airworthy by a ground engineer who carries an Air Ministry licence . . . For the crossing between Jersey and Portsmouth the route adopted has been planned so that the machine will never be more than 30 miles from land. In addition the machines will be equipped with the latest type of life-belts as standardised by the Air Ministry . . ." This was put rather differently by *The Aeroplane* which said: ". . . Although the D.H. Dragon is unquestionably one of the best light twin-engined commercial aeroplanes, and is very suitable for small operating concerns, it ought not to be used for such a long oversea crossing as that from Portsmouth to Jersey, in which the single stretch from the Isle of Wight to the French coast covers 60 miles of open and often tempestuous sea." The total distance was about 126 miles.

An advert in the *Jersey Morning News* of December 12 gave the programme for December which, on most days, began with a 10 am departure from Portsmouth followed by a 75 minute flight, and a return from Jersey at 11.30 am. (See Table 1) On December 13 the Channel was swept by the worst gale of that winter, so far, and at dawn on Friday, the 15th, Mr Thurgood collected his Dragon, G-ACMJ, and set off on the trial trip of Frank Wootton's painting, to Portsmouth and Jersey, which they reached at 10.30 am after a 54 minute crossing, aided by a favourable wind. With Mr Thurgood was Mr Greig and a Mr Sharpe. On the return flight they had two additional passengers, Captain H. Benest, M.C., and a *Morning News* reporter, who wired back that they had landed at 4.38 pm just as dusk was falling, that the crossing was a trifle bumpy, and that it took longer than expected because of the head-wind. He described the pilot, "Bill" Caldwell, as "a dour Scot", who was pleased with the crossing, and who considered the course was an easy one to navigate. Probably he replied "Aye" to the two questions put to him! In later years Mr Greig was to confess that this was his: "first and rather upsetting experience of air travel." (4)

All was now ready for the start, due to take place on Monday, the 18th, and, as advance bookings had been so good, arrangements were made to hire two extra Dragons, G-ACCE, from Brian Lewis Ltd., and G-ACET, from "Bill" Caldwell's old firm, Scottish Motor Traction. Two Dragons were used for the historic inaugural flight, which left on time at 10 am with just one passenger between them, and they landed at St Helier about eleven. Which two machines was not recorded, although 'MJ, christened *St Aubin's Bay*, is certain to have been one of them, and the two pilots were "Bill" Caldwell and E.A. Swiss, another recruit from Scottish Motor Traction. On the return at 11.50 there were seven passengers in one machine and five in the other, but it was 1.30 before they reached Portsmouth because of a strong head-wind. Their arrival was reported in the *Portsmouth Evening News* and all fourteen people were taken by Corporation omnibus into the town, where most of them caught the train to London.

Jersey Airways were using Portsmouth as their base for the simple reason that the beach at St Helier was tidal, and normally it was impossible for planes to stay there overnight. Portsmouth is located at the southern end of an island called Portsea Island, which is separated from the mainland by a channel so narrow that few people are aware of its existence. The Municipal Airport, (See Appendix 2D) opened in 1932, was in the extreme north-eastern corner of this island, 2½ miles from the city centre, bounded on the west by the Southern Railway line, and on the east by Langstone Harbour. It was a typical grass airfield of its time, levelled, drained, and sown by the celebrated Mr Hunter of Chester. In 1933 it had a service hangar, a club hangar, a control office, a Customs office, a manager's office, club premises, and a refreshment "chalet" (let out to tender). There were no landing lights, and no radio. Before the arrival of Jersey Airways it had been, to some extent, a little kingdom run by Portsmouth, Southsea, and Isle of Wight Aviation, but Jersey Airways obtained hangar space, and were given permission to operate air taxis should they wish to do so. The landing fee for a Dragon was 6/3d., on a sliding scale down to 4/- if more than 2,000 per annum. As P.S.I.O.W.A. had made some plans of their own with regard to Jersey it would be reasonable to suppose that they watched the activities of the newcomers with more than a casual interest. The time-table claimed that: "Corporation buses for all parts of the City meet all incoming planes" but added that: "Private cars depart 30 minutes before advertised times from Messrs Shaw's Offices, 87e, Commercial Road (almost opposite Portsmouth & Southsea railway station) to connect with departing planes at very moderate charges specially arranged for air passengers." A. Hume Shaw Ltd. were Jersey Airways' official Portsmouth agents.

The day following the inauguration was a quiet one, the Dragon arriving in Jersey at 11.30 with one passenger and leaving at 12.30 with two, but after that the weather clamped down over the Channel for most of the Christmas period. Instead of extra services there were hardly any. On the 20th the whole of Southern England was under a dense fog and the service cancelled, but Mr Speller, the A.I.D. Inspector in Charge at Supermarine-Vickers Southampton managed to find his way to Portsmouth and passed his observations on to the Air Ministry. He saw the two pilots, the ground engineer, and the three Dragons. "A question of compliance with para. IX (2) of Schedule 11 of the Air Navigation Order was investigated and it was found that scales were available at the Portsmouth hangar, these being of the 'Medical Supplies' type reading to 25 stone . . . Notes are taken of the weights of the passengers and baggage carried, and the Chief Pilot is insistent that he and his staff are very careful to ensure that the load carried is well within the max. permissible load. No load-sheet form is at present in use . . . Mr Stanton is the only ground engineer available . . . (not licensed in compass swinging or turn indicators), . . . The company have commenced operations at this time of the year with the impression that traffic will be at its lightest and that, in consequence, they will frequently make journeys with negligible payload. This loss will, they claim, be compensated for by the data accumulated. It is noted that the pilots do not hold a navigator's licence, but they assert that this is not necessary by virtue of the characteristics of the route traversed . . . The aircraft are equipped with 'Airvelope Life Saving Waistcoats'." (5) To this message the Air Ministry replied that Mr Stanton, if not licensed for compass-adjusting or turn indicators, was not qualified to sign daily certificates for aircraft operating beyond a radius of 20 miles from the point of departure. Furthermore, if the journey exceeded 100 miles over the sea the pilot needed a navigator's licence. Finally, load-sheets were to be instituted at once.

On December 21 visibility along the South Coast was down to 50 yards and again the service was cancelled. On the 22nd three passengers were flown to Jersey and twelve brought back, and on the 23rd one passenger was flown to Jersey and eleven brought back, but on the 24th the two Dragons found the fog too thick and they had to return to Portsmouth. No flying was attempted on the 25th, nor on the 26th, and although the planes took off twice on the 27th they failed to get through. The service ran on the 28th, but not the 29th, nor on the 30th, and it is not surprising to learn that bets were being made in Jersey as to how long the new air service would last. When the news came through, at the end of December, that an Imperial Airways' machine had flown into a 900 ft pylon in Belgium, in thick fog, killing all on board, Mr Thurgood may well have been having second thoughts about his investment in aviation.

However, the situation improved on New Year's Eve with two planes reaching Jersey at 2.40 pm with seven passengers, and leaving two hours later with thirteen. From January 2 the time-table was revised to connect with the 8.50 from Waterloo instead of the 6.30, and depart Portsmouth at 11.40 to reach Jersey at 12.55. Return was at 2 pm to land at Portsmouth 75 minutes later. These were the preferred times, and were used every day unless the tide intervened. When high water was predicted for the middle of the day the time-table was amended to suit, as shown on Fig. 1.

Jersey Airways' first D.H. "Dragon" on the beach at St. Aubin's Bay.
(By kind permission of the Jersey Evening Post)

"Bill" Caldwell in 'MJ actually left at 2.15 on the 2nd to reach Portsmouth at 3.30, and on the 3rd he was late getting to Jersey because of fog, but landed his six passengers and took off again at 2 pm with eight for Portsmouth. On the 4th the plane turned back after flying about in banks of fog for nearly an hour, but the weather was good on the 5th when Mr Swiss brought 'MJ down on the beach dead on time at 12.55, and there would be no more cancellations due to fog for the rest of the month. On January 9, the second Dragon, G-ACMC *St Brelade's Bay*, joined 'MJ on the service, and Jersey Airways settled down to improving weather conditions and no shortage of passengers. During January a "man from the Ministry" went down to Portsmouth and met Mr Thurgood, whom he described as: "another example of a man who has had some experience of road transport turning his thoughts and activities to transport by air. He frankly admits his complete ignorance of all matters aeronautical; he relies entirely on his pilots and ground engineers, and gave me the impression that he did not see any reason why it should be more difficult to operate an air service such as this than it was to maintain a bus service between two adjacent

86

towns. I fear that it is inevitable that we shall have just as much difficulty with him as we have experienced with Messrs Hillman and Scottish Motor Traction . . ." (5) Two of the Air Ministry's objections were parried by (a) Mr Stanton's application for an extension to his licence, and (b) the details of the route flown, which was given as 31 miles over land (Portsmouth-Spithead 3 mls., I.O.W. 10 mls., France 13 mls.) plus 95 miles over water (Spithead 4 mls., Channel 69 mls., France-Jersey 22 mls.) A route corresponding more or less, to a direct line from Portsmouth to Jersey passing over the Cherbourg prohibited area. There was no comment from the Air Ministry but the route used from the summer of 1934 on avoided France and passed over Alderney.

In the national press about this time there was a brief mention of the departure of Gordon Olley from Imperial Airways to start his own air charter company, Olley Air Service, which was registered on 10.1.34. He started with one D.H. Dragon, G-ACNA, painted silver with dark blue outlines, which was delivered on 28.2.34 but the significant factor was his backing by Sir Hugo Cunliffe-Owen, although just a rumour at this time. Olley's forceful personality, and Sir Hugo's finances were to play a big part in the development of British air transport. In the local papers Jersey Airways was well reported, but their activities were not fully approved, and some disquiet was voiced in the *Evening Post*. The "aerodrome" at St Helier (See Appendix 2C) sometimes called West Park, was nothing more than the sandy beach of St Aubin's Bay, which stretches in a gentle curve from St Helier, the main town and harbour, to St Aubin, some 2½ miles to the west. Between the high and low-water marks there is about 1,000 yards of sandy shore, which follows the curve of the bay and is bounded on the landward side by a 15 foot granite wall. West Park is on the outskirts of St Helier, and Jersey Airways used the beach immediately opposite for the loading and unloading of their aircraft. Wind and sea permitting the aircraft landed roughly parallel to the sea-wall at the West Park end of the beach. There were no facilities of any sort, and the huge disadvantage that every 12½ hours, or so, the beach was covered by the sea. In the summer, when not covered by the sea, it was covered with people. Writing under the name "Stylo" one contributor suggested that the use of the beach by the Airways was an encroachment of public rights, and involved considerable risk to the unwary. In the *J.E.P.* of January 13 the editor added his protest: "It is obvious that the company responsible . . . has received what they consider the requisite permission . . . one of the surprising aspects of the question when we recall the manner in which the former Bailiff, Sir William Vernon, so clearly laid down the rights of the public to unrestricted enjoyment of the beaches . . . July 30, 1927 when, following a fatality at a race meeting of a motor-cycle club held on Millbrook sands, the then Constable of St Lawrence, Mr John Le Marquand, was called before the Bar of the Royal Court and severely rebuked by Sir William . . . It is not surprising if one wonders why an exception should be made in the case of the present Air Service Company . . ." The editor appears to have overlooked the activities of Messrs Kirsten and Mace in 1930.

The beaches of Jersey were controlled by Major Giffard, His Majesty's Receiver-General, who, despite the complaints, did not feel obliged to justify his actions. He may have regarded it as a simple way of resolving Jersey's dilemma about an airport. If Jersey Airways could make a success of their service it would be a public demonstration of the need for an aerodrome; if they did not, then the States of Jersey could save themselves a good deal of unnecessary expense.

From the point of view of the pilot and the operator the use of a tidal beach causes problems, and that at St Aubin's Bay more than most. "The coastline of Jersey experiences one of the largest movements of tide recorded in the world. The vertical rise of the tide between low water mark and high water mark during the periods of spring tides can be as much as 12 metres (39.4'). During the third and fourth hours of a rising spring tide the rate of rise can be as much as 5 cm. (2") per minute . . ." (7) The reason is Jersey's geographical position. The width of the English Channel between Weymouth and St Malo is about twice the width between the Isle of Wight and Cherbourg and as the tidal stream flows through this restricted space the sea wells up in the Bay of St Malo and is trapped by the Cherbourg Peninsula, although some of it follows a curved path and surges out through the Race of Alderney.

At Guernsey the highest tide can rise 34 feet, at Jersey 40 feet, and at Mont St Michel it may reach 46 feet. By way of comparison the highest rise in the world is 53 feet (in the Bay of Fundy between New Brunswick and Nova Scotia).

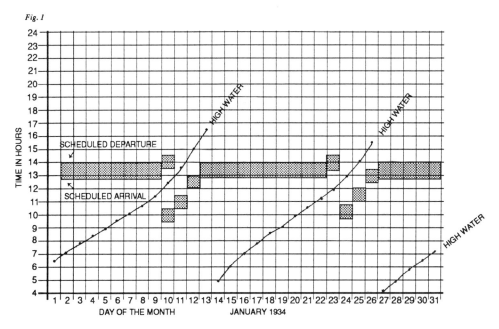

Fig. 1

TIME IN HOURS

SCHEDULED DEPARTURE

SCHEDULED ARRIVAL

HIGH WATER

HIGH WATER

HIGH WATER

DAY OF THE MONTH   JANUARY 1934

Spring tides occur about the time of the new moon and full moon when the sea reaches its highest levels at high water and lowest levels at low water. Neap tides occur about the time of moon's first and last quarters when the high water reaches its lowest level and low water its highest. Obviously spring tides have no connection with the springtime of the year but are related to the phases of the moon and will occur twice per lunar month, or approximately every 15 days. Until the start of the summer season Jersey Airways ran just one service a day with a time-table similar to that for January (Fig. 1) and, tide permitting, the aircraft was on the beach at St Helier for about an hour during the middle of the day. It so happens that, in Jersey, spring tides never occur in the middle of the day, they are always morning or evening tides, so by avoiding the beach within two hours either side of high water, as did Kirsten and Mace, Jersey Airways kept out of trouble during their first months of operation.

"Ebb tide is that between high water and low water lasting on average 6¼ hours; flood tide is that between low and high water, lasting about 5¼ hours . . ." (8) In other words high water at 10.30 am one day should mean that the morning high water on the following day would be at 11.30 am. However this time difference of one hour is only an average value and has it maximum value in the middle of the day so that the Jersey Airways' time-table was only disturbed by the tide on about four days in every

89

fourteen. Of course this time-table had been devised to suit a convenient train from Waterloo to Portsmouth and was not based on a study of tidal phenomena. They would learn more when they tried to run two services in the day as shown in a typical summer time-table – Fig. 2 (Correct, in fact, for August, 1935). The beach "aerodrome" came under the jurisdiction of the Harbour Master of St Helier, and aircraft were charged "harbour dues" at the same rates as ships; "light dues" based on tonnage! passenger fees at 1/3d. per passenger landed, and a cargo fee based on the weight of the package. There was no fee for departing passengers.

Gales interrupted the service in mid-January with winds up to 80 mph, the service being cancelled on the 17th purely on the weather forecast, and the first month of operation ended on the 18th with both planes leaving Portsmouth at 12.30 to run into a rain squall off the Isle of Wight. "Bill" Caldwell in 'MJ lost sight of the other Dragon but carried on to Jersey with his six passengers whereas 'MC returned to Portsmouth. On January 28 the Heston-Jersey service was inaugurated and Jersey Airways had a mention in *The Times* as well as a criticism in *The Aeroplane*: ". . . the right of the company to use a beach which is the property of the Crown and open to the public is questionable. The action of a company out for gain in encroaching on the rights of the public to the free use of the 'plages' of Jersey has already aroused feeling in the island and protests have appeared in the local press. A portion of the beach has been approved by the responsible authorities for use as a landing-place on the understanding that the company will take all reasonable precautions to prevent accidents, but there is difficulty in seeing what precautions the company can take to keep the thousands of holiday-makers off their lawful playground." The time-table for the London plane was so arranged that it landed and took-off from St Helier at the same time as the Portsmouth plane, which was sensible, as the public was kept off the beach, and the police, Customs, and air-line staff kept on the beach, for the minimum length of time. Also, the London plane could cross the Channel in company with the Portsmouth plane (just in case!) and, if need be, land at Portsmouth to suit traffic requirements. If numbers dwindled, one plane could take all, or if Portsmouth had too many and London not enough, the passengers could be shared out equally. On the opening day the Heston departure was scheduled for 10.55 to reach Jersey in two hours, and return at 2 pm to land Heston at 4. All went well, and 'MC, flown by new pilot, Flight-Lieut.

W.E. Knowlden, landed at West Park at 12.45. The weather was excellent, and the time of 1 hr. 55 min. included a wait at Portsmouth for 'MJ. Both returned at 2.15. The direct route from Heston to Jersey was about 174 miles, but a detour was required round the French prohibited area centred on Cherbourg, and the aircraft passed over Alderney to cover about 180 miles. (Table 1)

"The Heston Airport (See Appendix 2E) situated within a quarter of a mile of the Great West Road at its junction with the old Bath Road and within thirty minutes of the West End of London, is a model of aerodrome planning and construction . . . opened less than three years ago (i.e. 1929) it is already recognised as second in importance only to — Croydon . . . It is entirely the creation of private enterprise, being owned by Airwork Ltd. . . Commencing with a nucleus of two hangars, a central office building, and a restaurant, there has been added an up-to-date hotel, public enclosures, a series of show-rooms and offices and a new hangar capable of accommodating the largest types of aircraft. Important stages in the aerodrome's brief career have been its acquisition of full customs facilities . . . the installation of the radio transmitting station and meteorological bureau and the provision of complete lighting equipment for night flying. In this latter respect Heston affords exceptional facilities, for there has recently been installed the new Shadow-Bar anti-dazzle system of aerodrome lighting." (9) This Chance-Airwork floodlight system threw a moveable bar of shadow across the single 980,000 candle-power beam so that the aircraft was in shadow but the ground on either side was brightly lit and the pilot was not dazzled. It was replaced in 1935 by three floodlights, each of 1,250,000 candle power. The radio station worked on 833 metres and broadcast weather reports at regular intervals throughout the day. The best-known landmark in the vicinity was (and is) the Southall gasometer.

During the summer of 1933 Heston had been used by Spartan Air Lines for their I.O.W. service, and was the headquarters of the British Air Navigation Co., a charter firm which operated regular services in the summer to Continental resorts such as Le Touquet. It was the only British company to use the famous Ford Tri-motor. When Jersey Airways moved in, Airwork built a "traffic hall" with offices for the companies and the Customs, a news-stand, and a luggage-counter. Heston was the brain-child of Nigel Norman (later Sir Nigel) and Alan Muntz: ". . . both private

pilots and members of auxiliary R.A.F. squadrons . . . the site chosen . . .
lay near the village of Cranford, in market garden land now bordered by
Cranford Lane, Southall Lane, Wentworth Road and North Hyde Lane . . .
a large tract of land had been purchased by September, 1928. By this time
the two men had formed Airwork Ltd. to run and operate the aerodrome."
(10) As partners in Norman, Muntz, and Dawbarn they were highly
respected consultants in aerodrome design and construction. Just about 100
years before Jersey Airways' first autumn at Heston, 320 acres, which
included the landing area in use in 1934, was ploughed in one seven-hour
working day using 1,050 horses and 20 yoke of oxen!

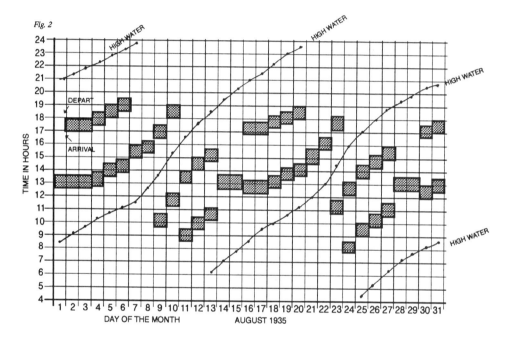

Fig. 2

The London office of Jersey Airways was in the Canadian National
Railway building at 17 Cockspur Street, a street mainly composed of
railway and steamship offices, which joins Whitehall to Pall Mall at
Trafalgar Square (The C.N.R. is still at No. 17). Free transport was
provided leaving 75 min. before the Heston departure time and this "free
private conveyance" met all incoming planes. 25 lb. of baggage was
allowed free, and 2d. per lb. charged for excess. Passengers were requested
to be at the Air Port: "with all baggage and ticket formalities completed
fifteen minutes before the advertised time of departure." Livestock could
not be carried as "personal baggage, or in the saloon of any air-liner". "A

machine of this type is also in regular use by the Prince of Wales. It is not affected by passengers moving about the cabin while in flight. With both engines mounted on the wings noise is reduced to a minimum, and the use of metal propellers ensures exceptional quietness . . . The totally enclosed cabin free from draughts, the absence of vibration, pitching, or rolling in flight have to be experienced to be fully appreciated. Clothing suitable for a journey of similar duration in a saloon car is quite adequate . . . Subject to ALL passengers being agreeable, smoking is permitted while in flight, but NOT on the GROUND . . ." (11) January ended with the justifiable claim that the service had only been cancelled on three days during the month. 120 passengers had been flown to Jersey and 176 from Jersey, and during most of the existence of Jersey Airways the monthly totals of people flying to Jersey was always exceeded by the numbers flying from Jersey, which was attributed to sufferings experienced on the boat and not a steady emigration of Jersiases.

The third Dragon, G-ACMO *St Ouen's Bay*, was delivered on February 1, and the survival of the company through the worst period of the year, plus the promising loads carried, attracted the watchful eyes of the railway companies; their archives, in addition to a complete set of Jersey Airways' traffic figures from January 1, contain a selection of newspaper cuttings beginning with one from *The Times* showing the London – Jersey air fare of £2. 19s. 6d. single, £4. 19s. 6d. return. Typed underneath were the equivalent rail and sea fares of £2. 10s. 0d. and £3. 6s. 9d. There were cuttings from the *Evening Standard*, one of February 7 headed: "STILL MORE HOLIDAY-MAKERS WILL FLY THIS YEAR", and another of February 28 in which their air correspondent said "Jersey Airways tell me their service . . . is going very well in spite of the weather". (12) But not entirely "in spite of the weather" because "Bill" Caldwell had his first skirmish with the Jersey tide on February 12 when he took off from the beach at about 2 pm and ran into fog on leaving the French coast at Cap de La Hague. He climbed above the fog bank but couldn't find Portsmouth and eventually turned back. Over France the weather was clear so he "fixed" his position and made another attempt, but ran into fog again off the Isle of Wight and decided to return to Jersey. Here the tide was coming in, with a high water of 32 feet due at 5.30 pm. A 32 foot tide would just about cover every square inch of sand, so, as soon as the machine was unloaded, it was hustled along the beach and pulled up the Millbrook slip with very little margin to spare.

Curious about the Jersey "aerodrome" the Air Ministry made enquiries, and were told that it was: "a circular area of sea, of radius ¾ ml. with centre Elizabeth Castle." It was licensed and approved for Customs and was, of course, the seadrome for flying-boats which had been in existence since 1928. However, the Air Ministry raised no objection to the use of the foreshore and, apparently, had no authority to do so, as Jersey was not obliged to consult them. The States, they were informed, wanted to make an aerodrome at St Peter's Barracks, but there was a delay over an exchange of land with the War Office. In addition, Jersey Airways were said to be negotiating for a site of approx. 100 vergées near Sorel, St John, but Mr Coutanche, the Attorney-General suspected they were only trying to create a nuisance value in order to be bought out by the Southern and Great Western railways.

JERSEY
AIRWAYS
LIMITED.

DAILY . SERVICES.
JERSEY — LONDON.
JERSEY—PORTSMOUTH.

WINTER
TIME TABLE

February & March, 1934.

Phones: 1221 St. HELIER.
2261 Portsmouth.
3640 Whitehall.

The next problem to agitate the official mind was the maximum permissible weight of the D.H. Dragon, which had been specified as 4,200 lb. by the makers. The Air Ministry advised Jersey Airways that this was too much for such a long oversea flight, especially as they had already had two cases of engine failure, and the Air Ministry suggested a limit of 3,850 lb. This was a recommendation only, and not obligatory, so Jersey Airways refused to accept it, on commercial grounds, and referred the matter to de Havillands. However, they did come to an arrangement with Airwork for the maintenance of their aircraft, and not long afterwards Airwork's John Parkes told an Air Ministry official that: "the first 25 hours scheduled inspection . . . on the first Dragon . . . indicated . . . a very indifferent condition . . . badly neglected . . ." On flying a Dragon on one engine he said that a lot depended on which engine had failed: ". . . in the case of one engine comparatively little rudder is required to keep the aircraft on course . . . in the case of the other . . . almost full rudder is required to hold its course and although the aircraft could be said to maintain its height even on that engine when fully loaded if allowed to circle gently over an aerodrome it certainly will not do so when being held on a course . . ." (5) In reply to Jersey Airways de Havillands expressed surprise because it was an indisputable fact that the Dragon, loaded to 4,200 lb. could maintain a height of 1,000 feet on one engine, as attested by the prototype at Martlesham Heath. They could only suppose that the Director of Civil Aviation was calling for some degree of prudence. In fact the Air Ministry was very concerned and their A.I.D. inspectors reported every case of a Jersey Airways' Dragon crossing the Channel with an all-up weight in excess of 3,850 lb. On February 24 'MC (Swiss) left Portsmouth loaded to 4,119 lb. On the 25th 'MO (Caldwell) left Portsmouth loaded to 4,159 lb. whilst 'MJ (Knowlden) left Heston loaded to 4,163 lb. On the 26th 'MO left Heston with the full 4,200 lb. "Bill" Caldwell said he had been told by a director that the 3,850 lb. limit was not a direct order, and they could not accept it because of the heavy financial loss. Somewhat frustrated the Air Ministry began to study the legal implications of putting out a more definite instruction on the subject, and, at the same time, initiated proposals for further tests at Martlesham on a D.H. Dragon.

On March 1 the Southern Railway held its annual general meeting, and the chairman, Gerald Loder, admitted that: "We have been carefully watching the development of transport by air . . . We are already suffering from a diversion of our cross-Channel traffic, particularly between London and Paris and, to a small extent, in our Channel Islands traffic . . ." (20) He went on to say that an air transport service was being planned by the main line railway companies, and on March 21, 1934 Railway Air Services Ltd. was registered with a nominal capital of £50,000 and its shares equally divided amongst the four railway companies and Imperial Airways. This company was to operate air services at the request of any of the railway companies individually, or in combination, and that railway or combination would become responsible for the operating costs of their particular route. About this time Spartan Air Lines, whose Spartan Cruisers had been flying twice daily between London and the Isle of Wight during the summer of 1933, invited the Southern Railway to share their losses. ". . . If, at the end of twelve months working, we (the S.R.) would like to develop the services Spartan Air Lines would welcome an input of capital from us so that the services could include a Channel Islands run, possibly with the absorption or co-operation of the Portsmouth, Southsea, and Isle of Wight Aviation Co. (who are contemplating running a Jersey service if the States go ahead with the projected aerodrome) . . ." (12) The Southern did accept this invitation and participated with Spartan during the summer, although Spartan ran the reduced winter service of 1934-35 on their own. In London there was a meeting between the S.R., the G.W.R., Imperial Airways, and Spartan Air Lines and Mr Collett said that the G.W.R. were anxious to co-operate with the S.R. in a Channel Islands service without which they would not consider a Birmingham to Southampton service. Urgent action was required because Jersey Airways had carried over 600 passengers during the winter months and by next year they would have created a vested interest. After considerable discussion it was agreed that if the aerodrome situation on Guernsey and Jersey could be cleared up the S.R. and R.A.S. would like to receive Spartan Air Lines' suggestions for operating the route with Spartan Cruisers. It was agreed that Mr W.D.L. Roberts should visit the Channel Islands as an unofficial representative of the joint Railway and Spartan interests.

A completely new company started operations in March, Provincial Airways, and their route was from Croydon to Plymouth, via Portsmouth and Southampton, with various other stops as required at places like Bournemouth and Torquay, and it continued, on demand, to Penzance and Newquay. They started with Fox Moths but soon replaced them with Dragons. This route had been pioneered in 1933 by a small firm with a big name, International Air Lines, which only lasted about a week but incurred the displeasure of some people at Croydon because its uniform was indistinguishable from that of Imperial Airways. Furthermore, some of the managerial and other non-flying staff sported pilot's "wings" and were said to frequent local taverns and cinemas whilst in uniform!

By March three more pilots had joined Jersey Airways: Jenkins, Glyn Roberts, and Eckersley-Maslin, the former chief pilot of P.S.I.O.W.A. On March 4 a retired naval dental surgeon in Guernsey, Mr Mark, received an S.O.S. from Bristol, where his wife's father, Sir Cecil Herslet, K.B.E., J.P. was seriously ill, and he asked Jersey Airways to divert one of their planes to Guernsey. The only landing place was Vazon Bay, and to avoid the possibility of a heavily-loaded machine sinking in the deep grey sand of this beach the spare Dragon was sent. This was G-ACMP *St Clement's Bay* which had only been on the service since February 27, and with Eckersley-Maslin as pilot and Miss McFarling of Bellingham's to complete the paper-work, they left Jersey at 1.35 and landed at Vazon Bay some fifteen minutes later. In less than five minutes they were on their way back with Mrs Mark, and she was transferred to the duplicate Portsmouth machine which left at 2.15. From Portsmouth Mrs Mark made a desperate cross-country dash to Bristol but arrived just too late; her father had died at 8 pm. This incident was mentioned in *The Aeroplane* of March 14 and within a week another plane had landed at Vazon Bay, albeit, unsuccessfully, as the machine ended up on its nose. The pilot, Mr Woods, said he had come to investigate the possibility of running an air service to Jersey and the mainland.

On March 14 the Portsmouth machine set out for Jersey but was driven back by gale-force winds from the south. As St Aubin's Bay faces south the beach is wide open to winds from that quarter, which could create problems in the vicinity of the high sea wall. The Heston machine managed to get through, and an eye-witness (there was never any shortage of them) reported that: ". . . When the plane came down the wind caught her, and caused her to tip sideways. The pilot skilfully righted the machine and taking her up again made a perfect landing. Some difficulty was also experienced in taking off . . ." (6) This was 'MP and she reached Heston in 50 minutes. On Sunday, March 18 the Portsmouth service was extended to Southampton where Mr Swiss arrived empty in *St Ouen's Bay* at 4.15 having dropped his seven passengers at Portsmouth. The first through passengers from Jersey to Southampton travelled on March 29, and the first from Southampton to Jersey on April 3. The planes left Southampton 15 minutes before the Portsmouth departure time, but in April this was increased to 20 minutes, and eventually half-an-hour had to be allowed.

The end of March coincided with Easter and six Dragons were now available, the two most recent arrivals being G-ACNG *Portelet Bay* and G-ACNH *Bouley Bay*. Extra services were run, many being duplicated or triplicated, and Mr Thurgood claimed he could have filled flying double-decker buses. For the first time the service ran twice in one day, and the early machine out of Portsmouth at 7.45 on Easter Thursday caught two Jersey fishermen by surprise. They were digging bait when this aircraft came in to land at 9 am, and if they hadn't thrown themselves flat on the ground they would have been hit. At least, so they said, but fishermen are notoriously prone to exaggeration. From Heston alone, over Easter, 130

97

passengers were carried to and from Jersey in 39 flights, which was pretty good going in those days. *The Aeroplane* reported that nearly 2,000 passengers had been carried since December 18, and: ". . . the striking success of the service . . . has lead the States of Jersey to spend £20,000 on the purchase of land for an island airport." This referred to a report relating to the establishment of an airport which was presented by Jurat de Gruchy on April 3 and, being adopted, the States voted £20,000 on April 5 for the purchase of land, and £1,000 for expert advice on airport layout, wireless, and similar matters. The complete traffic figures of Jersey Airways were published on April 25:-

From and To	Dec.	Jan.	Feb.	March	April 1 – 20	
Portsmouth	42	270	177	399	309	
Heston		19	172	362	346	
Southampton				21	121	(3)

Initially the extension to Southampton seemed a rather doubtful step because most of the passengers continued to board the planes at Portsmouth where a landing had to be made for Customs clearance, and this meant extra flying and an extra landing fee. To fly from Eastleigh the passenger had to pay an extra 2/6d. (or 5/- on the return), and be at the airport half-an-hour earlier, and if from the London area, as many were, they had to pay more to reach Southampton. However, Jersey Airways were looking to the future, when Southampton would have Customs facilities also.Its aerodrome had started life in the First World War as a U.S. Navy air station called Atlantic Park, and large hangars were built for the assembly of bombers from parts made in America, but the war ended before any of the components had arrived (See Appendix 2F). In 1932 the aerodrome was reopened by the Southampton Corporation and renamed Eastleigh. There was no night-landing equipment, no radio, no promise of radio, and no Customs, but there was a "half-hourly bus service" which "passes the aerodrome gates . . ." Mr L. F. (Frank) Payne was appointed manager in 1935. After ten years in the R.A.F. he had become chief pilot to Redwing Aircraft Ltd. at Gatwick as well as aerodrome manager. Later he was chief instructor to the Eastern Counties Aero Club and private pilot to Major Musker of the British Klemm Aeroplane Co. at Hanworth. The Jersey Airways' local office was again with the Canadian National

Railways at 134 High Street and in 1935 Mr W.L.G. Butt would join Jersey Airways as Southampton manager after eleven years with the C.N.R.

Jersey Airway Planes at Westpark, Jersey.

Dragons on the beach was the subject of this picture postcard, which was still on sale in 1936 judging by the postmark

In Jersey on April 6 Mr W.D.L. Roberts had interviews with Major Giffard (Receiver-General), Mr Duret-Albin (Solicitor-General), and Captain Allix (Harbour Master), and he was told that the only approved air port was the seaplane base at St Helier. The local authorities extended the airport regulations to cover aircraft landing on the foreshore without appreciating that this area was outside the approved zone. They realised their mistake after Jersey Airways had commenced their regular daily service, and they also realised that in the summer months the foreshore would be too crowded to allow many aircraft to land with safety. The Receiver-General did not think it advisable to stop Jersey Airways from using the sands because their service was a benefit to the public and they had spent a large sum of money on the assumption of continued operation. Also there was no alternative landing ground available. When asked if Spartan Air Lines could be granted similar landing facilities the Receiver-General said that no further permits would be granted and admitted that Jersey Airways had a monopoly. "Although the State hope to open the aerodrome next year and intend, at present, to control it themselves, I fear there is a grave risk of their plans being modified. The Jersey Airways have forced their hands once and obtained a temporary monopoly: it is quite conceivable they will do it a second time by purchasing another site and having it ready this summer. The State could hardly refuse to provide Customs facilities at a new site in place of those now provided on the beach. The Jersey Airways have adopted a bold policy to establish their position. In the light of their success to date they should have little difficulty in obtaining local finance for purchase and preparation of an aerodrome. Any company with strong local interests is bound to receive favoured consideration on the island . . . I could not obtain any reliable confirmation that Jersey Airways or any other concern were actually negotiating for the purchase of land – in fact in official circles the idea was considered ridiculous – nevertheless the Hotel hall porter and car driver mentioned the actual site that Jersey Airways had been closely studying . . . it is . . . apparent that . . . Jersey Airways is to make full use of their present advantageous position and extend their activities without delay . . . common knowledge that they intend to increase their fleet . . . endeavouring to buy . . . a footing in Guernsey . . . propose running to St Malo and Paris . . ." (27)

Mr Roberts then went on to say that if Jersey Airways did obtain local backing, built themselves an aerodrome or maintained their monopoly of the beach, and increased their fleet and range of air services then "their position will be exceptionally strong. Unless the railways are prepared to take the risk . . . essential to start a rival service before the summer . . . This can only be done by using sea planes or amphibians . . ." (27)

In Guernsey Mr Roberts saw Mr H.E. Marguard (States Supervisor) and Captain Franklin (Harbour Master) and found the situation was similar to Jersey but had not reached such an advanced state. The proposed site was at L'Ancresse and Mr Marguard told him there was to be a meeting of the States authorities on April 13 and he anticipated that a committee would be appointed to study the question of an aerodrome. It would be State owned and controlled and offers by Jersey Airways and others to carry out the work of levelling in return for priority rights had been refused. For seaplanes St Peter Port was superior to St Helier as it was more protected from the prevailing winds, the harbour entrance was wider and less affected by currents. There was thought to be no objection to alternative bases on the opposite sides of the islands for use when the wind was in the wrong quarter for the main harbours. In conclusion it was said that both Jersey and Guernsey State Authorities would welcome a proposal by the Southern and Great Western Railways for the establishment of a regular air service. "Both States would be less inclined to grant concessions to small private companies if they knew the Railways were supporting an alternative regular service . . ."(27)

On April 13th the Guernsey States considered a petition by Jersey Airways to construct an aerodrome on L'Ancresse Common with the result that a special committee was elected to investigate the whole question of an airport, and on April 21 Guernsey Aero Club, Limited was registered with a capital of £10,000 and founder members:- H.H. Randell, C.W. Noel, C.H. Smith, V.A. Lewis, J.G. Wheadon, Miss L. Collings and Mrs M. Collings.

So far, Jersey Airways' load factors had been 4.4 passengers per Dragon on the Portsmouth machines and 4.5 on the Heston machines, and it was decided that four of the Dragons should be fitted with radio. For Jersey a refuelling tanker was to be provided and a 32-seater bus after conversion into a mobile office and waiting room. Passengers descended to the beach by a flight of stone steps in the sea wall opposite West Park, and the bus could be driven down the slipway to the bottom of these steps before the arrival of the aircraft, and driven away again after their departure.

On May 1 the London office was transferred to 11, Elizabeth Street, S.W.1, on the north side of the Victoria Coach Station, and the Heston bus ran from Samuelson's Garage opposite. A new pilot, Mr Hay, appeared on the service, but his stay was short. According to the *J.E.P.* of May 12 he brought 'NG across from Portsmouth, had taken on seven passengers for the return flight, and then: ". . . taxied off down the beach, but the tail wheel dragged the machine around instead of . . . keeping the tail straight for the take-off. Mr Hay made several attempts, but was finally ordered to remain on the ground by an official of the company." Later, a director (no doubt, Greig) told a reporter: ". . . there was at no time any danger to the passengers . . . the pilot should not, however, have made so many attempts to get up . . . Once he had found the tail wheel was not functioning properly he should have throttled down immediately. Instead he chose to career about the beach for no purpose." With 'NG out-of-action Jersey Airways were forced to call on their Heston neighbours, BANCO, for assistance, and Mr Morton made a return trip for them that afternoon in the big Ford Tri-motor, G-ABHO.

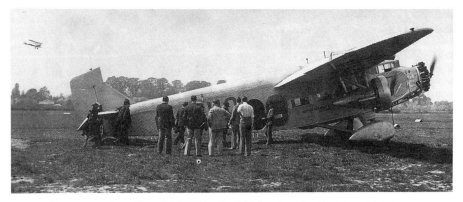

Passengers boarding BANCO's Ford Trimotor, G-ABHO, at Heston
(Quadrant Picture Library)

This machine caused quite a stir at West Park, and Mr Greig claimed that it was an experiment as they were interested in operating 15-seater machines. Soon after, or perhaps because of, Mr Hay's antics in careering about the beach the Constable of St Helier issued an official notice to say that the public was not allowed to use the beach at West Park when it was being used by Jersey Airways. This was queried, and it was announced that the Crown, being the owner of the foreshore, had granted a concession to Jersey Airways. The concession allowed them to use; "half a square mile with a centre 440 yards south of the second tower in St Aubin's Bay." It was assumed that by "second tower" officialdom actually meant the tower long known locally as the "First Tower"! and the beach aerodrome was roughly the stretch of shore between the swimming pool at West Park and the First Tower slipway. (See Appendix 2C) A stern editorial followed in the *J.E.P.* on the subject of "RESTRICTING THE PUBLIC", and letters appeared in the correspondence columns. One reader advocated audible warnings by siren, a red flag on a mast (as at rifle ranges), and demarcation flags for the landing area.

Coming in to land one afternoon Mr Jenkins found a young woman standing directly in his path. He was about seven feet from the ground, but managed to pull up just missing the woman, and go round again. When approached by Mr Greig and a policeman she declined to move, saying the sands were as much for her as the Airways. On May 19 the Southern Railway assistant docks and marine manager, Mr Biddle, a Jerseyman, made an unpublicised visit to Jersey and saw Mr Coutanche, the Attorney-

General, and Mr Duret Aubin, the Solicitor-General. In confidence he was told that there would be no monopoly of the aerodrome when it was constructed, nor the beach. All comers would be received on an equal basis. The whole purpose of his visit was to forestall the granting of any such monopoly.

The twice-daily summer service had been in operation since May 4, and as expected, they were very busy over Whit. On June 4 a completely new service was inaugurated from Jersey to Paris (Le Bourget). Naturally the times varied with the tides but the first machine was scheduled to leave Jersey at 10 am, arrive Le Bourget at 12.15 and depart 30 minutes later to reach Jersey at 3 pm. (See Table 1) It was to run on Mondays and Thursdays and Eckersley-Maslin made the inaugural flight in 'NH with one passenger, but returned with two. In 1934 Le Bourget was the premier airport of France, comparable with our Croydon, and about four miles north east of Paris (See Appendix 2G) To accommodate the Paris machine, which was also the spare Dragon for charters or emergencies, Jersey Airways were given permission to use the race-course at Quennevais. It was not licensed for passengers but a canvas hangar was built (later replaced by one of corrugated iron), and a ground engineer was based there. On June 10, during take-off from Quennevais the Dragon developed engine trouble, but managed to get down on to the beach. In order to allay any doubts in the minds of potential passengers it was announced that: ". . . 85% of known engine troubles occur within a few minutes of take-off due to the sudden strain on the engines!" (6) Presumably, the message intended was that there was no need to worry as the plane could always turn round and come back, (assuming it was safely airborne, of course!)

The first of the Railway Air Service routes was opened on May 7, 1934, on behalf of the G.W.R., by J.H. Lock in Dragon G-ACPX when he left Plymouth (Roborough) at 8.50 am for Teignmouth, Cardiff, Birmingham and Liverpool. The return from Speke was at 3.30 pm and the service ran every day except Sundays. It was really an extension of the Great Western Railway Air Service of 1933. In the far north Highland Airways were extending their routes to include Aberdeen, and on May 29 they flew the first regular air mail between Inverness and Kirkwall. This was the first serious attempt at a regular letter delivery service by air instead of by boat and it turned out to be quite successful. In the North West the Cutty Sark of British Amphibious Air Lines did not return to Blackpool, and the

Irish Sea was left to J.C. Higgins and his West Coast Air Services, but the lease to Stanley Park aerodrome at Blackpool was taken over by Midland and Scottish Air Ferries who had plans for a big expansion in a south-easterly direction. On April 6 Midland and Scottish had inaugurated a service between Liverpool and London with their fine new Avro 642, and this connected with two separate services, one to Belfast, via the Isle of Man, and the other to Glasgow. The inauguration ceremonies had been carried out by Mr Ramsey MacDonald, the Prime Minister, together with Lord Londonderry, the Secretary of State for Air. In London they connected with Mr Hillman's Paris machines at Romford but behind the scenes all was not well. The L.M.S. Railway were planning a Croydon-Birmingham-Manchester-Belfast-Glasgow service of their own, to be run by R.A.S. and as they were large share-holders in Scottish Motor Traction they put pressure on John Sword. Early in July he announced that he was closing down Midland and Scottish Air Ferries, ostensibly because of his increasing responsibility as general manager of Western Scottish Motor Traction and almost immediately, Hillman's took over the London-Liverpool-Belfast route.

In Jersey, the eighth and final Dragon, G-ACNJ *Rozel Bay* was delivered on June 8, (the seventh being G-ACNI *Bonne Nuit Bay)* and on the following day a record number of eight planes was used on a heavily augmented service. Possibly the first account in print of a day jaunt to Jersey by air appeared in *Airways and Airports* for July 1934 written by Evelyn Ayling, who made the trip on June 13. 'NJ was waiting at Heston: ". . . its silvered wings shimmering vividly against the contrasting green" of the flying field, (in fact, on the ground with the engines running the amplitude of the wing-tip vibration could be quite considerable). The lady was: "comfortably installed . . . in a pale grey upholstered saloon" and they took-off and headed south at 1,000 feet to run into a bank of mist at the coast, so they climbed to 6,000 feet and brilliant sunshine. The pilot, "a cheery young man, if he will allow me to say so – ably combined the duties of air host, directing our destinies . . . When we were soaring above the fog bank . . . he made a surprising announcement: 'You may smoke if you want to' . . . Aviation improvement number one since last time . . . My first sight of land was a glimpse of Alderney through a gap in the mist. It appeared under the starboard wing, a bright green shape set in a pale blue sea . . . Cap de la Hague on the other side announced the proximity of the

French coast. Our route lies six miles off this on a S.S.W. course . . . For a novelty, and to surprise my friends back in London I decided to make the return journey the same day . . . In doing this I struck what I imagine will always be one of the difficulties of air travel. The homebound machine was full! . . . somehow or other I was found a seat on the Dragon that roared its way along the mile of beach into the sweltering sky, not one wit dismayed by the addition of my eight-stone-four. I found out afterwards that some freight and heavy baggage was left behind for another machine to carry. It really was hot. Our pilot I noticed, very bronzed, had laid aside his smart blue tunic . . ." By June 18, after six months of operation, 5,400 passengers had been carried and over 1,000 Channel crossings made. Another two pilots had joined, Blythe and Duggan, and Eckersley-Maslin was appointed Air Superintendent with "Bill" Caldwell remaining as Chief Pilot.

Some of the problems of using a tidal beach have been discussed already, and an explanation given of how the winter time-table avoided the highest tides, more or less by chance. This was no longer the case with the summer time-table when two services were fitted into one day, (See Fig. 2), and towards the end of June it was apparent that the time table had been too optimistic.

On June 26, with a 33.7 foot tide due at 6.39 pm, three machines arrived late in the afternoon to find the beach almost covered by the incoming tide. The first machine down caught the water with its port wheel, spun round through ninety degrees, and ran straight into the sea. All the Jersey Airways' staff available rushed to the scene and managed to drag the aircraft back to dry land. It was hustled along the beach west of the First Tower where the passengers were attended to as quickly as possible, and the machine sent off again. The other two machines were signalled away, and after circling the bay they flew to the race-course where they stayed the night. The unfortunate passengers had to wait over an hour on the race-course for Customs and other officials. This event did not go unnoticed by the ever-watchful *J.E.P.*: ". . . the difficult task of compiling a time-table to fit in with the tides (despite a few close incidents when planes have landed and taken off on a minimum amount of beach) has been carried out with little inconvenience to passengers.

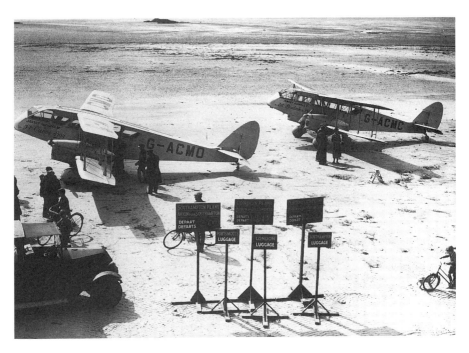

The next departure from Jersey is at 2 pm.
Musée de l'Air et de l'Espace, Paris ("Droits Réservés")

Somebody seems to have made a mistake on Tuesday for only one machine landed on the beach and then only with difficulty while two others were signalled to land on the race-course at Don Bridge . . . Although yesterday's time-table was advanced one hour it was found necessary to cancel the afternoon service at the last minute consequently many intending passengers were unable to make their journey."

The tide scored another success exactly one month later (July 26) when the Tilling-Stevens coach being used as a mobile office developed engine trouble after moving about 50 yards along the beach towards the slipway: "The coach gradually sank some feet in the soft sand and was slowly submerged and eventually battered to pieces by the pounding of the waves. This unusual sight was witnessed by the officials of the Company . . . and a large number of people. When the tide receded the vehicle presented a sorry spectacle. The chassis was eventually rescued and towed back to the garage . . ." (6) This incident was mentioned by a certain R.A.F. officer who was flying for Jersey Airways at this time during the week-ends, just for the experience. His name was D.C.T. Bennett, and he was to become famous as the leader of the Pathfinder Force, and reach the rank of Air Vice-

Marshal; ". . . We were operating into Jersey twice each day. Each pilot did his own paper-work and everything else, including looking after his passengers and their baggage, and running the aircraft single-handed . . . the beach becomes covered like a flash once the water starts its inward race. My flying . . . with Jersey Airways . . . came to an untimely end when some M.P. asked the Secretary of State for Air whether it was true that a regular Air Force officer was flying for a civil air line and thereby depriving a civil pilot of his livelihood. I had never taken any reward for my services . . ." (16)

It was now the high summer season and nearly 1,000 passengers a week were being flown. By August 4 the 10,000th passenger had been carried, and the Jersey Airways habit of flying in large flocks or coveys, due to the limitations of the tidal beach, brought them plenty of publicity. Even an inland paper like the *Nottingham Evening Post* carried a photograph of five Dragons en route for Jersey with the caption "Air Armada" and said that as many as six make the journey at the same time. During the August Bank Holiday eight Dragons went to and fro daily, and Jersey Airways' traffic figures were the envy of every other British internal air line. Since W.D.L. Roberts had warned of Jersey Airways' intentions their fleet had risen to eight aircraft and their routes extended to Paris, and now they were inviting local capital with the offer of 50,000 6% cumulative participating preference shares at £1 each. The advertisement appeared in the *Jersey Morning News* but was refused by the *Evening Post* on the grounds that the "moment is not opportune" as there is no proper aerodrome. It showed the directors as W.L. Thurgood of Cromwell Road, Ware and L.T.H. Greig of 3 Tynemouth Terrace, Jersey and the secretary was W.T. Scarborough of 8 Hill Street, St Helier. Of the nominal share capital of £120,000 authorised £16,600 had been issued and the balance sheet showed a pre-tax profit of £1,340 up to May 19.

In Guernsey the Aero Club, with directors H.H. Randell, C.W. Noel, C.H. Smith, and B. Bartlett, were buying up properties in the L'Erée district with the intention of making an aerodrome, and behind the Aero Club was Sir Alan Cobham who was hoping to start an air service to England when the aerodrome was completed if he could have it licensed for passenger-carrying aircraft. Cobham was one of the big names in British aviation, influential, but not backed by any strong financial group, although he had a number of business activities of his own. On July 20 the

Saro Cloud, G-ABXW *Cloud of Iona,* had arrived in Jersey with two of the Spartan Air Lines directors and spent the night in the harbour. It returned on August 29 in time for a conference between the local authorities and Messrs. Harrington (S.R.), Biggs (G.W.R.), Roberts (Spartan) and Lord (Saunders-Roe) all four having travelled over on the night boat. The subject of the discussion was a proposed service between Guernsey and Jersey. Meanwhile Mr Thurgood was said to be making approaches to the authorities of Guernsey, Alderney, and Sark for the use of landing grounds he had been to see recently but, if negotiations appeared to be unduly prolonged, he would consider starting a flying-boat service!

This threat was taken seriously by W.D. Roberts and the *Cloud of Iona* chartered by Spartan Air Lines to prevent Jersey Airways buying it. In addition Mr Roberts had placed an option on the two machines which were due to become available in the autumn. In a memo from Managing Director, Spartan Air Lines to Wing-Commander Measures of Railway Air Services, Mr Roberts explained that Jersey Airways were endeavouring to purchase an amphibian or flying-boat in order to obtain the Channel Islands mail contract, and as Spartan Air Lines have the first option on the only amphibian available, and R.A.S. are in the best position with regard to the Postmaster-General it is proposed that Spartan and R.A.S. shall co-operate together at the earliest date in an amphibian service to the Channel Islands.

Earlier in the year, Jersey Airways had made one of their Dragons available to Martlesham Heath, but this had coincided with a southerly gale which limited the amount of flying. In extremely bumpy weather conditions tests were carried out with a load of 3,850 lb. whilst the port engine was stopped and the starboard engine running at full throttle, and vice versa. The airscrew of the stopped engine was also stopped by stalling the engine. It was reported that the aircraft was easy to fly, and it maintained its height. In London these results were studied very carefully, and after much deliberation between various departments of the Air Ministry the Air Navigation Order was amended to include the following paragraph: "A flying machine registered in Great Britain and Northern Ireland and carrying passengers for hire or reward on a regular line or service of public air transport shall not, unless designed to manœuvre on the water, be flown over the sea or any area of water in such circumstances that, in the event of the stoppage of its engine, or one of its engines, it would be unable to reach land." (5) It was August before the final version of this amendment was promulgated in the form of "Notice to Airmen No. 74".

On July 30 the second of the Railway Air Service routes was opened, and this was between Cowes and Birmingham calling at Southampton and Bristol, and gave Jersey Airways a connection at Eastleigh with the Midlands, the West, and the North-West. Norman Edgar's Western Airways was now linking Bristol and Cardiff to Bournemouth where they connected with P.S.I.O.W.A. who were also running to London from the Isle of Wight in competition with Spartan Air Lines. But few routes could compare with the excellent traffic figures gleefully published by Jersey Airways, and these were being carefully watched by Whitehall Securities, the G.W.R., the S.R., P.S.I.O.W.A., and Sir Alan Cobham. The full R.A.S. network, complete with an air mail contract was due to start on August 20 with the L.M.S. sponsored Croydon-Birmingham-Manchester-Belfast-Glasgow service for which four-engined D.H. 86 aircraft had been ordered, and a mail and freight service by D.H. Dragon between Manchester, the Isle of Man, and Belfast. The actions of the railways were regarded with considerable distrust by the existing internal air-line operators whose financial resources were usually very much less than those of the railways although, to add insult to injury, the railways were in receipt of a Government subsidy for "not being able to run railways properly", so they said, "and the small air-lines helped to pay for it" they claimed "through the iniquitous tax on aviation fuel". (This tax was a sore point with pre-war aviators). It was fairly obvious that once a route had been pioneered by some intrepid aviator of the old school the railways would come along and set up a rival service to share the traffic so that both ran at a loss, and then the railways could afford to wait for the smaller man to go "bust". So it was thought by many people in aviation. When August 20 arrived and the R.A.S. 86's left Glasgow for their long roundabout trip to Croydon, loaded with special air mail covers, newspaper reporters, and the "top brass" of R.A.S., to make connections with the other planes at Birmingham, and then turn round at Croydon for the northward run home, Britain was struck by a gale of unprecedented ferocity, for midsummer. The inaugural mail service was reduced to a fiasco and the southbound aircraft forced to a halt at Manchester "after a terrific buffeting . . . during which the passengers were from time to time thrown from their seats . . . During one terrific 'bump' . . . Sir Harold Hartley (chairman of R.A.S.) was thrown up through the emergency roof exit, his head and shoulders smashing the canvas open . . ." One of the reporters said "I felt a tremendous crack as my head struck the luggage rack . . . Another passenger, who had been flung from his seat behind me, fell across me as I was shot into my seat . . . At the rear of the plane I saw Wing-Commander Measures (superintendent, R.A.S.) bleeding from a cut on his forehead . . . Sir Harold was unhurt, although shaken . . . The emergency exit through which he had crashed was flapping violently, filling the cabin with noise. Wing-Commander Measures stood up and held his raincoat over the opening . . . Passengers were told to hang on to their seats, but this was really unnecessary as everyone was doing so . . . One passenger hit the baggage rack with such force that it was knocked out of shape . . . (19)

In Jersey the very success of the air-line, with its "armadas" of Dragons, had become something of a problem because the beach was now crowded with holiday-makers, and on August 16 the editor of the *Evening Post* went down to see for himself: ". . . On several occasions we have protested at the danger to the public which exists from the regular use by aircraft of the public beach between West Park and First Tower. Between 5 and 5.30 pm . . . we watched the arrival of several . . . planes, and we have not the slightest hesitation in expressing our belief that there is not another place in the world which would tolerate such scenes as we witnessed. The beach from West Park slipway to the small group of rocks between the bathing pool and the promenade wall was crowded with folk. It was a glorious afternoon, hundreds of deck-chairs were out, children were running backwards and forwards . . . and sun-bathers were there in hundreds. The first of the Airways' planes appeared, flew out seaward, thence towards Fort Regent and, turning and shutting off its engines glided down from the harbours, to its prescribed landing place. Steadily losing height, the plane came down over the hundreds enjoying themselves on the beach. From twenty or thirty feet above their heads as it passed the foot of West Park slipway it came with a rush until, as it passed over the small group of rocks, its landing wheels could almost have been touched, and a shout went up as an elderly woman in its path ducked her head and the machine whizzed over with its wheels practically enclosing her. In a few moments a second plane followed in the same manner, not ten feet above the heads of scores and scores lying or running around the rocks. The landing of the third plane was a terrifying experience, for as it tore down a group of children appeared in its path. To many of the onlookers it appeared almost impossible that one boy at any rate could escape, but – and here we pay tribute to the skill of the pilot and acknowledge the coolness of the boy, who did not move – the machine flashed past him, wheels on either side of him and level with his shoulders, and landed a few score yards further on . . . Should a fatality occur – and under present conditions it appears almost inevitable – it will be difficult to ignore the culpability of the authorities . . ." Another problem for the Airways' staff was the large number of interested spectators who gathered round the aircraft on the beach and were difficult to disperse when the time came for the plane to move off.

There was a full moon on August 24, with 36 feet of water predicted for 7.16 pm, and eight machines arrived at the scheduled time of 4.15. All eight machines had to be turned round and dispatched as quickly as possible because the tide was coming in fast, but the last away (Mr Orchard in 'MJ) was left with a rapidly narrowing strip of sand. He opened the throttles and started his run, but the port wheel was caught by the advancing tide and 'MJ swung round and dashed straight into the sea. The five passengers were carried to dry land, but one angry lady got her feet wet because the stalwart employee who carried her ashore was big in build but rather short in leg. The value of the mobile office was then demonstrated when it was driven along the beach and hitched to a tow-rope to bring 'MJ out of the water. Once on dry land the Dragon was hauled away by private car and left on the First Tower slipway.

The following day was a Saturday, and because of heavy week-end bookings a Provincial Airways' Dragon, G-ACKD *Saturn*, had been hired to help out. It was on the beach beside *St Clement's Bay* and both were about to take-off when, for some reason, *Saturn* spun round on one wheel and rammed *St Clement's Bay* head on. Both machines were damaged and left for the mainland later in the day without passengers. This was a very sad day for Jersey Airways because early in the evening the prophecies of the *Evening Post* came true, although not in the manner anticipated. A small boy of ten, Denis Dutot, was struck by a plane and killed, and a another little boy, Raymond Potigny, was injured, but recovered after some time in hospital. With high water due at 8.05 pm, Jersey Airways,

111

learning from experience, had advanced the 6 pm departure time by 30 minutes, but there were eight machines to leave and it was nearly a quarter to six before the last one, G-ACMO *St Ouen's Bay* began its run along the beach. The pilot was Geoffrey Wood; it was his first day on the service and only his second take-off from West Park. There was no wind, and the aircraft were taking off in the westerly direction to become airborne somewhere between the two groynes. "I taxied out on to the centre of the beach well clear of the wall" said Mr Wood. "Soon after I had opened my throttles the aircraft started to swing to the right. I immediately applied full left rudder in order to check the swing, but the aircraft continued to swing to the right and I throttled back my port engine. She still swung to the right and I saw that an accident was unavoidable. I then throttled back my other engine, stopping it, and pulled on the brakes. I was too late to avoid an accident . . ." (6) The two boys were close to the groyne and, in the normal course of events, they were well out of harms way. "At the time of the accident . . . the sea was not very much more than 200 feet from . . . the sea wall, and the available runway over hard sand was further restricted in width at one point by a low groyne . . . extending about 60 feet from the sea wall . . ." (32) The plane hit the sea wall near its junction with the second groyne. None of the occupants was injured and the damage to the machine was slight, but the two little boys were struck by the wheels.

The Air Ministry Report attributed the accident to errors of judgement on the part of the pilot; arising from his lack of experience in handling twin-engined aircraft and added a note "The Dragon (D.H. 84) aeroplane, like other twin-engined and single-ruddered aircraft, is liable to develop a swing at a critical speed during the process of taking-off, more particularly when the machine is heavily laden and therefore slow in gaining flying position. The tendency to swing – always to the right in the case of the Dragon – appears to start when the tail is about to lift off the ground, and the swing is likely to develop rapidly unless checked in its initial stage by means of the engines. The directional instability of the aircraft at this critical period, that is, before the machine has gained sufficient speed for the tail controls to become effective, would certainly appear to be due to the slipstream of the starboard airscrew being deflected against the side of the fuselage and fin by reason of the direction of rotation of the engines." On this occasion 'MO was taking off at just 84 lbs. below the max. permissible all-up weight. The pilot had completed five years service in the R.A.F. with 690 flying hours, all on single-engined aircraft. Eight months after leaving the Air Force he took his 'B' licence, following his first period of Reserve training, but did no more flying for another twelve months and then, after his second period of Reserve training he joined Jersey Airways. Four days before the accident he had carried out 2 hours 40 mins. flying at Heston in a Dragon, including landing tests, and his licence had been endorsed to cover this type of aircraft. On the day of the accident he had flown the machine to and from Jersey in the morning with passengers, and had returned to the Island from Heston in the afternoon. In passing, the Air Ministry Report said that ". . . Under the terms of the licence issued by the Island Authorities the Company were entitled to use nearly half a mile of fore-shore on the St Helier side of the bay as a landing and taking-off ground for their Public Transport aircraft at any time when the tides were not less than 2 hours from full-flood . . . From 2 hours before to 2 hours after the time of high-water the fore-shore was closed to all air traffic (After the accident, these times were extended to 2½ hours)."

Jersey Airways could equally have been blamed for an "error of judgement" in using such an inexperienced pilot. The beach at St Helier was no place for learners. In Monday's issue of the *Evening Post* the editorial was headed "J'ACCUSE", and the Island authorities blamed for the tragedy. An immediate and searching enquiry was demanded.

The same Monday (August 27) another hired Dragon, G-ACCR of Commercial Air Hire Ltd., took off from West Park and set course for England, but by 3 o'clock it was back on the beach. According to one of its passengers, Mrs Smith of Maidstone, : ". . . We were going along very nicely, and I was thoroughly enjoying the trip. We had rounded the point of the French coast over which aeroplanes are not allowed to fly, and had just passed Alderney, when the pilot – whom I consider a very tactful man – conveyed to us that he had been recalled 'by wireless' . . . I did not believe him at the time, and heard, when we reached here, that there was only petrol in one tank . . ." Mr Greig tried to bluff it out: ". . . The machine is only hired by us. Apparently the pilot was not satisfied with something and came back. There was no danger . . ." *The Evening Post* made no comment but concluded their report by saying that the machine was to leave again for Heston "after refuelling"! Taking-off in a Dragon with insufficient petrol was easily done because the normal arrangement was to have a single petrol gauge on the instrument panel serving both tanks. It could be switched to either tank but, until the button underneath was pressed, it read "zero". G-ACCR had started its air-line career with a small firm flying between Barnstaple and Lundy Island, but hit a stone wall on Lundy and came to grief. After repair it went to Commercial Air Hire for early morning newspaper flights to Paris, and any other odd jobs later in the day.

At the beginning of September time-tables were still being adjusted to give wider margins from high water, and for a time the beach was relatively free from incident, although there was a minor mishap on September 4 when 'MP landed in the afternoon and managed to tear off a wheel spat and a tyre in turning to taxi up to the mobile office. Passengers were off-loaded as quickly as possible and 'MP towed up the beach clear of the 25 foot tide. However, over at Heston Mr Israel had a very narrow escape when taking 'MJ up on a test flight. One engine cut out and the plane dived straight into the ground. Mr Israel received only slight injuries but 'MJ, presumably, went back for another overhaul. Pilots at the end of August were:- Caldwell, Eckersley-Maslin, Swiss, Jenkins, Knowlden, Israel, Oakley, Orchard, Blythe and Wood, and by this time 14,100 passengers had been carried, during the summer months at 1,000 per week or 4.5 per flight (on average). From September 17 the service to England was reduced to once daily and the Paris service was closed down completely on September 27.

The new winter time-table repeated the pattern of the previous winter with arrivals at 12.30 pm and departures some 60 minutes later, except when high water forced a change, but the margin was now 2½ hours, except for a couple of days when the h.w. level was only about 26 ft. This two or 2½ hour margin was a reasonable rule-of-thumb arrangement but in theory it is possible to calculate the height of the sea at any state of the tide by a well-known formula ("The Rule of Twelfths") using tidal data published well in advance. The limiting height in St Aubin's Bay for aircraft operation would have been reached when the space between the end of the groyne and the water's edge was almost equal to the wing span of the aircraft, say perhaps something like 26 ft. However, tide tables are calculated for an assumed barometric pressure (29.9") and a variation of 1" would introduce an error of about 1 foot in the predicted height. Strong winds, too, have an effect, and if the sea were a foot higher than estimated it would be about 150' farther up the beach, depending on local contours.

Guernsey continued to attract attention. There was activity at L'Erée, and Spartan Air Lines appeared to be planning an inter-island amphibian service, and once the Jersey airport opened Jersey Airways would have no monopoly rights to its use. It was all very sinister thought a writer in the *Jersey Morning News* of September 13. The most suitable site for an aerodrome on Guernsey was L'Ancresse, he said: ". . . but here strong vested interests have to be considered, the Rifle Association, the Golf Club, the Race Club, join hands with those who object to the amenities of a public common being sacrificed . . ." Regarding Spartan's application to run an inter-island service he observed that: ". . . behind Spartan Air Lines it is not difficult to perceive the guiding hands of the Railway Companies making their next move in this game of aerial chess. Not a big move to start with but *'C'est le premier pas qui coute'* . . . In October the *Cloud of Iona* reappeared, making trial flights around the islands, including a flight to Alderney on October 26 with a party of businessmen. The pilot was none other than Flying Officer R.C.H. Monk who, the previous year, had flown the Cutty Sark G-ABBC between Blackpool and the Isle of Man. His erstwhile rivals, Blackpool and West Coast Air Services had just reached the end of their financial tether and the company had now been taken over by Olley Air Services, although retaining its name, and its pioneer pilot, J.C. Higgins. In Scotland another remarkable character, Eric Gandar Dower, had built himself an aerodrome at Dyce, near Aberdeen, and started an Aberdeen-Glasgow air service using a Short Scion flown by an equally remarkable character, Eric Starling. The former Midland and Scottish Air Ferries route from Glasgow to Campbeltown and Islay was now being operated by another road transport man, George Nicholson, who had run a Mondays and Saturdays Newcastle-Carlisle-Isle of Man service during the summer as Northern Airways but were now calling themselves Northern and Scottish Airways. In what may have seemed a counter move in the game of "aerial chess" a company called Guernsey Airways Ltd. was registered in Guernsey on November 24 as a wholly-owned subsidiary of Jersey Airways, but all was revealed on December 1 when Channel Island Airways, Ltd. was formed with a capital of £100,000 as a holding company for both Jersey and Guernsey Airways. 50% of the shares were held by Whitehall Securities and 50% by Mr Thurgood and associates. The chairman of the new company was J.A. Perree, a well-known Jersey farmer and businessman.

The reason for the new company, Channel Island Airways, retaining the old name of Jersey Airways was their reluctance to make an application for the transfer of the beach landing arrangements from the original company, and it was thought that the Jersey Islanders would prefer the old name. No doubt, the name Guernsey Airways was considered to be more appropriate for services available to the Guernsey Islanders, and there was the advantage that the names Channel Islands, Jersey, and Guernsey would not be available to any other companies. Messrs. Thurgood and Greig had met the Spartan people at their headquarters, 53 Parliament Street, and despite the earlier reports, which may have been bluff, of course, Mr Thurgood condemned flying-boats on the grounds that they had a lower reserve of engine power and faced a greater risk of forced landings due to mechanical troubles. He said he had been hoping that Spartan would have started their service with Saro Clouds because they would have burnt their fingers! A few days later Mr Thurgood had met two of the directors of the Southern Railway and intimated that he would not be unwilling to come to some working arrangement with the S.R. and, as a result, there were fruitful discussions between the general manager of the S.R., the Hon. Clive Pearson, and Mr Thurgood. On December 14 the S.R. sent a memo to the G.W.R. board of directors to advise them that the proposed service to the Channel Islands to be operated by Railway Air Services as soon as a landing place was available was recommended, but, as Whitehall Securities were providing Jersey Airways with strong financial backing it would be more advantageous to co-operate with them than to compete.

By the end of 1934 Portsmouth had been provided with a mobile radio station, and four of the Dragons had been equipped with R/T. They could be heard reporting to Portsmouth on 862m immediately after leaving Jersey, and when passing Alderney, and the Heston machines switched over to 900m when ready to contact Croydon. The machines fitted were 'NH, 'NI, 'NG, and 'NJ, and used the call-signs of Normandy-Hanover, Normandy-Italy, Normandy-Gibraltar, and Normandy-Jerusalem respectively. However, the big news, made possible by the increased capital, was the order for six brand-new D.H. 86's at a total cost of about

£50,000. The 86 (See Appendix 1D) had been designed in four months for use on the Singapore-Brisbane service of Qantas Empire Airways which linked up with the Imperial Airways' Indian route. Imperials had reached Cape Town by mid-1932 so that their two principal objectives had been achieved by the end of 1934 when the route to Brisbane was completed. With similar ideas K.L.M. had opened their regular Amsterdam-Batavia service in 1931 using the very reliable Fokker F.XVIII. In Europe each country tended to run its own national air-line, and, if possible, build its own national air-liners, although the Dutch Fokkers and German Junkers did tend to cross frontiers for use by foreign operators. But how far Europe had fallen behind the U.S.A. was realised when the Douglas D.C. 2 began to appear in the colours of Swissair and K.L.M. and when, in the England – Australia Air Race of October, 1934 a K.L.M. Douglas D.C. 2, PH-AJU, came second to our special racing machine, the first D.H. Comet.

"JERSEY AIRWAYS' NEW FLEET" said *Flight* for November 15: "Six D.H. 86 four-engined machines to be put into operation next year . . . Once or twice since the Jersey line opened the D.H. Dragons have reached their objective safely on one engine, and the new machines should completely remove any possibility of failure over the long sea crossing, for they can fly fully-loaded on any two of the four Gipsy Six engines fitted . . ." At the Air Ministry they were still trying to decide what to do about Jersey Airways' Dragons, and they sent out a circular letter to all internal air-line operators using Dragons (although mainly aimed at Jersey Airways):

> *"Gentlemen,*
> *I am directed to refer to Article 9 (1A) of the Air Navigation (Consolidated) Order, 1923 and to say that the Air Ministry would be glad to receive an assurance that you have taken steps to ensure that the loading of aircraft employed by you on regular lines or services involving flights over the sea or inland waters meets the safety requirements mentioned in that article."*
>
> *Air Ministry – 24.11.34. (5)*

With their letter to Jersey Airways they must have included the results of the Martlesham Heath tests because Jersey Airways wrote back on

November 28 noting:

> "... *that in the opinion of the Air Ministry D.H. 84 aircraft can only be expected to maintain a height of 1,000 feet in bumpy weather, with one engine stopped, at a total weight of 3,860 lbs. We further note your reference to Article 9 (1A). We would point out, however, that bumpy conditions are normally experienced only over land, to which Art. 9 (1A) does not apply. We are not clear as to the height which a D.H. 84 can be expected to maintain in bumpy weather at a total weight of 4,200 lbs. . . Whilst it is clear that these machines will not maintain 1,000 feet . . . it is not yet clear whether an actual forced landing would result. We should be glad to hear whether any further information on this point is available. Meanwhile additional precautions will be taken, and we would advise you that the regular use of D.H. 84 aircraft will be discontinued as soon as our D.H. 86 machines become available . . ."*

L.T.H. Greig (5)

This was followed by a letter from Mr St Barbe of de Havillands dated 1.12.34:

> "... *Somewhat embarrassed and not a little surprised to learn from a number of commercial operators of D.H. 84's of a letter from your Department interpreted by them as possibly a restriction on the all-up weight of that type under certain conditions . . . So far as we are aware . . . there is nothing in the Air Navigation (Amendment) No. 3 . . . stating that a machine is required to maintain any specific height in the event of a stoppage of one of its engines. The regulations merely stipulate . . . must be able to reach land . . . The tests somewhat inconclusive . . . in bumpy weather . . . 1,000 feet . . . at 3,860 lbs. Had the tests been continued they would have undoubtedly revealed that a height of 500 feet can be maintained at a higher weight, and 200 feet at a still greater one. The 1934 Dragon . . . all-up weight 4,500 lbs. has a higher*

ceiling on one engine than the 1933 model . . . Actually a fully-loaded Dragon (4,500 lbs.) with one engine stopped has a gliding angle of 1 in 75 which would enable it to cover a distance of no less than 17 miles from a height of 1,000 feet . . . From a height of 2,000 feet . . . 34 miles . . . therefore safe for a sea crossing of 50 miles or more. Not taking into account the weight of fuel consumed, hence it becomes lighter in flight . . . glide further . . . Also possible to jettison luggage and other gear . . ." (5)

They concluded that the purpose of the Air Ministry's letter was to sound a note of caution, but requested confirmation of this interpretation. Faced by these arguments the Air Ministry could only confirm, rather weakly, that their "whole purpose . . . was to convey a warning . . ." (5)

November had seen Jersey Airways offering special week-end excursions to London for £4. 5s. 0d. to attend the Armistice Day services, or to see the Lord Mayor's Show, and on December 12 the Jersey States voted to continue work on the aerodrome. Even with the winter time-table in force the tide still managed to create problems, as on December 15, when, with a mere 28.7 foot tide predicted for 1.30 pm there seemed to be ample time for two machines scheduled to arrive at 10.15, but there was a strong and gusty wind from the south and they did not arrive until 11. The southerly wind, aided by the usual "low" associated with southerly gales, had piled the tide right up the beach so that the normal landing place was impossible, and the bus had to be moved towards the First Tower: ". . . Even then the landing was none too easy and one of the machines actually landed on the water's edge but, magnificently handled by her pilot, she was swung round on one wheel and brought to rest. Passengers disembarked, the Customs formalities were rushed through . . . and the outgoing passengers embarked, but the tide gained considerably . . . infinitesimal space of dry beach left when the machines took off . . . the wind was blowing dead into the bay so the machines had to take off seawards. Both got off safely but it was a near thing, for a spectator informs us that one of them skimmed the water with her wings as she rose." (6)

For landings in bad visibility with no wind, or a dead cross wind, Jersey Airways had decreed that they should be made in a westerly direction, that is, by an approach over the harbour, and, once again, Christmas brought its quota of fog, but nothing like the continuous blanket of the previous Christmas. On the 22nd Heston was blotted out, but the passengers were taken by coach to Kenley where they were picked up by Dragons flown in from Portsmouth. In all, six plane loads left Portsmouth for Jersey that day, and there were eight plane loads to Jersey on the 23rd, four from Heston and four from Portsmouth. On Christmas Eve there was one plane from Heston and one from Portsmouth, but on Christmas Day there was fog over London, and both departures were from Portsmouth taking two passengers to Jersey and returning with fourteen. Whilst awaiting the arrival of the two planes a party of Airways, Harbour, Customs, and Police officials upheld the spirit of the season in the mobile bus on the beach. According to *The Aeroplane* eight Dragons were filled on December 22nd, 23rd, and 24th, and on the 22nd they had to charter two Spartan Cruisers to make a total of ten planes, but perhaps their informant had been upholding the spirit of the season, also!

During 1934 Jersey Airways carried 19,761 passengers, or nearly 20,000 since the start of operations, but only 105 used the Paris service. Heston accounted for 7,000 passengers in 1,765 aircraft movements at an average of four passengers per machine, and most of the remaining passengers had flown from Portsmouth and Southampton at an average of 5.32 passengers per machine, (74% capacity). At a later date Mr Caldwell recalled that, although Jersey Airways started to use Southampton in the spring of 1934 the service was via Portsmouth, but during the winter of 1934/35 their headquarters were re-established at Portsmouth where they took delivery of their first 86, and it was March before they moved back to Eastleigh. Final figures for the year 1934 showed a profit of £5,150.

Note

Martlesham Heath was the aerodrome used by the Air Ministry's Aeroplane and Armament Experimental Establishment.

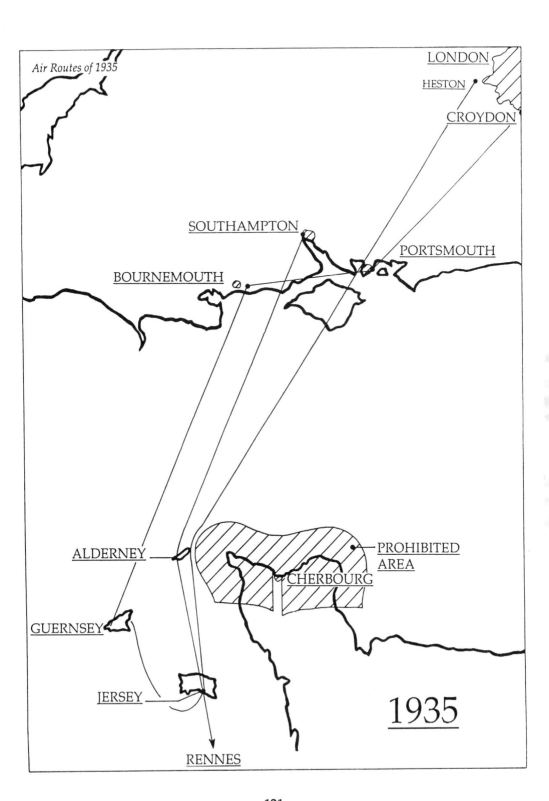

Air Routes of 1935

LONDON

HESTON

CROYDON

SOUTHAMPTON

PORTSMOUTH

BOURNEMOUTH

ALDERNEY

PROHIBITED
AREA

CHERBOURG

GUERNSEY

JERSEY

1935

RENNES

Jersey Airways' D.H.86, G-ACZN, "St. Catherine's Bay" on test at Hatfield
(Quadrant Picture Library)

THE SOUND OF FOUR ENGINES (1935)

At the beginning of 1935 the outlook for Jersey Airways was far better than it had been twelve months earlier. In addition to the mobile radio station at Portsmouth there were wooden sheds on the Jersey airport site housing a radio station under the control of Mr Duggan, a former G.W.R. mailboat wireless-operator, and it would soon be equipped with D/F. The Jersey airport was now a definite proposition, and new aircraft with four-engined reliability were on order. Provided these big 86's could be put down on the beach without too much trouble all would be well. Financially they had the support of the wealthy Whitehall Securities Corporation, and in January came the news that the G.W.R. and S.R. jointly were to take a one-third interest in Jersey Airways, the remaining two thirds being equally divided between W.S.C. and Thurgood (and associates). With the two most powerful groups in British internal air-lines behind them Jersey Airways were in a a strong position.

On January 8 the single daily services from Portsmouth/Southampton and Heston were supplemented by a new service to Rennes, an important rail centre, 85 miles S.S.E. of Jersey in the Ille-et-Vilaine department of Brittany, which could effect considerable savings in time for travellers heading for Western France, Bordeaux, Biarritz, and Spain. It would run on Tuesdays and Fridays and this was confirmed by the local paper, *L'Ouest Eclair*: "Un service régulier . . . fonctionnera à partir d'aujourd hui 8 Janvier le mardi et le vendredi . . ." The fare was £1. 7s. 6d. single, £2. 5s. 0d. return and the airport was at St Jacques-de-la-Lande about 4.4 miles S.W. of Rennes. (See Appendix 2F). "Un service automobile en correspondence . . . sera assuré par M. Delory, Rue Baudrairie. Le départ pour l'aéroport aura lieu le 50 minutes avant l'heure fixée pour l'arrivée de l'avion. Le retour à Rennes aura lieu dès le depart de l'avion pour Jersey . . . 5 francs . . Les horaires . . . au hall de dépêche du journal chez M. Delory . . . et au bureau du Tourisme à la gare." These times varied with the tide as usual, but the inaugural flight was scheduled for 11 am, and at 10.30 two Dragons came over from the racecourse where they had spent the night. A 37.2 ft. spring tide had been on the ebb since 8.44 am but the sea was still high up the beach, and the two machines circled waiting for a space to clear with an audience of about 70 people. Eckersley-Maslin came in first: ". . . so low that it appeared almost to scrape the groyne at the First Tower, and when it touched the sands one wheel was in the edge of the water while the opposite wing was almost touching the sea wall. Then the other machine (Blythe) also landed, but this pilot made two attempts before he succeeded." (6) The Dragons left on time with five passengers each, some bound for Switzerland by the 12.49 pm Rennes-Paris express. The flight took 42 minutes against the 50 allowed and: ". . . Rennes was bathed in sunshine and the aerodrome gay with bunting, the French tri-colour and the Union Jack being conspicuously displayed. The residents of the district looked on it as a great occasion and, with the President of the Rennes Chamber of Commerce, assembled to welcome the pilots and passengers and gave them a great reception." (6) But the *Evening Post* was critical of the morning's display: ". . . Since the unfortunate accident . . . stringent regulations were made . . . and the Airways prohibited from landing at certain states of the tide . . . Apparently the regulations are not stringent enough or else there is something wrong with the administration of them." What Eckersley-Maslin did with a Dragon would have been impossible with an 86 and at no time in the future did Jersey Airways ever compile a time-table with less than the stipulated 2½ hours interval from high water.

Although the Air Ministry had accepted de Havilland's superior logic regarding the all-up weight of the Dragon, their officials at Portsmouth and Heston had not, and they told the Jersey Airways' pilots in no uncertain terms that they were not to take-off with a max. weight exceeding 3,850 lbs. Whereupon Greig threatened to remove the radio sets from the aircraft and reduce the amount of fuel in the tanks. He wrote to Bertram on January 28: ". . . I enclose . . . a copy of instructions which I have . . . been compelled to issue . . . during the last day or two definite instructions were given to our pilots . . . not to exceed an all-up weight of 3,850 lbs. . . . it is impossible for me to countenance the loss of 350 lbs. of payload in addition to 75 lbs. for radio equipment and petrol for five hours duration . . . 3,850 lbs. without wireless and with full tanks, only leaves me about the equivalent of four passengers. If 75 lb. is taken off this for wireless I am left with three passengers only, which is completely uneconomic." (5) Mr Bertram was the Deputy Director-General of Civil Aviation at this time, and a typical civil servant, being a product of St Paul's School and Pembroke College. He was not one of the "old hands" from the days of the R.F.C.

The first 86 (See Appendix 1D) to be ready was G-ACYF *Giffard Bay*, and it was due to make its first flight to Jersey on February 6 with the Director-General himself, Lt.-Col. Sir F. C. Shelmerdine, on board, but departure was postponed until the following day due to a last-minute hitch. Perhaps this had something to do with the north-easterly gale blowing hard on the 6th, because the 86 could be a rough ride in gale force winds, and to throw the D.G.C.A. out through the emergency exit in the roof would be bad publicity. However, Sir Francis had other engagements on the 7th when, at 10.34, the new 86 took off from Heston with nine passengers on board:- Thurgood, Greig, Fountain Barber (Jersey Airways' publicity manager), Maurice Jackaman (Airports, Ltd.), Mortimer Sharpe (*Aeroplane*), Taylor (*Flight*), Jones (*Daily Herald*), the Countess of Drogheda, C.B.E., (the first woman to fly the Channel) and, for reasons best known to Jersey Airways, His Excellency Cxatia Saraci, First Secretary of the Albanian Legation and Chamberlain to King Zog!

"Averaging 156 mph with a fair following wind, Jersey Airways' first D.H. 86 'Express' flew its maiden trip from Heston to St Helier last Thursday. The outward distance was covered in 1 hr. 11 min. and the return in 1 hr. 35 min. showing an overall speed of 137 mph . . . Apart from the modified Qantas-type nose, to accommodate full dual-control, and the Dowty hydraulically-operated split trailing-edge flaps, the Jersey 'Expresses' are very completely equipped. Delivery No. 1, which was flown by Mr B.A. Blythe – with the moral support of Capt. Broad (of de Havilland's) – has a Kollsman sensitive altimeter, a Smith rate-of-climb indicator, a Sperry artificial horizon and directional gyro, and a Smith turn-and-bank indicator. The sensitive altimeter is an interesting and, incidentally, expensive instrument indicating altitude changes to a minimum of twenty feet. Two hands move over a scale of one to ten, the 'hour hand' giving the thousands and the 'minute hand' giving the hundreds of feet. Adjustments to suit changing barometric pressures can be made very simply and quickly . . . The rate-of-climb indicator . . . enables a pilot to judge the descent . . . in relation to his passengers' ear-drums. All normal blind flying is carried out on the Sperry, and the turn indicator is fitted as a check and to comply with c. of a. regulations, the artificial horizon, of course, does not function in aerobatic attitudes. In addition *Giffard Bay* has Standard two-way radio. Somewhere towards Alderney

125

on the outward journey the station on Jersey received a message from Barton, Manchester, to the effect that the 86 was calling Jersey! (According to the *Jersey Morning News* the actual transmission was: 'Hello Jersey Airport – This is Jersey 'YF calling. We are now over St Catherine's Point at 3,000 feet and shall arrive in Jersey about 12.40 – Terminé.') This year, it is hoped, Jersey will have its own complete D/F station, but in the meantime the machines obtain bearings from Portsmouth when necessary, and the pilots can usually obtain a 'fix' through that station and Croydon. This year, too, will see a D/F station at Heston, and the chain will then be complete. Although the beach at St Helier is nothing if not extensive, it is often necessary to land and take-off slightly across wind. A Dragon can be handled satisfactorily under these circumstances, and on Thursday it was shown that even the much larger and heavier 'Express' responds gamely to 'aileron against rudder' tactics. Nevertheless, the pilots will undoubtedly breathe sighs of relief when the long-awaited aerodrome is laid out." (20)

The Jersey Airways' 86's had seats for fourteen passengers, and the engines were started by portable batteries kept on trolleys at each aerodrome and plugged-in to a connection in the belly of the fuselage. After lunch the 86 took various local dignitaries on a trip around the Island before returning to Heston. However, aerial car ferries were still in the future, as the advert in the *J.E.P.* headed "YOUR HUMBER DELIVERED BY AIR" was on behalf of Boudin's bicycle shop. Although, as *Flight* had said, the Dragons had "reached their objective . . . on one engine . . . once or twice . . ." during 1934, the Airways had managed to keep this news from the Press, but early in 1935 (Feb. 18) their luck ran out, and *Portelet Bay* was observed on the shingle undergoing repairs, and attracting attention which led to rumours: ". . . of a more or less sensational nature (!) . . . bound for Jersey yesterday with five passengers and a full load of luggage . . . a few miles the other side of Alderney the pilot, Mr Jenkins, realised something was wrong with one engine, and that he would have to carry on with only one . . . The passengers . . . blissfully unaware because the rush of air kept the airscrew turning . . ." (6) Three days later Jersey was the centre of a 75 mph hurricane and *St Ouen's Bay*", just back from overhaul and pegged down on the race-course overnight for the Rennes service, was torn from its moorings, and tossed about on the ground. Before it could be securely lashed to the refuelling lorry some damage was caused to the port wing.

During February Eastleigh was approved as a Customs airport, and Jersey Airways abandoned the Portsmouth call. Sadly the minutes of the Portsmouth City Council recorded that: "Jersey Airways are not to use Portsmouth as a main port of call during the coming season. Purely on account of certain facilities afforded at Southampton which could not be provided at Portsmouth." They did not say what these facilities were, but the *Jersey Morning News* put it down to the poor transport facilities to and from Portsmouth aerodrome compared with Southampton where there was a railway halt 50 yards from the traffic offices at the aerodrome. In fact there were many advantages, including lower landing fees, and bigger hangars with lower rents. Rail connections to the Midlands and West were better, and fast trains to London more frequent. Southampton, of course was a major seaport, especially for passengers, and it was the port used by the Channel Island steamers of the S.R. whilst the G.W.R. steamers ran from Weymouth, which could be reached via the Southampton-Bournemouth line. Both railways now had an interest in Jersey Airways and there would be arrangements for the interchange of passengers and facilities for luggage in advance. Up to the end of January the scheduled time for the Jersey-Heston flight was 120 minutes, in February this was reduced to 90 minutes (with the arrival of the 86), but in March it was increased to 105 minutes, because Portsmouth was omitted from the time-table after February 28, and extra time allowed for a journey via Eastleigh. The original 75 minutes for the Jersey-Portsmouth flight had been reduced to 60 minutes in February, but from March 1 the 75 minutes was restored for the direct Southampton-Jersey service.

Jersey Airways now decided to carry out their own maintenance, and one of the ground engineers taken on at the end of February was George Cook, who held licence No. 125. George had joined the R.F.C. in 1914, and after the war he had worked for a number of well-known firms, such as B.A.T. and the Aircraft Disposal Co., but in 1921 he sailed to America in the *Mauritania* with the Savage sky-writing outfit. When Cyril Turner, in an S.E. 5, wrote "Hello, New York" in smoke 10,000 feet above the city all traffic stopped, and it was headlines in every newspaper. A few days later a million dollar contract was signed. Eventually, however, the sky-writing faded away, and George came back to England and rejoined the A.D.C. Then he toured Britain, first with C.D. Barnard's air display, and later with Cobham's, but after a year at the Yapton Flying Club and a brief return to Cobham he joined Jersey Airways. About two months after the move from Portsmouth all maintenance was transferred to Eastleigh, an engine overhaul shop was installed and c. of a's carried out. At the end of March the Rennes service was discontinued, the States committee concerned refusing to renew the permit for the route because of the Colorado beetle. It is not active during the winter months but comes to life in the spring and, as Rennes was in the Colorado beetle zone, the Jersey potato growers were seriously alarmed at the thought of these beetles arriving by plane. Just in time for the Easter rush the second and third 86's were delivered:- G-ACYG *Grouville Bay* and G-ACZN *St Catherine's Bay*.

On 4.4.1935 United Airways was registered with a nominal capital of £50,000 and directors Balfour, Ballardie, Roberts, and Thurgood, but it was wholly owned by Whitehall Securities as Mr Thurgood did not take up his option of a share-holding. The basic inspiration for its formation came from R.C.H. Monk, who was flying the *Cloud of Iona* for Saunders-Roe. After five years in the R.A.F. he had joined National Flying Services, which was a company offering aero club facilities, private tuition, and charter services, at various aerodromes up and down the country, including Stanley Park, Blackpool, where Flying Officer Monk was based. When N.F.S. went out of business he had flown passengers between Blackpool and the Isle of Man in a Saro Cutty Sark, but spent most of his time joy-riding at Blackpool. At the end of the 1933 season he ceased to operate because of an agreement with the Blackpool Corporation to use a larger aircraft after a certain date, but he was unable to obtain the Saro Cloud he wanted, and early in 1934 he joined P.S.I.O.W.A. as a pilot but quickly moved on to Saunders-Roe. After N.F.S. the lease to Stanley Park had been taken up by Midland & Scottish Air Ferries, but they would not be renewing it, and it would soon be open to tender. Monk had pointed out the excellent joy-riding prospects at Blackpool just as Jersey Airways was expecting a surplus of D.H. Dragons, the very machine for the purpose, and the Isle of Man routes would be ideal for Spartan Cruisers with the reliability of three engines. Blackpool was still anxious to be on the map, as far as air services were concerned, and for their airport to be the "Croydon of the North" was the laudable ambition of many councillors of aerodrome sub-committees in widely separated parts of Northern England. Blackpool had gone one better than most by having two aerodromes, both owned by the Corporation. The official "municipal" aerodrome was Stanley Park, but the Corporation had little interest in club flying, and positively disliked joy-riding; they wanted proper air services. Some rate-payers were complaining about the cost of Stanley Park, and others complained about the noise. A regular Liverpool-Blackpool-Isle of Man air service had been started in 1933 by Blackpool and West Coast Air Services but, much to the annoyance of the aerodrome committee, they used another aerodrome at Squires Gate, on the south side of the town. The Corporation then bought up the whole of the Squires Gate Estate, which happened to come on to the market, but "West Coast" had a lease, and could only be moved by consent. Somewhat reminiscent of the Avro tender of 1919 for the joy-riding monopoly of Blackpool's South Shore, the negotiations for the lease of Stanley Park for 1935 were brought to a successful conclusion when United Airways agreed to a suggestion that they should run a regular service between Blackpool and London, in addition to the proposed Isle of Man services. Heston was chosen as the London terminus, and a few weeks later, when United bought controlling interests in both Highland Airways and Northern & Scottish Airways the Whitehall Securities chain stretched from Jersey to the Orkney Islands.

To add to the complexity of the situation over the Irish Sea the L.M.S. Railway and the Isle of Man Steam Packet Company, jointly, arranged for Railway Air Services to operate a service on their behalf, under the name of Manx Airways, initially between Manchester, Blackpool, and the Isle of Man, but later extended to Liverpool. According to *The Aeroplane* the fares were about the same as those of B.W.C.A.S. "with which the railways are working in friendly competition" (!) On the other R.A.S. services the G.W.R.'s Plymouth route continued on from Birmingham to a new terminus at Nottingham, while the joint G.W.R./S.R. service continued at one end from Birmingham to Liverpool, and at the other from Southampton to Portsmouth and Brighton, with a separate service from Southampton to Cowes and Sandown. On the L.M.S. main line from Croydon to Belfast and Glasgow, Manchester (Barton) was replaced by Liverpool (Speke) on 1.11.34, but the Summer service included both places. Much to their annoyance, R.A.S. lost the mail contract (from 1.12.34 to 30.11.35) to Hillman's. It has been said that Mr Hillman put in an uneconomically low tender just to obtain the prestige, as he was about to float Hillman's as a public company, and he had to restore the London-

Belfast service he had just closed down (on 30.9.34) and extend it to Glasgow. Hillman's Airways, Ltd. was duly registered on December 12, 1934, and on the very last day of the month Mr Hillman died of a heart attack at the early age of 45. Major McCrindle was appointed managing director in April 1935 and there was considerable expansion with new routes to Ostend and Brussels, and from Liverpool to Manchester and Hull, and three D.H. 86A's were added to their fleet of seven Rapides, four Dragons, and sundry smaller craft. Provincial Airways, also expanded during 1935 with services from Southampton to Hull, via Leicester and Nottingham, and from Nottingham and Leicester to Le Touquet and Paris. A new company, Crilly Airways, opened up in the Midlands with services from Leicester to Bristol, Norwich, Northampton, Nottingham, Liverpool, and Skegness, but nothing more was heard of Eastern Air Services, and another new company, North Eastern Airways inaugurated a service from Heston to Newcastle and Edinburgh connecting with Aberdeen Airways, who also ran from Aberdeen to Wick, Thurso, and Kirkwall, in fierce competition with Highland Airways. On April 14 Spartan Air Lines after a year at Croydon, transferred their London terminus back to Heston in direct competition with P.S.I.O.W.A. who reopened their Heston-Isle of Wight summer service on the following day. Between Heston and Croydon there was a shuttle service called the Inner Circle Air Line run by Commercial Air Hire, of the Paris newspaper flights. The year promised to be a busy one for internal air-line operators, and on April 15 the new radio-control system came into force, with Croydon responsible for the Thames Estuary, Kent and Continental areas, and Heston controlling the area bounded by Brighton, Oxford, Leicester, Bedford, Clacton, and Stapleford Abbotts. Aircraft from Jersey to Heston remained in the Portsmouth zone until they crossed the boundary just north of Petersfield. By the end of April the fourth 86, G-ACZO *Ouaine Bay* had arrived.

The final instalment of the long saga concerning the all-up weight of the Dragon was sent to Bertram by Greig on April 10: ". . . the real position was that the A.I.D. officer at Portsmouth, upon at least one occasion, refused to permit our aircraft to take-off at a weight exceeding 3,850 lbs., and the subsequent correspondence was in the nature of a diplomatic counter-attack in case any definite regulations were foreshadowed . . . In actual fact . . . our aircraft were not deprived of their radio or their petrol . . . In any event I do not propose to pursue this question further because the whole of the Dragons are coming off the Jersey run and being replaced by six D.H. 86's and two D.H. 89's . . . Most . . . of our Dragons will be transferred to our associated companies, though we may sell one or two and will probably keep one Dragon in Jersey for trips between Jersey and Alderney, and any charter work which may arise . . . construction on Alderney is proceeding very satisfactorily . . . may be used as a stepping stone to Guernsey, the Alderney to Guernsey section being operated by amphibian . . . pending . . . a proper aerodrome on Guernsey . . . At the present moment the selection of a suitable site appears to be largely obscured by the activities of a noisy minority who are putting forward claims in respect of L'Erée which . . . is a white elephant that they are anxious to have taken over by the States, or alternatively to use as an excuse for opposing the creation of a State owned aerodrome with the object of keeping the air traffic to Guernsey as their private monopoly . . . We now have our own maintenance arrangements at Southampton . . . and on the 15th inst. we will also create our own maintenance organisation at Heston . . ." (5) Jersey Airways had decided to make an aerodrome on Alderney, and thanks to the enthusiasm of the inhabitants had very little difficulty in obtaining the land, although the 150 vergées required had about 60 owners, some owning just a few perches. Perhaps the fact that the land could still be utilised to a certain extent and that it is a common practice to tether cattle in Alderney, may have had some bearing on this. The aerodrome was on the Blaye, a plateau in the south of the Island, and some trouble was experienced with rock outcrops which had to be removed and the holes back-filled with soil. Two tractors were at work, but on Guernsey, the aerodrome at L'Erée, in the hands of a rival firm, was now an accomplished fact.

Sir Alan Cobham, K.B.E., A.F.C. was one of the famous names of pre-war aviation. Born in 1894, he had joined the army in 1914 and transferred to the R.F.C. in 1917. After the war he went joy-riding in the ubiquitous Avro 504K, and then became a noted taxi-pilot, flying thousands of miles across Europe and North Africa. He raced in the King's Cup, and made a series of long-distance flights to the Cape, Australia, round Africa, and to the Belgian Congo. At the outset of his "Round Africa" flight he had left Hamble on November 20, 1927 in the Short Singapore, G-EBUP, and passed over Bellegreve Bay and Guernsey where, he claimed "we could scent the faint aroma of flowers in the air . . ." (68) It was all good publicity for British aviation, and for Sir Alan, too, as when, with a fine touch of showmanship he landed the D.H. 50 seaplane on the Thames at Westminster after the flight to Australia and back for which he received his knighthood in 1926. He became even better known through his National Aviation Day Campaign, or Cobham's Air Display as it was generally called. In 1929 he toured the country with one aircraft, the D.H. 61 Giant Moth, G-AAEV, and called at 110 different places in 21 weeks giving free rides to school children (at the expense of Sir Charles Wakefield), free rides to mayors, town clerks, and "hordes of councillors", followed by normal joy-rides for the fare-paying public. The idea was to arouse interest in municipal aerodromes and, hopefully, obtain commissions for Sir Alan's other business of aviation and aerodrome consultant. This was followed in 1932 by his air display proper, which visited 168 towns and cities starting in London (Hanworth) and ending at Chingford on October 16 having travelled as far north as Inverness. Using a mixed collection of aircraft numerous "turns" were put on, including aerobatics, wing-walking, air racing, and comic acts, with joy-rides all day long in planes of various sizes up to the "giant air liner". The object was to make everyone "air-minded" and, at the same time, earn an honest penny for Sir Alan and his merry men. Why one had to be "air-minded" was not explained.

South Africa was toured in the winter of 1932, and in 1933 the show was split in two to cover a wider area, opening in Dublin for the first time on July 1. One of the items was to call for a volunteer wing-walker from the crowd, whereupon a certain Martin Hearn would appear disguised as a country bumpkin and board the plane. After take-off the "yokel" climbed out of the cockpit to lurch about the plane and eventually fall overboard. This was actually a dummy, inflated with a bicycle pump, whilst the real Martin Hearn kept out of sight in the cockpit. In Dublin the dummy wasn't blown up hard enough "and it hit the ground with a soft thud instead of bouncing. People screamed, a priest ran out to give the Last Sacraments, and one lady had a baby on the spot . . ." (21) Wing Commander Bullmore gives Liverpool (Speke) as the scene of this event. Serious accidents were rare, and the displays a great success with hardly anyone in the country failing to see one. By 1935 the show included Westland Wessex, G-EBXK, which had been the prototype Westland IV, and in March, 1935 Sir Alan bought three more from SABENA, the Belgian national air-line. He intended to open a regular service from Guernsey to the mainland using L'Erée and an aerodrome at Christchurch, near Bournemouth.

Cobham's "Wessex", G-ABAJ, when in service with SABENA
(Pamlin Prints)

The Wessex (See Appendix 1E) was a high-wing monoplane with three 105 hp Genet-Major engines and a cruising speed of 95 mph. It could land in fairly small fields and was supposed to have the ability to fly on two engines. Back in 1930 M. Renard of SABENA had said that his pilots had

133

managed to obtain a ceiling of 5,000 ft. on two engines with full load. Between Christchurch and Croydon an Airspeed Envoy was to be used, and Cobham had G-ADBA, a series 1 model with Cheetah IX engines. The Envoy (See Appendix 1F) was a fast, modern monoplane with a retractable undercarriage and two radial engines giving a cruising speed of about 150-170 mph. Renamed the "Oxford" it was to become a familiar sight in the wartime skies of Britain as a training machine.

The field at L'Erée was owned by the Guernsey Aero Club, in which Sir Alan Cobham had a considerable interest, and they possessed just one aircraft, an Avro Avian. In 1934 when Cobham's project was initiated Jersey Airways had been just a small firm with the luck to pick a profitable route and be given permission to use the beach at St Helier, but once Jersey airport was completed they would be wide open to competition. However by the spring of 1935 they were backed by two powerful groups and a rival firm would be unlikely to break their grip of the Jersey routes. But no beach landing grounds were available on Guernsey, although Vazon had been used in an emergency, and the only existing aerodrome was L'Erée. If a licence for commercial operation could be obtained and a satisfactory service run the States might be tempted to abandon the idea of making their own aerodrome on grounds of expense, loss of good agricultural land, and interference with amenities, and as L'Erée was privately owned the owners would have a virtual monopoly, as feared by Mr Greig. Unfortunately for Sir Alan, the Guernsey States Aerodrome Committee, with expert advice, favoured a site at La Villiaze. L'Erée (See Appendix 2J) lies at the same latitude as St Peter Port but on the opposite coast about six miles away by road. The landing area was an irregular-shaped depression on the rectangular promontory between Rocquaine Bay and Perelle Bay. On the N.W. perimeter it was separated from the sea by a road, "La Rue de la Rocque", and a stone dyke giving protection from high tides, and both were well above the general level of the aerodrome surface. To the W.N.W. was the Fort Saumarez Martello tower rising to 98 feet, to the S.E. was L'Erée hill, and to the N.E. some ground rising to about 50 feet. The lowest part of the aerodrome was below the level of high water spring tides, indicating possible drainage problems, and there were sundry granite mounds in various inconvenient places. Take-off run was very limited, and the only favourable factor was the cheapness of the land due to its low agricultural value. The three

SABENA Wessex, OO-AGC (G-ABAJ), OO-AGE (G-ADEW), and OO-AGF (G-ADFZ) were ferried from Brussels to Penshurst, via Croydon on March 7, 11, and 28 respectively, by Cecil Bebb and, after various checks, flown on to Ford in Sussex where Sir Alan kept his display machines.

Flying Officer Bebb had joined the R.A.F. in 1921 at the age of sixteen, and taken his C.F.S. Instructor's Course in 1929. From the R.A.F. he went to Southern Aircraft, Ltd. as a pilot, and then to Cobham's Air Display. "I had decided to leave his Circus" (early in 1935) recalls Captain Bebb, but Sir Alan said "No – I am going to start an air-line to Guernsey, the Scilly Isles, and Dublin, and I want you to survey the situation in Guernsey and the Scilly Isles – Guernsey was problematic due to the small landing area . . ." On April 25 trial landings were to be carried out at L'Erée so Captain Bebb in G-ABAJ, with Sir Alan Cobham and an Air Ministry

Captain Cecil Bebb

official on board flew from Portsmouth to Guernsey: "It was a lovely morning though rather hazy" and they flew on until they could see "greenhouses glistening in the distance . . . As I was circling the field Cobham came rushing up to the cockpit and said 'My God! The wind is blowing the wrong way – Go and land on one of those sandy beaches!' I said I was going to do a couple of dummy runs, and if I feel confident enough not to finish up hitting the sea wall I will land on the third run. So I came down over the rocky mound in a stalled condition, cut the engines on the boundary, and – Clonk – we were on the ground in one piece. Cobham nearly kissed me! No trials to-day I thought . . ." but Cecil Noel suggested there could be a wind change in the afternoon with the change of tide: ". . . and sure enough the wind swung round to the south-west, so I said put on ballast the equivalent of two passengers, next run four passengers, and the third, six, and there I stopped, and Collins (the Air Ministry inspector) licensed the field for a Wessex with six passengers." (76)

At the Guernsey Royal Court on April 29, 1935 the Guernsey Aero Club was granted a temporary licence for the use of L'Erée aerodrome by aircraft of the Wessex type. When Advocate V.G. Carey asked whether Jersey Airways would be able to use L'Erée, Advocate Randell, acting for the Aero Club, said "No"; it was a privately-owned aerodrome and only those who applied for, and were given a licence, could make use of it. Four days later (May 3) Cobham Air Routes Ltd. was registered with a nominal capital of £30,000 and two directors, Sir Alan and Lady Cobham. The same day Captain Bebb flew to Guernsey in G-ADEW with Cobham Air Routes' staff, including R.B. Mortimore the business manager, for a meeting with Aero Club members:- Advocate Randell (chairman), Cecil Noel (director), Deputy Bartlett (director), and Clifton Smith (secretary). Cobham himself was down with 'flu. Later another Wessex arrived (G-ABAJ) flown by Captain Rodney Beresford with engineers Meacock and Sutherland on board, but he burst a tyre on landing and the Wessex lurched round with a damaged undercarriage and a bent propeller. He had found the aerodrome without difficulty, he said: "but the wind was in an unfavourable quarter for landing . . ." When asked about the suitability of L'Erée Mr Mortimore, with more tact than truth, claimed that: ". . . The planes have had no difficulty in coming down or taking-off . . . there are inferior aerodromes to this in England . . . There was a difficult wind to-day, but it rarely blows from that quarter . . ." (22) A large crowd had gathered to witness the unique sight of three planes on the ground at the same time on the only licensed aerodrome in the Channel Islands, and at the end of the day Mr Bebb returned to the mainland in 'EW leaving 'AJ behind for repair . . .

The proposed service was scheduled to leave Croydon (See Appendix 2K) daily at 9 am and 2.30 pm to reach Guernsey in two hours, with return flights at noon and 5 pm, and adverts began to appear in the Guernsey papers:

"EXPRESS AIR SERVICE GUERNSEY-LONDON VIA BOURNEMOUTH, SOUTHAMPTON, PORTSMOUTH – SERVICE TWICE DAILY IN EACH DIRECTION – AIRCRAFT WESTLAND WESSEX THREE ENGINES SIX PASSENGERS. Sure, comfortable, speedy – Road transport provided between airport and town at all points – SERVICE COMMENCING JUBILEE DAY Book now at Bougourd Brothers, Esplanade and Pollett – Tel. 1128 Sole local agents BOOKING Seats must be booked 24 hours in advance.

LONDON OFFICE: Cobham Air Routes Ltd., Coastal Chambers, 172 Buckingham Palace Road, London, S.W.1 Fares/Times on application."

Sir Alan Cobham and Mr. Outram at L'Erée before the inaugural flight of "Wessex", G-ADEW", to Christchurch on May 6,1935

(By kind permission of Mrs P Mackenzie)

It was the Silver Jubilee of King George V that was being celebrated on May 6, but there was no ceremony attached to the inaugural flight when Captain Ogden, the third of the Cobham Air Routes pilots, brought G-ADEW into L'Erée just on 11 carrying Sir Alan and insurance men to inspect the damaged machine. 'EW took-off again at 12.15 pm with Mr V.A. Lewis, of the *Guernsey Star*, and Mr Outram of the insurance co., who was seen off by Sir Alan Cobham. The Wessex reached Christchurch just after 1.30 pm, and half-an-hour later Mr Lewis continued on to Croydon. After spending an hour in London he set out on his return flight and landed at 6.15 pm, again in 'EW, but with Mr Bebb as pilot. The second flight of the day had been put back until 6.30 pm for the benefit of Mr Simpson-Smith who was operating on the Bailiff of Guernsey, Mr A. Bell. During the first week the cross-Channel leg was flown by Messrs Ogden and Bebb alternately whilst C.H. Colman, the Airspeed test pilot probably flew the Croydon section. On May 8, no doubt as a publicity "stunt", Lord Donegall of the *Sunday Dispatch* and the Hon. Anthony Vivian arrived in Guernsey for a visit lasting just 40 minutes. An *Evening Press* reporter was driven out to L'Erée by Mr Newton, the Bougourd Bros. manager, to await their arrival and: "at 11.20 am a faint speck was seen high in the sky and five minutes later the great plane was at rest in L'Erée, Pilot W.H. Ogden making a splendid landing with hundreds of feet to spare when the plane came to rest . . . Lord Donegall said they left London at 9.10 am . . . and reached Bournemouth, via Portsmouth. They crossed the Channel in one hour . . . extremely interested in the beautiful coastline . . . fascinated by the appearance of so many glasshouses . . ." But the 40 minutes soon went by: ". . . and Mr J. Sutherland, the engineer-in-charge of L'Erée Station, having got the monoplane ready, with the aid of the ever-willing Jack Ferbrache . . . Pilot Ogden once more entered the plane . . ." with the two recent arrivals and two other passengers. ". . . Mr Blunden is at present the manager at L'Erée . . . and arriving yesterday was Mr G. Button to assist in tuning-up and repairing the Westland Wessex monoplane which is under an improvised canvas marquee." (22)

Initially the fare to London was £3. 5s. 0d. single, £6. 4s. 0d. return, but the latter was reduced to £5. 14s. 0d. on May 9, possibly because *The Aeroplane* had compared them with Jersey Airways fares of £2. 19s. 6d. and £4. 19s. 6d. A Miss Spencer was the first lady passenger and she left on the 12.00 plane on May 9 with Captain Bebb and three other people. On the 5 o'clock plane Captain Ogden had four passengers including Mr Goodge of Boot's the Chemists in St Helier who crossed from Jersey on the up mail-boat, and a Mr Elliott who had arrived on the morning plane. On May 10 Captain Bebb landed at 11.20 am with Meacock, the ground engineer, and returned at noon with two delegates to the Rotary Conference at Margate. The second machine of the day arrived empty, and returned with only Mr Meacock on board. And so the service continued, seldom fully booked, sometimes empty, and of the passengers, some were staff, and others journalists, travel agents, Aero Club members, and no doubt various friends and relations who could possibly claim free tickets or a certain amount of discount. However, Mr Simpson-Smith looked like becoming a "regular" because he flew to Croydon again on May 12.

On the first day of the second week there was no morning plane because of a radio fault, but Captain Bebb came through in the afternoon, and the following day he took over his regular duty of flying the Envoy between Croydon and Christchurch. The afternoon plane of the 14th flown by Captain Ogden left L'Erée at 5.35 pm carrying Mr Vernon Ricketts, of the *Daily Express*, Mrs Ricketts, and the Hon. Anthony Vivian, and once more a little publicity was generated: "London-Guernsey, sixty-three minutes. How does that look beside the ten hour land and sea schedule? . . . Sir Alan Cobham has already made a two hour connection to the island from Croydon. I flew on it last week. From Croydon to Bournemouth via Portsmouth's lawn-surfaced airport I went in the sleek, speedy Envoy, cruising at 150 mph. But at the coast one must, at present, change machines. A lumbering old Wessex tri-motor with its cruising speed of about 90 mph picks you up . . . but it is only a temporary arrangement. The faster Envoy can't land safely on Guernsey's present little aerodrome at L'Erée. But they are going literally to dynamite cottages and walls away to make the airport big enough for anything to get down on. You feel quite an intrepid pioneer landing at L'Erée, with its canvas hangar – also temporary. The fisherfolk turn out in force with a company of the townspeople to watch the still novel spectacle . . . The headquarters of Guernsey's small but enthusiastic flying club is L'Erée. It has only one Avian at present. On the windy day I was over there the sturdy little machine was securely shackled to the ground with ropes and huge metal pulleys to stop it turning over. . . Guernsey, still under the Conqueror's feudal law, imposes its own regulations on the club. No flying is allowed during chapel hours on the Sabbath . . . Moving spirit in the club is . . . Cecil Noel. Ex-service pilot of weather-beaten aspect. A Guernseyman. Tawny hair strewn above his sun-tanned face . . . He told me he had flown the little single-engined machine four times between Guernsey and the mainland . . . Noel has one great trial. He has to run the little Guernsey airport, where he tries desperately hard to plant grass seed on the extensive bare patches. The rain holds off. And every time a machine taxis or takes off it blasts the loose seeds and dust over its enthusiastic spectators." (23)

There was no afternoon plane on the 15th, but the following morning it ". . . ran to schedule despite inclement weather . . ." (23) and left at noon on the return with Deputy Bartlett and Miss Newton for Croydon and Mr Schneider for Bournemouth. Mr Bebb flew the afternoon service in addition to his two return trips in the Envoy, and brought Simpson-Smith in at 4.45. He left at 5 pm with one passenger for Bournemouth, one for Portsmouth, and Mr Beresford for Croydon. The weather caused another interruption on the 17th when Mr Davison, of the Truchot Motor Works, decided to make his first flight and left Bournemouth for Guernsey at 3.55 pm. Good progress was made for 45 minutes, "Then" said Mr Davison "we ran into a driving rainstorm. The pilot was flying blind. We could see nothing, and after flying for an hour and twenty minutes the pilot decided to turn back. It was impossible to see any landmarks. Eventually Swanage was sighted and the plane landed safely at Bournemouth about two and a half hours after taking off." (22) Later Mr Davison flew with the same pilot to Southampton and returned to Guernsey by boat, quite thrilled by his experience.

Rodney Beresford came on to the service on Sunday, May 19, and flew both Guernsey trips, but there was no morning service the following day because of the weather. Mr Ogden now alternated with Mr Beresford on the Guernsey leg but the afternoon plane on the 21st came in empty and left empty, as did the morning plane on the 22nd, and it was reported that the afternoon plane would be cancelled if there were no bookings. However, this plane arrived with the rare load of five passengers, but as these included Mr Mortimore, the business manager, Terry Bougourd, and a Mr and Mrs Lewis (perhaps V.A. Lewis of the *Star* and his wife) there can't have been much profit on the trip. Mr Ogden left at 5.15 with two passengers. However, traffic figures improved considerably on the 23rd: "There was a busy scene at L'Erée aerodrome this morning, when a large crowd of friends seeing off the Glee Singers increased the usual crowd of sightseers . . . Our representative was privileged to watch this morning the routine work of the Air Port. With planes arriving and departing twice daily, the office and ground staff are kept well occupied. As soon as a plane lands the ground engineers drag across the portable petrol tank to commence refuelling while two Customs officers are waiting to examine baggage. Mr C.A. Noel is in charge of the Aerodrome, and he has to examine the time-sheets and logs of the pilots. An office has been taken in a nearby house, "Les Sablons", and there a typist is kept busy with the secretarial work which is increasing as the number of passengers daily are steadily rising . . . there is usually a knot of people watching the air-liners glide gracefully down to the landing ground, and they are much interested in the pilots with their smart uniforms and golden-barred epaulettes, and their wireless ear-phones . . ." (23)

The Glee Singers were to join one of the largest choirs ever assembled under one roof (over seventeen hundred) to take part in a Royal Command Performance at the Albert Hall held for the benefit of "indigent musicians". Sir Walford Davies hoped that those who listened-in on the wireless would pay something towards the cause as the numbers of performers was so great that there was not much space for an audience! The Glee Singers flew to Bournemouth but continued on to London by rail.

The aerodrome at Bournemouth was situated on the main London road about one mile east of Christchurch. (see Appendix 2L). Formerly just an A.A. landing ground it was now owned by Bournemouth Airport, Ltd., with Sir Alan Cobham as chairman of the board of directors, and on May 31 a subscription list was opened for the issue of 28,300 preferred ordinary shares at £1 each. It was described in *Aero* of July, 1935: "Bournemouth Airport only started a year ago, but already they run thirty-two services a day, and they envisage a future in which they may rival Croydon itself. And I don't see why they shouldn't. The aerodrome is on the main road, is centrally situated for most European countries, and has excellent flat ground for miles around. At the present moment the arrangements are fairly primitive, consisting merely of a temporary building for offices; combined waiting room and café; a marquee as a hangar; and a post with a notice-board nailed to it to indicate the rigours of a Customs examination. But the plans for the future are little short of grandiose. Quite a big building is to be put up even in the first instance . . . Control tower, central hall with kiosks, bedrooms and rest-rooms for visitors, a café and well-arranged Customs facilities, all have their place in the new building. Outside are to be tennis-courts, tea gardens, a swimming pool, and there is even a rumour of speed-boat racing which will be flood-lit at night . . . Their idea is to bring out to Christchurch . . . a whole lot of people who have never yet given flying a serious thought. When these people see scores of air services arriving and leaving regularly, they are much more likely to want to try that form of transport for themselves . . ." A hangar was to be erected to house the Wessex on the Guernsey service as they were normally kept at Portsmouth and ferried across in the morning, although this was treated as an additional regular service to that of the Envoy from Croydon. In the summer of 1935 Christchurch was used by the P.S.I.O.W.A. machines coming from Ryde, via Shanklin, Western Airways machines from Cardiff, via Bristol, and the Provincial Airways machines on the Croydon-Plymouth route. To the alleged "thirty-two services" Cobham Air Routes contributed ten! to wit:- Two Envoy arrivals and departures (to and from Croydon), two Wessex arrivals and departures (to and from L'Erée), and one Wessex arrival and departure (to and from Portsmouth) . . .

One of the big events of the pre-war years was the Irish Sweep, and V.A. Lewis, the enthusiastic air correspondent of the *Guernsey Star*, decided to fly to Dublin to watch the draw take place. He planned to fly to Croydon by Cobham Air Routes, on to Belfast by Railway Air Services, and thence to Dublin by chartered Fox Moth. Rather rashly he told his readers he would leave Guernsey at noon on Friday, May 31, and be in Dublin by 7.30 pm the same day, but fog intervened, and the morning plane for Guernsey could not take-off. The afternoon plane managed to leave at about 4.30 but then the fog descended on L'Erée and it had to return to Christchurch without landing. Poor Mr Lewis was marooned in Guernsey until 12.25 pm the following day when the Wessex departed with a full load: ". . . We passed over the mailboat short of Alderney, and very soon afterwards we struck fog – lots of it, a thick bank the end of which we could not see. Up we went above it, and in a few minutes we were again in the sunshine with a white bank of fog obliterating everything below. Approaching the English coast the engines were throttled down and we came through the fog . . . we made Bournemouth aerodrome without the slightest difficulty . . . Once in the Envoy we flew above fog, clouds and everything else – and were there in a very few minutes . . . at Croydon ten minutes behind schedule – which means we caught up 15 minutes on the late start . . ." (24) He left Croydon at 3.10 in the R.A.S. D.H. 86 and found more fog as they approached Ireland, but his further adventures do not concern Cobham Air Routes, except his return at 11.45 on June 5 with Mr Ogden.

An ominous event for Cobham Air Routes had been the arrival in Jersey on May 22 of Saro Windhover, G-ABJP, now the property of Guernsey

142

Airways, and its flight to Guernsey and Alderney the same day. As an amphibian the Windhover could land on a beach, a normal aerodrome, or on the sea, and if it were to fly between Guernsey and Jersey on a regular basis passengers could continue to the mainland by Jersey Airways. This would be an alternative to the Bournemouth route. The Windhover (See Appendix 1C) followed normal Saro practice in having a single wooden wing mounted directly on an "Alclad" hull, and it had three 120 hp Gipsy II engines, with a small auxiliary aerofoil spanning all three.

Guernsey Airways' Saro "Windhover" being refulled on the beach at St. Helier
(By kind permission of the Jersey Evening Post)

On 25.9.31 it had opened a twice-daily service between Gibraltar and Tangier which lasted about four months, and then 'JP lay in the open at Gib. until the summer of 1932 when it was hired by the Hon. Mrs Bruce for an attempt on the world endurance record. Despite a crash at Alicante, 'JP took-off on its record-breaking attempt at 14.00 hours on August 1, 1932. The world record was 23 days . . . and Mrs Bruce hoped to stay in the air for a month, being refuelled from a Bristol Fighter via a 1" hose-pipe. The machine came down after two hours. The second attempt lasted 15 hours, and the third and final attempt, 54 hours 13 minutes, which was a long way short of the intended duration but would have rated as a British record had they carried a sealed barometer. To save weight Mrs Bruce left it behind so the record was unofficial. Little more was heard of 'JP until it arrived in the Channel Islands, where it was well received, the *Guernsey Evening Press* giving ample space to: "AIR SERVICES – JERSEY AIRWAYS INTRODUCE FAST AMPHIBIAN – PLANE BUILT FOR ENDURANCE RECORD."

D/F apparatus had now been installed at the Jersey airport site, and two new pilots, K.T. Murray and O.C.A. Hankey, joined Jersey Airways in May from Air Service Training. On May 24 a night landing was made on the racecourse by the aid of car head-lights and "every available lighting facility" when Douglas Brecknell arrived at 9.30 pm with Harley Street specialist Mr T. Izod Bennett. On May 25 Sir Herbert Walker opened new offices at Victoria Station for Channel Island Airways and Mr J.B. Elliott (later Sir John), then assistant traffic manager of the S.R., said they were determined not to be out of the air business . . . "We shall experiment . . . will spend money, and are prepared to lose money for a time in order to give the country a chance of supporting an internal air service. The present policy of the railways is not to run a route in competition with fast frequent main line services but to link by air towns which were difficult of access by rail." (23) On June 1 the twice-daily summer service started, and the Heston-Jersey time was reduced to 90 minutes, indicating direct flights with the heavier summer loads. Posters appeared in Guernsey advertising a forthcoming Guernsey Airways amphibian service with fares to Jersey of 12/- single, 18/- return, and flying times to Jersey, Southampton, and London of 15, 90, and 120 minutes respectively. Both Guernsey Airways' and Cobham Air Routes' time-tables were published in Bradshaw's International Air Guide for June (and subsequent months), as shown Fig. 3, and it will be seen that Cobham's were now allowing themselves 75 minutes for the Guernsey – Christchurch leg and 2 hrs 15 min. for Guernsey to Croydon, with the afternoon departures at 2.45 pm from Croydon and 5.30 pm from Guernsey, whilst Guernsey Airways increased their inter-island flying time to 20 minutes and later to 30 minutes. On May 30 the Wessex G-ADFZ made its first trip to Guernsey, flown by Rodney Beresford, and the service settled down to a set pattern of Ogden in 'EW flying one return trip per day and Beresford in 'FZ flying the other, whilst Cecil Bebb made two daily trips between

Croydon and Bournemouth with great regularity in the Envoy, 'BA. On the Friday before Whit Sunday Mr Ogden managed to fit in an extra Wessex service from the mainland and the *Star* of June 8 proudly reported that there had been 30 passengers between Guernsey and England in the previous 24 hours.

Fig 3a

---

9 A   JERSEY – GUERNSEY
                           GUERNSEY AIRWAYS

JERSEY – GUERNSEY
Services by flying boat leave 15 minutes after arrival of London and Southampton services, see tables 10 and 11.
Flying time 20 minutes.

GUERNSEY – JERSEY
Services by flying boat leave Guernsey 35 minutes prior to departure of London and Southampton services from Jersey, see tables 10 and 11.

Fares on application to Company

June 1935

---

9 A   JERSEY – GUERNSEY
                           GUERNSEY AIRWAYS

Services by Amphibian operate between Jersey (St. Aubin's Bay Sands) and Guernsey (St. Peter Port Harbour).

Duration of flight 30 minutes:- Time of Services on application to the Company.

FARES:- Single 12/-; Return 18/-
Baggage allowance 25lbs; Excess Baggage ¼d. per lb.

For conecting services between London and Jersey and between Southampton and Jersey, see Tables 10 and 11.

July, August, September 1935

Fig 3b

19 LONDON – PORTSMOUTH – BOURNEMOUTH – GUERNSEY
(Daily)
COBHAM AIR ROUTES

Miles	Airports of					Airports of				
0	LONDON	dep	–	09 00	14 45	GUERNSEY	dep	12 00	17 30	–
58	PORTSMOUTH	arr	–	09 25	15 10	BOURNEMOUTH	arr	13 15	18 45	–
83	PORTSMOUTH	dep	09 00	09 35	15 20	BOURNEMOUTH	dep	13 25	18 55	19 10
83	BOURNEMOUTH	arr	09 20	09 50	15 35	PORTSMOUTH ...	arr	13 40	19 10	19 30
	BOURNEMOUTH	dep	–	10 00	15 45	PORTSMOUTH ...	dep	13 50	19 20	–
183	GUERNSEY	arr	–	11 15	17 00	LONDON	arr	14 15	19 45	–

Distance and Time allowance for conveyance between Airport and Town Terminus

TOWN	AIRPORT	TOWN TERMINUS	Miles	Minutes
LONDON	Croydon	Coach Station, 172, Buckingham Palace Road...	13	60
PORTSMOUTH	Portsmouth	A. Hume Shaw Ltd, 87E, Commercial Road	5	15
BOURNEMOUTH	Christchurch	To Centre of Town	6	20
ST. PETER PORT	L'Eree	Bougourd Bros., Town Quay Esplanade, St Peter Port	6	15

FARES

	PORTSMOUTH			BOURNEMOUTH			GUERNSEY		
	Single	Return	Ex. Bag.	Single	Return	Ex. Bag.	Single	Return	Ex. Bag.
	s. d.	s. d.	s. d.	s. d.	s. d.	s. d.	s. d.	s. d.	s. d.
LONDON	20 0	38 0	0 2	30 0	57 0	0 3	65 0	118 0	0 5
PORTSMOUTH	–	–	–	11 0	20 0	0 2	46 0	87 0	0 4
BOURNEMOUTH	–	–	–	–	–	–	35 0	67 0	0 4

Ex. Bag – Excess Baggage per lb.
Children under 3 years accompanied by an Adult 25% between 3 and 7 years 50% of above fares.
(No free baggage allowance).   Free baggage allowance 25 lbs.

June 1935

Whit Sunday (June 9) was chosen for the inauguration of the amphibian service (daily, except Wednesdays), and: ". . . For the first time in insular history two air services were in operation from Guernsey . . . the plane moors in the harbour (see Appendix 2B) and the passengers are landed and

146

embarked by the S.R./G.W.R. tender . . ." (22) Piloted by Eckersley-Maslin the amphibian had an auspicious start:-

Jersey Dep. scheduled	Guernsey Arr. actual	Passengers	Guernsey Dep. scheduled	actual	Passengers	Jersey Arr. scheduled
8.25 am	8.40 am	2	9.15 am	9.25 am	5	9.35 am
10.25 am	10.35 am	5	3 pm	3.15 pm	5	3.20 pm
4.10 pm	4.25 pm	5	5 pm	5.10 pm	5	5.20 pm

But over on the other side of the island Mr Ogden arrived empty at noon and left with four at 12.30 pm, while Mr Beresford arrived at 5 pm with two passengers and left at 5.30 pm with another two. This typified the two operations. The Wessex crossed twice daily with an average of about three passengers, at somewhat variable times, interrupted on occasion by the weather (although boosted on the 14th when they brought the Dagenham Girl Pipers to play nightly at eight in the Candie Gardens), and the Windhover ran three services a day with good loads, but they too had their interruptions. On Sunday, 16th, V.A. Lewis of the *Star* went down to the White Rock in plenty of time to catch the plane: ". . . and after wandering about that bleak and uncomfortable area for a long time I happened across a scribbled note on a board. Unfortunately it was undecipherable . . ." However, outside the railway's booking office on the New Jetty another notice said: "All seaplane services to Jersey suspended until Tuesday, June 18th." No reason was given. On the 21st there was fog. "Residents on the east and south coasts . . . were surprised to see the machine flying very low as Pilot Eckersley-Maslin tried to find a gap in the fog. People all over the Island gazed skywards when they heard the drone of the aircraft's powerful engines, and caught occasional glimpses of its hull. The machine came down within a few feet of the surface off Moulin Huet and flew around the Pea Stacks when it disappeared. It passed over the roof-tops at Jerbourg and again vanished." (23) Taking off on the last trip of the day at about 7.10 pm on June 28 as Eckersley-Maslin brought 'JP up to flying speed and a height of about ten feet, she dropped back, but instead of just touching the crest of one or two waves in the usual way, the nose dug in to an extra large one with such force that the impact damaged the bow and strained the hull. One lady passenger was slightly injured when her nose made contact with the back of the seat in front.

After an examination at St Helier the Windhover was withdrawn from service and sent to Southampton for repair. It was sufficiently airworthy to make the trip under its own steam but perhaps Mr Greig, with all the authority of his recently-acquired pilot's "A" licence, was not sufficiently sympathetic concerning the Flight-Lieutenant's little mishap because Eckersley-Maslin resigned from the company at the end of June. The inter-island service was now at a standstill, but between June 9 and 28 the amphibian operated on thirteen days and carried 288 passengers.

Towards the end of June an attempt was made to run a Plymouth-Jersey service by a Mr C.W.R. Cann (formerly a Plymouth Fascist leader, said *The Aeroplane*") who was managing director of Whoopee Sports Ltd. (manufacturers of floats for seaside bathing resorts), for which Dragon 'NJ was chartered from Jersey Airways. Apart from reducing the journey time to one hour from fifteen hours it was hoped that the G.P.O. would be interested, and for demonstration purposes a number of envelopes were posted at 5 am on Friday, June 28 in the Plymouth area addressed to the airport at Roborough. These were delivered in time to leave on *Rozel Bay* with "Bill" Caldwell and five passengers after a civic send-off by a large party of local dignitaries, including Mrs Pillar, the Lady Mayoress. The Dragon " . . . a handsome lithe aluminium grey biplane with two motors purring . . ." wrote the man from the Western Independent and: ". . . after rising from Roborough and watching Plymouth slip away from under us we make out the Yealm, Bigbury, and Mothecombe before proceeding still seawise, aslant of Start Point, and creeping out over what looks like a remarkably empty Channel of gently rippling water . . ." they landed at St Helier at 1.15 pm and the envelopes were re-addressed, re-stamped and posted in time for the 4.15 pm collection. In due course the letters reached their Jersey destinations, but the Post Office was not impressed, apparently, as no further flights took place, although a bi-weekly (Mondays and Fridays) service had been intended. On July 13 the *Western Morning News* reported that a Customs office had been established at Roborough, but: ". . . these provisions have been rendered inopportune at present by the suspension of the air service . . ." Probably they did not realise, until their arrival at St Helier, that the Jersey aerodrome was just a tidal beach and fixed times were not possible. It appears that there was one positioning flight from Jersey to Plymouth, and the one ceremonial inaugural flight from Plymouth to Jersey with five passengers.

Jersey Airways' D.H. "Rapide", G-ADBV, "St. Ouen's Bay II " in front of the sea wall at St. Helier
(By kind permission of the Jersey Evening Post)

The accident to the Windhover was a serious blow to Guernsey Airways because Alderney aerodrome was progressing well and they had intended to link Jersey, Guernsey, and Alderney by amphibian as soon as the aerodrome was licensed, and connect Alderney with Southampton by D.H. Rapide. The D.H. 89, or Dragon-Rapide (Appendix 1D) as it was first called, was a Dragon with all the improvements of the 86, such as 200 hp Gipsy-Six engines and highly-tapered wings, and Jersey Airways bought two, G-ADBV *St Ouen's Bay II* and G-ADBW (not named). In addition, the company had received their last two 86's, G-ACZP *Belcroute Bay* and G-ACGR *La Saline Bay*, and of the Dragons only 'NJ remained.

It would be reasonable to assume that the news of the Windhover's misfortune was received with equanimity by Cobham Air Routes, whose L'Erée aerodrome had been inspected on June 25 by Sir Alan Cobham, G.P. Olley, and J.W.S. Comber (an Olley director). Schedules were amended slightly on June 26 by advancing the noon departure from L'Erée to 11.45 am and all subsequent arrivals and departures along the route by the same amount, so that the second Croydon departure was 2.30 pm again, and the second Guernsey departure 5.15 pm. By the end of June traffic was improving slightly and Mr Bebb flew an extra service to Guernsey in 'FZ on June 29. On July 3, Captain Ogden left L'Erée at about 5.30 pm with one passenger, Mr C.F. Grainger of 66, Heathhurst Road, Sanderstead, Surrey, one of the principals of Grainger and Hutley's, produce merchants of Spitalfields. He was a frequent visitor to the Channel Islands and had stopped in Jersey for a couple of days and then crossed to Guernsey for a brief business transaction, but was too late for the Weymouth boat and caught the plane instead. From Portsmouth he was joining his wife and children at their summer cottage at Seaview, I.O.W. At 6.20 pm 'EW sent out a radio message reporting trouble with the starboard engine. Ten minutes later there was a second message saying that the plane was losing height. At 6.40 pm there was a third and final message but the transmission was completely incomprehensible which indicated, probably, that the trailing aerial was dragging through the water. 'EW's last position was estimated at three to four miles from the Needles, on course for Christchurch. Visibility was about 40 miles and the sea was calm.

Two aircraft left Portsmouth for the area, and an R.A.F. flying-boat left Calshot. The Yarmouth (I.O.W.) and Swanage lifeboats joined the sea search together with a steamer and several small craft, and Mr Bebb took off from Christchurch at 7.20 pm and did not return until nine.

THE EVENING POST THURSDAY JULY 4 1935

GUERNSEY PLANE MYSTERY

SINKS WITHOUT TRACE IN SIGHT OF LAND

PASSENGER WELL KNOWN IN JERSEY PICKED UP BUT NO TRACE OF PILOT

DESTROYER, PLANES AND LIFEBOATS JOIN IN SEARCH

THE MISSING PLANE

The 'R' class destroyer *Rowena* put to sea from Portland and carried on after dark with the aid of her searchlights. Nothing was found – no trace of pilot, passenger, plane, or wreckage, and although there had been plenty of shipping about at the time, no eye-witness came forward. It was a complete mystery because the Wessex was considered capable of flying on any two of its three engines with a load much greater than one passenger, and, with a reasonable landing, should have floated on the surface for a time, especially in perfect weather conditions. W.H. Ogden was a most competent pilot, with about 3,000 hours to his credit, and was very strong physically. He was ex. R.A.F., 35 years of age, married, and lived at Bognor Regis. He had flown for Sir Alan in Africa.

At nine o'clock the following morning, when all hope had been abandoned, a small steamer, the *Stanmore* of London, signalled a message to Prawle Point (Devon). They had Mr Grainger on board, but the pilot was a casualty. Like Hawker and Mackenzie Grieve in 1919, Fred Grainger had been picked up by a ship without wireless; she was bound from Shoreham to Fowey, but it was evening before she arrived and low tide. She stopped opposite the offices of brokers Hannan, Samuel & Co. and sent Mr Grainger ashore in a small boat. Watched by a crowd of spectators he entered the broker's offices by the back door and remained inside, inaccessible to the gathered journalists. To a written message offering to fly him back to London he replied "No concern on God's earth would get me into another plane to-night". Captain Herbert, of Llanon, Cardiganshire, told journalists that: ". . . on reaching a point about ten miles off Anvil Point, 22 miles from the Needles, at about five past eight we noticed something floundering in the water. You couldn't call it swimming for the object seemed to be in the last stages of exhaustion. In ten minutes we got Mr Grainger aboard and saw that he was nearly finished. We set to work on him by turns, and after applying artificial respiration for 2½ hours Mr Grainger was sufficiently recovered for us to rig him out in a change of clothes and put him to bed." (22) According to Mr Grainger they had left Guernsey at 5.40 pm but not without difficulty in starting the starboard engine. After some time in the air this engine began to give trouble, eventually stopping altogether: ". . . the pilot warned me that he might be compelled to land on the sea, and he and I both put on lifebelts. The two remaining engines were apparently unable to bring the plane to land and the pilot had to make a forced landing about ten miles from the coast . . ." (22) When the plane hit the water Mr Grainger was flung into the gangway of the cabin: ". . . the next moment I had scrambled up, opened the emergency exit in the roof and was in the water . . ." (6) The plane sank in about 15 minutes and there was little hope for Captain Ogden who was stuck right down in the cockpit. Mr Grainger travelled up to London on the night sleeper and was met at Paddington by his parents. Hatless, face swollen, one eye discoloured, and without an overcoat, but carrying a brown-paper parcel under his arm, he went off in a saloon car to his parent's home in Tulse Hill. He said later: "After a time I found the water very cold and my limbs became numb, but the lifebelt held my head up. I prayed to lose consciousness and then the thought of my wife and children strengthened me. I doubt whether I could have lasted another ten minutes." From London Mr Grainger then set off for the Isle of Wight, crossing to Cowes in a motor-launch, and meeting his wife on the pontoon, where she had been waiting about an hour for his arrival: "Oh! you naughty thing" exclaimed his wife, as he stepped ashore. (22)

Although the service struggled on with Mr Beresford in 'FZ there were now serious doubts about these six-year old machines, but as L'Erée was only licensed for the Wessex there could be no service without them. On Sunday, July 7, Rodney Beresford left L'Erée at 11.45 am with three passengers, and that was the last schedule flight of Cobham Air Routes Ltd. from Guernsey. Before it could be restarted L'Erée would have to be improved and extended to permit the use of modern aircraft, but Sir Alan had had enough: ". . . I found it hard to get good engineers, and very hard indeed to find enough passengers to enable this operation to pay its way." (21) 'FZ went to the air display and survived a collision with an Avro 504N over Blackpool the following September. The Envoy, G-ADBA, and the Cobham interests in L'Erée and the Guernsey Aero Club were taken over by Olley, and Cecil Bebb joined Olley at the same time to become a well-known charter pilot. His best known exploit was the flying of General Franco from Las Palmas to Tetuán to start the Spanish Civil War for which he received the Spanish Order of Merit and the Order of the White Cross. After spending most of World War Two as a test pilot Captain Bebb returned to Olley Air Service and was chief pilot from 1946. The Air Ministry accident report concluded that the starboard engine of 'EW failed completely after about 25 minutes flying, possibly due to a broken induction fan. This was followed in the next half hour by a loss of power on one, or both of the other engines due to over-heating. Failure to make a successful forced landing may have been due to the passenger's last moment action in moving from the front to the rear of the cabin, and: ". . . the pilot took an unnecessary, but not wholly unjustifiable risk, in attempting to complete the sea passage on only two engines. His safest course of action would have been to turn down wind and head for the French coast . . ." (25)

On the main Jersey Airways' lines to Heston and Eastleigh the numbers carried continued to break records, and the whole fleet of 86's was in operation, but not entirely to the satisfaction of the other users of the beach, nor the J.E.P.: ". . . the first of the Jersey Airways' machines (on the afternoon of July 9) . . . passed so close over the heads of people near the Bathing Pool as to frighten them. The machine was gliding down and so was unheard by some of the people until apparently on top of them. Two ladies are said to have been so frightened that they were seized with a fit of hysteria and had to return home . . ." The previous day six people had appeared before the Constable of St Helier for alleged disobedience of

153

police orders in crossing the sands after being told not to. At the end of the month two machines arrived early, before the Morris car used by the police, so that the three constables on duty were unable to clear the area properly on foot. There were a number of people on the beach when the plane landed, only avoided by "what seemed to be a miracle". Later, Jersey Airways said they would fire a Verey light in future to stop planes landing before the beach was clear. However, the original misgivings of *The Aeroplane* had long since evaporated due, no doubt, to the air-line's obvious success, and Jersey Airways were often mentioned, thus:- "Passengers from Jersey sometimes ask what is the white line on the surface of the sea between the Casquets and Sark. This is the mark of an overfall due to the meeting of the two tidal currents, and it is so reliable that in thick weather a pilot, who may have inadvertently passed East of the island of Alderney instead of over it, is practically certain to catch sight of the overfall and to know that he should then change course for Jersey . . . Punctilious visitors to Heston should not air their knowledge if they notice a Jersey machine leaving a few minutes behind schedule . . . The reason for leaving late is, generally, that the weather report indicates a tail wind and . . . pilots dislike arriving early . . ." (They could be fired at with a Verey pistol!) ". . . Passengers from Jersey to London begin to learn that passing Portsmouth is a signal for putting on hats and gloves . . . If a machine has come over the sea at 6,000 feet it may travel very quickly after Portsmouth because it will be descending at, say 300 feet per minute, for the last 17 minutes and may be averaging 155 mph air speed." From July 22, thanks to the railway connection, there was inter-availability of air tickets with rail and boat tickets, as well as the facility for sending heavy luggage in advance by rail and boat. A boat passenger with a 19-day first-class return from Southampton to Jersey costing 47/- could return by air for an extra 19/-.

As a temporary measure Guernsey Airways arranged to borrow the Saro Cloud, G-ABCJ (See Appendix 1C), and restarted the inter-island service on August 5, Bank Holiday Monday. 'CJ was the prototype Saro Cloud now re-engined with two 340 hp Napier Rapier IV's, and fitted with a small auxiliary aerofoil behind and below the engine nacelles. Seven passengers could be carried with a crew of two, and the pilot, Mr Brent, had just completed five years service in the R.A.F. As before there were three services per day, tide permitting, except on Wednesdays (the day set aside for overhaul), and there was another auspicious start:-

Guernsey Arrive	No. of passengers	Guernsey Dep.	No. of passengers
2pm	4	2.30 pm	7
4 pm	3	5.30 pm	6
7 pm	3	7.30 pm	5

The above times were maintained until the tide forced a change on the 8th but on Saturday the 10th the service had to be cancelled because of carburetter trouble, and there was no service until the 15th when the amphibian left Jersey at noon for Guernsey. In the afternoon it left Jersey again at 2 pm but continued on from Guernsey to Alderney to make the first landing on the new aerodrome. The passengers included Mr Greig and an Air Ministry inspector to examine and report on the new aerodrome. One of the other passengers was the *Guernsey Star* correspondent: "After a flight of only seven minutes, the retractable undercart was lowered and a perfect landing made on the new aerodrome . . . The plane had come practically to a standstill before half of the aerodrome surface had been traversed . . . A small group of onlookers, the younger ones quite wildly excited, gathered round the plane, but the numbers soon swelled until 'half Alderney' seemed to be there . . ." The aerodrome looked rather like the Sahara Desert, he said, and on the return: ". . . after taxiing out to the far end of the 'drome we had to wait a few minutes for the dust to die down." The surface was level, except for a hard patch in the centre caused by solid rock, and it was covered in about a foot of dust but grass seed and rain would soon change that, he thought. On the following day (16th) 'CJ flew three trips to Guernsey and back and carried 33 passengers, but the next day the service had to be cancelled again, and then postponed indefinitely. A crack had been found in one of the propellers. Guernsey Airways expressed their regrets: ". . . to the many intending passengers . . . the irregularity of the service has arisen through a series of minor mechanical difficulties with the machine, which was hired at considerable expense . . . the hired machine proved totally unsuitable for commercial purposes and it was impossible to obtain certain essential spares sufficiently rapidly . . . to suspend the service completely until the return of the Company's own machine . . . The delay in the repairs to the Windhover has arisen from the recent great expansion in military aircraft requirements." (22)

155

The prototype Saro "Cloud", G-ABCJ, re-engined with Napier "Rapiers", probably in St Peters Port. August 1935 (Carel Toms Collection)

Jersey Airways, also, had their problems on Saturday, August 17. At Heston a tyre burst as Mr Israel was taking off at 10.45 am in 'ZP. He kept going but then the other tyre burst and the machine swerved round but he managed to keep it on an even keel and none of the thirteen passengers was injured. After a slight delay Commercial Air Hire's "Big Avro" took over the service. This was G-ACFV, the twin-engined version of the two Avro 642's built, and originally the pride of Midland & Scottish Air Ferries. It had two Armstrong Siddeley Jaguar VID engines and could carry 16 passengers at 150 mph. It must have attracted a good deal of attention when it landed at West Park; and Mr Orchard attracted even more when he brought 'ZO in at about 5 pm and his port wheel-brake seized throwing a sudden strain on the starboard undercarriage leg which collapsed. The starboard wing was damaged and the tip of the starboard propeller broke off, narrowly missing the occupants of the nearby official car. *Ouaine Bay* was completely immobile with a 38 ft spring tide due at 9.38 pm. Motor lorries and mechanics were mustered in great haste and, with one lorry lashed to the starboard side, the starboard undercarriage was removed. A second lorry was lashed to the port undercarriage leg and very slowly, with the incoming tide only yards away, the whole assembly was moved along the beach towards the First Tower. At the slipway the damaged wing had to be supported on a cart-axle whilst the 86 was towed up tail first, and a great crowd lined the promenade to watch a ". . . thrilling race with the tide . . ." (26) Towards the end of the month 'ZO was shipped to England aboard the S.R. cargo steamer *Haslemere*. With two 86's out of action the "Big Avro" continued to fly for Jersey Airways, but she had to be taken off the service on the last day of August and hauled up the First Tower slip to the disappointment of her 16 passengers. The problem, said the *Morning News* was ". . . lost combustion . . ." in the port engine(!) and two new pistons were to be fitted.

The Avro 642, G-ACFV
(Quadrant Picture Library)

During August, 825 passengers flew from Heston to Jersey, and 927 from Jersey to Heston, in 187 Channel crossings by 86 and Rapide (and Avro 642), and 1,862 passengers flew from Southampton, and 2,002 to Southampton, in 289 crossings by 86, 51 by Rapide, and 33 by Dragon, an average of ten passengers per machine. The inter-island service ran for one week when 77 passengers travelled to Guernsey and 86 from. The total number of passengers for the first eight months of 1935 was 17,672, an increase of 25% on the same period of the previous year.

"Travelling by Jersey Airways from Southampton, the machine flies over the docks, with a panoramic view of the whole area of Southampton Water and of the Hamble Estuary, over the Solent with its yachts, over the Isle of Wight and, by virtue of the regulations, over Alderney, with the French coast ten miles to the left. Returning by the direct route to Heston, passengers can see the whole of the Isle of Wight with its multitudinous resorts, the forts of the Solent, Portsmouth, Hayling Island, the South Downs, Brooklands, and, if they are lucky, most of London spread out to the right. While flying last week with Mr Blythe . . . we saw the *Bremen* in the docks and, while we were returning, making its way to Cherbourg, as well as an aircraft-carrier, complete with destroyer, steaming out of Portsmouth . . . the pilots know all there is to be known about beach landing in all conditions . . . Mr Blythe came in to both St Helier and Heston without even 'rumbling' in accepted transport manner, adjusting his approach at Heston with the hydraulically operated flaps. He glides the Express at about 80 mph, crossing the boundary at 75 mph, so that the machine sits down almost as soon as it is held off, with little or no tendency to float . . . The Kollsman sensitive altimeter allows the machine to be brought gently down either to the beach or into Heston in conditions of very bad visibility once the barometric pressure has been verified . . ." (20) Mr Blythe left Jersey Airways in September to join Cook Strait Airways in New Zealand. Normally he shared the Heston run with Israel, and they were the only pilots in the company (at this time) with second-class navigator's tickets. Mr Orchard, who flew on the Southampton run, followed Mr Blythe to Cook Strait Airways very soon afterwards. In September severe gales disrupted services and both of Heston's radio masts were blown down so that Croydon had to take over traffic control. By this time the broadcasting of the regular met. reports had been transferred to Borough Hill, Daventry. On the worst day of the gales (September 17) only one plane landed at Heston and that was a Spartan Air Lines machine from Cowes. As usual, everyone made record flights; one 86 did the 184 miles from Jersey to Heston in 60 minutes, which adds up to a 140 mph cruising speed plus a 45 mph tail wind, and the Spartan Cruiser managed to fly from Cowes to Heston in 24 minutes.

October saw the return of the Windhover, and on October 12 the licence for Alderney was granted, so it seemed that all was ready for the start of the new services. In addition to the inter-islands amphibian service, and the Alderney-Southampton Rapide service, the 86's of the mainland services were going to land at Alderney on request. In order to run to a regular time-table it was decided that the amphibian would use the harbour at St Helier whenever the tide prevented the use of the beach, and on October 5 the Windhover was brought over from Southampton to try out the mooring arrangements and rehearse the appropriate drill. It flew back to Southampton afterwards, but returned on the 14th and reopened the Jersey-Guernsey section at the winter frequency of one return trip per day (except Wednesdays), but the link with Alderney was held up because of a problem concerning Customs facilities. Frank Brent left Jersey at 10.45 on the 14th to inaugurate this latest attempt at an amphibian service, but there were no passengers and he arrived at St Peter's Port at 11.15. Return was scheduled for 1.45, and this routine was maintained, as far as possible, with the exception that the departure was advanced to 1 pm when there were passengers transferring at Jersey to the mainland service. The routine was upset at the end of the month by gale force winds such that one plane made the Jersey-Southampton trip in 35 minutes. The amphibian service was cancelled on November 1 because the water was too rough off St Peter Port, and the following day it set out from Jersey but had to return because of the huge swell outside the Guernsey harbour. It was November 5 before a landing could be made there, and continued bad weather prevented another landing until November 9. The service was cancelled again on the 10th and this erratic mode of operation continued. On Saturday night (16th) gusts up to 75 mph at L'Erée tore the Aero Club's hangar to pieces, and badly damaged the Avian. On Monday, 18th one passenger was taken to Guernsey and three brought back, but on the 19th the service was postponed indefinitely and once again the Windhover was returned to Southampton for extensive repairs. According to the air correspondent of the *Guernsey Star*: "Flying to London was a very ordinary affair except for the cramped journey from Guernsey to Jersey. I don't wonder that amphibians are unpopular if that is the best they can do. The Windhover is a veritable hen-coop with wings. You can't move a limb and you sit in an atmosphere of petrol fumes with the mechanic continually climbing over your knees . . . Taking off the sea, you spend most of your time ineffectively trying to keep dry. Water literally pours in from the supposedly closed windows."

Frank Brent did not stay with Guernsey Airways, but has left a very interesting account of the inter-island service from the pilot's point of view. He used the pseudonym "Windline" and did not name the firm or the places, but they are all too obvious:- ". . . The service is operated from a tidal beach at the home port (St Helier) and a small harbour (St Peter Port) at the other island. No suitable mooring site being available, the aircraft is kept inland at a landing-ground, actually the oval enclosed by the local racecourse (Quennevais). A lonely grandstand and a small hangar are the only buildings and, because of its size, the amphibian has to be picketed out . . . On arrival in the morning one is greeted by the ground engineer . . . The three engines previously warmed, are started and run up, the 'Daily Certificate of Safety' signed, and the Flight Engineer climbs aboard, pulling up the ladder (literally) after him. On one occasion this ladder was inadvertently left outside hooked on the footrail during a rather bumpy flight and on landing was found hanging on the undercarriage . . . Perforce choosing the longer runway (the other is useless except in a near gale) after a last look round and a burst on each engine 'just to make sure' the throttles are pushed forward. The wind is across our run . . . and the sensation of drift over the rough surface most unpleasant, but being lightly loaded the machine is quickly airborne. The tide down in the bay is out far enough to permit a landing on the sands, after which we taxi up to the company's mobile traffic office – two motor coaches driven down on the beach when required . . . Now comes the collection of the mass of forms without which no departure for 'Foreign' can be made – passenger lists, manifests, notices of departure, load sheets, journey log – all to be checked and signed, and except the load sheet, presented to the Customs for clearance. The passengers, baggage, and cargo being aboard and satisfactorily disposed as regards load distribution, we take off on our journey. As soon as the island is cleared the under-carriage is raised, an operation always of interest to passengers, who can see the 'works' out of the cabin windows . . . Visibility good, wind only about 15 knots, and sea slight. There seems to be rather a heavy swell running with the wind, however, promising to be troublesome for the alighting at our destination which, because of the smallness of the harbour, must be effected outside in the open sea. On arrival it is indeed found that there is no option but to alight crosswind along one of the swell crests, very gingerly, with a thought for the wing floats . . . The harbour is entered through a narrow gap in a massive sea wall, a flagstaff-surmounted castle on one hand and a watch tower on the other. Entry must not be made if the 'harbour closed to vessels entering' signal is made from the tower, for, apart from the penalty of a fine, it would be most embarrassing to meet an oncoming ship – a flying boat under way being neither able to go astern under its own power nor to stop unless the engines are switched off, in which case very little control is retained . . . Approach to the mooring buoy is made with the centre engine stopped and the undercarriage lowered to act as a 'water-brake', this

160

taking the place of the drogues used on flying boats. In a strong enough wind it is possible to lose all way thus; and even to drift astern, but to-day this cannot be done, so the Engineer, who stands in the forward hatch with a 'Grabit' boathook and line, must be sure he picks up the spreader of the buoy at the first attempt. Engines have been switched off, the mooring gear is shackled up, and the waiting motor boat tender comes alongside. Passengers and cargo are transhipped, and, after a glance at the bilges, we go ashore there to be greeted by the company's representatives. The first call is at the Customs, where passenger lists, journey log etc. together with a completed 'Air Navigation Report' are presented to secure 'clearance inwards'. There is now just time, before we are due out again, to call on the Harbour Master to ask him if he can get the owners of certain crabpots laid rather close to our moorings to move them so as to give us more swinging room, and to enjoy a coffee and a cigarette at a nearby cafe in a narrow cobbled street running up the hillside from the quay . . . Back to the traffic office, the inevitable sheaf of 'ship's papers' is collected, 'clearance outward' obtained at the Customs, and the waiting passengers shepherded into the tender lying alongside the steps in the quay wall. After putting us aboard, the tender takes a slipline through an eye aft below our rudder so that we can be towed astern clear of the buoy. With the moorings ready to slip, engines are started, and the tender tows us astern as the Engineer casts off forward. After the line on our stern is slipped by the tender, at a given signal, we turn and taxi out of the harbour, warming up the engines on the way . . . The wind has veered a bit and risen considerably, knocking up a nasty short sea, so that taxiing crosswind is a dirty business, the frequent 'flap-flap-flap' of the water thrown up through the airscrews making one feel thankful for their Schwartz protection. The swell is still running, but the wind and sea compel a take-off more or less into the wind, so after a clearing burst on each engine in turn, and a pause to await one of the smooth spots which are usually to be found at intervals in any sea, the throttles are opened. In a smother of spray, with stick hard back, we gather speed, crossing the swell crests at a fairly acute angle. Presently the stick can be eased forward for a few seconds, and then back to lift the aircraft into the air as it rises to the scend of the sea, but having only just got flying speed, we touch the surface again once or twice before finally climbing away on the course home . . . The tide is so far in on our return that a sea alighting has to be made, and as there is a heavy surf breaking some care is needed in taxying ashore to avoid being swung into wind broadside to the beach or else lifted on a roller and dropped with a bang after it has broken. After unloading and 'clearing inwards' at the Customs we wallow back into the sea, taking each of the first few breakers well over the bows, and take off for the landing ground. Here, with a side-slip to cheat the usual cross wind and a rumble to dodge the rabbit-holes, one more 'happy landing' is made. The aircraft is taxied to its pickets, having assured the waiting G.E. . . . who is ready with a freshwater hose for the benefit of 'Old Man Corrosion', that apparently no bits have fallen off since the morning, the Journey Log times are totalled and the book closed for the day." (43)

The uncertainty of these flying-boat services, especially in winter, showed that an aerodrome on Guernsey was essential. In Jersey there had been no argument about the site, only whether the expense was justifiable; in Alderney there had been no argument at all; in Guernsey there had been much discussion and three possible sites, one in use, and another under active consideration. In October, G.P. Olley had flown into L'Erée, with Sir Hugo and Lady Cunliffe-Owen and, as the successors to Cobham Air Routes, a third powerful group had joined the Railways and Whitehall Securities in the Channel Islands arena. Sir Hugo was the chairman of the British-American Tobacco Co. and had a large financial interest in the Olley enterprise. Despite allegations made at the time in various quarters there is no reason to doubt that the Guernsey States Aerodrome Committee and their consultants, Norman, Muntz, and Dawbarn had any motive other than the provision of the best possible aerodrome for the island, with due regard to cost, amenities, and other relevant factors, and, of the three sites available; L'Erée, La Villiaze, and L'Ancresse, they favoured La Villiaze. The use of L'Ancresse would have interfered with the golf course, the rifle range, and the age-old "common rights" enjoyed by the "Habitants" for hundreds of years, but the chief obstacle was the lack of soil suitable for grassing down. It would have been necessary to bring in large quantities from elsewhere. L'Erée was too small, although enlargement was possible to a certain extent, but its main defect was its low-lying situation which, apart from drainage considerations, would be unsuitable for the blind-approach equipment then coming into use at modern airports. Instead of an aerodrome in a depression the ideal for the Lorenz-type blind-landing techniques available at that time was an

162

elevated situation with good approaches as at La Villiaze. On the other hand, did Guernsey need a large modern airport? Considerable space was taken up in the Guernsey newspapers on the relative merits of the various sites, and on October 29 Captain Olley joined in with a full page advertisement in the *Star* extolling the merits of L'Erée. Jersey Airways offered to pay 4% interest on the States capital outlay on La Villiaze for a five-year monopoly, or they would make and run the airport if granted a concession for a number of years. Olley offered L'Erée to the States at cost price plus 6% per annum at any time up to ten years from its completion (in an enlarged form). When the debate opened on the morning of October 30 the public gallery of the States was packed, and the audience included Sir Hugo, Captain Olley, and J.W.S. Comber. At the end of an all-day sitting, by a single vote, it was decided to acquire the site at La Villiaze. Modern blind-landing methods do not have the same limitations as those of the Thirties, and to-day's visitors to Guernsey may be told that "they built the airport in the wrong place – it is too high"! and according to Captain Olley's advertisement daily observations over a period of seven months found that La Villiaze was unusable on 47 days owing to "low cloud producing fog conditions", whereas L'Erée was only unusable for 30 minutes on account of a bank of fog enveloping the Island.

On November 7 Israel's 86 was the only aircraft to take-off from Heston, and the only one to land there. He left to schedule in the morning in almost zero visibility, and returned in the afternoon when fog had been replaced by a blinding rainstorm.

At the end of 1935 an Australian D.H. 86, VH-URT, crashed, and because of two earlier crashes involving Australian 86's the Australian Ministry of Defence suspended the airworthiness certificates for aircraft of this type. However, the ban on the "CONDEMNED AIR LINER", as the *J.E.P.* put it, was lifted a day or so later. The year drew to its close with a typical beach incident on December 30 when a Rapide made four attempts to land in a 35 mph cross-wind. The first machine to arrive, an 86, landed safely, but the smaller 89 was in difficulties, and each time it came down a gust caught it and forced it up again, until, after the fourth attempt, the pilot made a final circuit and headed back to Southampton.

During 1935 Jersey Airways' pilots included Caldwell, Orchard, Swiss, Blythe, Israel, Brecknell, Oakley, Jordan, Murray, Hankey, Dade, and Walker. Douglas Brecknell was the youngest. The oldest was E.W. Jordan, who had transferred from Rapides to 86's to take Blythe's place on the Heston run, and K. Murray had spent some of his time, joy-riding at Blackpool, perhaps on loan to United. On the Jersey-Heston route 213,000 miles were flown and 8,569 passengers carried, together with 103.7 tons of freight and excess baggage, and the figures for the Southampton route were 238,000 miles flown, 15,957 passengers, and 184.3 tons of freight, etc. Only 4,000 miles were flown on the Rennes service, with 93 passengers, and 1.2 tons of freight, whilst between Jersey and Guernsey there were 387 passengers, and 1.6 tons of freight, with 3,000 miles flown. Due to the size of the 86 approx. 25% more passengers were carried on the main routes, but 25% fewer miles flown.

The audited accounts for the year ending 31 December, 1935 show that Jersey Airways made a profit of £3,574, Guernsey Airways a loss of £2,911, and Channel Island Airways a loss of £525. The combined effect was a profit of just £138. Each company kept its own accounts although operating as one. Jersey Airways' profits were down on the £5,150 of 1934 and Mr Greig ascribed this to:-

(a)   The 1935 Silver Jubilee as the most severe cause.

(b)   The series of Imperial Airways and K.L.M. crashes early in 1935 and the loss of the Cobham Air Routes' Westland Wessex.

(c)   The staff had to be carried over the winter of 1934/35, but not the winter of 1933/34.

(d)   The reduction of a twice daily to a once daily service in mid-week all through the summer months to increase average loading. This proved to be a mistake.

(e)   The additional costs involved in the change from Dragon to 86:- wages, maintenance, insurance, depreciation, etc.

(f)   The total passenger traffic to Jersey in 1935 was 8,000 down compared with 1934, nevertheless air-line passengers increased by 4,873.

On 30.9.35 a private company called Allied British Airways was registered with a capital of £100. On 29.10.35 it was renamed British Airways, and it became a public company on 11.12.35. At the beginning of January, 1936 its nominal capital was increased by £245,140 beyond its registered capital of £100, for the purpose of acquiring the undertakings and assets of Hillman's, United, and Spartan Air Lines. United, of course, had a large share-holding in Highland Airways and in Northern & Scottish. Since becoming a private company the Hillman finances had taken a turn for the worse; in the financial year ending March 31, 1933 the aviation side of Hillman's business had lost £1,603, in the following year £4,698, but in the six months ending September 30, 1934 they claimed to have made a profit of £3,547. However, at the first annual general meeting of the new company, Hillman's Airways Ltd., Sir Charles Harris reported a loss of £39,766 up to the end of September, 1935 due to their considerable expansion. Working capital was dangerously low when the offer of support came from United and Spartan, and this offer was accepted by the share-holders. Whitehall Securities now had a footing in Europe.

Note

The writer, just 14, was at Speke in 1935 for the Cobham Air Display and recalls the wing-walking item. I was trying to make up my mind whether to volunteer when the "yokel" beat me to it. The fall to earth must have been quite realistic because I remember saying to my chum: "I suppose it was a dummy." Anyone rushing on to the field would have been considered part of the act, but if any lady gave birth it was not in our immediate vicinity.

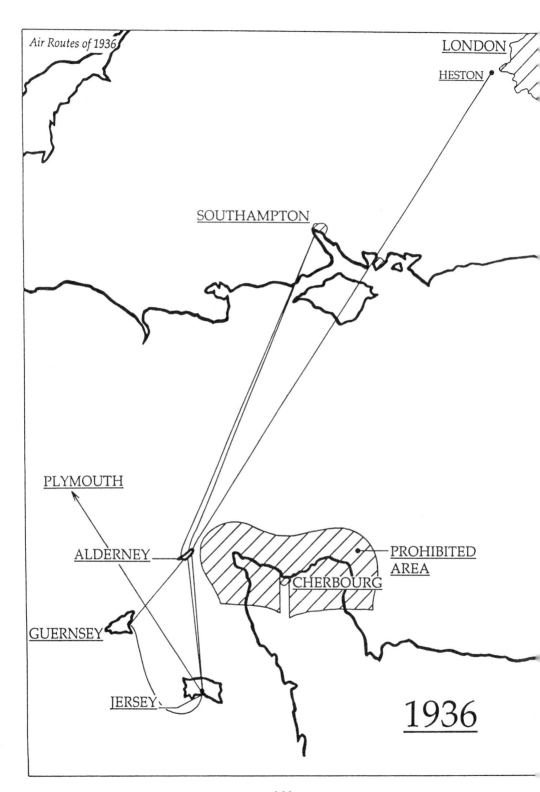

Air Routes of 1936

LONDON

HESTON

SOUTHAMPTON

PLYMOUTH

ALDERNEY

PROHIBITED AREA

CHERBOURG

GUERNSEY

JERSEY

1936

A STEPPING STONE TO GUERNSEY

January, 1936 brought the usual cancellations due to fog, dense in the London area, but on a normal day there was a steady four or five passengers in and out of Heston by Rapide to transfer to an 86 at Eastleigh for the trip across the Channel. At week-ends these figures were roughly doubled and an 86 would fly direct from Heston. Traffic from Eastleigh was always heavier, one of the reasons being the Londoner who took the train to Southampton and joined the plane at Eastleigh instead of Heston. This saved about £1 on the return fare, and indicated that rail was preferable to air travel over short and medium distances, probably on grounds of cost, comfort, and convenience. On the other hand, flying was much better than travelling by boat, and the extra expense was justified by the time and misery saved.

During the quieter winter period Jersey Airways tended to shed a few pilots and, in addition to the two departures for New Zealand, John Dade left to become an instructor at the Maidstone Aero Club at West Malling. He was only 21, and had just spent a year as a first officer on 86's. In February D. Brecknell and K. Murray qualified for their second-class navigator's tickets, whilst on February 11 Mr Israel had a skirmish with the elements flying an empty machine below cloud. He: ". . . watched the rain hit his wings and there solidify with alarming rapidity." (20) The plane gradually lost height as the ice built up, but the light load helped and he managed to land at Eastleigh just as the instruments froze up. The 86 was said to be very prone to icing trouble, and ice had been known to form almost everywhere, including the lower surface of the wing from leading edge to trailing edge.

"Icing" at this time was a comparatively recent phenomena to British pilots, although well-known in America. It is true that icing of the carburetter had been experienced over many years, initially as a baffling mystery when engines lost power and the pilot was forced to land. The engines were then found to be in perfect working order as the ice in the carburetter inlet had melted by the time the mechanics arrived on the scene. Possibly this was the origin of a tale, often heard in pre-war days, of the secret ray able to stop aero engines. It was well known, said the rumour, that someone had been flying in the vicinity of a certain "hush-

hush" establishment when suddenly his engine cut and he was obliged to come down. Subsequent inspection, of course, found the engine in perfect running order! The icing experienced by Mr Israel was quite different with the ice building up on the leading edges of wings, struts, wires, and airscrews to reduce the flying characteristics to such an extent that ultimately control of the aircraft could be lost. Little was heard of it in Britain until the "Thirties".

Pictures appeared in *Flight* in 1934 showing ice on a Hawker Hart as, quite by chance, their chief photographer happened to be flying with Hawker's chief test pilot when they encountered conditions favourable to ice formation. Towards the end of 1935 Lockspeiser read a paper to the Royal Aeronautical Society entitled: "The Prevention of Ice Accretion on Aeroplanes" which explained a system being developed by Dunlop in which ethylene-glycol plus a certain amount of ethyl alcohol was spread along the leading edge of the wing through a porous leather strip. Widely used in America were Goodrich de-icers in which rubber casings were fitted to the various leading edges and pulsations of compressed air inflated and deflated these casings to break off the ice. The ice tended to form when ascending or descending near cloud, it was thought, and did not occur at very low temperatures, or in clear air. By 1937 *Flight* was complaining that although ice accretion was a real danger: ". . . the newspapers have now discovered . . . (it) . . . and apply it as a certain cause of almost every crash." By 1938, to move on another year, the favourable conditions had been defined as 15-32°F in stratified cloud, 0-32°F in cumulus, normally in cloud but could occur under a warm layer from which rain was falling (as discovered by Mr Israel). From November, 1938 there was an Air Ministry order requiring all British transport aircraft to carry an approved de-icing device. European aircraft of American manufacture, such as the Douglas D.C.2 and the Lockhead Electra, were fitted with Goodrich de-icers, but little more was heard of the Dunlop "Anticer" and the crude British answer was a horrible brown paste called "Kilfrost" smeared along the leading edge of the wings (and occasionally one's clothes). There was a feeling amongst British pilots that this practice was inferior to the methods used by their foreign competitors.

Although various Alderney services had been shown in Bradshaw's International Air Guide since October, 1935, the Windhover was still out of action, and no attempt had been made to inaugurate the request stop of the mainland 86's. This may have been due to the need for some additional drainage and re-seeding, or it may not have been good economics to arrange for traffic staff and Customs to deal with just a few passengers. Whatever the reasons the aerodrome was virtually ready for use.

G-ACZR "La Saline Bay" at Eastleigh (R.A.F. Museum)

It was on the west side of the Blaye, 290 feet above sea-level, and the entrance, and primitive airport office, reached by a narrow twisting roadway, were on the south side opposite the Telegraph Tower (See Appendix 2M). Enlarged and modernised it is still in use to-day, although the airport buildings are now on the north side, nearer to St Anne. On February 13 Dragon 'NJ landed with Mr & Mrs Greig on board, and arrangements were made for Miss Wilma Le Cocq to go to Jersey for training as Alderney's representative of Jersey Airways. Wilma, an attractive young lady, with blue eyes and blonde hair, from a well-known local family, was to run the aerodrome and the local office until the war. The Windhover was recommissioned in March, and took Greig and Thurgood to Alderney on March 18. On March 27 the first Alderney request stop was made by a Heston-bound 86 which landed two passengers, Mr Gordon Rice and Mrs Faul. Both returned to Jersey the following day with "Bill" Caldwell coming through from Eastleigh, and as Mr Rice was a solicitor it is assumed that the purpose of their visit was a legal matter. They were not the first fare-paying passengers between the two islands because there had been a day excursion from Jersey on March 10 in Dragon 'NJ.

On March 30 there was a day trip to Dinan by 86 for 30/-, leaving Jersey at 9 am and returning from Dinan at 3.45 pm. Another new service was due to start on Friday, April 3, and this was a twice-weekly service to Plymouth (Tuesdays and Fridays). Regular advertisements for it appeared in the local press, sponsored by Bellingham's, modestly describing themselves as: "Jersey's one and only 100% efficient travel bureau", and the inaugural flight was scheduled to leave Jersey at 10.30 am to reach Plymouth at 11.45 am, but visibility in Jersey was so bad that the plane could not take-off. At Roborough, Plymouth's municipal aerodrome, the Lord Mayor was waiting to give a civic welcome, so 'NJ was sent from Eastleigh. Unfortunately, visibility in the Channel Islands remained poor all day and 'NJ had to stay on the ground. The Lord Mayor left at 4.30 pm, and 'NJ managed to get away at 11.15 am the following morning with two lady passengers. The fare for the 120 miles was £2.15s. single, £4 return, and the scheduled time of flight 75 minutes. Despite the adverts there was no rush to use this service and it was April 10 before the first Jersey passenger, Engineer-Commander McEun, landed at Plymouth. Roborough had been used as far back as 1923, but was opened officially by the Prince of Wales in July, 1931, (See Appendix 2N) having cost the city council £20,000. At an altitude of 460 feet, the take-off run was 500 yards min, and 775 yards max, and there was a hangar with offices. The hangar was a large corrugated-iron affair with a control tower located on the highest part of the roof. The aerodrome is still in use, and the old hangar survives in an excellent state of preservation (currently painted royal blue), and although the control tower is no longer on the roof, the original iron framework of the old tower remains. The George Hotel too, is still close at hand but the liquids on sale no longer include aviation spirit! For many years cattle were grazed on the aerodrome, and the northern end was used as a sports field, with polo in the summer and warnings of rugby football posts in the winter, but early in 1936 the lease was taken over by Whitney Straight and the above hazards removed. The manager was Flight.-Lieut. Knowlden, who had left Jersey Airways to join Crilly, and he was assisted by K.T. Murray, also from Jersey Airways.

Provincial Airways ceased to operate after the end of the 1935 summer season, so the only other Plymouth operator at this time was Railway Air

Services, but their service was not due to start until May 25 when the route would be Bristol – Weston – Cardiff – Teignmouth – Plymouth with arrival scheduled for 12.35 pm and departure at 4.20 pm. There would be a connection at Bristol with the joint G.W.R./S.R. service from Brighton to Liverpool.

Fig. 4a

JERSEY – GUERNSEY – ALDERNEY (Inter Island Service)
(Service Daily except Wednesday, unless otherwise stated, commencing from April 3rd or 4th)
GUERNSEY AIRWAYS

Services by Amphibian operate between JERSEY (St. Aubin's Bay Sands or St. Helier Harbour), GUERNSEY (St. Peter Port Harbour) and ALDERNEY.

Miles	Airports of		A	B	C	Airports of		A	B	C	
0	JERSEY	dep	10 45	–	–	ALDERNEY	dep	13 00	14 00	16 00	–
25	GUERNSEY	arr	11 15	–	–	GUERNSEY	arr	13 30	14 30	16 30	–
	GUERNSEY	dep	–	12 00	13 00	15 00	GUERNSEY	dep	–	–	–	17 00
50	ALDERNEY	arr	–	12 30	13 30	15 30	JERSEY	arr	–	–	–	17 30

A On Weekdays only.   B Sundays only.   C From April 9th to 14th only.
Air/Rail/Steamer Interavailability of tickets applies between Jersey and Guernsey only

Fares

	Single			Return			
	£	s.	d.	£	s.	d.	Baggage allowance 25 lbs.
JERSEY - GUERNSEY	0	12	0	0	18	0	
JERSEY - ALDERNEY	0	15	0	1	2	6	Excess Baggage ½d. per lb.
GUERNSEY - ALDERNEY	0	12	0	0	18	0	

For connecting services between London and Jersey and between Southampton and Jersey, see Tables 10 and 11.

SOUTHAMPTON – ALDERNEY – GUERNSEY
(Service Daily except Wednesday, unless otherwise stated, commencing, from April 3rd or 4th)
GUERNSEY AIRWAYS

A Service will be operated by Land 'plane between SOUTHAMPTON (Eastleigh Airport) and ALDERNEY and by Amphibian Aircraft between ALDERNEY and GUERNSEY (St. Peter Port Harbour)

Miles	Airports of		A	B	C	Airports of		A	B	C
0	SOUTHAMPTON	dep	11 45	12 45	14 45	GUERNSEY	dep	12 00	13 00	15 00
100	ALDERNEY	arr	12 45	13 45	15 45	ALDERNEY	arr	12 30	13 30	15 30
	ALDERNEY	dep	13 00	14 00	16 00	ALDERNEY	dep	13 00	14 00	16 00
125	GUERNSEY	arr	13 30	14 30	16 30	SOUTHAMPTON	arr	14 00	15 00	17 00

A On Weekdays only   B Sundays only   C From April 9th to 14th only
See Table 11 for conveyance etc, between Southampton and Eastleigh Airport.

Heavy baggage facilities in advance by Rail Steamer and interavailability of Air/Rail Sea Tickets in association with Southern and Great Western Railways. On the direct service between Southampton and Alderney, the local fare between Guernsey and Alderney has to be paid.

FARES

	Single			Return			
	£	s.	d.	£	s.	d.	
SOUTHAMPTON – ALDERNEY	1	15	0	3	0	0	Excess Baggage 2d. per lb
SOUTHAMPTON – GUERNSEY	1	15	0	3	0	0	Excess Baggage 4d. per lb
LONDON – GUERNSEY	2	19	6	4	19	6	

¶ Transfer to London Service 23 · extra.
Children under 3 years, free, from 3 to 7 years 50% of fares Baggage allowance 25 lbs

---

April 1936

The long-awaited Southampton-Alderney-Guernsey service was finally inaugurated on April 6, 1936, and the details are given on Fig. 4. The Windhover pilot was now Bill Halmshaw, and the inaugural trip from Guernsey to Alderney took 33 minutes against a 40 mph head-wind. The passengers were Mr Kane, of the *Guernsey Star*, a Mr Pritchard, and Peter and John Newton, aged five and six respectively. Mr Pritchard returned to Guernsey in the amphibian with three passengers from England, but Mr Kane and the two boys carried on to Eastleigh in the Rapide to become the first passengers on that route in that direction. They crossed at 6,000 feet, and the pilot, Douglas Brecknell, brother of Adrian Brecknell, the Guernsey Airways' man at St Peter Port, circled the King George graving dock to give them a better view of the *Queen Mary*.

Figure content (timetable):

JERSEY – GUERNSEY – ALDERNEY (Inter Island Service)
GUERNSEY AIRWAYS

Services by Amphibian operate between JERSEY (St Aubin's Bay Sands or St Helier Harbour)
GUERNSEY (St Peter Port Harbour) and ALDERNEY.

Miles	Airports of		D	A	B	D	Airports of	A	B	¶D	•D		•D
0	JERSEY	dep	10 45	-	-	-	ALDERNEY	dep	13 00	14 00	-	17 15	-
25	GUERNSEY	arr	11 15	-	-	-	GUERNSEY	arr	13 30	14 30	-	17 45	-
	GUERNSEY	dep	-	12 00	13 00	16 15	GUERNSEY	dep	-	-	17 00	-	18 15
50	ALDERNEY	arr	-	12 30	13 30	16 45	JERSEY	arr	-	-	17 30	-	18 45

A Not on Wednesday or Sunday. B Sundays only.   D Daily except Wednesday.
• From May 29th.   ¶ Until May 28th.
Air/Rail/Steamer Interavailability of tickets applies between Jersey and Guernsey only.

Fares

	Single			Return			
	£	s	d	£	s	d	Baggage allowance 25 lbs.
JERSEY – GUERNSEY	0	12	0	0	18	0	
JERSEY – ALDERNEY	0	15	0	1	2	6	Excess Baggage ¼d. per lb
GUERNSEY – ALDERNEY	0	12	0	0	18	0	

For connecting services between London and Jersey and between Southampton and Jersey, see Tables 10 and 11.

SOUTHAMPTON – ALDERNEY – GUERNSEY
GUERNSEY AIRWAYS

A Service will be operated by Land 'plane between SOUTHAMPTON (Eastleigh Airport) and ALDERNEY and by Amphibian Aircraft
between ALDERNEY and GUERNSEY (St Peter Port Harbour).

Miles	Airports of		A	B	¶D	Airports of		A	B	¶D
0	SOUTHAMPTON	dep	11 45	12 45	16 00	GUERNSEY	dep	12 00	13 00	16 15
100	ALDERNEY	arr	12 45	13 45	17 00	ALDERNEY	arr	12 30	13 30	16 45
	ALDERNEY	dep	13 00	14 00	17 15	ALDERNEY	dep	13 00	14 00	17 15
125	GUERNSEY	arr	13 30	14 30	17 45	SOUTHAMPTON	arr	14 00	15 00	18 15

A Not on Wed. or Sun.   B Sundays only   D Daily except Wednesday   ¶ From May 29th.
See Table 11 for conveyance etc. between Southampton and Eastleigh Airport.

May 1936

Business was quite good on the inter-island routes, and by April 9 the *Guernsey Evening Press* was saying: ". . . It is now of daily interest to watch the sky southwards shortly after 11 o'clock for the arrival of the fine triple-engined Saro Windhover in flight from Jersey."

Easter Sunday was on April 12, and special twice-daily flights from Jersey to Alderney were run over the Easter week-end using 86's. It cost 15/- single and 22/6 return, took 15 minutes, and gave: ". . . a full view of the Channel Islands." Miss Le Cocq, very smart in her new uniform, was managing the aerodrome and running the office in St Anne. She drove the Customs officer out to the airport, completed all the paper-work in the tin hut on the edge of the field using the tractor top as a table, and coped with the passengers. There were no telephones on Alderney and all bookings had to go by telegram, well in advance. Wilma's weather reports also went by telegram. The airport groundstaff was old Sam Allan, who acted as porter, loader, groundsman, refueller, and operator of the starting batteries. Such were the charms of Miss Le Cocq that, in due course, it was alleged there was a huge waiting list for the job of assistant to old Sam. Rather inconsiderately the Windhover went u/s. on Easter Monday and was sent to Southampton for the repair of "two broken braces", but the service was resumed on the 14th, and interrupted again on the 21st when Mr Halmshaw landed at St Peter Port at 11.15 am and decided that the sea was too rough for further activity. The amphibian was still rolling heavily in the pool next morning, and there was such a big swell running outside that Halmshaw probably took-off from within the harbour when he did make a move. He was fairly adept at dropping the Windhover into confined spaces and landed inside St Helier harbour a few days later (25th). He came down from the racecourse in the morning when the tide was high on the beach and landed on the sea, but found it too rough to taxi through the pier heads so he took-off again, landed inside the harbour near the Weymouth boat's berth, and taxied along until he was opposite the Victoria Pier. Halmshaw was a very experienced flying-boat pilot; he was a native of Barnsley and had studied law at Sheffield University, but finding law somewhat unexciting had joined the R.A.F. at the age of 23. After initial training at Sealand and five years with 201 and 210 flying-boat squadrons he transferred to the Reserve in March, 1936, joining Jersey Airways almost immediately afterwards.

Passengers on the 86's that left St Helier at 5 pm on March 31 had an excellent view of the famous airship *Hindenburg* heading west towards the Atlantic. She passed Cap La Hague at 5 o'clock and was sighted by the Jersey Airways' machines at 5.10 pm about ten miles north of Alderney. They were close enough to read her registration number, LZ129. But the passengers on the 86 that left Jersey for Heston on Easter Saturday (April 11) had a much less pleasant surprise when they were struck by lightning. They flew into a cloud over Haslemere whereupon there was a blinding flash of lightning and an explosion. No one was hurt, but the radio was put out of action, the compass affected, and fabric torn away from the underside of the fuselage. Israel was the pilot and Samuels the wireless-operator. It is thought nowadays that lightning is only a minor hazard: "few if any airplanes have been knocked down by lightning . . ." (28), but at that time they were not too sure. First reports on the crash of a K.L.M. Douglas D.C. 2 at Rutbah at the end of 1934 put forward the theory that the plane had been struck by lightning and all the occupants electrocuted, although later reports contradicted this. Nevertheless, the idea of sitting inside a metal aeroplane containing large quantities of aviation fuel with lightning flashing all around, did not appeal to everyone, judging by the correspondence in the Press and articles such as "Flying Through a Thunderstorm" by O.K. Whiting, a passenger on the night plane from New York to Miami: ". . . There was a terrific flash of lightning – it seemed to start almost level with us, and crash down zig-zag to the earth below. For a few seconds the plane was lit up in a blinding light. Every detail could be seen . . . Outside the flashes seemed to follow each other every few seconds. By their light I could see our wings glistening in torrential rain . . ." (44) Mr Whiting admitted to being terrified.

Between April 25 and June 19 travellers on the Plymouth route were able to witness the sad end of the famous four-masted Finnish barque *Herzogin Cecilie* aground on the Ham Stone, off Salcombe. She had just left Falmouth after an 86 day crossing from Australia and this was to prove her last voyage. All the mainland services were running well, apart from minor incidents, and the twice-daily summer service started at the end of May, but the inter-island service was handicapped by having only one machine. This ran regularly enough during the first half of May, but was out of action in Guernsey on the 16th with engine trouble and a broken bracing wire. It returned to service on the 17th, and made a very neat landing within St Peter Port harbour on the 21st when the sea outside was too rough, but damaged an undercarriage strut and the Alderney call had to be omitted until the 24th. As with the other mainland services, the Guernsey-Alderney service was doubled up at the end of May, and a special trip to Dinard was made on June 2 for Major and Mrs Giffard and a friend, accompanied by Mr Greig. Having deposited the passengers the amphibian was taking-off for the return when the port engine seized up solid with a broken crankshaft. Take-off was aborted, and the amphibian brought back to harbour. A new engine was flown to Dinard on the following day, but work was only possible for three hours at a stretch because of the tides, and it was June 6 before 'JP could be flown to Jersey and Eastleigh for the work to be completed. The amphibian was back in normal service on the 8th, but on the 9th, whilst refuelling at Guernsey after an unsuccessful attempt to reach fog-bound Alderney, a defect was found in the ignition system of the centre engine, said to be similar to the fault that had lead to the wrecking of the port engine. From June 12 the service was disrupted by fog, but 'JP flew again on the 20th, only to be grounded on Alderney on the 23rd with engine trouble. A ground engineer was flown across and the trouble partly rectified, but it was 10 pm before the passengers reached Jersey and 'JP berthed in the harbour overnight. It was operational again on June 26 but on the 29th there was more trouble when Dragon *Rozel Bay* overshot the Alderney aerodrome. Coming in to land with six passengers, the pilot, Mr Martin, ran out of airfield and hit a bank, breaking the starboard propeller and damaging the undercarriage.

Mr Martin was fairly new to Guernsey Airways and claimed that his brakes failed. He was given the choice, he said, of charging six cows or a bank, so he chose the bank. One of the passengers, a Mr Head, had left Beckenham that morning with Miss V. Edwards and caught a train from Waterloo at about 8.30 for Eastleigh, where they had boarded the Dragon. He said: "the pilot seemed to have difficulty in positioning the plane for the descent, and circled twice over the landing ground before attempting the landing . . . The plane made a perfect landing . . ." and it was some time before it dawned on Mr Head, who was sitting right behind the pilot, ". . . that the plane would over-run the aerodrome . . ." (22) The Windhover took them on to Guernsey but they had to stay the night because of fog. By July 2 *Rozel Bay* had been repaired and flown to Eastleigh, but the Windhover was dogged by bad weather, mostly fog, and the service was only intermittent. On July 9, as 'JP taxied along the beach at West Park after the day's flying the undercarriage suddenly folded up into the flying position dropping the hull on to the sand, and there it had to stay until the tide came in. Once afloat the amphibian was able to take-off but, instead of flying to the race-course for the night, it landed in the bay and taxied into harbour. The undercarriage was completely unserviceable and 'JP would have to go to Eastleigh for repairs.

Saro "Cloud", G-ABXW, "Cloud of Iona" in St. Helier harbour.
(By kind permission of the Jersey Evening Post)

In Guernsey the Aero Club, who were not giving up without a fight, had acquired more land at L'Erée to extend the existing length of run from 350 yards to about 600 yards, whilst at La Villiaze the land-owners were demanding "six quarters a vergée". In Jersey the aerodrome was going ahead, and more money was requested for additional items, such as £30,000 for night-flying facilities, but they denied they were trying to outdo Croydon. The inter-island service was restored on July 12 when another amphibian was brought into use. This was G-ABXW, a Wright Whirlwind engined Saro Cloud called the *Cloud of Iona* (See Appendix 1C). It was not her first visit to the Channel Islands, and she had made the first commercial flight to Alderney in 1934.

'XW had been christened *Cloud of Iona* by the Duchess of Hamilton at Cowes on July 15th, 1932, for an Edinburgh-registered company called British Flying Boats, Ltd., the managing director of which was Lord Malcolm Douglas-Hamilton, one of the Duchess's four pilot sons. When first taken over, the *Cloud of Iona* had seats for eight passengers and a crew of two, and with two engines of nearly twice the power of the Windhover's it could carry a much bigger load.

On July 23 St Peter Port had to be missed after three attempts to land on the rough water outside the harbour entrance, and on July 27 'XW was delayed on Alderney until the evening because of water in the petrol supply. The fuel system and tanks were drained and the problem apparently solved. On July 28 she was flown to Eastleigh for the fitting of radio and four extra seats, but only three additional seats were fitted and the radio could not be found. The previous owner had installed radio but both transmitter and receiver were removed before Guernsey Airways took the machine over. 'XW returned on the 30th, now with seats for eleven passengers, but no radio, and Bill Halmshaw was not too happy about it, although the extra seats would be very useful over the imminent Bank Holiday week-end.

Note

A vergée is about 2,150 sq. yds in Jersey, and 1,960 sq. yds. in Guernsey.

The *Hindenburg* was a German Zeppelin launched in 1936. Length 803 ft., diameter 135 ft., and gas capacity 7,000,000 cu.ft.

The *Herzogin Cecilie* was built as a cadet training ship and launched in 1902. Steel hull, four masts, barque-rigged, 3,342 tons.

The famous Cunarder *Queen Mary* was launched in 1934, 80,000 tons, 1,020 ft. long, maiden voyage May, 1936.

BANK HOLIDAY (1936)

In the 1930's August Bank Holiday was taken very seriously, and everyone felt obliged to go somewhere for the occasion, be it only Hampstead Heath. This year, 1936, would be no exception; London's great termini would be besieged, hundreds of extra trains would run, records would be broken on the cross-Channel ferries, and the beaches of Blackpool, Brighton, and Southend would be so packed that hardly one square inch of sand would be left uncovered. Weather permitting, of course. The problem of travel was of secondary importance compared with the problem of weather. Forecasts then were much less reliable than they are to-day, but, regardless, the papers were full of them, and the advice of "experts". On Friday, July 31, the weathermen were gloomy; at 10 am at Portsmouth the barometer was falling, by 7 pm a depression would be moving eastwards between the Faroes and Norway. The *Southern Daily Echo* said the holiday rush was "soaring to its peak this afternoon" but the outlook was "Showers certain – some bright sunshine possible".

Over in Guernsey three people were planning a week-end in Jersey. They were 28 year-old Ernest Appleby, his 24 year-old fiancée, Elsie Marley, and their school-teacher friend, Miss Maud Bean, who was 31. Mr Appleby, a steady young man with good prospects in the Guernsey Civil Service, had been working for the past eighteen months in the showrooms of the Electricity Board. He lived at St Andrew's and had won a scholarship from his local school to the States Intermediate School. Elsie worked at Mr Mauger's nursery in L'Islet; they were buying a house, and planned to marry in November. The Marleys lived at Les Sauvagées, St Sampson's and, after tea with the family that Friday afternoon the engaged couple had left at about five o'clock and caught a bus into St Peter Port in time for the last amphibian flight to Jersey.

Maud Bean taught at the Hautes Capelles School, and when it broke up for the holidays she had rushed home to Cocagne to collect her things and taken the bus into St Peter Port with her mother to meet her friends at the harbour. This would be her second trip to Jersey by amphibian, and she was looking forward to seeing her brother, who worked in Jersey at Boot's the Chemists. Her mother had come to see her off.

Five more passengers waited to join the plane, including another engaged couple who came from the Sparkhill district of Birmingham, 20 year-old Claude Willis of Evelyn Road, and 23 year-old Margaret Davies of Hendon Road. Their fortnight at a Jersey holiday camp was nearly over and they were due to return to England on the following day. As a final fling they had made a day-trip to Guernsey for their first experience of flying. Claude worked for Frank Wilde and Glover, auctioneers, of Waterloo Street, Birmingham, while Margaret was in the Income Tax office in Newhall Street. She was wearing white shorts and a brown jumper, but had bought or borrowed overalls for the flight, and the two engaged couples soon made a jolly party together on the quay.

The *"Cloud of Iona"* at Alderney airport *(via Mr. Arthur Robert)*

Also from the English Midlands came Miss Alice Judd, of 3 Westgate Road, Rugby, who was staying at the Bay View Hotel in Jersey. She had flown to Jersey from Heston on July 18, and had celebrated her 49th birthday on holiday. Years ago she, too, had been engaged to be married, but her fiancé "went off and married someone else". Miss Judd had been employed for many years by a local building firm, and was a very competent business-woman and secretary. She was a keen tennis player, an accomplished soprano, a member of the Rugby Philharmonic Society, and a regular member of the local Methodist church. She sang in the choir and was frequently its soloist. A determined and strong-minded character, it may have been that her fiancé felt unequal to such high standards. Before returning to England she had decided to visit a former member of her church who was married to a Guernseyman and living in St Peter Port, so earlier in the day she had gone down to West Park to join the *Cloud of Iona* for the morning trip to Guernsey. Miss Judd was a popular guest wherever she went because of her voice and fondness of music, and some of her fellow-guests went along to see her off and take a few "snaps" of the event. Miss Judd's friend was Mrs Emily Diddams, who lived over a cake-shop in the Pollett, and the visit came as a complete surprise. When the time came for Miss Judd to leave, Emily couldn't go down to the pier because of the children, but her window overlooked the harbour and she decided to watch the plane's departure from this viewpoint.

The two remaining passengers belonged to Jersey, although Mr Viel, son of the late Centenier Viel of St Saviours, lived in Paris, having retired from an executive position with Bon Marché, the well-known Paris store. He was on holiday in Jersey, staying at Farmers' Hotel in Gloucester Street, and he had come to Guernsey with his sister, Mrs W.J. Simpson, whose husband, the stationer of Library Place, was in the Overdale hospital with chronic asthma.

The Holiday Snaps The Cloud of Iona preparing to leave Jersey (31.7.36).
Capt. Halmshaw (centre), Miss Judd (right),
(via Mr D Judd)

179

The Holiday snaps. The Cloud of Iona leaving Jersey (31.7.36.).
(via Mr. D. Judd)

The amphibian for which they were waiting, G-ABXW *Cloud of Iona"*,
was coming from Alderney. Normally it made two trips to Alderney from
Guernsey in the day, the last one being scheduled to leave St Peter Port at
4.15 pm to land on Alderney at 4.45 pm. This particular afternoon Friday,
31st July, Bill Halmshaw, the pilot, had just found time to call in at the
little Alderney post office, where he bumped into Arthur Robert, a post-
office engineer from Jersey who was working on the Alderney radio set,
(their only link with the outside world). Arthur had twice flown between
Alderney and Jersey in the amphibian and they exchanged a few
pleasantries. "He was a tall man, very affable, well-liked in Alderney"
recalls Arthur. (6) He was smiling as he walked out of the post-office.
Back at the aerodrome Francis Sotinel, a cheerful young Jerseyman, who
had served in the French Air Force until he joined Jersey Airways earlier
that year, would be making his usual checks. It was only recently that he
had been made flight mechanic in place of Eric Melville, who had grown
too heavy.

At 5.25 pm the *Cloud of Iona* took off from Alderney and landed on the
sea, 40 minutes later, outside the entrance to St Peter Port harbour, just as

the G.W.R. mailboat *St Helier* was leaving for Jersey. A typical Channel packet of nearly 2,000 tons, with two sets of Parson's geared turbines giving her a speed of 18 knots, she had arrived from Weymouth an hour earlier. This was the regular run for which she had been built in 1924, and her commanding officer, Captain Pitman, watched the arrival of the amphibian as he set course for Jersey.

As soon as the *Cloud* had entered harbour and picked up her buoy, the tender went alongside to collect the passengers and the pilot. There was a strong gusty wind from the south-west, rough seas and blinding rain; a heavy sea fret made visibility poor, and the cloud base was exceedingly low. Bill Halmshaw didn't like the look of it so he went to the 'phone and rang through to Jersey. It was 6.35 pm and he was given the latest state of the weather there:- wind, west-by-north, 40-45 mph, visibility, 1,000 yards with clouds on the hills, sea very rough, and the tide was falling rapidly. He spoke to Mr Wieland in the first floor office above Bellingham's. Wieland went across to the window and peered down Mulcaster Street towards the harbour; the weather was poor but, he thought, flyable. In fact the weather was deteriorating, and it continued to deteriorate until about 11 pm that night. Bill Halmshaw was undecided. The more adventurous of his passengers urged him on. They all had good reasons for wanting to be in Jersey that night, especially those due to return to England on the following day, but Captain Halmshaw was an experienced flying-boat pilot of a cautious Yorkshire disposition and not one to be influenced by light-hearted holiday-makers. However, in the end he decided to "have a go". If the sea was too rough he would be able to land on the beach as the tide was on the ebb.

At 7 pm 'XW slipped from her buoy and proceeded out of harbour into the open sea, watched by Adrian Brecknell, Mrs Bean, and various other interest spectators. She taxied out a mile or more, turned towards the land, and took-off into the wind. At 1905 hours (in service language) she left the water and commenced a gentle, right-hand, climbing turn through 270 degrees, until she was heading towards Jersey at a height of 150-200 ft. P.C. Grainger, on duty at the White Rock, watched the machine make a perfect take-off to pass over Jethou, as did local pilot George Renouf. From the bottom of Bosq Lane Mr J.W. Way saw it flying low over Belle Grève Bay: ". . . the machine was flying northwards, and as it turned seawards it was getting lower and lower . . ." When it disappeared into the mist he concluded it was about to land outside the harbour. (22) On board the motor-boat *Fire-Flax* within the harbour, T.E.G. McCathie and J.G. Wheadon: ". . . saw a plane shortly after seven flying comparatively low, going towards Jersey, south of the Ferriers . . ." (a group of rocks off Jethou). (22) Emily Diddams didn't see the plane at all: ". . . the night was too foggy."

The time-table allowed thirty minutes for the flight, but twenty was usually sufficient. For those waiting at West Park this was the last duty of the day, and on such a day, with heavy rain driving in off the sea, they would be glad to finish and get off home. They waited, patiently or impatiently, according to their natures, but, as the minutes ticked by, impatience gave way to anxiety. What had happened to her? The amphibian service was not noted for clockwork regularity and had suffered its ample share of delays and cancellations, but by eight o'clock there was a feeling that something had gone wrong. Mr Wieland went to the telephone and rang through to Guernsey. Where is 'XW? – She left at five past seven, replied Mr Brecknell, and has not returned. The implications were ominous, and urgent action was called for, but what action could they take? The *Cloud of Iona* had no radio, and nothing was known of her whereabouts.

Mr Wieland at once notified the Air Ministry that the aircraft was overdue, so that all shipping was warned of the missing amphibian, and asked to keep a good look-out. He then advised M. Delalande, the French Consul in Jersey, who informed the French air and naval authorities, and all ports between Cherbourg and Brest. In Guernsey Mr Brecknell had contacted the lifeboat service immediately and told them that the amphibian had failed to reach Jersey. At 8.15 pm two maroons went up from St Peter Port to summon the lifeboat's crew, and fifteen minutes later the lifeboat *Queen Victoria* was launched. Alerted by the maroons, many of the townsfolk gathered at the White Rock to watch Coxswain Fred Hobbs take the lifeboat out with a crew of seven and Adrian Brecknell of the Airways. Up in the Pollett, above the cake-shop with her three children, Mrs Diddams heard the maroons, and she wondered if Miss Judd's aeroplane was "all right".

The normal bad weather route of the amphibian was to pass just to the south of Sark and set course for the north-west tip of Jersey to close Grosnez Point, where the land rises to 300 feet, and then follow the coast down to

La Corbière light. This conspicuous landmark, perched on a 90 ft rock, is the "Land's End" of Jersey, and the amphibian rounded Corbière and Noirmont Point to reach St Aubin's Bay.

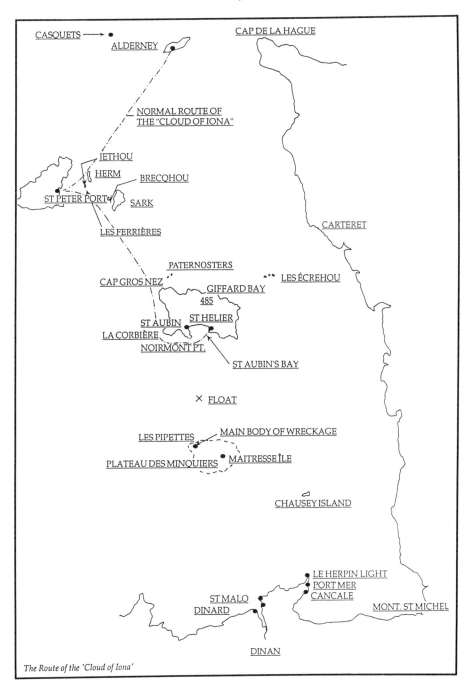

The Route of the 'Cloud of Iona'

Not very far from the route used by the mailboats, such as the *St Helier*, which had arrived at Jersey at 8 pm, just as Mr Wieland was on the 'phone to Guernsey. On board the *Queen Victoria* Coxswain Hobbs had very little in the way of information, but he was in constant touch by radio, and he decided to steer for Jethou and the Ferriers to follow in the probable track of the *Cloud of Iona*. Visibility was extremely poor, heavy rain falling, a big sea running, and darkness approaching. The sun would set at 8.53 pm, and it was estimated that the *Cloud of Iona* would run out of fuel at 8.45 pm.

On the cinema screens of Jersey a hand-scribbled notice was flashed: A flying-boat was missing – Would any members of the lifeboat's crew, and Captain Pitman of the *St Helier* please go to the entrance foyer? Young Jack Beuzeval, of Jersey Airways, comfortably settled in the "Forum" watching Jan Kiepura and Gladys Swarthout in "Give Us This Night", read the message and guessed it was the *Cloud of Iona*. He left immediately. At this time Jersey did not possess a power-driven lifeboat and it was proposed that the *St Helier* be sent out, but, in the end, it was decided to sail the States tug *Duke of Normandy* as soon as she could raise enough steam. Phone calls were made to places near the amphibian's probable route, and first reports said that the amphibian had been seen to the north of Sark flying low in a north-easterly direction, but later calls could confirm only that it had been heard shortly after six (at which time it was flying from Alderney to Guernsey), and not later than that. Sark lighthouse heard the amphibian on its way to Guernsey, but did not hear it flying towards Jersey at seven o'clock, nor did they know anything about it drifting in the sea off the Sark coast, as reported by someone on the north-west coast of Jersey.

SECOND EDN.   GUERNSEY EVENING PRESS, SATURDAY, AUGUST 1, 1936

TEN ON MISSING AMPHIBIAN

CLOUD OF IONA UNABLE TO REACH JERSEY IN BLINDING RAINSTORM

THREE SARNIANS ON PLANE   R.A.F. AIRCRAFT JOIN IN SEARCH

LIFEBOAT RETURNS AND GOES OUT AGAIN

A Mr Warn claimed to have seen it come down off Jethou, and the islanders made a search on foot. Herm, too, was searched on foot, but another report that the *Cloud of Iona* had been seen in flames was not taken too seriously!

At about 9.30 pm, T. McCathie and J. Wheadon, who, from the *Fire-Flax*, had watched the amphibian take-off, left St Peter Port in the yacht *Dodo* with Captain F.W. Noyon, to search between Sark and Jersey. At 10.30 pm the States tug *Duke of Normandy* put out from St Helier and steamed towards La Corbière in bad weather and heavy seas. At about 10.40 pm the *Dodo* sighted the *Queen Victoria*, which had scoured the west and east coast of Sark and proceeded along the north coast of Jersey as far as Ronez until redirected by R/T to the north of Sark.

Late into the night, Airways, Railways, and Harbour officials sat huddled in the Harbour Office of St Helier discussing the various possibilities, and what steps to take next. The railways, of course, ran most of the ships on the Channel island routes; those from Southampton belonging to the S.R., and those from Weymouth the G.W.R. For Mr Wieland, Captain Benest, Peter Lee, the ground engineer, and many more, there was a long night ahead, and in the office in Mulcaster Street about half-a-dozen of the staff were busy answering telephone calls from anxious relatives, the Press, and the numerous other people involved one way or another. Mrs Halmshaw sat up most of the night waiting for news, as did the families and friends of the other passengers and crew, who were aware of the situation. In Guernsey Mr and Mrs Bean were listening to radio messages from the *Queen Victoria*", thanks to local radio dealers, Ogier Brothers of St Sampson's. Poor old Mrs Judd was on her own; she was a widow, and Alice Judd's brother was also away on holiday, but the news did not reach the mainland until the following morning.

At 11.20 pm the *Duke of Normandy* returned to harbour from Corbière because of heavy seas, but at 1 am the French Government tug *Pintade* sailed from Cherbourg to join in the search. The *Queen Victoria* was instructed to anchor in a sheltered position until half an hour before dawn, and by 2 am she was moored in the lee of Brecqhou. The private motor yacht *Dodo* remained at sea until 2.30 am. For those waiting on shore the night dragged slowly by, with not a scrap of news from any source. There were plans to bring aircraft into action at dawn, and a feeling that the amphibian must be somewhere to the north-east of a line joining Jersey to Guernsey because of the strong south-westerly wind. There was hope that it might have reached the French coast, perhaps at some remote part of the Cherbourg peninsula. The last plane to arrive in Jersey from Southampton that Friday afternoon was a chartered Dragon flown by a Mr Williams, who had refused to make the return trip because his radio was not working properly. It was hoped that he might take-off at first light to make an air search, but the weather remained bad, and he did not go. However, flying-boat N 9900 (a Supermarine Southampton of 201 Squadron) took off from Calshot with Flight-Lieut. Dunn in command and a crew of six; Bill Caldwell took-off from Eastleigh in a Jersey Airways' 86, and the *Queen Victoria* slipped from her mooring off Brecqhou. French aircraft also took part. After a fruitless search of the French coast lasting three hours Bill Caldwell returned to Eastleigh. By 6 am the *Queen Victoria* was off La Corbière when she was instructed to search the north coast of Jersey. She sighted a number of steamers on the busy holiday routes but no sign of the *Cloud of Iona*". By 6.30 am she was off Grosnez Point, altering course to the east in improving visibility as wind and rain abated. For the Bank Holiday rush six machines (four 86's, one 89, and one Dragon) had been booked for Jersey that Saturday morning, at 8.30 am from Heston, and 8.45 am from Eastleigh, and each machine flew a different course to cover as wide an area as possible. On the return flight the chartered Dragon was substituted for the Jersey Airways' Dragon which was retained in Jersey to fly when and where wanted.

During her night voyage from Guernsey to Weymouth the G.W.R. cargo vessel *Roebuck* had made a wide detour, and all other ships had kept a good look-out, but nothing had been seen. At 10.20 am the *Queen Victoria* came into St Peter Port for fuel and a replacement transformer for the transmitter. At 10.40 am the Singapore N 9900 alighted on St Aubin's Bay to refuel, and ascertain the latest situation. They reported a large patch of oil four miles south-west of Alderney, as did one of the French flying-boats taking part. While Captain Benest took the R.A.F. crew to the Yacht Hotel for a well-earned lunch, Mr Martin took off in the spare Dragon, with Mr Greig, to investigate a report of wreckage in the vicinity of Les Ecréhos. Nothing was found, and upon their return the N 9900 departed to continue her search. At 12.25 pm the *Queen Victoria* sailed again, and the *Guernsey Evening Press* announced that: "on enquiry from Jersey Airways at 12.45 there was still no news." According to the *Portsmouth Evening News*, a port official, speaking to the Press Association from Jersey shortly after

1 pm, said: ". . . The island is alive with rumours . . . unofficial reports that a French machine had sighted a big patch of oil off Alderney. The weather is very bad for the search . . . thick mist . . . makes aerial survey difficult . . ." The *Jersey Evening Post* said: " . . . There is only one thing in the news to-day of local importance, that is the missing amphibian. The sympathy of the whole island will go out to the relatives of the missing passengers and crew in their growing anxiety as to the fate of the machine. Rumour after rumour that the craft was safe have buoyed up their hopes, but no definite news has come to hand, and all they can do is to wait."

As the *Jersey Morning News* said on the following Monday: ". . . The words 'any news' has been on everyone's lips." One of the more sensational stories came from two Londoners, Mr F.W. Newark, of Kingston-on-Thames, and his daughter, Mrs Gasson, of New Maldon, who claimed to have seen the *Cloud of Iona* on the surface of the water near Corbière when they were arriving in Jersey by the *St Helier* on the Friday night, and suggested that it may have been run down. They told a reporter they were on the lower deck of the *St Helier* as she crossed St Ouen's Bay at about 7.15 pm. ". . . We were looking through the square windows of the shelter part when I saw a flying-boat on the water . . ." said Mrs Gasson. ". . . I told my father and he looked at it through his field-glasses. It was so close that I could distinctly see the passengers. The plane was moving with her propellers whirring on a course which converged with that of the steamer. I heard the engine spluttering. My father ran through the saloon to see it from the other side but when he got there he could see nothing of it and wondered what had become of it. In the bustle of departure we forgot all about in and it was not until to-day that we learned that an air-liner was missing . . . We thought . . ." added both Mrs Gasson and her father, ". . . in the light of after events, that the machine's wing may have been struck by the '*St Helier*' and it was overturned . . ." (6) Captain Pitman thought the story was "highly improbable".

By 2 pm on the Saturday afternoon the weather was clearing, and the sun broke through to cheer the lifeboatmen and help the airmen see the surface of the water. In Jersey, at about 2 pm, a telegram was received from the Préfet Maritime in Cherbourg; a French aircraft had sighted an aluminium float nine miles south-east of Corbière lighthouse, and the tug *Pintade* was being sent to pick it up. At 3.50 pm a message came from the N 9900: "Quantity of plywood and aircraft fabric floating about in the

187

vicinity of the Minquiers. Winding in to investigate." It was normal practice to use a trailing aerial consisting of a length of wire with a weight on the outboard end which was wound off its drum to hang below the aircraft. In order to fly very low this aerial had to be wound in, and the aircraft was no longer in contact with base. Soon another message was received: "Have searched in the vicinity of the Minquier reef and located a considerable amount of fabric and plywood easily recognisable as aircraft material. Continuing search to the west."

Was this the *Cloud of Iona*? The Plateau des Minquiers, or "Minkies" to the Channel Islanders: ". . . consists of numerous rocks and shoals lying on a plateau of about 130 square miles, the centre of which is situated 12 miles south of Jersey and 18 miles north of St Malo. The highest rock, Maîtresse Île, is 10 metres high, and situated near the middle of the plateau." (29) This area was the setting for a novel (and film) by Hammond Innes: ". . . I knew them by reputation: a fearful area of rocks and reefs that we call the Minkies . . ." (30) This ". . . Plateau des Minquiers is bordered by innumerable dangers . . ." (29), and local knowledge is essential, as well as daylight. It was too late to set out at once so a search-party was arranged for 4 am on the following morning (Sunday). The Guernsey lifeboat, which had been about four miles off the French coast near Cap de Carteret at 3.30 pm was ordered to return to harbour, which it reached at 7.15 pm after twenty-three hours on duty.

Dawn that Sunday morning was a dull, grey affair, with a high wind, a choppy sea, and showers of blinding rain, and it was nearer 5 am before the three boats left St Aubin's little harbour, and one of these soon turned back with Captain Benest on board, soaking wet from an unsuccessful attempt at changing boats in mid-stream. The leader of the expedition, in Capt Benest's *Diana*", was F. Lawrence, a well-known local pilot and second coxswain of the lifeboat, and with him were Greig and Lee of the Airways, W. Picot, and R. Lawrence. The other boat was the *Lady Annabelle* manned by her owner, Mr Le Marquand of the Bel Royal Garage, and four friends, with a photographer and a journalist from the *Evening Post*.

By the time the two boats reached the Minkies the journalist had lost interest in the proceedings, but he revived a little, when, three miles north of Maîtresse Île, the *Diana* picked up a piece of wood about two feet square with a hole in the middle.

The second of the "Cloud of Iona's" two engines is hoisted into the yawl wedged in the rocks of Les Pipettes
(By kind permission of the Jersey Evening Post)

All eyes went to Peter Lee, the ground engineer, as he looked at it very carefully. Yes, he said, it was part of 'XW's emergency exit, and one of the few wooden items in the metal hull. A clear indication that the wreckage was indeed that of the *Cloud of Iona*, and that she had broken up. The last slender hope of finding survivors was Maîtresse Île, which is not completely covered at high water, and has several cottages used at one time by stone-masons. A flag was flying from the mast on this tiny island, and they made a landing, but it was only a fishing party from Jersey. They had been on the Minkies since Friday and they had neither seen nor heard the amphibian. After a meal on dry land the search-party set off again and threaded their way through the maze of narrow channels between rocks and sandbanks under the expert guidance of Mr Lawrence, studying every rock through field-glasses. More wreckage was found about ¾ ml. west of Les Pipettes, including a cushion, parts of the wings and ailerons and a wooden fairing from the petrol tank. Beyond all doubt the *Cloud of Iona* had disintegrated, and there was no hope of finding anyone alive.

Channel Island Airways Ltd. issued the following statement:- "Prolonged search by every means at the disposal of the Company has failed to locate the actual place at which the missing air liner disappeared. Wreckage, verified as part of the flying boat, has been found near the Minquiers Rocks, which indicate the disaster took place between that position and Jersey. The search is to continue. The Company expresses its deepest regret to the relatives of those who must now be presumed to have lost their lives." This presumption was borne out in the following week by a series of melancholy reports of bodies being found in the sea, or washed ashore, along a wide stretch of the French coast from St Malo to Cherbourg. The body of Alice Judd was found by the Fisheries Pinnace *Mont St Michel* in a bay about three miles east of Port Mer and five miles south of the Herpin light, and was taken to Cancale where there happened to be some Jersey people on holiday. ". . . On going down to the quay we saw the body lying on a lower landing stage. It was covered with a tarpaulin and surrounded by a great heap of flowers. While we were there, women came up with more flowers, which they added to the pile. As each came up, she would kneel down, make the Sign of the Cross, and remain on her knees for a few moments in prayer. The reverence with which that body was treated by the simple fisher-folk of the village was most impressive . . ." (26) Miss Judd now lies in the Rugby Cemetery. Bill

Halmshaw and Frank Sotinel were buried in graves alongside each other at the Mont-à-l'Abbé Cemetery in Jersey. On the same day Ernest Appleby was buried at St Andrew's where he had been a chorister for many years: ". . . The house which he had just purchased overlooks the St Andrew's Cemetery site. All the blinds were drawn to-day." (26) Margaret Davies was buried in Robin Hood Cemetery, Birmingham, but the body of her boy-friend, Claude Willis had not been found. His father wrote to Mr Mustart of the Jersey Holiday Rendezvous, to thank him for personal effects, and he enclosed an account of Miss Davies' funeral: ". . . the grave is being kept open for a week or ten days, in the hope that my son's body may be found, and laid with her. – Our thanks also go out to all those who so heroically assisted in trying to locate the wreck, and who have given us such valuable assistance . . ." (6) Claude Willis's body was never found, but all the others were eventually returned to their next-of-kin.

Mr Appleby was picked up by a Jersey boat about six miles north of St Malo and brought in to St Helier, which made it necessary to hold an inquest. The search had come to an end; but not the story, for many questions were being asked. On August 3 the editor of the *Evening Post* had raised one point: ". . . which has surprised, and is agitating the minds of a considerable section of the public. It is the question of a plane, amphibian or otherwise, carrying on a public flying service without the provision of radio . . ." At the inquest Mr Greig told them ". . . 'XW had been temporarily on service . . . about three weeks. Prior to that it was in the possession of Spartan Aircraft, Ltd. It was originally obtained on temporary loan and an agreement to purchase was made a few days before the accident. It was actually the property of the Company . . . The machine was only partially fitted with wireless, but there was no radio station on watch within 100 miles so that it could have made no difference anyhow. As soon as it was decided to purchase the machine instructions were issued to the Marconi Telegraph Co. to inspect the machine with a view to supplying the balance, and arrangements had been made for a Marconi engineer to inspect the machine in Jersey on the morning of Saturday, August 1st . . . All pilots had absolute discretion to cancel a flight or turn back . . . The practice on this machine was to leave Jersey with fuel for the day's flying . . ." This did not satisfy the editor.

". . . Some points in the evidence offered by Mr Greig . . . call for criticism . . ! No station within 100 miles! He appears to have forgotten the G.W.R. mail steamer *'St Helier'*, able to send and receive messages, was actually crossing from Guernsey to Jersey between six and eight that evening . . . No station was on watch because the aircraft had no radio. Had she had radio the St Peter's airport radio station would have been on watch (the station which any owner of a wireless set may hear speaking to Jersey Airways' planes on any day of the week) . . ." Normally ships and aircraft used different frequencies, but in an emergency Jersey Airways were allowed to use the ship frequency of 600 metres.

Some six months later Guernsey Airways Ltd. was convicted at Guernsey for having flown the *Cloud of Iona* on three days without wireless, and fined £300 (at that time the biggest fine ever levied by a Guernsey local police court) and costs. The regulation infringed laid down that an aircraft carrying ten or more occupants must have wireless. Obviously, radio would have made a tremendous difference on the night in question, but the fault was something of a technicality in that the flight would have been quite legal with one less person on board. The Dragons flew from Portsmouth to Jersey without radio during most of 1934, and sometimes carried eight passengers over the much greater distance. The *Cloud of Iona* had been granted a dispensation for flights from Liverpool, Blackpool and the Isle of Man not exceeding 20 minutes duration and 10 miles range, when in the hands of a previous owner, and Guernsey Airways had written to the Air Ministry on July 25 for a dispensation covering the inter-island service but the amphibian had come to grief before the Air Ministry could reply.

On Friday, August 14, Walter Gallichan and George Maroe, of La Rocque, returned from a fishing trip with the news that they had found the smashed hull and engines of the *Cloud of Iona* wedged in the rocks of Les Pipettes. On Sunday, 16th, following an exploratory visit the previous day, a tricky salvage operation was mounted by the States tug *Duke of Normandy*, the yacht *Diana*, and a yawl, which was rowed into position on the Pipettes at a convenient state of the tide to be left high and dry as the tide receded. Sheerlegs were erected, block and tackle rigged, and eventually both engines were recovered, as well as other important parts including the compass, instrument panel, control wheel, rudder bar, Verey light pistol and several cartridges, and some personal effects. The engine throttle controls were handled very carefully so as not to disturb the various lever positions. The yawl was successfully floated off on the next tide.

The Conclusions of the Air Ministry investigation, published in February, 1937, were:-

1. That the aircraft was forced to descend into the sea by reason of a sudden and probably complete loss of engine power which occurred when the aircraft was within sight of Jersey.
2. That it is not possible, on the evidence available after the accident, to arrive at any definite opinion as to the cause of the loss of engine power.
3. That the pilot successfully brought the amphibian aircraft on to the water but that it was subsequently swamped by heavy seas.
4. That all possible rescue measures were instituted without undue delay, but that the weather conditions, coupled with the lack of knowledge as to where the aircraft had come down, strongly militated against the success of these operations. (31)

This did not placate the *J.E.P.* Far from it: ". . . The mountain has laboured and brought forth a mouse . . . More than six months and a couple of questions in Parliament have been required to produce this report – and what does it tell the public – Nothing whatever that we did not know already. The Inspector tells us . . . 'The aircraft was forced to descend into the sea by reason of a sudden and probably complete loss of power' – we hardly supposed that the ill-fated aircraft had been shot down. A few things that public would like to know more about . . . The weather conditions; they were bad, very bad, were they too bad for the machine to cross, if so, who was responsible . . . Jersey officials, Guernsey representative, or the pilot. Petrol – How much was taken on in the morning; were the tanks refilled in Guernsey . . .?" The questions raised by the exasperated editor were left unanswered.

It is now possible to examine the Air Ministry records (32), which show that Captain Wilkins had completed his Report by August 31, 1936. That nothing appeared until six months later may well have been due to the court case pending, as the Conclusions were published within a few days of Guernsey Airways being fined £300. The full Report was not published, only the Conclusions, and these differ in places from the original version of August 31, thus:-

Para. 1. Instead of "loss of power" the original said the aircraft was forced to alight on the sea: "by reason of a failure of one or both engines." It did not say "within sight of Jersey".
Para. 2. The original draft had the additional comment:- "in view of the fact that there were no survivors or witnesses of the accident, and

Certainly the final version was very bland and non-committal. No blame was attached to anyone or anything, and the subtle change from "engine failure" to "loss of power" included the possibility of running out of petrol, which is the easiest way of causing air-locks in fuel pumps.

From the full Report we learn that 'XW was inspected and certified as airworthy by a qualified engineer on the morning of July 31, and that the tanks held 120 gallons of petrol, which was the usual amount for the day's flying. At 7.05 pm the crew of the motor-boat used as a tender saw her take-off and set course for Jersey. At about 7.10 she was sighted by a ship, still flying on a direct course for Jersey, and about ten minutes later she was heard at Grosnez Point. From the evidence of people who heard the aircraft pass (it could not be seen, the clouds were almost on the ground – or water!) the pilot followed the coast past Corbière to St Aubin's Bay, when the aircraft was seen momentarily to emerge from the clouds at about 7.30, as well as being heard by two other people. From then on – nothing – until the sighting of the wreckage, apart from three children from L'Erée in Guernsey, who claimed to have seen a flying boat off Lihou Island (west coast of Guernsey) at 8.15 pm on the Friday evening, flying south!

A study of the wreckage and the marks on the rocks showed that the hull of the aircraft, with both engines attached, had floated on to the reef in an inverted position. The bow portion, some six feet long, had been damaged by the action of the sea whilst lying on the rocks, but the keel was straight and there was no evidence of a heavy nose-dive. Both airscrews were intact except for minor damage to the tips caused by contact with the rocks. The undercarriage legs were in the "down" position, and the tell-tale switch was on suggesting that the pilot intended to land ashore. When the salvaged engines were stripped down no defects could be found apart from corrosion resulting from immersion in sea water. The petrol pump of the starboard engine was in a more advanced state of corrosion, internally, than the port, suggesting that there was no petrol in this pump at the time of the forced landing. The running switches were in the "on" position. ". . . Before the aircraft left Alderney on the last flight, the flight-engineer checked the amount of petrol then in the tanks by

194

means of a wooden dipstick. It would appear that the tanks then contained not less than 70 gallons of fuel. It has been proved in service that, with the engines running at normal cruising speed, the consumption of this aircraft was 26 gallons per hour. The flight from Alderney to Guernsey occupied 40 minutes. When the amphibian left Guernsey on the fatal flight, therefore, the tanks contained sufficient fuel for a flight of about 2 hours duration. Experience has shown that fuel was drawn from the starboard tank more rapidly than from the port. If, on the flight in question, this effect for any reason became exaggerated, there is a possibility that movements of the aircraft, while flying in the very boisterous atmospheric conditions in the vicinity of Jersey, may have caused the small quantity of fuel in the bottom of the tank to surge sufficiently to uncover the tank outlet temporarily and thus cause one or both fuel pumps to become air-locked."

That the wreckage was found on the north-west edge of the Minkies aroused no comment, although 'XW was over St Aubin's Bay at a very low altitude at about 7.30 pm and, had a loss of power occurred then, there was no reason why a forced landing could not have been made very near to Jersey, even in St Aubin's Bay. Perhaps the Inspector assumed that the aircraft came down just outside visibility distance and was carried on to Les Pipettes by the strong tidal currents of the area? The Admiralty chart of the Minkies, (No 3656) tabulates the speed and direction of the tidal current at a point close to Les Pipettes (position 'D') and this information has been used to plot the movement of a floating object dropped into the sea at this position at 8 pm on 31st July, 1936 (i.e. three hours after high water at St Helier with a tide about half way between spring and neap). See Fig. 5. The object drifts on to Les Pipettes at about 5 am the following morning, after a total movement in a southerly direction of only 2 miles (neglecting the effect of the strong south-westerly wind). Conversely, if the inverted hull of an amphibian drifted on to Les Pipettes at 5 am on the morning of August 1st, 1936 it is reasonable to assume that its starting point would have been somewhere near position 'D'! The accuracy of the data used will decrease with distance from position 'D', but the accuracy of the result is not important as its sole purpose is to show the improbability of the *Cloud of Iona* having drifted on to Les Pipettes from a position near St Aubin's Bay. The obvious conclusion is that the loss of power did not occur when the amphibian arrived at 7.30 pm and some other reason prevented it from landing. This could only have been the very poor visibility.

Fig. 5

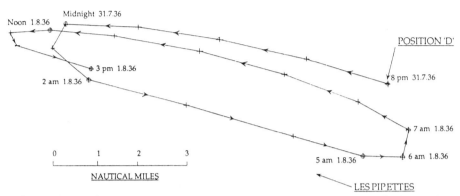

ESTIMATED MOVEMENT, DUE TO TIDE,
OF A FLOATING OBJECT IN
POSITION 'D' AT 8 PM ON 31.7.36.

At 6.35 pm the Jersey weather report, probably recorded a little earlier, gave visibility as 1,000 yards. The weather deteriorated continuously until 11 pm, and the sun was setting. Cloud was on the hills, and the highest point of Jersey is only about 450 feet, and hardly reaches 300 feet in the centre of the Island. Off the west coast "the clouds were almost on the ground" said the Report. With a south-westerly wind driving into St Aubin's Bay against an ebbing tide the mist and spray would merge with the base of the cloud. Looking down Mulcaster Street from No. 1 Mr Wieland may well have seen as far as the harbour, but had he gone outside and looked behind and up towards Fort Regent on its hill he would have seen nothing but cloud. There seems little doubt that when Bill Halmshaw made his approach he was forced to turn away in almost zero visibility. It was probably not the first time he had been in such a situation, and he may have been half expecting it, but he would never have left St Peter Port without sufficient fuel for his return and an ample margin to spare. On paper he had fuel for 90 minutes flying when he arrived off St Aubin's Bay but that would have meant flying until the tanks were bone dry so, in practical terms, he had about 60 minutes, of which 30 minutes or more had to be allowed for a possible return to Guernsey, which left 30 minutes at the outside for flying in the St Aubin's Bay area. Most pilots in these circumstances would make another attempt after circling away, clear of danger, and fixing their position on some low-lying landmark, but long before fuel became a problem they would be heading for a suitable alternative. For a return to Guernsey or a diversion to St Malo the wheels would have been lifted into the "up" position so it must be assumed that Bill Halmshaw was still hoping to make a beach landing in St Aubin's Bay when he suffered his complete loss of power, and the above assumptions would make the time somewhere between 7.30 pm and 8 pm. If a second attempt was made the engines were not heard again over St Aubin's Bay, and if he tried to pin-point his position on some conspicuous part of the Minkies he was not heard from Maîtresse Île, which lies on the eastern side of the plateau. Had he been off Lihou Island at 8.15 pm, as claimed by the three children it would have been too late for a return to Jersey with a reasonable fuel margin for a diversion and he would have gone straight to St Peter Port. Both St Peter Port and St Malo were more sheltered from south-westerly gales than St Helier, and Bill Halmshaw was familiar with the Dinard-St Malo area after his enforced stay there in June with the Windhover.

For the amphibian to come down miles from help and sheltered water in the vicinity of the dangerous Minkies Reef indicates that the loss of power took Bill Halmshaw completely by surprise, as at 8 pm he should have had about 26 gallons of fuel left. The *Cloud of Iona* could not maintain height on one engine, but in the event of an engine failure the pilot would try to stay airborne as long as possible by taking whatever steps he could, such as increasing revs. on the remaining engine. The setting of the controls or other evidence must have indicated to the Inspector that no such action had been taken hence his verdict that the loss of power was "complete", meaning that both engines stopped almost simultaneously. For two completely independent engines with separate electrics to stop simultaneously could be an extraordinary coincidence, or a shortage of fuel, if the two supplies were inter-connected. Details of the *Cloud of Iona's* fuel system are not available, and no tanks or associated pipe-work were recovered from the wreckage, but it would have been similar to that of the R.A.F.'s Saro Clouds with engine-mounted fuel-pumps taking fuel from tanks in the wings. As the engines were high above the wings the pumps "sucked" the fuel up the pipes and if air entered the system fuel could no longer flow, and the system had to be re-primed by hand-operated priming pumps on the engine. R.A.F. Saro Clouds had the two tanks (port and starboard) inter-connected through a collector box, and there was a balance pipe between the carburettors of each engine, so that fuel could be taken from either tank by either pump, and both engines could use one tank or one pump. Suitable isolating valves and cocks were provided. The *Cloud of Iona's* piping arrangement was probably much simpler but it would have been explained to the Inspector, and as he considered that an air-lock due to the low fuel level in the starboard tank could stop both engines, then this must have been possible.

Obviously any mechanical failure in the fuel system would have allowed fuel to leak away and air to enter the pipe-lines, and in earlier times the copper pipes used had sometimes fractured due to work-hardening caused by vibration in service, but, by the time of the Saro Clouds, the copper pipes were restricted to a few straight lengths where vibration was minimal, and flexible hose, such as "Petroflex" used elsewhere. The aircraft was four years old, but had not seen a great deal of service, and had been used by the makers (nominally Spartan Air Lines) since the end of 1933. For a mechanical fault to develop in the midst of Bill Halmshaw's other problems would have been a very unlucky set of circumstances, and the more probable cause of the disaster was the low level of fuel in the starboard tank, as suggested by the Inspector. The Report said that the flight-engineer checked fuel levels before leaving Alderney and ". . . it would appear . . ." they had ". . . not less than 70 gallons . . ." Not a very convincing statement considering that the fuel level was probably the vital factor in the whole affair. If the quantity of 70 gallons on Alderney was correct then the *Cloud of Iona* would have had 26 gallons left by 8 pm which should have meant 13 gallons in each tank but for the fact that the starboard tank emptied more rapidly than the port tank. No figures were given and the amount was probably marginal although measurable resulting in, say, 10 gallons in one tank against 16 in the other. Each tank could hold 100 gallons (perhaps 94 would be more exact) so that 10 gallons represented a fairly low level. There was probably a small sump in the bottom of the tank with an outlet to the pipe-work leading to the fuel pump, and the tank would have been fitted with one or more baffles to prevent the fuel surging about in bad weather. However, with a very low fuel level a baffle would act like a dam wall, and if the plane tilted in a direction such that the fuel drained away from the sump area the baffle would restrict the flow of fuel from the high side of the tank towards the sump. If, at the same time, a sudden gust lifted the plane in the air, fuel could have been thrown from the sump and the fatal ingress of air permitted. It is most unlikely that such a contingency had been anticipated by any of those concerned with the *Cloud of Iona"*, especially with 26 gallons on board, but this was the disadvantage of having fuel pumps above the level of the fuel tanks. The ideal arrangement is to have the fuel pumps below the level of the fuel tanks but this brings the added complication of a separate source of power to drive the pump.

It was not suggested that the *Cloud of Iona* ran out of petrol, only that a sufficiently low level in the starboard tank combined with a sudden manœuvre, perhaps caught by a gust in a steep bank, allowed air to enter the fuel system, and it is difficult to estimate what that level might have been. Also, as no explanation is given for the starboard tank emptying more rapidly than the other it is difficult to suggest any reason why this should become exaggerated as the levels in both tanks dropped. However, some consideration can be given to the accuracy of the 70 gallons said to be on board when the amphibian left Alderney. There is little doubt that this figure would have been obtained from the copy of the load-sheet retained on Alderney. Each service flight of an air-line had to be covered by a load-sheet, giving the weight of everything on board, passengers, crew, baggage, freight, mail, oil, petrol, and removable equipment, such as radio, and these weights were added to the empty weight of the aircraft to give the total which was not to exceed a certain laid down maximum. The object was to avoid overloading, and the traffic staff were usually given the fuel quantity in round figures for conversion to lbs. weight by a simple table. A measured quantity of, say, 66½ gallons could well be rounded up to 70 gallons for a load-sheet, and, from overload considerations, this would be an error in the correct direction.

How this fuel quantity was to be obtained was not laid down, although it was a simple matter in a normal aircraft to read the gauges on the instrument panel, but with the *Cloud of Iona* it would have been left to the flight-engineer to climb up on the wing and use the dipstick. Alternatively, the fuel remaining at any given time could be obtained by subtracting a figure based on time in the air at a known fuel consumption from the quantity last measured. This must have been done at St Peter Port because the Report makes no mention of the fuel quantity at the *Cloud of Iona's* last port of call and, no doubt, Adrian Brecknell confirmed that he had used an estimated value. According to Mr Greig it was the practice to leave Jersey in the morning with enough fuel for the whole day's flying, and for an aircraft performing a regular series of flights every day of about three hours total duration starting with 120 gallons, as did the *Cloud of Iona*, and returning with about 40 gallons (the equivalent of 1 hour 40 min. flying) there was no real need for a dipstick check between flights, except perhaps as a routine precaution, provided no additional flying had been required. When the amphibian landed on Alderney for the second time that Friday it had been in the air about two hours and used, by calculation, 52 gallons of fuel. Subtracted from 120 leaves 68 and rounded off to 70 gallons is exactly the figure given on the load-sheet!

As the unfortunate flight engineer was lost with his machine there was probably only one person on Alderney in a position to confirm that Sotinel "dipped" the tanks before his last departure and that would have been old Sam Allen. It was Bank Holiday and the planes fully booked and Miss Le Cocq would have been far too busy dealing with all the passengers and their luggage, and trying to complete the paper-work. The amphibian was scheduled to arrive at 4.45 pm and the Southampton Rapide at 5.15 pm, and there would have been luggage and freight for Sam to transfer between the two aircraft and to and from the St Anne transport. Squally showers were falling and the only shelter on this bleak and windswept field was the tiny tractor hut perched nearly 300 feet above the sea not far from the edge of the cliffs. The *Cloud of Iona* left ten minutes late and old Sam would have had a very busy half-hour. There were no telephones on Alderney and if asked, at a later date, whether the tanks were checked by dipstick he could well have been a little unsure, or even mistaken. Sotinel may have been up on the wing for some other purpose. The amphibian was only on dry land for two 30 minute periods during the whole day's flying, and other little jobs may have been necessary. Alternatively, as the traffic people were always in a hurry for the fuel quantities to complete their load-sheets an estimated figure may have been given in the first place and the check made later. If the actual quantity was less than the estimated figure then the load-sheet could have been left unaltered although the pilot kept informed, obviously.

Considerations such as above may account for the Inspector's lack of conviction when he said that "it would appear" that the tanks held no less than 70 gallons. Also, it would be reasonable to assume some small margin of error in this figure. We have no information regarding to the accuracy of the dipstick, nor how much skillful interpolation was required to use it. If it was not used on Alderney then there would be an additional small error due to the difference between estimated fuel consumption and flying time and actual consumption and engine running time. It was suggested earlier that the *Cloud of Iona* suffered its "loss of power" at about 8pm with 10 gallons in the starboard tank. Obviously any small error could bring this time forward or reduce the figure of ten gallons, and make the "boisterous weather" theory quite plausible.

The belief that the amphibian made a successful forced landing was deduced from the state of the keel, all damage being due to the pounding on the rocks and not from diving out of control. Also, none of the bodies showed signs of severe injuries before or after death from drowning. All wore their life-belts, and in some cases these were still inflated. They must have left the machine before it turned over and drifted on to Les Pipettes.

Various bits and pieces of the aircraft would have torn away before and after drifting on to the reef, and the plywood and fabric reported by N-9900 was probably from the wings. The position of the float "nine miles south-east of Corbière" is quite compatible with the location of the hull because a watertight float sitting high in the water would be very much influenced by the strong south-westerly winds during the night. Wing-tip floats were very vulnerable, and probably amongst the first items to part company. Although the *Pintade* was sent to collect this float it evidently failed to do so because the Report mentions only one wing-tip float, from the port wing, which was washed ashore at Anneville. The wing-tip floats of the Saro Cloud, incidentally, were quite some distance inboard.

Local opinion at the time is expressed by Peter Manton (now Senator the Rev. P. Manton) who was then a keen young meteorologist: ". . . I clearly remember the weather on the evening of the *Cloud of Iona* tragedy. Thick drizzle and fog with a westerly wind about force five inside a warm sector. No hope of finding the Island . . . We have never really got over it. Those of us who were around can never forget the impact . . ." (35)

Stories and legends surrounding the *Cloud of Iona* continue to linger on in the Channel Islands. There are still some who think it was run down by the *St Helier* off Corbière, from whence it drifted on to the Minkies. Those who saw it going down off Sark were probably confused by the very low height at which it was flying. In Guernsey some still hold that Bill Halmshaw was "ordered" to make the flight, by whom is not specified, but this would have been contrary to normal practice, and Bill Halmshaw and other flying-boat pilots had refused to fly in bad weather on a number of occasions. The belief that the passengers urged the pilot on, or tried to, comes from Alice Judd's nephew as a piece of family folklore which must have originated in Guernsey. A "Mystery Rocket" from the direction of the Paternosters (north of Jersey) reported by a Jersey motorist was seen on the night of Monday, August 3, and is therefore hardly relevant to the *Cloud of Iona* drifting many miles to the south of Jersey 72 hours earlier. One story still told (in Guernsey) is that Bill Halmshaw had collected a fresh chicken and a dozen eggs in a cardboard box packed with sawdust and when the aircraft was found the eggs were still unbroken. If so, this was not mentioned in the Jersey papers, nor the Inspector's Report! All that remains of the *Cloud of Iona* to-day are a few fading photographs, a few fading memories, and one of the airscrews, now housed in the Jersey Motor Museum.

The inter-island service was "suspended", and although the repairs to the Windhover were completed in the following month it was never used again. The Rapide service between Southampton and Alderney was suspended, also, and contact with Alderney reduced to the "request" stops of the mainland 86's. However, all was well with the Jersey Airways' main lines. On August 27 four 86's left St Helier just after 11 am and when off Cap La Hague they sighted an airship heading west at 3,500 ft. Once again it was the *Hindenburg* bound for the U.S.A. and recently the subject of questions in the "House" concerning its journeys over Britain. The summer service ended on September 30 with flights reduced to once daily and the Plymouth service was discontinued, for the winter it was thought, but actually for good, because the Devon terminus was transferred to Exeter in the following year. The very first landing on Jersey's new airport took place on November 7 when, delayed by 60-70 mph head-winds, Douglas Brecknell arriving with twelve passengers, found that the tide was too high up the beach for a safe landing in the strong cross-wind and was given permission to land at St Peter's . The 86's used about 40 gallons of fuel on the cross-Channel trip and took off with at least 80 gallons in the tanks. Brecknell had about 50 gallons remaining when he landed at 10.15, and he left half-an-hour later to reach Eastleigh at 11.30. The wind was still strong on the following day, and although the Dragon managed to get down on to the beach at about 11 the 86 that arrived at the same time made several attempts before returning to Eastleigh. The Southampton machine had to turn back again on November 11, and the year ended with a number of cancelled services for the usual winter hazards of rough weather, fog, and on one occasion: ". . . the presence of ice on the wings . . ." (6)

The results of the year's operations varied slightly with the source of the information due, probably, to some confusion as to whether the passengers flew by Jersey Airways or Guernsey Airways. In round terms the number of passengers carried was up by 25% on 1935, and the miles flown up by 15%. According to Air Ministry figures for regular British air lines excluding Imperial Airways, Jersey Airways came seventh in route mileage, viz:- British Airways 2,500; Railway Air Services 1,072; Northern & Scottish 716; Blackpool & West Coast 664; Crilly 580; North Eastern 395; and Jersey Airways 335, with Guernsey Airways 16th out of 17 with only 50 miles. This low figure shows that Guernsey Airways were responsible for the amphibian services only, between the islands, and that the Southampton-Alderney route was attributed to Jersey Airways (contrary to the information in Bradshaw's International Air Guide). In terms of miles flown Jersey Airways came fourth, viz:- British Airways 1,540,000; R.A.S. 849,000; Northern & Scottish 523,000; and Jersey Airways 522,000, with Guernsey Airways one of the bottom three with 10,000, but in terms of passengers carried Jersey Airways came top with 30,061, followed by B.W.C.A.S. 30,000; P.S.I.O.W.A. 28,690; R.A.S. 22,103; British Airways 19,642; Northern & Scottish 15,117, and Guernsey Airways 11th with 1,877. Speke Airport (Liverpool) had the most aircraft arrivals (neglecting Croydon) with 5,365 against Eastleigh's 2,643, but Eastleigh had 13,443 passenger arrivals compared with Speke's 8,309. Of the Jersey Airways' passengers, 9,382 used Heston, 21,150 Southampton, 382 Alderney, and 315 Plymouth. The Heston total included 158 Heston-Alderney passengers, and the Southampton total 644 Southampton-Alderney passengers. Audited accounts for 31.12.36 show that Jersey Airways made a profit of £4,288, Guernsey Airways a loss of £2,735, and Channel Island Airways a profit of £9, to give a combined total profit of £1,562. To celebrate the firm's third anniversary a staff dinner was held at the Dolphin Hotel in Southampton's High Street, and this was followed by a few speeches and a mass migration to the Hippodrome.

For 1936 the newly-formed British Airways, with its board of directors comprising Roberts, Balfour, and Ballardie of Whitehall Securities, and McCrindle, Grenville, and d'Erlanger from Hillman's, did not reopen the former United Airways' services from Heston to Liverpool and Blackpool, nor the former Hillman's services from Essex Airport to Liverpool so that the route from London to the North-West was allowed to become a monopoly of the L.M.S. section of R.A.S. In July, 1936 the former Hillman's and United operations to the Isle of Man and Belfast were handed over to the W.S.C. controlled Northern & Scottish to compete with B.W.C.A.S. and Manx Airways. British Airways were concentrating on European services and moved their base to Gatwick, a promising new airport with its own station on the Southern Railway line to Brighton, although, in addition to their Paris, Amsterdam, Hamburg, Malmo, and Stockholm services, and their night mail to Cologne and Hanover, they continued to run the Spartan Air Lines/Southern Railway joint service to the Isle of Wight from their new Gatwick base. The former Jersey Airways' Dragon, G-ACNI late *Belle Croute Bay*", was used on this run, suitable repainted. British Airways were given a subsidy for their Scandinavian service, which upset a number of people, including Members of Parliament, because a comparatively new firm, British Continental Airways, which had been operating to Belgium since July, 1935, and later to Lille and Amsterdam, had made a survey trip over their proposed Scandinavian route in December, 1935, followed by an inaugural flight on February 7, 1936, whereas British Airways did not make their preliminary survey flight until five days later. However, as Sir Phillip Sassoon explained, negotiations with British Airways had been in progress long before B.C.A. gave any indication of their interest, and the eventual outcome was a merger between the two companies, described at the time as a "shot-gun wedding" because of the pressure the Air Ministry put on British Continental. This made British Airways approximately one sixth Hillman's, one sixth British Continental, one third W.S.C., and one third d'Erlangers, Ltd. Crilly Airways faded away in 1936, but a new company called Irish Sea Airways started a Dublin – Isle of Man service, and a Dublin – Bristol service which was extended to Croydon in the September. Irish Sea Airways was a joint venture by Blackpool and West Coast Air Services and a newly-formed Irish Company called Aer Lingus.

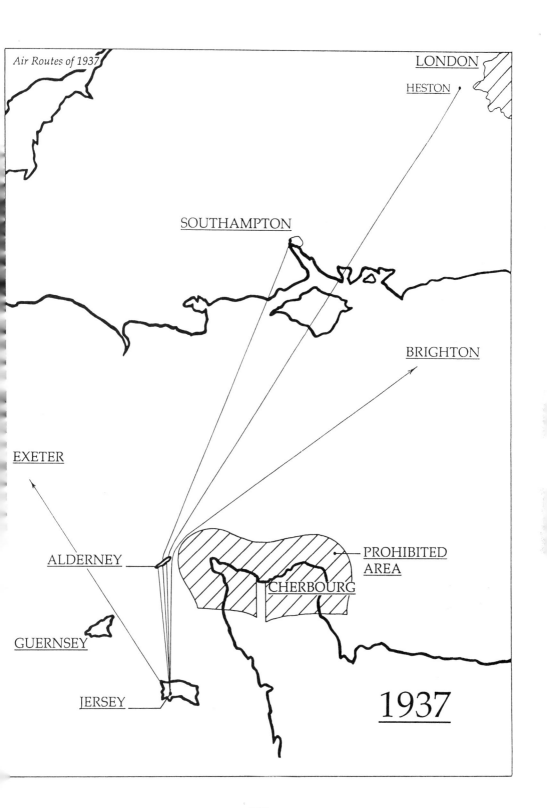

Air Routes of 1937

LONDON

HESTON

SOUTHAMPTON

BRIGHTON

EXETER

ALDERNEY

PROHIBITED
AREA

CHERBOURG

GUERNSEY

JERSEY

1937

As the managing director of a profitable British internal air-line L.T.H. Greig was probably unique, and towards the end of 1936 he had read a paper before the Royal Aeronautical Society on "The Economics of Air Line Operation". This was given two and half pages in *The Aeroplane*, entirely without comment, and two pages in *Flight* which, unusually, was a little unkind in places. The paper contained nothing new or startling, they said, and Sir Francis Shelmerdine had already covered the majority of its points in a previous lecture; the discussion was not so much a discussion as a series of separate talks, and the questions asked were mainly rhetorical! (By no means an uncommon state of affairs at the meetings of learned societies). No doubt they were referring to the first Brancker Memorial Lecture delivered by Sir Francis the previous year, but if Mr Greig was not entirely original he was, at least, abreast of current thinking, which had advanced a good deal since the then Secretary of State for Air, Captain the Rt. Hon. F.E. Guest, O.B.E., D.S.O., M.P., had astounded his audience at the Second Air Conference in 1922 by saying that: ". . . England has shown itself to be so well railroaded as to render it unattractive, and certainly unprofitable, to develop aircraft lines from a commercial point of view. I am almost of the opinion that it is true of Europe generally, and that the prospects of an aerial commercial success in Europe are not very great and will not be for many, many long years to come . . ." (36) He amplified his ideas at the inaugural dinner of the Daimler Airway two months later: ". . . Although in England, through want of space, the weather conditions, the excessive comfort and speed of other forms of transport, civil aviation had, apparently, not become popular . . . We were merely the heart of a great Empire which had great stretches of country which were unbridgeable except by air . . ." (37) Actually, this was not very different from the view of the Advisory Committee of Civil Aviation, which had, in 1920, recognised that ". . . The British Isles, with their regular fast train services, did not offer much scope . . ." (38) and "owing to climatic conditions and their relatively small area, are not suitable for an early development of Civil Aviation . . ." (39) Indeed, if the British air lines of the time were unable to make a profit on such a potentially lucrative route as London to Paris, there was not much point in trying to run between London and Leeds. Nevertheless, there was still a hope for aviation above the far-off deserts and jungles of the Empire. Certainly, in the ensuing ten years, few internal air lines survived for long, and few were actually inaugurated, whilst our national air-line, Imperial Airways, plodded on slowly but surely towards the Cape and the Far East.

By the mid-Thirties British trains were still too fast for the average 120 mph air-liner when the distance from the town to the airport was taken into account. As Shelmerdine had pointed out: ". . . Taking a journey of 100 miles and allowing 20 minutes for each terminal road journey, 10 minutes for loading and unloading. 15 minutes for taxiing and circuits, and 37 minutes for the trip at 160 mph" (a very high speed for the time) ". . . the total is 1 hr. 42 min., or an average of 58.8 mph between town centres. If the journey begins or ends in London the position is worse because it takes 40 minutes . . . to reach the airport . . . On the same basis a 200 mile journey may average 86 mph . . . a 300 mile journey 101 mph . . . and a 400 mile journey 112 mph. Meanwhile railway speeds are increasing . . . the fastest train of the day between London and Liverpool (180 miles) takes 3 hrs. 35 min., which is 50.4 mph. The fastest air-line takes 2 hrs. 50 min. which is 63.7 mph . . ." (40) Mr Greig was not even hopeful for journeys over 350 miles in competition with efficient rail services. From London to Edinburgh at 170 mph would take 3½ hours centre to centre, he said, against seven hours by rail, but the fares would be high, and the air service could not run with "train-like regularity". Another factor, not mentioned by any of the speakers, was the excellent restaurant car facilities on the trains. In 1935 the air service just mentioned left Speke at 11.10 am to arrive Croydon at five past one, and the passenger was taken in to London with the immediate problem of food, whereas the rail passenger could enjoy a good four-course meal and a bottle of wine on the journey, hence the 45 minutes saved by flying was lost having lunch. Again, over longer distances the sleeping-car offered many advantages. The rail passenger could arrive in London first thing in the morning, spend a whole day in town, and then return the same way, whereas the air passenger had to travel during the daylight hours so that he did not reach London until lunch-time, and there was probably no plane back until the following day, which meant a night in a hotel and only half a day in town.

Obviously then, prospects for air-lines on the main trunk routes were not promising, but although Britain is not well-endowed with deserts or impenetrable jungles there are large stretches of sea, often storm-tossed and turbulent, and this was were the aeroplane could compete in both speed and comfort. As Sir Francis had said: ". . . Routes over water are different. An air journey between London and Belfast averages 72 mph against the fastest surface journey of 27 mph." He also mentioned, incidentally, that air fares ranged from 3d. to 10d. per mile, with 4d. the average, and that Imperial Airways charged 5½d per mile on their Paris service. Mr Greig echoed that an air line over the sea: ". . . offers very substantial inducements in time-saving and comfort." In terms of distance over water Mr Greig had chosen the best available route. Despite their closeness to the French coast, the Channel Islands' trade, commerce, and holiday traffic is mainly with England, and this involved a boat journey of many hours duration until Jersey Airways, in December 1933, reduced the time from St Helier to Portsmouth to 75 minutes.

On the question of landplanes versus flying-boats Mr Greig had no doubts about the merits of four-engined landplanes, for which a forced landing due to engine failure would be very unlikely, but he thought the fuselage should be designed to float for as long as possible. Although Imperial Airways had 29 flying-boats on order they were to overcome the special difficulties met on the Imperial routes and they would not be suitable for operation around the British Isles. The limiting factor was the need for sheltered water. He said that the minimum average load for economic operation on most air-lines was 50% capacity, and that speed could be: ". . . a very expensive luxury, indeed . . ." He gave no details of the economics of his own air-line because the tidal beach made their operations "radically different". Or that was his excuse for not divulging such information. However, the new Jersey airport was nearing completion and Jersey Airways would soon achieve complete normality, to the relief of all concerned.

On March 10th, 1937 aircraft of Jersey Airways made their last schedule departures from the beach at West Park, and in the afternoon the new airport was opened by Mrs Coutanche, wife of the Bailiff. It was a very quiet opening with just 200 guests; there was no air display, and the general public was excluded, although invited to apply for tickets which, in strict rotation, would permit them a conducted tour of the airport buildings at a later date. Two special machines arrived from Heston, and the principal guests were lunched at the St Brelade's Bay Hotel with the

Piers and Harbours Committee while the visiting Pressmen had lunch at the Grand. After a mere 30 minutes of speeches the airport was duly declared open and the guests taken on their tour of inspection, many remaining to watch the departure of the two planes for England at 4 pm. St Peter's airport (See Appendix 2P) had a total area of 77 acres, and an east-west run of 980 yards with a white concrete fog-line, although the north-south run was only 528 yards. There were four G.E.C. floodlights and the larger of the two hangars, some 220 feet by 100 feet, was leased to Jersey Airways, and could hold their entire fleet of six 86's, two Rapides, and one Dragon.

The newly opened airport on the cover of a Jersey Airways timetable

The Airport Controller was Lt.-Cdr. C.W. Phillips, R.N.(Ret'd.) who, after the normal naval officer's education at Osborne and Dartmouth, had served as a midshipman on H.M. ships *Dragon* and *Valiant*, and as a sub-lieutenant on H.M.S. *Ramillies*, before going to the R.A.F. for flying training. As a Lieutenant: R.N. he had been appointed to various aircraft-carriers and a battleship, but retired from the Fleet Air Arm in 1933 to become personal pilot to Sir W. Lindsay Everard, a well-known Leicestershire M.P., and manager of his private aerodrome at Ratcliffe. The Assistant Controller was C.V.P. Roche, who had flown on the Western Front with No. 24 Sqdrn. until wounded in 1916. Becoming an instructor, and then a ferry pilot, he was mentioned in despatches before leaving the R.A.F. for the Instone Air Line and later Imperial Airways. For the past three years he had been the airport manager at Hull. In addition there was F.S. Maxwell, with the title of Overseer, who had just spent six years at Heston. Jersey airport still flourishes, larger and busier than ever, with the original terminal buildings embedded within the additions of later years. In time for the visiting journalists the Airways produced a "hand-out" entitled "We Think You Ought To Know" which gave a number of interesting facts about the air-line and included an "AIR JOURNEY LOG" showing that the route of March, 1937 passed directly over Cap de la Hague.

It was a great day for all concerned, particularly the pilots of Jersey Airways, but it was the end of an era, too, for all the staff, and the first floor of No. 1 Mulcaster Street was vacated, as well as the beach at West Park. The late Mr J.W. Beuzeval remembered the limited accommodation; the General Manager (Greig) and his secretary, Miss Le Selleur, in one office ". . . the rest of us being parked in the general office under the . . . eye of the Traffic Manager . . ." (Wieland). The "rest of us" consisted of W. Scarborough, company secretary, Mrs Bowkes, accounts clerk, Frank Vigot and Jack Beuzeval, traffic clerks, and messenger boy Clodiez. "Of course, as time went on more people were engaged, but for office duties only . . ." and just three, Vigot, Beuzeval, and Wieland carried out beach duties until the airport opened. ". . . On the beach we had one licensed engineer, two fitters, and one refueller – the loading and unloading of the aircraft was carried out by licensed harbour porters." Jack's salary was 25/- per week to begin with, and he started work at 9 am and took turn and turn about with Frank Vigot decoding the reservation telegrams from the mainland booking offices, which quite often lasted until about 9 pm. They were required on the beach twice a day (in the summer) ". . . and sometimes on three occasions, particularly when the Saro Cloud returned when the tide was up . . . On some occasions the amphibian landed in the sea and if the beach was completely covered would taxi up the First Tower slip and disembark passengers . . . On Sundays one duty consisted of office plus beach whilst the second man merely had to attend the twice daily arrival of the aircraft. Our social life on the Sabbath therefore was somewhat precarious. Particularly annoying if you had had the good fortune to meet a charming young visitor." (34)

Within a week of the airport being opened there was an unusual visitor in the shape of G-ACEU, the sole landplane version of the Short Scion Senior, which had come for evaluation by Jersey Airways. On March 18 it was giving joy-rides, and was flown by at least three different pilots. Nothing came of the trials and eventually 'EU went out to the Middle East. It was now Jersey Airways' policy to make St Peter's their home base, instead of Eastleigh, and pilots, engineers, stores, and aircraft were to be concentrated at the new headquarters. Naturally this did not suit everyone and Douglas Lucke, who had been with company about twelve months, handed in his resignation; his wife didn't want to live in Jersey and he had found himself another job as a flying instructor under the R.A.F. expansion scheme. Flying Officer D.W. Lucke, ex R.A.F., 27 years of age with 2,000 hours flying experience, had been born in Mexico, of Canadian parents. While staying at his London flat he received a mysterious telephone call inviting him to a certain London aerodrome. There he met an Australian, a New Zealander, and ". . . the toughest-looking guy I have every come across . . .", an American named Semons ". . . dressed in a beret, a leather flying coat and high Spanish boots, . . . three days growth of hair on his face . . ." (6) Lucke was offered £50 to fly Short Scion G-ADDN from Rochester to Bordeaux and on to Santander. The Spanish Civil War had been running its cruel course since the summer of 1936 and aircraft were at a premium, both sides buying planes and inducing pilots to ferry them out of the country and then on to Spain. The Government policy of "Non-intervention" prohibited such activities, much to the disgust of some people whose business it was to make or sell aircraft, but Lucke did not go through with the deal and "blew" the story to the Customs and the C.I.D . . . He said the gang was badly "wanted" by Scotland Yard.

The opening of St Peter's and Jersey Airways' transfer from Eastleigh had an immediate effect on the time-table. Until March 10 the well-established winter routine was in force with planes arriving from the mainland at lunch-time (tide permitting) to remain about an hour. From

March 11 the routine was reversed and both mainland machines left St Peter's at 10.30 am and arrived back at 3.15 pm. The Heston flying time remained 90 minutes, but the Southampton time was reduced to 60 minutes, and 45 minutes had to be allowed for the journey from St Helier to the airport. Over Easter (25th – 31st) there were two services during the day, and in April the Eastleigh machine left at 10 am and the other 30 minutes earlier, but it did not leave Heston until 3.30 pm. Joy-rides were available on Sundays, and on April 12 the *Daily Sketch* began to arrive by air, closely followed by the *Daily Mirror*. A big publicity campaign was launched by R.A.R. Wieland with 300,000 leaflets, 10,000 posters, and 10,000 showcards being sent out. The poster, by Lawson Wood, was thought to be very clever and attracted much favourable comment. On May 1 a service to Alderney was inaugurated leaving St Peter's at 1.30 pm and Alderney at 2.05 pm on Mondays and Fridays with a 25 minutes flying time, although the first flight had to be delayed until 3 pm because of fog on Alderney. With the approach of summer the May time-table had both mainland services leaving the Island at 9.15 am with the Heston machine due back at 12.45 pm and the Eastleigh machine at 6.20 pm with extra services at week-ends and over the Bank Holiday, as usual. On May 31 new services were inaugurated between Jersey and Brighton and between Jersey and Exeter. Mr Greig travelled on the Brighton plane, which was *St Catherine's Bay* flown by J. Israel, with chief radio-operator J. Lyons, and the passengers included four-year old Sheila Tyrrell and her nine-month old brother, Gerald. (The very old and the very young always qualified for a line or two in the paper in those days). The 86 was met by Lord Amherst, manager of Shoreham Airport, and a large gathering of civic dignitaries. Lord Amherst who held a 'B' licence and was still an active pilot, had joined the Olley group (which ran the airport for the municipalities concerned) from the defunct British Air Navigation Co. of Heston. The reason for the larger than usual collection of mayors and aldermen was the fact that the airport, opened in 1935, was a joint venture by the three adjacent towns of Brighton, Hove, and Worthing, and it was located on the west bank of the river Adur, opposite Shoreham, about six miles from Brighton and four from Worthing. (See Appendix 2Q).

The site, on the north side of the L.B. & S.C. railway line, had been an R.F.C. training aerodrome during the First World War, but during the 1920's another aerodrome came into use also on the north side of the

railway line but west of Salt Farms Road and this was used by the
Southern Aero Club and Southern Aircraft Ltd. It was called Lee's Barn
and was restricted to aircraft like the Avro 504K.

This shows the Jersey Airways' D.H.86, G-ACZN, "St. Catherine's Bay" landing at
Shoreham

The new aerodrome had been built on the site of the original R.F.C. flying
field and Lee's Barn abandoned. It had good approaches over the sea and
the river, and an attractive group of airport buildings in the "modern"
style of the day. Very little has changed, and steps have been taken
towards the "listing" of the terminal building as a fine specimen of 1930's
"art-deco" aerodrome architecture. The chapel of Lancing College remains
a conspicious landmark. Before the lunch in the airport lounge, members of
the Press and the civic party were taken along the coast in the 86 as far as

Newhaven with a Rapide in company which accounts for the many photographs of *St Catherine's Bay* in flight over various parts of Sussex. In addition to the children, two others had the honour of making the first flight from Jersey to Brighton as fare-paying passengers, Mrs Tyrell, their mother, of Five Mile Road, Jersey and Mr Leslie Wyse of Brighton. The distance was 150 miles, the fares 55/- single, £4 return, and the flying time 75 min. The service was once daily on Fridays, Mondays, and Tuesdays, and twice daily on Saturdays and Sundays, but from July 2 it was twice daily on all five days leaving St Peter's at 9.30 am and 3.30 pm and Shoreham at 11.15 am and 5.15 pm.

Shoreham was also the terminus of the Railway Air Service line from Liverpool, via Birmingham, Gloucester, Bristol, Southampton and Ryde, and there were other services to Ryde, as well as a Sunday service to Cardiff during July and August.

The Exeter service was flown by "Bill" Caldwell in *Ouaine Bay* with Martin as First Officer, and two passengers, C.T.W. Clerk and F.J. Smith, both of Guernsey, who were the first passengers to land at the new aerodrome. They were met by a formidable body, including the Mayor of Exeter, the Sheriff of Devon, the Deputy Mayor, the Deputy Town Clerk, and the Chief Constable. In addition, as the aerodrome was being run by the Straight Corporation, Whitney Straight had flown in from London in his own Miles "Whitney Straight", to be joined by Col. L.A. Strange, now a director of the Straight Corporation and Flying Officer Mouatt, the airport manager. Mr Clerk was interviewed by the *Exeter Express & Echo*: ". . . the plane was very steady. There was no motion at all over the sea and only a few bumps when we got over land. Conversation could be carried on quite ordinarily, as if one were in a train . . ." Mr Clerk was last in Exeter in 1916 at Streatham Hall when it was a hospital for wounded officers, but he and Mr Smith were flying on to Plymouth. The occasion was referred to as the "formal" opening of the new Exeter airport (See Appendix 2R) because the "official" opening would not take place until the airport buildings were completed, but the actual first landing had occurred on May 10 when S.W.A. Scott, of Air Dispatch, flying a Leopard-Moth, brought films of the Coronation of King George VI. Before the arrival of *Ouaine Bay* at 10.30 am, two Short Scions, G-ADDV and G-ADDX, belonging to Plymouth Airport Ltd. (that part of the Straight Corporation running Roborough) had flown over from Plymouth as a goodwill gesture, and after the welcoming ceremonies *Ouaine Bay* took various dignitaries on the inevitable free flights over the city of Exeter and the surrounding countryside. At about 12.20 pm the Railway Air Services' Dragon, G-ADDI *City of Cardiff'*, flown by J. Nicholas, hove in sight bringing various railway officials, including the ubiquitous Wing-Commander Measures. Exeter was now a "request" stop on the R.A.S. Bristol-Cardiff-Plymouth service, which was due at Exeter at noon (southbound) and 4.45 pm (northbound). 'DI took off from Clyst Honiton at 12.35 pm, half-an-hour late, with Messrs Clerk and Smith amongst the passengers, perhaps the first fare-paying passengers to leave the new airport. This R.A.S. service brought Bristol, Cardiff, and Plymouth within 60, 35, and 25 minutes respectively of Exeter, whose airport is still Clyst Honiton, 4½ miles east of the city, just south of the main London (A30) road.

A First Day cover flown by Jersey Airways on 1.6.37.

Fares from Jersey to Exeter were £2.15 single, £4 return (the same as for Brighton), but the distance was only 120 miles with a one hour flying time. The service ran Friday to Tuesday (inclusive), except Sunday, and there were two services a day in the high season leaving St Peter's at 9.30 am and 3.30 pm and Clyst Honiton at 12.15 pm and 4.55 pm. Improvements continued to be made to the aerodromes used by Jersey Airways and during 1935 night-flying equipment had been installed at Eastleigh, and they now had three 1,250,000 candle-power floodlights, and a red neon beacon flashing "SN", as well as D/F wireless and weather reports. Heston had been extended to cover about 180 acres, and the Air Ministry had put aside £550,000 for its purchase, whilst in Jersey they were giving the finishing touches to their flashing beacon. May 4 was remarkable because the Aurora Borealis was visible as far south as the Channel Islands, but May 6 was the day of a disaster in New Jersey that hit the head-lines all over the world when the *Hindenburg* burst into flames landing at Lakenhurst after a journey from Frankfurt. The Zeppelin was completely destroyed with a loss of 35 lives. Jersey Airways flew their longest charter to date

(700 mls.) when D. Brecknell took a lady patient, Miss A. Mees, to Rotterdam in a Rapide, but a big event in their history was the inauguration of the Air Mail service on June 1.

At 6.25 am Captain B. Walker in Rapide 'BW left St Peter's unobtrusively with 335 lb of mail and landed at Eastleigh at 7.37 am. In the opposite direction, "Bill" Caldwell left Eastleigh at 7.50 am in 86 'YF with 229 lb of mail and arrived St Peter's at 8.50 am: ". . . At the appointed hour . . . *'Giffard Bay'*, . . . was reported approaching the island and soon afterwards she could be seen silhouetted against the almost cloudless sky, her hull shimmering in the sun's rays – a thing of beauty indeed. Flying just above the cockpit was the blue Royal Mail Air pennant and on the bow stood boldly out the words 'Royal Mail' surrounding the crown. A perfect landing was effected just before the appointed hour and when the official party arrived the plane taxied up in front of the main building . . ." (6) In fact "Bill" had arrived about ten minutes too soon and taxied into a far off corner of the airfield to await the official reception party which included the Lieut. Governor and the Bailiff.

There was surprise in some quarters that, despite the new air mail, letters were taking the same time as before, generally speaking. It was difficult for the Post Office to improve on their existing methods because letters were normally posted during the day and taken to their destination at night, by train or boat. The air-lines operated by day. Mail for Jersey was collected by day and sent over on the night boat. Only letters arriving too late for the night boat went on the early morning flight from Eastleigh. Similarly, in Jersey only mail posted after the latest time to catch the night boat and before 5 am the next morning was flown to the mainland. There was no extra fee for carriage by air and the Post Office decided which route was the quicker, which was convenient for the Post Office, nor was it necessary to apply the blue "air mail" vignette. Unless familiar with the system recipients had no means of knowing whether their mail had arrived by sea or air but for the benefit of philatelists and others letters sent to the Jersey Airways' offices for carriage on the first flight were rubber-stamped:-

JERSEY AIRWAYS LTD   FIRST AIR MAIL FLIGHT   1ST JUNE 1937.

Green ink was used by the London office, blue by Jersey, and violet by Southampton. Variations were provided by stamp dealers, and some covers had meter stamps, that is they were printed with a stamp and the slogan:- JERSEY AIRWAYS / VICTORIA RLY STATION / PHONE VICTORIA 5692/5 – 1½ HRS LONDON – FARE £5 / OR FROM EXETER – SOUTHAMPTON – BRIGHTON.

The first of June was also the starting date of the full summer service, and as it was the first to be compiled free from tidal considerations it is given in full below:-

HESTON (90 min.) Fares now £3 single, £5 return.

Dep.	St Peter's	9.30 am D	11.30 am P	4.30 pm D
Dep.	Heston	11.30 am D	1.30 pm P	6.30 pm D

SOUTHAMPTON (60 – 65 min.) Fares now £1. 17. 6 single, £3. 2. 6 return.

Dep. St Peter's	6.25 am W	8.30 am M	9.15 am T	9.30 am S	12.30 pm M
	1.30 pm E	3.30 pm M	4 pm D	6.30 pm F	7 pm M
Dep. Eastleigh	7.55 am W	10.00 am M	11.00 am S	12.15 pm T	2 pm M
	3 pm E	5 pm M	5.30 pm D	8 pm F	8.30 pm F

D Daily; E Daily except Wednesdays; F Fridays & Saturdays; M Mondays, Fridays, Saturdays & Sundays; P Fridays, Saturdays, & Sundays; S Saturdays, Sundays & Mondays; T Tuesdays, Wednesdays, & Thursdays; W Weekdays.

Flying time to Jersey was 65 minutes, but from Jersey only 60 minutes, possibly an allowance for the prevailing winds, although the 6.25 am ex. Jersey was given 65 minutes for some reason.

At the beginning of June the first through electric train from Waterloo arrived in Portsmouth to open the longest stretch (74 miles) of main-line electrification in the country, and this brought Portsmouth into consideration again as a port of call for Jersey Airways. The *Daily Mirror* of July 1 carried an article on Miss Le Cocq of Alderney airport as "the girl who made an island air-minded" and Wilma, now Mrs Colin Bragg and still living on Alderney said in a recent interview (1985) "They were very happy days" and told of how she was warned of aircraft movements by telegram. "Whenever one arrived for me the telegram boy would cycle round the island until he found me . . ." (41) Perhaps there was a waiting list for his job, too! On July 5 there was a special charter from Jersey to Dinard for the benefit of thirteen passengers from the Southampton steamer who had missed their connection to St Malo by the S.S. *Brittany*. The month of July was particularly misty in Jersey and on the 12th five machines had to return to the mainland without landing. It was the month, also, of the year's mishap, fortunately a minor one, when, on the 25th, the Heston machine taxied out for take-off, but collided with a Miles Whitney Straight and the 86 "is now unserviceable". August Bank Holiday broke more records with 572 passengers into Jersey and 549 out and 631 passengers carried in one day would be Jersey Airways' highest ever. In common with most other British air-lines at this period Jersey Airways presented each passenger with a small packet containing a wad of cotton wool, five pieces of chewing gum, and a thin glass phial of smelling salts wrapped in a protective covering to prevent splinters damaging the fingers. These were supplied free of charge by Boot's the Chemists, and it was reported that on one occasion a poor old lady had to be rushed to hospital on landing having misunderstood the instructions and stuffed the chewing-gum into her ears! (However, not a Jersey Airways' passenger.)

An advert in "Popular Flying" for June, 1937

As the nights were drawing in the last scheduled arrivals at St Peter's on Fridays and Saturdays at 9.35 pm sometimes required floodlights and, as the local paper carefully explained, all four floodlights did not go on, just the one that would be behind the plane as it landed. By September 3 the Jersey beacon was in operation, and as early as September 13 the 8.30 am machine from St Peter's to Eastleigh reported icing conditions. No more planes took off until 4.30 pm in the afternoon and, as all the day's flying had to be compressed into a few hours, notices were flashed on to the cinema screens to round-up off-duty pilots. On September 21 the Bailiff of Guernsey cut the first sod at La Villiaze airport site and, the very same day, three Air Ministry officials arrived, to inspect L'Erée once more and make another report. The Aero Club was hoping to start an inter-island service with a Short Scion equipped with wireless. The winter time-table came into force on September 27, and the previous Saturday (25th) the season's last air delivery of newspapers took place. This summer service for holiday-makers had been run at a dead loss, said the *Newspaper World* incurring "terrific" expense in the order of several thousand pounds. Mr Greig agreed that it had cost several thousands but pointed out that the rates charged were substantially below normal for air freight, and the average cost was just under ½d. per copy. There was a special excursion to Paris on September 28 leaving St Peter's at 4.45 pm to arrive Le Bourget 90 min. later, and leaving Le Bourget the following day at 4 pm. The fare was 63/- return and 22 passengers travelled in two planes, including traffic manager R.A.R. Wieland and the wife he had married that morning. A similar very convenient excursion leaving Jersey on October 13, and returning on the 14th brought them back. From November 1 it was decided that the Heston service should be operated by four-engined machines only, flying direct to Jersey, and the practice of taking the less numerous mid-week winter passengers as far as Eastleigh by Rapide would be discontinued. This changing of planes, and the extra flying time involved, had not been at all popular with the passengers. By now Jersey Airways possessed only one twin-engined machine because Rapide G-ADBV had been sold during 1937, for £3,000, as well as the old Dragon 'NJ which had gone for £1,340 8s. 2d.! Also from November 1 the Air Ministry took over air traffic control at Portsmouth with Mr Halliwell as Chief Controller, and by the end of November Heston had become Air Ministry property, but was managed by Airwork Ltd. who obtained a seven-year lease on their other business premises. The first 86 to have a complete overhaul on Jersey was *Ouaine Bay* and on December 1 Mr Israel took it up for a 20 min. test flight. It had taken a couple of months, said H. Greig, maintenance manager (and brother to L.T.H.), and *Grouville Bay* was half finished. All machines were being fitted with a thermometer just below the cockpit window to measure the outside air temperature, a useful guide to the possibility of "icing". During December trips to Dinard were advertised for the 9th, 18th, 22nd and 30th, departing St Peter's at 9 am and Dinard at 9.30am for 27/6d. single and 45/- return. On Christmas Eve there was a scheduled departure from St Peter's at 4.30 pm and this was Jersey Airways' first night flight with passengers on a regular service, although conditions were roughly comparable for the 6.25 am mail plane.

At the beginning of 1937 the Maybury Report had been published, and one of its recommendations was the "rationalisation" of internal air routes with a central junction aerodrome approximately where Ringway is today. Another recommendation was that all air routes should be licensed, and for those routes radiating from the "central junction" to the major cities this licence should be exclusive, that is, a monopoly for a fixed number of years. In May, 1937 Northern & Scottish had abandoned operations from the Isle of Man and across the Irish Sea to leave the field free for a new company called Isle of Man Air Services Ltd. which was formed in September, 1937 from Blackpool & West Coast Air Services and its rival, Manx Airways. Its composition was one-third Olley Group, one-third L.M.S., and one-third Isle of Man Steam Packet Co. B.W.C.A.S. remained in being as a partner with Aer Lingus in Irish Sea Airways, but dropped the Blackpool from its name. About the same time (August, 1937) a new company called Scottish Airways was formed to take over the operations of Highland Airways and Northern & Scottish. British Airways held 50%, the L.M.S. 40%, and David MacBrayne, Ltd. 10%. The former Northern & Scottish routes to the Islands were flown by Scottish Airways on behalf of a subsidiary company called Western Isles Airways in which David MacBrayne, the steamship company predominant in that area, held a much larger stake. There would be no more internal air-line operations under the name of British Airways, and the last relic of Spartan Air Lines, the Gatwick – Isle of Wight service did not reappear in 1937.

Although the Southern and Great Western Railways had agreed to take a one-third interest in Jersey Airways, this agreement was not put into effect until the Jersey airport was commissioned, as the railways had not wanted to be associated with the dubious beach landing-ground, and it was October, 1937 before the transaction was completed and they became jointly equal share-holders with the other groups. Mr K.W.C. Grand of the G.W.R. and Mr H. Mansbridge of the S.R. joined the board of Channel Island Airways, and Mr Perree resigned to become President. The end of the year results came as an unpleasant shock as Jersey Airways had made a loss of £9,963, Guernsey Airways a loss of £2,069, but Channel Island Airways a profit of £3,307 (due in the main to interest on capital invested). Comparison with 1936 was complicated by the huge increase in mail and freight to 131,719 and 710,449 lb. respectively. Passengers increased by 7% to make a total of 33,314 (21,982 via Southampton, 8,866 via Heston, 1,091 via Brighton, 857 via Alderney, and 518 via Exeter), but miles flown increased by just over one-third to 682,621, due to the special mail and newspaper flights. Some of the factors responsible were the adverse effect on traffic of the Coronation, the increased cost of labour and materials due to rearmament, increased insurance on flight risks (from 8% to 11%), increased cost of ground transport (St Helier to St Peter's cost £1,561, Victoria to Heston went up from £880 to £1,138, and new transport at Southampton cost £881). Fees for landing were up from £1,286 to £3,710.

As Guernsey Airways did not operate during 1937 the loss of £2,069 was quite heavy. Claims and expenses connected with the loss of the *Cloud of Iona* amounted to £736, and £829 went into depreciation, insurance, and other charges on the Windhover. In addition, an ominous note in the balance sheet warned that: ". . . They may be further liability for compensation arising out of the loss of the *Cloud of Iona* . . ." as Mr Simpson a 60-year old Londoner who had been an invalid from chronic asthma for the past six years was claiming for the loss of his wife in the accident. The combined result of the three companies was a loss of £8,725.

Nine months of operation from Jersey's new airport had been completely free from untoward incident, but had cost nearly £10,000 and there would be some anxiety about the financial prospects of 1938. Would this loss be repeated, or even increased with twelve months' residence at St Peter's, and what effect would the opening of Guernsey airport have on the balance sheet?

Notes

The *Brittany* of 1,522 tons gross with two sets of Parsons' turbines and a speed of 16 knots was built by Denny and launched in 1933 for the Southern Railway's services between the Channel Islands and France (Granville and St Malo) as a replacement for the *Vera*". The *Brittany* survived until 1972 when, as the Finnish *Alandsfarjan* she ran aground off Sweden in fog and became a total loss.

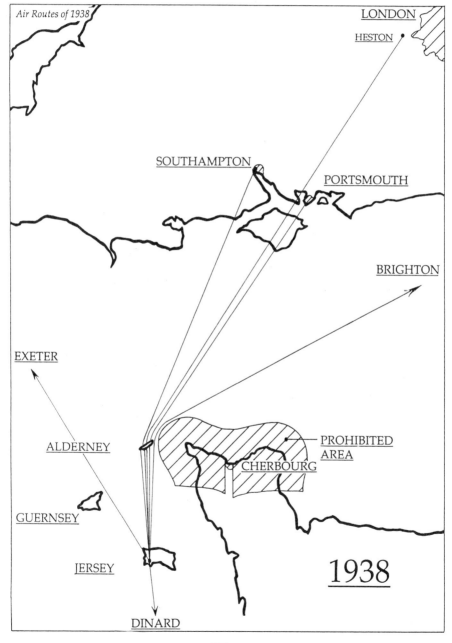

Air Routes of 1938

1938

No great changes were planned for 1938 except, perhaps, to the financial end results. Brighton and Exeter would reappear in the summer time-table, there would be a brief return to Portsmouth, and for a few weeks in the high season there would be a joint service to Dinard with Air France. The basic routes were now firmly established and all that was required to complete the network was Guernsey airport. From January 1 the times of the London plane were changed to 11.30 am from St Peter's and 1.30 pm from Heston to connect with the Guernsey steamships. There were the usual winter delays due to fog and storm, and the cancellation of the Heston service on a Monday was immediately apparent to the Jersey cinema-goers because there were no news reels that night. Other freight about this time, according to the Airways' regular advert in the *J.E.P.* included:- ". . . radio sets, spare parts, shell fish, carpet fasteners, motor tyres, inner tubes, a battery, films, watches, caviare, paté de foie gras, dogs, day-old chicks, a kitten, and a bird . . ." Perhaps this winter's bad weather was attributed to increased sun-spot activity because the Aurora Borealis was visible in the Channel Islands again on January 25.

THE D.H. 86 14 SEATER AIR LINER, "THE LA SALINE BAY"   G.2935.

Postcards of the air-liners were popular in Jersey, especially amongst air travellers who wrote: "This is our plane. . . . . . ."

With the heightening international tension there was an increase in military aviation and early in January, during exercises, a French plane was reported down in the sea 12 miles off Corbière, but it could not be found by the Jersey Airways' machine that took off to look for it. The overdue aircraft, presumably a flying-boat, had managed to return to Cherbourg. In February another French plane was down about 4 miles S.W. of Guernsey, and two Jersey Airways machines picked up the message off Cap La Hague and made for the given position but again they found nothing. Eventually the French crew were reported to be safe with no details regarding the fate of their aircraft. On February 8 there was a huge blast at L'Erée where they were trying to remove a hill to enlarge the aerodrome: ". . . Three charges shook the earth for a considerable distance around, and the air was thick with granite and debris. The hill was rent in two, and several photographers had narrow escapes . . ." (6) One chunk of granite hit and completely wrecked the camera in a girl's hand.

£17,550 of new shares in the Aero Club were issued to Olley Air Service on account of cash advanced, and this gave the Olley group a controlling interest. On February 28 a "request" stop at Portsmouth became available on the normal Jersey-Heston service with fares of 43/3d. single, 66/9d. return. In March the fares on the Jersey-Southampton route were increased to 42/6d. single, 66/- return, but there were cheap holiday and week-end tickets at about 10% less. "Holiday" tickets were available from Jersey on Wednesdays, Thursdays, and Fridays, and "Week-end" tickets were available between October 1 and April 30. Joy-rides could be had for 6/6d. at St Peter's between 3.30 pm and 4 pm on Thursdays and Saturdays.

Jersey Airways' pilots in April, 1938 included W.B. Caldwell, J.M. Israel, D.F.C. Brecknell, E.W. Jordan, A.G.M. Cary, B. Walker, and G. Rayer and the

A JERSEY HOLIDAY *By Air*

PORTELET BAY, JERSEY

New Cheap WEEK-END And HOLIDAY TICKETS

NINETY minutes of luxurious aerial travel, and you are there. You can enjoy from the start every minute of your holiday in this island jewel of the ancient Duchy of Normandy, so full of beauty, history and romance.

You see the loveliness of Jersey as your 'plane glides down to the fresh, green turf in the heart of the Island. You catch glimpses of beautiful bays, in which you will spend long, sunny days, bathing in the sparkling surf, basking on the golden sands, walking and resting amidst all the grandeur of rocky shores.

You will love the quaint, old-fashioned town of St. Helier, whilst the villages and lanes of Jersey, through which you must pass to savour each fresh delight of the coast, are a sheer joy. Whether you use the excellent service of buses, or whether you walk from place to place in this charming island, you hear the pleasant patois of the smiling islanders who hail the King of England.

HOLIDAY RETURN FARES.

From SOUTHAMPTON	...	...	59 6
From PORTSMOUTH	...	...	60 3
From LONDON	...	...	90 -

Also Direct from EXETER and BRIGHTON.

JERSEY AIRWAYS

Send for Illustrated Folder—it tells you all about Advance Luggage, Special Ticket Facilities and inter-availability of air-rail-steamer tickets. Apply at Jersey Airways, Ltd., Victoria Railway Station, London, S.W.1.

14-Seater
4-engined
Machines

Over 33,000 passengers were carried to Jersey last year

traffic staff was augmented by the arrival of F. Miller from Northern & Scottish Airways. He became deputy to the Traffic Manager. There was the usual Easter rush (April 14 – 19) and: ". . . so heavy was the air traffic yesterday . . . (18th) . . . that night fell before the day's flying was completed. Passengers on the last two machines . . . had the experience of approaching a darkened field, picked out by red obstruction lights, and gliding to earth straight into the glare of a broad beam of light . . ." (26) By now St Peter's had been in use for over a year and, human nature being what it is, complete harmony did not exist between all the personalities involved, in fact, "friction" was reported in certain quarters. When, towards the end of April, an aircraft was reported down in the sea, the airport controller, Lt.-Cdr. Phillips, took off to look for it in a borrowed Leopard Moth. The report was a false alarm, but the Lt.-Cdr. suggested that it would be a good idea to have a light aircraft available at the airport for use in an emergency, otherwise Jersey Airways would have to bring out an 86, find a pilot and crew, and warm up four engines, which might take an hour. The following day there was a letter in the *J.E.P.* from Mr Greig to say that a Jersey Airways' machine could be ready to take-off, in an emergency, in less than fifteen minutes, and that a single-engined machine without radio would not be suitable. He also mentioned that Jersey Airways had never made charges for S.O.S. searches in the past, and had not considered doing so. This was followed, a few weeks later, by another letter from Greig: ". . . this company and its staff maintain most cordial relations with control and radio staff at Heston, Portsmouth, Southampton, and the management at Shoreham and Exeter (neither of these has radio). In so far as Jersey is concerned the company's flying personnel have unanimously expressed to me their appreciation of the assistance afforded to them by the Radio Staff at the Airport . . ." (6) The omission of the St Peter's control officers was all too obvious. By the end of April airport control at Eastleigh had been taken over by the Air Ministry in accordance with their current practice for the more important aerodromes, with J.D. Parkinson as supervising control officer, the former senior control officer, Sq-Ldr. Malet having gone to the S.B.A.C.

In May G-ACZP was chartered by R.G. Maltwood for a 1,250 mile trip to Cannes to collect his father. The pilot was J. Israel (at the request of the charterer) with First Officer Challis, and Flight-Engineer M. Lovell. 'ZP, incidentally, was to outlive all other 86's and survive until 1958. Another

86, G-ACZR *La Saline Bay*, went up on a test flight in May for c. of a. renewal, after a thorough overhaul during which it had been fitted with Lorenz short-wave approach apparatus, as well as the latest Standard radio, and both R/T and W.T could be used while the machine was on the ground. 'ZR was scheduled to make an appearance at the Royal Aeronautical Society's Garden Party. In the Lorenz system a beacon was located on the aerodrome which transmitted a continuous signal along a narrow beam coinciding with the correct direction of approach. To the left of the beam there was a zone of dots, and to the right a zone of dashes. At about ¼ of a mile and 2¼ miles from the perimeter of the airfield two beacons, the inner and outer marker, sent a cone of signals vertically upwards so that the pilot could check that his height was correct for the corresponding distance from the touch-down point. In the vertical plane the main signal could be considered as being composed of an infinite number of beams, of different curvatures and field strengths, but all tangential to the surface of the aerodrome. Another instrument showed the strength of this field by the movement of a needle against a scale and, with practice, the pilot descended, hopefully, along the curved flight path most suited to his type of aircraft by staying within the correct beam as indicated by the needle registering a constant field strength. Not many British aerodromes had Lorenz but the numbers were expected to increase.

On May 28 the summer time-table came into force, and the Brighton and Exeter services were resumed, whilst from June 1 there was a contract for more than three tons of newspapers daily from Eastleigh to Jersey which required three 86's. The mail contract was renewed and, in addition to the 6.25 am and 7.55 am departures from St Peter's and Eastleigh respectively, there were departures from St Peter's with mail at 3.30 pm on weekdays and 10.30 am on Sundays. At 11 am on June 13 a three-engined Air France Wibault (See Appendix 1G) landed at St Peter's with a party from Paris and Dinard including René Briend

and Jean Schneider, commercial director and secretary-general, respectively of Air France. They had come in connection with an air service to Jersey, and when they left for Paris at 4.14 pm Mr Greig and Mr Joualt (of Boutin's Agency) went with them. On June 28 Rodney Beresford, who had flown for Cobham Air Routes and fairly recently joined Jersey Airways, took off from St Peter's in *Giffard Bay*, renamed *General Murchison*, for the Far East. Plane and pilot were joining Wearne's Air Services for the Singapore-Penang run. Fog was troublesome in June and G. Rayer had to land *Belcroute Bay* on the beach on the 22nd. With permission from the Constable of St Helier the 86 was left on the First Tower slip, but J. Israel coming in half-an-hour later (6.30 pm) managed to find a hole in the fog and land at St Peter's. On such landings Peter Manton recalls: ". . . When I heard a bump at 6 am one foggy morning I was unable to see the plane taxi on to the hard standing. I asked the pilot how he got in. 'Oh, I let down over St Aubin's Bay' he replied . . . 'flew up Beaumont Hill, and turned left at the garage' . . ." (35) On the 23rd the three newspaper machines had to return to Eastleigh, and the mail plane couldn't get through to St Peter's until 10.40 am. Rapide G-ADBW was sold to Airwork during the month which made Jersey Airways the only British air-line to have an all four-engined fleet. Imperial Airways were now using Southampton again as a base for their flying boats and two of the pilots on the new 'C' class flying boats were none other than those pioneers of the early days, Horsey and Bailey.

The Air France Paris-Dinard week-end service was inaugurated on July 9, but the first through flight to Jersey did not take place until August 8 when Durman landed his Wibault at 7.56 am. This was a "guest" flight bringing the Mayor of Dinard, the President and Vice-President of the Dinard Aero Club, Frontin of l'Ouest Éclair, Joualt of Boutins's and René Briend. The Wibault had seats for ten passengers and could cruise at 140 mph. It was scheduled to leave Le Bourget every Saturday at 1.15 pm, reach Dinard (See Appendix 2S) ninety minutes later, and return on Monday leaving Dinard at 9 am. The Dinard-Jersey service was allowed 20 minutes and left Dinard at 3.15 pm on Saturday, 8 am and 5.30 pm on Sunday and 7.30 am on Monday. Jersey at 5 pm on Saturday, 8.45 am and 6.15 pm on Sunday, and 8.15 am on Monday. Jersey Airways opened their service on August 9 and this ran on Tuesdays and Thursdays with 25 minutes allowed for the flight leaving Jersey at 1.35 pm and Dinard at

2.30 pm. The 86 used was the one scheduled to leave Eastleigh at 12.15 pm and it was possible to leave Manchester at 9 am by R.A.S. and be in Dinard at 2 pm. *Ouaine Bay* made the inaugural flight with A.G.M. Cary at the controls as far as Jersey. "At 12.28 pm yesterday I was at the Southampton Airport (wrote 'Contact' of the *Southern Daily Echo*). At 2.20 pm, less than two hours later, I was at Dinard, charming resort on the coast of Brittany. And on the way I had looked in at Jersey for half-an-hour. Sounds incredible, doesn't it!" They crossed the Channel at 1,000-1,500 ft. and at Jersey "Bill" Caldwell took over. ". . . Twenty-three minutes after getting away from the handsome white and red terminal building at Jersey Airport we glided to the airfield at Dinard, leaving St Malo on our left . . ." The Deputy-Mayor was there to greet them when they arrived at "Dinard's aerodrome-cum-racecourse . . ." and British and French flags were fluttering together in the breeze of a perfect summer's day outside the spotlessly-clean hangars. Inside upturned champagne glasses on a flower-decked table told of good things to come. In addition to Mr Greig the party included R.A.R. Wieland, W.L.G. Butt (Southampton manager) and J.R. Jenkins (London manager). The first Air France service machine, Wilbault F-AMHM *L'Intrepide"*, with pilot Chouard and radio-operator Fabre came through to Jersey on August 13. The one fare-paying passenger was accompanied by the Mayor and Mayoress of Dinard, Joualt of Boutin's, Costa de Beauregard of Air France, and Mdme. de Beauregard. The plane landed at 4.45 pm after flying from Paris to Dinard in 105 minutes and from Dinard to Jersey in 18. A large party met the plane and the indefatigable M. Delalande offered one of his vin d'honneurs in the airport restaurant. *L'Intrepide* left at five past five with ten passengers.

Over the August Bank Holiday planes were arriving at St Peter's as late as 11 pm and local people turned up in large numbers to watch the night landings, and at one time there were three or four hundred cars parked at the aerodrome and along the approach roads. The airport controller now had an assistance controller of the same name, Flight-Lieut. Phillips, who had come from Speke. On August 18, Nigel Norman, one of the Guernsey airport consultants, took off from Jersey in his Leopard Moth, G-ACNN, an early example of personal number plates, and made the first landing on the Guernsey airport site at La Villiaze. Out in Singapore the newly-arrived Rodney Beresford received severe injuries when the cockpit canopy of the little Hillson Praga monoplane he was flying came adrift causing him to crash. He returned to England but never recovered and died soon afterwards. During June and July the Portsmouth "request" stops were augmented by direct services at the week-ends and the full 1938 time-table for August, 1938 is given on Table 3. On August 17 Guernsey-born Councillor Stranger cut the first sod on the site of the new Cunliffe-Owen factory which was to be built at Eastleigh for the manufacture of the British version of the Burnelli OA-1 a twin-engined 15-seater with a "lifting fuselage", whilst Captain Olley and Frank Payne looked on. On Alderney a lady visitor who had fractured her knee-cap was put on board an 86 sent over from Jersey and flown to Southampton but finding this four-engined air-liner so comfortable she decided to fly in it all the way back to Birmingham. Obviously "not short of a bob or two" as the saying was. Eastleigh by now was a place of great activity, and in addition to the air-line and aero club flying the first few Spitfires were just beginning to trickle out of the factory. There was a Fleet Air Arm station on the site currently with Swordfish of 810, 820, and 821 squadrons for H.M. Ships *Ark Royal* and *Courageous*, heading across the Atlantic, on board the *Georgic* were the first of two Lockheed 14's for British Airways and these would be assembled in the Jersey Airways' hangar. At the end of August five foot high white-washed letters appeared on the only field on Lihou saying "THIS ISLAND FOR SALE". It was meant for passengers on the Exeter route but Sir Stephen Demetriada saw it from the Southampton plane and chartered an 86 to cruise over Lihou while he took photographs.

L'Intrepide's busiest week-end started on September 3 (Saturday) when it landed at St Peter's at 3.49 pm with 10 passengers and left at 5.42 pm with five. It returned in the morning at 8.28 am with ten day-trippers, took off at 8.51 am with ten for Dinard, and came in again at 6.48 pm with nine to leave at 7.02 pm with the ten excursionists. On Monday morning it arrived at 7.54 am with five and left at 10.47 am for Dinard and Paris. This service was suspended for the winter on September 12. The summer newspaper contract ended on October 2, but a new contract was signed and from October 24 two 86's left Eastleigh every morning at six with the London dailies. The rest of the Eastleigh routine was the arrival of the mailplane at 7.30 am and its departure at 7.55 am, followed by the arrival of the service 86 at 11.30 am and its departure at 2 pm. As from October 10 Jersey airport and the air space within a five mile radius became a "controlled zone". The main effect was to improve safety in bad weather because aircraft

230

were not allowed to enter this zone without permission from Jersey control when visibility was less than 1,000 yards in any direction.

Wilbert 282 F-AKEL "La Rapide" about to leave Le Bourget for Dinard
(Musée de l'Air et de l'Espace, Paris. Droits réservés)

If one machine had permission to land, others had to wait their turn at specified altitudes. This state of affairs was known as "QBI" conditions, from the code letters in the official "Q" code for wireless messages. Earlier in the year, when answering a question in the House, Colonel Muirhead had stated that, unofficially, "Q" meant "Quite" and "I" meant "Impossible" (laughter). Summer services ended at the beginning of October, and those to Brighton and Exeter closed down for the winter. The Alderney service was reduced to Fridays only, leaving St Peter's at 9.20 am and 2.20 pm and leaving Alderney 30 minutes later. An interesting rumour about this time concerned replacement aircraft for the D.H. 86's. One possibility was said to be the Douglas D.C. 3, better known today as the Dakota.

More "friction" was generated at St Peter's on October 10 when Douglas Brecknell landed his 86 from the west instead of the east as directed by the control officer. With the wind virtually nil this may not have seemed a matter of much importance, but it soon developed into a full-scale legal battle in the Royal Court. Although the Jersey newspapers were of a very high standard, the *Evening Post* in particular giving excellent accounts of British and foreign affairs, there was a tendency to cover local matters in minute detail, and the attempted smuggling of two bottles of cognac could well rate two whole columns in the *Morning News*. Hence, Mr Brecknell's "alleged infringement of the Air Navigation Order" was given considerable space and headed, in large letters: "WELL-KNOWN PILOT AT ROYAL COURT". However, the details do tell us something about the airport routine which began at 5.35 am when the controller went on duty. His first job was to make out a weather report, and by his observations, visibility was six miles, and wind velocity – calm. At 6.45 am he made another observation; the wind-sock was hanging dead, but the vane on the control-tower indicated some wind from the west. Two planes were expected from Eastleigh, and just before 7 am a signal was received from Jersey Airways' G-ACZO saying she had passed Cap La Hague, followed by a signal from G-ACZR to say she was near Cap La Hague. To indicate the correct direction for landing, which was from east to west, the controller arranged for the ball to be hoisted, and for the "T" to be laid out opposite the terminal building. At a later date, the various authorities consulted agreed that there was very little wind, but "West by North" at 1 mph would have been a reasonable description, although the Corbière lighthouse-keeper may have been nearest the mark when he said that the wind was variable, and they often got "catspaws" off the land.

In reply to a signal from 'ZO requesting the weather at St Peter's Lt.-Cdr. Phillips replied: "Wind calm, land from east to west". Aloft in 'ZO Captain Brecknell pointed out some smoke to his wireless-operator, Arthur Challis, and as this appeared to be moving in a westerly direction a signal was sent "I am landing from the west", which he promptly did, touching down at 7.11 am. Captain Bernard Walker in the second plane thought there was an easterly drift of wind, and when he received a message giving the weather at the airport he landed in a direction from south-east to north-west at 7.12 am. His machine, 'ZR came to rest about 300 yards from the perimeter. After the arrival of 'ZO some heated words were exchanged, and when asked why he had landed from the wrong direction Captain Brecknell replied that he was accustomed to landing from the west (when there was no wind), and that it was futile to waste the company's money. Aircraft from the mainland approach St Peter's from the north, but most aerodromes required a left-hand circuit, or part circuit before landing. As Captain Brecknell was in no mood to apologise, the controller threatened to charge him before the Royal Court, and Brecknell in return threatened to report the whole affair to Mr Greig. However, before this argument could be transferred to His Majesty's Attorney-General, on the one hand, and Advocate Bailhache on the other, a much more serious event was to appal the inhabitants of Jersey.

Douglas Brecknell joined Jersey Airways in August, 1935 from Western Airways. Educated at Bristol Grammar School and the "Conway" he had studied engineering at Bristol University and spent about six years in the West Country engineering works founded by his grandfather.

The weather report from Jersey airport at 10 am on Friday, November 4, 1938 read: Visibility, three to four miles; Wind, W.S.W. 15 mph: Cloud, 10/10 at 120 ft. (Ten-tenths cloud meant that the sky was completely obscured). Previously there had been fog, and it was still quite misty. G-ACZN *St Catherine's Bay* had left St Peter's at 6.28 am, that morning for Eastleigh, and taken-off from Eastleigh at 9.11 am to return to St Peter's at 10.23 am. The pilot was A.G.M. (Geoff) Cary, an ex R.A.F. officer, who had joined Jersey Airways the previous winter after a spell in India. He was married, lived at St Brelade, and was an excellent player of golf, tennis and squash. With him was Jack Lyons, the senior operator, an ex-merchant navy man who had just obtained his pilot's "A" licence, and their next mainland trip was scheduled for 10.30 am, but three planes were leaving and because of the weather they were taking off at intervals, the first at 10.43 am, the second at 10.48 am, and 'ZN last, at 10.52 am.

Frank Vigot was the traffic clerk dealing with 'ZN, and its passenger list of:-

Major and Mrs Voisin,
Captain, Mrs and Bridget Swan,
Sister J. Hansford,
Mr T. Cox,
Mrs L. Wall,
Mr F. Berry,
Mr S. Spring, and
Mr H. Kearsley.

Most of the passengers were well-known in Jersey:- Major Gerald Voisin had been commissioned in the Jersey Militia, but transferred to the Royal Guernsey Light Infantry in 1917 and served on the Western Front. He resigned from the Militia in 1929 to devote more time to the family business, a prominent Jersey store. Mrs Voisin came from Shropshire, and they were off to England for a christening. Captain W.D. Swan, Royal Engineers, was the second son of Lt-Col C.T. Swan of Jersey and an Old Victorian. His wife, Rozel, was the eldest daughter of Lt-Col Beazeley, also of Jersey, and they were returning to India from leave with their

14-month old daughter. They were due to sail from Southampton on the troopship *Neuralia*. 27-year old Janet Hansford was leaving the Jersey General Hospital to take up another post near her parents who lived at Frome in Somerset. She was an only child. Chartered accountant Thomas Cox, married with two children, had been over to see his brother, who ran the Lucas C.A.V. Rotax station in David Place, and audit his accounts. Mrs Lucy Wall was a widow, born in Dublin in 1889, but living at Cranleigh in Surrey. She had been staying at the Royal Hotel and was on her way to America to see her son; Frank Berry, of New Malden, Surrey, a married man of about sixty, had been to the Jersey Gas Co. on behalf of Fletcher, Russell and Co. gas appliance manufacturers of Warrington; Stuart Spring of Malvern, was a representative for the Skefco ball-bearing company; Harry Kearsley, of Southport, was very well-known in the Island, having arrived in the potato season every year for the past 35 years. He was on the staff of Swift's, the Manchester fruit merchants, and for some years had dealt in tomatoes as well as potatoes. One of his many friends had asked him to stay on an extra day and cross together on the boat, but Harry had refused to be pursuaded.

In addition, there were two prospective passengers on the mail-boat just arriving from Guernsey. One was Harry Opie of Guernsey, a stevedore with Messrs Loveridge, but much involved in local boxing. Harry was the trainer of Guernsey boxer Billy Barker, who was billed to fight at the end of November, but had taken ill in London, and wanted Harry to go over to see him as quickly as possible. For the first time in his life Harry had decided to fly. The other prospective passenger was Louis Morris, of 52, Shaftesbury Avenue, London. Described as a film magnate, he was connected with Regal Cinemas Ltd., and because the boat was running late, he had sent a wireless message to the airport asking them to "hold" the aircraft. Taking taxis, both men rushed out to the airport and arrived about five minutes before 'ZN was due to take-off. But they were not allowed to board the plane. Frank Vigot had completed the passenger list, the load-sheet, and all the other paper-work, the passengers were on board, and the engines were being warmed up. Mr Morris protested vigorously, but the officials were adamant. To allow more passengers to join would require a revision of all the documents, and cause too long a delay.

APPALLING AIR DISASTER

Plane in Flames at St. Peter's

FOURTEEN DEAD

Many Well-known Residents Among Victims

When the pilot was ready Frank Vigot signalled to the control tower, and permission to take-off was given. The plane moved forward; little Bridget Swan waved good-bye to her grandma through the cabin window, and 'ZN taxied out to the end of the fog-line. Turning on to the white line the throttles were opened, and the plane gathered speed, the tail came up, and 'ZN was airborne. It took off in the east to west direction and was soon lost to sight in the low-lying clouds, but was audible in the direction of St Brelade (to the south of the aerodrome) turning on to a left-hand circuit and moving towards St Peter's church (to the east of the aerodrome) before setting course for Eastleigh (to the north). At 10.52 am 'ZN transmitted a message: "QBF 300ft. ASC" meaning ". . . I am in cloud at 300 ft. and climbing". Suddenly, from the direction of St Peter's, the 86 emerged from the cloud base in a steep left-hand side-slip and dived towards St Peter's Farm and the narrow lane leading from the Don Bridge road to St Peter's Common. This lane was separated from the fields on either side by earth banks, each topped with a hedge, and at that precise moment delivery man William Le Page was driving Tyler's van along it towards the Common. On his right-hand side was St Peter's Farm, belonging to Mr Laurens, and on his left Mr Huelin's Seadua Farm, and he could distinctly hear a plane overhead flying very low: ". . . to my horror, as I was a short distance away, I saw the plane loom out of the mist right in front of me. I realised there was going to be a crash, stopped, and the plane hit the field, bounced, and crashed across the road . . ." (6) The 86 had struck the ground in a field called "La Bataille", skidded and bounced through the hedge, to smash into the bank on the opposite side of the lane, and come to rest in the lane about 100 yards in front of Mr Le Page. ". . . The plane was perfectly whole when it came out of the mist, the engines were 'all out'. The plane was at an angle of 45 degrees and appeared to be on a fairly even keel . . . there was a terrific explosion and a huge sheet of flame shot out. It was at least 50 feet high and 30 feet in width . . . There was not a bit of plane to be seen in the flames . . ." (26) Mr Huelin was working on his farm only 80 yards away and he and his son ran towards the plane which was: ". . . burning fiercely, and had, he imagined, exploded, for several bodies were pitched among the mangolds in his field, these included the baby . . . The propellers were going up to the time the plane struck the ground, the engines were making a much louder sound than usual. He did not see any flame or smoke until she struck. The first body he saw in the field had all the clothing alight. The heat from the plane was awful. There were four bodies in the mangolds and one in the grass. They were all dead . . ." (26) On the other side of the lane two men had been busy mowing La Bataille field with scythes, Edmund Le Cornu, the foreman and Pierre Le Saux, a French labourer who: " . . . saw the machine when it was almost upon us, so I threw myself to the ground instantly, and as I did so the plane just grazed me . . ." (26) Pierre was unhurt except for a scratch over the eye, but Mr Le Cornu was killed instantly. He was only a few yards away from Pierre, but was carried a considerable distance by the aircraft, and had every shred of clothing torn from his body. They were both so accustomed to aircraft that they took no notice of them.

At the airport friends and relations had stood gazing after the vanishing aircraft, trying to follow its movements by sound as it was swallowed up in the clouds but, from the balcony outside the control-tower, look-out man Sydney Gallichan saw the plane diving into the ground. He shouted through the window to the duty control officer, Flight-Lieut. Phillips, who immediately sounded the alarm. The airport clock showed 10.53 am. In less than two minutes the fire engine had reached the burning wreckage some 500 yards away to the east, closely followed by the ambulance, and then the fire-engines from St Helier. Lou. Morris, who had been talking to his driver in the car park when he saw the plane crash, was one of the first to arrive from the airport: ". . . She was very low; all at once she struck, bounced, and burst into flames. My chauffeur and I ran as hard as we could over fields and hedges to the scene . . . As we ran so the petrol tanks exploded and there was a great burst of flame. Bodies were flung out . . . the airport warning siren went and the firemen and ambulance were on there way round the road in seconds . . . Airport men did their utmost to extinguish the flames, but it was hopeless – not a thing could be done . . . It was a ghastly sight, one which I shall never forget. I am thankful now that I was not allowed on board . . ." (6) There were no survivors.

Parts of the machine had been flung far and wide, a landing wheel was found fifty yards from the crash point, and the tail wheel an equal distance in the opposite direction. Passenger's luggage and effects were scattered over an area of about 100 square yards, a partially burnt book – *Travelling to Freedom*, a child's toy, silk stockings fluttering from the brambles, and beside one of the engines, a sheepskin flying boot. ". . . The scythe, which Mr Le Cornu was using . . . lying across the pile of torn and burnt articles, made a grim symbol . . ." (26) Amongst all this debris, one of the few items completely untouched by the flames was the Last Will and Testament of Mrs Wall: ". . . I bequeath all my property to my son, Patrick Wall, c/o Investment Trading, 930, Ingraham Buildings, Miami, Florida." (26) "To-day" said the *Evening Post* "the blackest page in the history of Jersey aviation has been written". According to the *Morning News* the chief control officer said that: ". . . from the ground, nothing could be seen to account for the crash" and with visibility at 4,400 yards and witnesses' statements that all four engines appeared to be running ". . . the mystery is made even deeper."

A post-mortem on the pilot found no evidence of any diseased condition which could have caused the accident. Load sheets and other documents were examined and found to be in order, although it must have been an anxious time for Norman Bull, the ground engineer who signed the daily certificate pronouncing that 'ZN was safe for flight, and Cyril Tubb, the other ground engineer, who had signed that the engines and instruments were in every way fit for service. In the following April the Air Ministry

Report was published and said that the machine took off and disappeared into cloud almost immediately. One minute later, about 500 yards east of its original starting point, it emerged from the clouds at a height of about 120ft in a distinct left-hand side-slip which the pilot could not correct before the crash. The Inspector concluded that there was an error of airmanship on the part of the pilot: ". . . who, when making a climbing turn in a cloud, inadvertently allowed the machine to fall into a side-slip at a height which did not permit the recovery of normal control . . ." (6)

TABLE 1

FROM ST. HELIER, JERSEY

TO	MLS.	MINS.	AV.MPH	SHILLINGS SINGLE	SHILLINGS RETURN	PENCE PER MILE SINGLE	PENCE PER MILE RETURN
Portsmouth	126	75	101	32.5	55	3.1	2.62
from 18.12.33 to 17.3.34							
Southampton via P'mouth	140	105	80	35	60	3	2.57
from 18.3.34 to 31.1.35							
as above	140	90	93	35	60	3	2.57
from 1.2.35 to 26.3.35							
Southampton direct	129	75	103	35	60	3.26	2.79
from 27.3.35 to 10.3.37							
Heston	181	120	91	59.5	99.5	3.94	3.3
from 28.1.34. to 31.1.35							
as above	181	90	121	59.5	99.5 (winter)	3.94	3.3
from 1.2.35 to 28.2.35							
as above	181	105	103	59.5	99.5 (winter)	3.94	3.3
from 1.3.35 to 31.5.35							
as above	181	90	121	59.5	99.5	3.94	3.3
from 1.6.35 to Oct.1936 (winter-summer-winter)							
as above	181	105	103	59.5	99.5	3.94	3.3
from Oct. 1936 to 10.3.37 (winter)							
Plymouth	120	75	96	55	80	5.5	4
from 4.4.36 to 29.9.36							
Guernsey	25	30	50	12	18	5.76	4.3
from 9.6.35 to 31.7.36 (with interruptions)							
Paris	208	135	92	75	125	4.3	3.6
from 4.6.34 to 29.9.34							
Rennes	85	50	102	27.5	45	3.9	3.2
from 8.1.35 to 29.3.35							
Alderney on request by D.H.86	39						
First passengers on 27.3.36 but service was intended to be from Alderney to the mainland. From 6.4.36 to 31.7.36 Jersey could be reached by amphibian, via Guernsey. From 1.8.36 to 10.3.37 the 86 was the only connection.							
FROM ST PETER'S AIRPORT, JERSEY							
Southampton	129	60/65	129/119	37.5	62.5	3.49	2.91
from 11.3.37 to March, 1938							
as above	129	60/65	129/119	42.5	66	3.95	3.07
from March, 1938 to Sept. 1939							
Portsmouth	126	60	129	43.25	66.75	4.12	3.18
from 28.2.38 to 30.9.38							
Heston	181	90	121	60	100	4	3.3
from 11.3.37 to Sept. 1939							
Heston, via P'mouth		95	114	60	100		
from 28.2.38 to 28.5.38							
as above		100	109	60	100		
from 29.5.38 to 30.9.38							
Exeter	120	60	120	55	80	5.5	4
from 31.5.37 to 2.10.37 and 28.5.38 to 26.9.38							
Brighton	150	75	120	55	80	4.4	3.2
from 31.5.37 to 2.10.37 and 28.5.38 to 26.9.38							
Guernsey La Villiaze	24	15	96	13.5	22	6.8	5.5
from 5.5.39 to Sept. 1939							
Alderney	39	25	94	15	22.5	4.6	3.5
from 1.5.37 to 30.10.37							
	39	20	117	15	22.5	4.6	3.5
from Nov. 1937 to May, 1939							
Dinard	50	20	150	22.5	42.5	5.4	5.1
from 9.8.38 to Sept. 1938 and May 1939 to Sept. 1939							

From November 4 the Friday afternoon departure from Eastleigh was advanced by one hour to connect with the Alderney plane leaving Jersey at 2.20 pm. Through passengers were charged a supplementary fare of 3/- only. As the morning newspaper service, or "Dawn Patrol", required two 86's to leave Eastleigh at 6 am one was flown back at 10.30 am as a duplicate to the normal service and the second left Jersey in the afternoon to make an additional one way service. Because of the gravel sub-soil Eastleigh never became water-logged and in bad weather was a convenient haven for air-liners unable to use their normal base. Thanks to this beneficial sub-soil, perhaps, or the prevailing weather conditions, there was a prolific crop of mushrooms and one aircraft worker was fined 10/- for trespassing on the landing area despite the numerous notices everywhere prohibiting this dangerous activity. The new 175' x 150' hangar was nearing completion and this was capable of holding five of the new 123' wing span Armstrong Whitworth Ensigns being constructed at nearby Hamble for Imperial Airways. Another new development at Eastleigh was the production of the Foster Wikner monoplane. On November 20 *Grouville Bay* with George Rayer as pilot and radio-operator B. Worsley and four passengers made a 39 minute crossing from St Peter's to Eastleigh. *Straightaway* the house magazine of the Straight Corporation had some kind words to say about Jersey Airways and reported 379 passengers on their Exeter service during the season just ending.

On December 5, 1938 Jersey airport control was made an "Area Station" responsible for all radio communication with aircraft, direction-finding, safety and traffic control within the limits of its area, which included all the other Channel Islands, and was bounded by the Portsmouth area, the Exeter area, and the French areas of Tours and Le Bourget. However, Portsmouth would not be used again by Jersey Airways. After the closure of the revived Portsmouth service at the end of the summer season an analysis of the figures showed that Portsmouth passengers were not generally additional passengers but simply passengers diverted from other routes and there was no net gain. In the Royal Court the case against Mr Brecknell continued and Mr Caldwell was called as witness. He said that the grass was very short and there was a tendency to skid and take a longer run. The 86 weighed 4½ tons. At St Peter's aircraft needed all the room at their disposal and great care was necessary. If he felt that he had to land contrary to the direction indicated he thought he would ask permission. It was dangerous for two planes to land from opposite directions almost at the same time. Captain Cumming, Director of Training for the Straight Corporation was called to give expert evidence. He said the wind-sock was not reliable for light winds and smoke was better at less than force two. After Brecknell's signal stating his intention he submitted that it was up to control to reply, give further instructions, or tell him not to land. On December 12 Mr Brecknell was fined £10 and £2 costs, but on December 17 he was granted the Right to Appeal.

Ironically, also on December 17 the early morning newspaper plane, G-ACYG, arriving at St Peter's from Eastleigh, piloted by Vernon Gorry Wilson, collided with the fence on the far side of the airfield. "I LANDED ACCORDING TO INSTRUCTIONS" said the head-lines. (6) Captain Wilson had only just joined Jersey Airways and this was his first landing at St Peter's. He was a most experienced pilot with over 7,000 hours to his credit after service in the R.A.F. and with Imperial Airways flying numerous types of aircraft, light and heavy, in various parts of the world. He was the sole survivor of the *City of Khartoum* accident in which Short Calcutta, G-AASJ, ran out of fuel on the night of 31.12.35 within sight of Alexandria and all three engines suddenly stopped. The pilot was in the open cockpit and was picked up five hours later by H.M.S. *Brilliant* but nine passengers and three crew were lost. "I came in about 7.30. It was dark and I couldn't see the wind-sock. I had a radio message from the control stating it was calm, the wind 'T' was out for me to land from the north-east corner . . . so I obeyed that signal. The floodlights too, were on at that quarter of the field. I landed down the fog-line and then found that, owing to the heavy dew, the grass was so wet that the machine would not pull up. I had a full load . . . I skidded several hundred yards with the wheels locked and suddenly realised I was going to hit the fence . . . it was a very minor accident, but an annoying one, as it should not have happened. I was told that there was no wind, yet there was a wind of at least seven miles an hour, and I landed down it in accordance with instructions. That is all I can tell you. Except that the wind had not altered at all since I landed and, as you can see, the wind-sock shows that the wind is blowing from the north-east corner of the field." (6) The duty control officer, Flight-Lieut.

Phillips, declined to comment.

A similar mishap, but rather less serious, happened in the last week of December, and on the very last day of 1938. J. Israel badly damaged the ex Isle of Man Air Services D.H. 86B, G-ADVK, only delivered to Eastleigh on December 8. Israel, with radio-operator P. Moss and five passengers was landing at St Peter's at about 3.30 pm in misty weather, and on very sodden turf. He landed from the west, and was heading slightly towards the north fence, but when he applied the brakes the wheels locked and the machine slid forward over the wet ground. The port wing hit the northern floodlight with great force and the plane was spun round to finish up about fifteen yards away with its nose projecting over the roadway. One wing was completely torn off and the other damaged. Mr Heaton, company secretary and accountant since 1937 was one of the passengers. The longest hold-up in Jersey Airways' history took place from December 19 to 23 when snow caused cancellations over five whole days. There was one service to and from Heston on Christmas Eve, but no planes on the 25th, 26th, or 28th. In fact, December 28 was the first day since 1928 on which no transport plane managed to cross the English Channel.

During 1938 Jersey Airways carried 34,962 passengers and 1,200,000 lb. of freight, only slightly more than in 1937, but much more important, at a profit. The most surprising piece of news came when Mr Greig announced that he was "severing his connection" with Jersey Airways. He could not discuss his reasons for leaving, and he did not know what his future plans would be. A fairly clear indication that his sudden departure was not pre-meditated! His brother, H. Greig, resigned from his post as maintenance manager not long afterwards, and about six months later Mr Thurgood sold all his shares in the company and resigned from the board. A series of events which could be construed as tending to confirm a suspicion of some disagreement at board level! Perhaps, as "Neville Shute" said in his autobiography, senior executives can be divided into "starters" and "runners" and by this time Jersey Airways was well and truly started.

The process of re-grouping the major British internal air-lines, with Whitehall Securities and the Railways playing a predominant role, continued throughout 1938, and British Airways became a wholly European operation. Captain Balfour resigned all his directorships and became Under-Secretary of State for Air, with Sir Kingsley Wood as Air Minister, and the Hon. Clive Pearson, head of Whitehall Securities, and now a director of the Southern Railway, had taken over as chairman of British Airways, with W.D.L. Roberts stepping down to vice-chairman. Towards the end of 1938 Great Western & Southern Air Lines Ltd. was formed to take over the operations formerly carried out for the G.W.R. and the S.R. by Railway Air Services, and those of Olley's Channel Air Ferries, so that R.A.S. henceforth was restricted to the Croydon-Birmingham-Manchester-Liverpool-Belfast-Glasgow route flown for the L.M.S. This complicated intermarriage of various former rivals did not affect Jersey Airways directly, but it gave their board of directors a very useful insight into other people's problems and activities. The Jersey Airways' chairman, W.D.L. Roberts, was also chairman of Scottish Airways, and vice-Chairman of British Airways. Keith Grand had been a director of Railway Air Services since its inception, and before that he had been involved with the Great Western Railway Air Service of 1933. He was now a director of the newly-formed Great Western & Southern Air Lines. Mansbridge was a director of Hay's Wharf Cartage, and a member of the Southern Railway's board Standing Committee on Aerial Transport. J. de C. Ballardie, who had been chairman of both Highland Airways and Northern & Scottish, and was one of the original British Airways directors, retired at the end of 1938, and his place was taken by the Hon. H. Morgan-Grenville.

The recommendation of the Maybury Committee to license internal air lines was implemented on September 16, 1938 when the provisions of the Air Navigation (Licensing of Public Transport) Order, 1938 came into force. To obtain a route licence the company had to submit its proposals to the Licensing Authority, who made them public, normally by placing notices in *Flight* and *The Aeroplane*. If more than one company applied for the same route a public enquiry was required but in general, "sitting tenants" were given favourable treatment. The object was to give one company a complete monopoly of the route for a fixed period, usually seven years for a long-established service. Jersey Airways made four applications (Nos. 31 to 34) for the routes from Jersey to Southampton, London, Exeter, and Brighton, which were received by the Authority on October 14. As there were no objections, nor other applications, provisional licenses were granted, followed by full licenses on 21.7.39. Those for Southampton and London were for seven years, and the others for two. Actually, the regulations did not apply to the Channel Islands, only to the U.K. so it was fortunate that there was only one company to consider.

One item that must have appeared on the board meeting agenda of the Airways about this time would have been the question of replacement aircraft. W.D.L. Roberts, of course, knew about the experiences of British Airways; their problems with the D.H. 86A before conversion to 86B (42) and the pros and cons of their mixed fleet, which included Fokker F.XII's Junkers 52's, and Lockheed Electras, with Super-Electra on order. The latter to become better known as the Lockheed 14, or Hudson. Priority in Britain was going to military aircraft under the urgent rearmament schemes, and it would be years before de Havillands could supply a true replacement for the 86 (the Heron). However, they did have a rival to the American Lockheed on the drawing-board, and this was the D.H. 95, Flamingo, an all-metal, high-wing monoplane with two Bristol sleeve-valved radial engines, and a retractable undercarriage. (See Appendix 1D) The Air Ministry was doing all it could to help, and to encourage sales as, apart from performance, its success depended very much on selling price. With a metal aircraft there was a high initial outlay on jigs and tools, and to reduce this outlay to a small proportion of the selling price it had to be spread over a large number of aircraft. The Flamingo would have a max. economical cruising speed of about 200 mph on about 1,000 hp, whereas the 86 cruised at 145 mph on about 700 hp, and it would reduce the flying time on the main Jersey-Southampton run from one hour to about 45 minutes carrying 18 passengers instead of the 86's fourteen (when full loads were available, but would use 48 gallons of petrol against the 36 gallons of the 86. It would cost more than twice the price, and the all-metal construction and radial sleeve-valved engines could be a new experience for most of the existing ground engineers at St Peter's. As the saving of 15 minutes on the Southampton route was really negligible compared with the time taken by the boats, and as they had no need to fear a rival air-line because of the licensing system, the chief effect would be on the balance sheet.

There was good news for all internal air-line operators on December 12 when a White Paper on Civil Air Transport Services announced that £100,000 had been set aside for subsidizing internal air-lines over a period of five years. The rate of subsidy was to be 6d. per capacity ton-mile in the first year, decreasing by ½d per year to 4d. in the last year. Various conditions were laid down, but if new aeroplanes were produced, deemed to be specially suitable for internal air line services, then the top rate could be granted during any year for the operation of such machines. Obviously, the new Flamingo would qualify for this top rate. On December 28, 1938 the Flamingo made its first flight, and the first company to place an order for this new aircraft would be Jersey Airways.

The end of the year financial results showed a profit by Jersey Airways of £4,773, and a loss by Guernsey Airways of £527, but a small profit of £178 by Channel Island Airways made a total net profit of £4,425. No operations were carried out by Guernsey Airways and the major item in its Profit & Loss Account was a loss of £152 on the sale of the Windhover to the Percival Aircraft Co. of Luton for £200.

Note

In the Channel Island Airways' estimates for 1939 the speed and fuel consumption figures allowed for the D.H. 86 were 115 mph and 37 gals./hr. compared with 170 mph and 62 gals./hr. for the D.H. 95.

TABLE 2

FROM ALDERNEY

TO	MLS.	MIN.	AV.MPH.	SHILLINGS SINGLE	RETURN	PENCE PER MILE SINGLE	RETURN
Southampton	100	60	100	35	60	4.2	3.6
	from 6.5.36 until August, 1936						
as above by D.H.86	100			35	60	4.2	3.6
	from 1.12.36 to 10.3.37						
Heston by D.H.86				59.5	99.5		
	from 27.3.36 to 30.11.36						
Guernsey St. Peter Port	25	30	50	12	18	5.8	4.3
	from 6.4.36 to 31.7.36						
Guernsey La Villiaze	See under Guernsey, La Villiaze						
Jersey St. Helier	See under Jersey, St. Helier						
Jersey St. Peter's	See under Jersey, St. Peter's.						
FROM GUERNSEY, LA VILLIAZE							
Southampton	118	60	118	42.5	66	4.3	3.4
	from 5.5.39 to Sept. 1939						
Heston	172	90	115	60	100	4.2	3.5
	from 5.5.39 to Sept. 1939						
Alderney	26	15	104	11.5	18	5.3	4.2
	from 5.5.39 to Sept. 1939						
Exeter	96	50	115	55	80	6.9	5
	from 27.5.39 to Sept. 1939						
Brighton	140	75	112	55	80	4.7	3.4
	from 27.5.39 to Sept. 1939						

In the above tables "Sept. 1939" means the outbreak of war, or the imminence of war, as some services were terminated towards the end of August, and not exactly on Sept. 3rd.

FROM GUERNSEY, L'ERÉE (Cobham Air Routes)							
Bournemouth	100	75	80	35	67	4.2	4
Portsmouth	125	100	75	46	87	4.4	4.2
Croydon	183	135	81	65	114	4.3	3.7
	all from 6.5.35 to 7.7.35						

THE FINAL CHAPTER (1939)

In 1939 Channel Island Airways would reach full maturity, and the years of growth come to an end with the opening of Guernsey airport which would allow the complete route system to be neatly slotted together into its final pattern. Furthermore, they would have a total monopoly of these routes, a Government subsidy to fly them, and the latest type of British aircraft, the Flamingo. They had mail and newspaper contracts, the strongest financial backing, and they were hand-in-glove with the operators of the alternative rail and boat services.

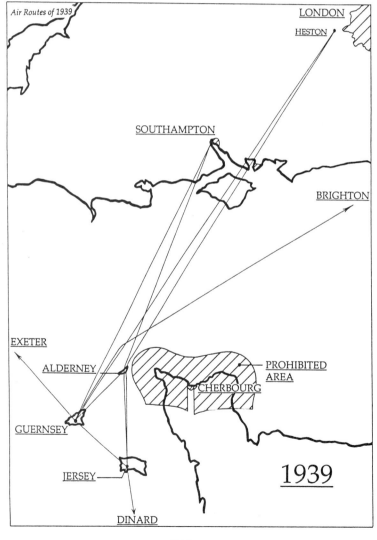

In the precarious world of civil aviation the outlook for both air and ground staff looked almost too good to be true! But there was one dark cloud on the horizon, daily growing more and more ominous, and this was the international situation. Britain was making tremendous efforts to re-arm, but in our weakness we had been forced to accept humiliating accommodations with the dictators. Germany, Italy, and Japan were pursuing aggressive policies, and Franco was winning the Spanish Civil War. Early in the previous year (1938) Hitler had sent his troops into Austria and occupied Vienna. In the autumn he had demanded concessions from Czechoslovakia, and Chamberlain, the British Prime Minister, had flown to Munich to meet Hitler. On September 22 he had again flown to Germany, and when he returned a "State of Emergency" had been declared. This was the "Munich Crisis". The Royal Navy was mobilized, and trenches were dug in the parks, but that was about the limit to our "scabre-rattling" capability. Of modern aircraft the R.A.F. had but two squadrons of Hurricanes and a handful of Spitfires. For the third time Chamberlain saw Hitler, and when he flew back to Heston on September 30, in a B.A.. Lockheed Electra, he had waved in the air a scrap of paper which, he said, meant ". . . peace – in our time". Everyone cheered, but some were doubtful, even Chamberlain, and our efforts to re-arm were redoubled.

G-ACZO "Ouaine Bay" at Heston in 1939 with the new insignia of Guernsey and Jersey Airways (R. Giddings, Poole)

On January 2, 1939 Mr G.O. Waters arrived in Jersey to take over as general manager. After many years in shipping G.O. ("Jo") Waters had joined Imperial Airways at Croydon, and on the formation of Railway Air Services he had been seconded as Commercial Assistant to that company. Towards the end of January bad weather dislocated services, Heston was unusable after heavy rain, and a rather belated Air Ministry notice to Airmen advised pilots to take care when landing at Jersey because of surface water and soft patches. On January 24 "Bill" Caldwell notched up his 3,000th cross-Channel flight and, with the departure of Greig, must have become the longest serving member of the staff. The new chief engineer, to replace Mr H. Greig due to leave on February 18, was Mr A. Lowe from Imperial Airways.

In February, Lt.-Cdr. Fletcher, Labour M.P. for Nuneaton, asked the Secretary of State for Air what action had been taken by the Air Ministry on the report that a British air-liner was nearly struck by a projectile from a British warship in the Channel; if the aircraft was flying over an officially recognised route; and if it belonged to the company that had requested the establishment of an officially recognised air route for its traffic over the Southampton area. Captain Balfour (Under-secretary of State) replied "The incident in question was reported to the Admiralty, and arrangements were made for the interchange of information between that Department and the Air Ministry regarding the areas in which naval exercises are carried out and the routes followed by aircraft on scheduled services. The aircraft, which belonged to Jersey Airways, was not on an officially-recognised air route and was outside the area over which any such route could competently be prescribed. Jersey Airways is the company that asked for the establishment of an officially-recognised air route in the Southampton area". An amusing version of this incident is told by Captain Balfour (the late Lord Balfour of Inchrye): ". . . A Queen Bee, pilotless, wireless-controlled Tiger Moth was flown in mid-Channel. The Queen Bee could only fly straight so here was an opportunity for the Navy to justify their claim that their new multiple pom-pom . . . could shoot out of the sky any aircraft within range . . . After a lot of shooting . . . the Admiral turned to his Gunnery Officer. 'Very strange, Commander, but we don't seem to be able to hit that aircraft.' The Commander put his glass to his eye and replied: 'No Sir, But I think it is a good thing, Sir, as we seem to have been firing at the Jersey Airways' machine for the last five minutes' ..." (33)

The British Industries Fair was held in February, and the States of Jersey participated for the first time. Every day fresh milk, cream, and butter was flown over by Jersey Airways.

JERSEY AIRWAYS
regular daily services

FROM

LONDON in 90 Minutes

180 MILES NON-STOP DIRECT FROM HESTON AIRPORT

SOUTHAMPTON in 1 hour

Also direct from Exeter & Brighton during the Summer Season

WINTER & SUMMER

HOLIDAY TICKETS

These cheap tickets are issued for travel on any Wednesday, Thursday or Friday, provided the return journey is made on or before the following Monday fortnight, excepting on Saturdays in July and August when a supplement is payable.

FREE

Illustrated literature and Time-table containing interesting photos and details of facilities for Advance Baggage and Air-Steamer Ticket Interavailability from Jersey Airways Ltd., Dept. O.G., The Airport, Jersey, C.I. Telegrams: "Chanair, Jersey." Phone: St. Peters 200, Jersey.

FARES

	Single Tickets	RETURN	
		ORDINARY valid 3 months	"HOLIDAY" or "WEEKEND"
LONDON - - -	60/-	100/-	90/-
SOUTHAMPT'N	42/6	66/-	59/6
EXETER and BRIGHTON - -	55/-	80/-	—

An advertisement of 1939

At the end of the month another D.H. 86B, G-AENR, arrived at Eastleigh for Jersey Airways. It had come from Isle of Man Air Services, and was a former stable-companion of G-ADVK with the old Blackpool & West Coast Air Services. In March a party was held at the "Pomme d'Or", and dinner at eight was followed by George Formby in "It's in the Air" at the Forum. The Jersey Airways' party had been a regular annual event but Mr Greig's departure probably made it inappropriate at the end of 1938, and this one allowed the new general manager to meet his staff. One of the guests was Lt.-Cdr. Phillips from the airport, perhaps a diplomatic gesture to reduced any remnants of friction, although Douglas Brecknell did not attend. W.L.G. Butt from Southampton and Jenkins from the London office were amongst those present, and the ladies included Miss Le Selleur and Miss MacFarling. The winter time-table, limited to Heston, Southampton, and Alderney had faced the usual hazards of snow, ice, fog, and flood, but the arrival of spring brought no great improvement in the weather, and West Park was to prove a very convenient emergency landing-ground.

On April 6 a French seaplane came down some five miles S.E. of Jersey, and there was an intensive search by the Jersey lifeboat, Jersey Airways, French aircraft, and a submarine, but it was not found until the following morning. It had drifted all through the night to reach a position off Cap Frehel, about ten miles west of St Malo, where it was taken in tow. There were no allegations that it had been shot down by the British Navy! On April 16 the Heston-Jersey machine was delayed at Eastleigh because of bad weather reports from Jersey, but eventually it took off at 7.14 pm and managed to find its way into St Peter's. Captain Rayer, with wireless-operator Bateman and ten passengers took off just one minute later, but found thick fog at St Peter's and landed on the beach in the dusk at 8.33 pm. The 86 spent the night on the slipway. On April 25 Squadron-Leader Glencross in command of Handley Page Harrow K7026 was approaching the Channel Islands above cloud on a long-distance night flight from Feltwell, Norfolk when both engines iced up. It was 5.50 am and as they came down they sent off an S.O.S. The Guernsey lifeboat was launched, Jersey Airways and R.A.F. machines made a search, and the Channel steamers joined in, but the plane could not be found. The Harrow had emerged from the clouds close to Alderney, and just managed to touch down in a field, but bounced over the hedge into the next field, which turned out to be Alderney aerodrome. They had tried to send a message as they landed but the aerials were swept away and all contact lost. There were no telephones on the island and the Squadron Leader was found sitting on the Post Office steps when it opened at 9 am. The damaged Harrow was left on Alderney until replacements parts could be obtained, but it was August before Rollason's, the well-known Croydon firm could complete the repair work. At Eastleigh the Cunliffe-Owen factory had been opened and their first machine, G-AFMB, was being test flown. Additional D/F facilities were going to be provided to assist with the flight testing of the anticipated large numbers of Spitfires.

Preparations were going ahead for the opening of the Guernsey airport, and Flight-Lieut. Swoffer was appointed chief control officer. Frank Swoffer had been an air traffic controller at the Empire Air Base on Southampton Water, but his experience stretched back to the days of the R.F.C. when, at one stage, he was left for dead in the mortuary (after spinning in from 200 ft). Before transferring to the R.F.C. he had been in the Army, and was wounded at Hill 60. After the war he went flax farming in East Africa, but rejoined the R.A.F. in 1922. His second-in-command was none other than Cecil Noel, who must have realised there was not much future now for L'Erée. La Villiaze (see Appendix 2T) was slightly larger than St Peter's with runs of 800 yds. SW-NE, 900 yds. NW-SE, and 1,000 yds. WNW-ESE, and it had costs £101,500, excluding hangars. The annual outlay was estimated to be £3,936 (£2,600 for salaries) against an estimated income of £3,972. Full night-landing facilities were available, with four floodlights, a rotating beacon, and the usual boundary and obstruction lights. Marconi D/F was in operation, and there was a concrete fog-line. Unlike Jersey, the authorities decided to put on a bit of a show for the opening ceremony which was to take place on May 5 and 600 seats were available on written application. Guernsey Airways had applied for their licenses in November, 1938 (Serial Nos. 56 – 59), the routes being Guernsey to Exeter, Heston, Southampton, and Brighton respectively, and two year provisional licenses were granted from May 5, 1939 (the opening day), followed by full licenses in July. The opening ceremony was performed by the Air Minister himself, Sir Kingsley Wood, and a squadron of Ansons gave a display of formation flying. The modified "C" class flying boat *Australia* was demonstrated by none other than D.C.T. Bennett, the R.A.F. officer who had flown for Jersey Airways in 1934, and he made several very low passes over the aerodrome. One unrehearsed item was provided by the Vickers Wellington bringing Air Chief Marshal Sir Cyril Newall. There was a down-draught near the airport boundary, and the Wellington came in a shade too low. It was caught in the down-draught and dropped on to the boundary fence, tearing away some of the fence and some of the Wellington. Naturally Jersey and Guernsey Airways joined in the activity, and the first plane to leave La Villiaze took W.L.G. Butt back to Southampton with a gift of "rare island blooms" (two to three dozen yellow arum lilies) to be presented to the Queen as she left Portsmouth on the *Empress of Australia*. Other visitors that day included an Airspeed Oxford, Captain and Mrs de Havilland in a hired Rapide (their own Dragonfly having a defective air speed indicator), and Shell's Hornet Moth, the only single-engined machine.

On May 8 the London dailies were on sale in Guernsey, and the Guernsey air mail was inaugurated when Captain B. Walker left Eastleigh at 8 am in G-ACZP to reach La Villiaze at 8.59 am. As with the Jersey air mail, there was no extra fee, and the G.P.O. decided whether the letter went by sea or air. On normal weekdays the night boat left Southampton at 11.45 pm, and mail too late for this went by air. Mail carried by sea was delivered by the 8 am post, and mail carried by air was delivered in St Peter Port (and parts of St Sampson) by the 10.45 am post. The biggest saving, some 22 hours, was in the period October to May at the week-ends because there was no night boat on Sundays.

FIRST FLIGHT COVER

Airmail Service,
Southampton to Guernsey,
Channel Islands.
Inaugurated May 8th,
1939.

BY AIR MAIL

Mr. R. Terbrache,
Wairoa,
Green Lanes,
Guernsey,
Channel Islands.

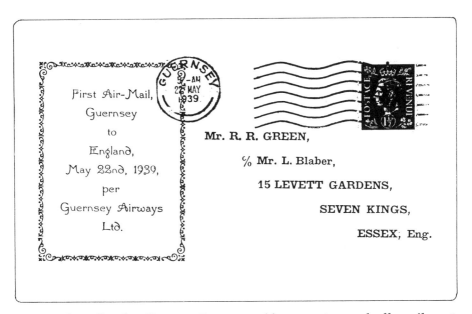

First Air-Mail,
Guernsey
to
England,
May 22nd, 1939,
per
Guernsey Airways
Ltd.

Mr. R. R. GREEN,

% Mr. L. Blaber,

15 LEVETT GARDENS,

SEVEN KINGS,

ESSEX, Eng.

For the benefit of collectors Guernsey Airways stamped all mail sent through them with a special cachet, although, in the normal course of events, mail is carried in sealed bags, delivered to one aerodrome and collected from the other by G.P.O. staff, and the air-line personnel have no access to it. In the opposite direction the Guernsey air mail service started on May 22 when Captain John Pugh in G-ADVK with radio-operator T. McCave left St Peter's at 6 am and landed at La Villiaze 15 min. later with inter-island mail. He then took off from La Villiaze at 6.28 for Eastleigh with the Guernsey mail for the mainland, as well as nine passengers including a journalist and a photographer from the *Guernsey Evening Press*, so a very full account of the event appeared in that night's paper. They crossed at 2,000 feet, and landed at 7.25 am to be met by W.L.G. Butt of the Airways, and L.F. Payne, the airport manager. There were two despatches of mail daily from Guernsey, and the latest times of posting at the Smith St. head office were 5 am and 2.15 pm. The early post obtained delivery in London and much of Southern England in the morning or early afternoon, and as far north as Leicester the same day, whilst the second despatch obtained delivery the following morning. John Pugh had only recently joined Guernsey Airways, but had flown for Jersey Airways for a brief period some years earlier. He was best known for his two years of meteorological flying during his R.A.F. service when he ascended almost daily to 28,000 ft. from Duxford. He had flown with the Hon. Mrs Victor Bruce on her attempt at the endurance record in the Saro Windhover. In 1935 he flew between Heston and the North West for United Airways, and then spent two years on the night mails from Croydon to Cologne and Hanover before going out to Singapore as chief pilot to Wearne's. The chief control officer at Eastleigh, J.D. Parkinson, was being replaced by Arthur Russell, who had been flying since 1912. He was in the R.F.C. and R.A.F. from 1913 until 1927 and he spent three years as a prisoner-of-war after being shot down by the German "ace", Boelke. From 1927 to 1937 he was at Croydon and in October, 1937 he was appointed Area Control Officer at Manchester. Mr E.O. Rounds, Jersey Airways' assistant manager at Eastleigh was to leave soon, also, for the Straight Corporation. He had been at Eastleigh about twelve months after a year at Heston as traffic manager. He held a Master's ticket and had been at sea until 1934 having completed his education on the *Worcester*. At a rather higher level, K.W.C. Grand, on the board of all the Channel Island Airways companies, as well as G.W. & S., was appointed principal assistant to the G.W.R. General Manager. Eastleigh airport was costing the rate-payers about £4,500 per annum but, undeterred, work was starting on a new £50,000 terminal building. More Lockheed 14's were on their way across the Atlantic for erection in the Eastleigh hangars, but these where for Aer Lingus and probably for the Croydon-Dublin service. Landing fees at Eastleigh were 9d. per 1,000 lb. calculated on the max. laden weight of the machine, plus 1/6d. per passenger embarked or disembarked, and 1/6d. per 150 lbs. of freight embarked or disembarked. In Guernsey new offices for Channel Island Airways were being built on the South Esplanade, St Peter Port.

An abbreviated summer service started as soon as La Villiaze opened, but, in compliance with their licences, direct services to Heston and Eastleigh from Jersey were flown by Jersey Airways and those from Guernsey by Guernsey Airways. In the high summer season the Exeter and Brighton services would be shared. The maximum subsidy for any one company had been fixed at £15,000 but Channel Island Airways were hoping that Jersey Airways and Guernsey Airways would be treated as two separate companies. Instead of JERSEY AIRWAYS LTD the 86's now carried a winged emblem containing the coats of arms of the two islands with GUERNSEY & JERSEY AIRWAYS beneath.

On May 10 Douglas Brecknell who had now flown over 4,000 hours in 25 different types of aircraft, arrived from Eastleigh with eight passengers at the scheduled time of 6.05 pm, but there was fog at St Peter's so he landed at West Park. He was due to leave St Peter's for Guernsey and Southampton at 6.30 pm so, under the circumstances, he did well to get away from West Park at 6.50 pm with his three passengers. His brother, Adrian, formerly the station officer at Guernsey in the flying-boat days was now at a diamond mine in Transvaal, and in his place was E.V. Wieland (brother to R.A.R.). The Guernsey Airways' superintendent was A.W. Berry, who had come into aviation after 20 years in shipping, and in addition to H. Wellock, station engineer, there was a cashier, six clerks, and two young ladies for secretarial work. The Alderney service now ran to Guernsey instead of Jersey, as Guernsey is the nearer, and has closer political ties, but it was a severe blow to former patrons of the direct Jersey-Alderney service who had to catch the 6 am plane to Guernsey and change, for which they were charged an extra 18/- on the return fare. Jersey Airways' joint operation of the Dinard route started on May 23, and again it was on Tuesdays and Thursdays leaving St Peter's at 1.55 pm and Dinard at 2.30 pm with 25 min. flying time. The Exeter and Brighton services were resumed on May 27, via Guernsey, and this gave a reporter from the *Guernsey Star* an eventful day. He arrived at La Villiaze just before 11.30 am and a card was thrust into his hand which said "SIT HALF WAY ALONG PLANE"; the door slammed, and they were off. The pilot was G.F. Hales and the radio-operator A.H. Clapham, and there were three other passengers, one of whom was Mr Berry the superintendent. At Exeter they were met by Mr Parkhouse, the airport manager, and Mr Brumham, the station officer for G.W. & S. Air Lines. Returning to La Villiaze the Star journalist then flew to Shoreham with Captain Israel, and again they were looked after by the local G.W. & S. station officer. In June the long-drawn out case of Simpson v. Guernsey Airways ended with an amicable settlement, and Lt.-Cdr. Phillips left St Peter's to take an appointment with the Admiralty, whilst R.F. Bulstrode left the Eastleigh control tower to take charge of Ringway. From Guernsey little Olive Gallez was flown to Eastleigh in 39 minutes by Jersey Airways and on to Heston in a special plane provided by the *Daily Express*. From Heston she was taken to Great Ormonde St. Hospital to have an open safety-pin removed from her throat by Mr Simpson-Smith, Cobham Air

Routes' old customer.

The week-end service to Dinard restarted on July 1 and, said L'Ouest Éclair: "Les Dinardais ont pu voir évoluer au-dessus de la ville vers 11 heures hier le superbe avion trimoteur Wibault de la Compagnie Air France que effectuait le premier service aérienne de Paris à Dinard pour la saison 1939 . . ." (72) Unfortunately the Wibault was not seen over Jersey until the following week-end because the pilot taxied on to an unfinished part of the aerodrome and the heavy machine sank in the mud.

Passengers boarding a Wibault 283 at Le Bourget
Musée de l'Air et de l'Espace   (droits réservés)

This year the Wibault was scheduled to leave Le Bourget at 11 am and was allowed 110 minutes for the flight. The Jersey flights left Dinard at 1.05 pm on Saturdays, 8.30 am and 6 pm on Sundays, and 7.40 am on Mondays with a 25 min. flying time. In the opposite direction there were flights from Jersey at 2 pm on Saturdays, 9.30 am and 6.45 pm on Sundays, and 8.25 am on Mondays. The Saturday afternoon departure on July 22 was delayed about six hours when one of the engines refused to start and the Air France mechanic Richard Albert received a nasty blow on the arm while swinging the prop. It is not known whether this was the same mechanic (Air France mechanics were usually called by their Christian names) as the Richard who climbed on to the wing of a Farman Goliath over the Channel, back in September 1924, to repair some damage, and being unable to do so, lay on the wing with one leg dangling in space and held the two ends of a broken pipe together for 45 minutes until the pilot was able to land at Lympne. The Colorado beetle was still cause for concern and aircraft landing from Dinard were thoroughly inspected, the interiors vacuum-cleaned, and the dust-bags burned. Passengers and baggage were liable to inspection, also. At Eastleigh on July 1 the white ensign was raised as the Admiralty took over the Fleet Air Arm base, now H.M.S. *Raven*, in accordance with the latest policy, and the aerodrome was being fitted with Lorenz blind-landing equipment at a cost of £4,500.

The D.H. "Flamingo", G-AFUE, at La Villiaze in 1939 (R.A.F. Museum)

Also the shortest landing run of 800 yards was being increased to 1,000 yards, and the white chalk fog-line moved to coincide with the Lorenz beam. After numerous complaints the Jersey-Alderney fares were reduced to £1 single, 31/6d. return, and the times adjusted to allow a 7.40 am departure from St Peter's. On Sunday, 2nd July there was a surprise visit to St Peter's by the prototype Flamingo, G-AFUE, flown by Geoffrey de Havilland, jnr. on test. After two local flights it returned to Heston and Hatfield. This machine, which was on loan, had seats for 12 passengers, but the production models would carry 18. The following day it was flown to Eastleigh in the evening, and spent the Tuesday morning on practice landings before flying to Jersey and back via Guernsey to make its first landing at La Villiaze. There were more practice landings on the Wednesday and a return trip to Hatfield and on the 6th it was flown to Jersey with Mr Israel as co-pilot. The Flamingo spent the whole day in Jersey on local flying, presumably for the benefit of the Airways' pilots, and stayed overnight before returning to Eastleigh in 45 minutes. This was Friday, July 7 and in the evening two Ansons, lead by Flight-Lieut. Joualt, arrived over St Peter's at the same time as the Airways' Exeter and Heston machines, but the airfield was shrouded in mist and both 86's landed on the beach, followed by one of the Ansons. Flight-Lieut Joualt was recalled to Thorney Island whilst he was still circling and waiting for the mist to clear. According to *The Aeroplane* the pilot of the beach Anson asked one of the Airways' pilots if he could picket down for the night: ". . . and was given permission most heartily. Later, when the liner was about to leave for the airport, the Ansoneer asked why, to which the Jersey pilot replied that the tide was just beginning its usual 40-ft. rise and he was forbidden to picket out under water . . ." On July 10 the final link in the air mail system was made by the first despatch of inter-island mail from Guernsey to Jersey and it was during this month that Mr Thurgood resigned from the board and sold all his holdings so that Channel Island Airways became 50% Whitehall Securities, 25% G.W.R. and 25% S.R.

On July 8, with Mr Caldwell as co-pilot, the Flamingo was flown to Birmingham for the official opening of Elmdon aerodrome. More flights followed with mails and newspapers over the Heston and Eastleigh routes and on July 12 a party of London Press men, including Charles Brown, the photographer, were taken on a tour of the Islands. 'UE was scheduled to leave Heston at 10 am, circle Alderney at 10.50 am, and cruise over Sark, Herm, and Jethou to arrive Guernsey at 11.10 am. In fact it landed at La Villiaze at 11.05 am.

A couple of days later more journalists, some from the aeronautical press were given a similar day out with Bill Caldwell at the controls (without Geoffrey de Havilland in company), hence this flight of the Flamingo was well and truly reported:- "Clouds hung low over Heston on the morning of July 14, and QBI placards over the control tower railings . . ." They flew at 3,000' in cloud at 180 mph until they crossed the coast into clear weather ". . . probably quieter than any other machine of its class, and sheer smoothness of travel is helped considerably by the fact that it is normally flown at a good deal less than 60% full power. More important . . . is the ample power reserve which this fact implies . . . apart from single-engined performance, this means, with constant-speed airscrews, that the take-off is very short indeed . . . A steep approach and short landing largely depend on piloting skill, but a good take-off and initial rate-of-climb can only, so to speak, be designed into the machine . . . Some 25 degrees of flap are used for the take-off . . ." The wind at La Villiaze was from the same direction as it was on the opening day ". . . when the short, down-hill run embarrassed both civil and military pilots . . . The Flamingo sailed in 30 feet over the fence (repaired) and pulled up near the middle of the aerodrome . . . The runs used on this day were about 700 yards . . ."

The D.H. "Flamingo", G-AFUE, crossing the coast near Portsmouth (R.A.F. Museum)

The high wing layout and good view was much appreciated "Both on the way to Jersey via Guernsey and during the return journey the Flamingo was being generally flown at about 52% full power – 460 hp from each engine . . . Whilst the prototype has normal constant-speed airscrews the later production machines will have de Havilland Hydromatics, with a consequent improvement in the already good single-engined performance figures and an increase in the maximum possible all-up weight . . . On the outward journey Alderney was reached, against a 20 mph head wind, in two minutes less than an hour, giving an average speed of 167 mph, while the entire run from Jersey to Heston was afterwards made in 52 minutes, an average of 226 mph. The ground speed thus averaged out at 196 mph for the two journeys . . ." (3, 20)

The young de Havilland test pilot was back with the Flamingo on the 15th as it was intended to go into regular service with passengers on that date, but there was a problem with the oil system and it was the 20th before the first fare-paying passenger was able to step on board. Geoffrey de Havilland's log-book shows the extent of the day's flying:-

The figures in brackets are the scheduled times.

(0800)	(0900)	(0915)
0745 Dep. Eastleigh	0835 Arr. Guernsey	0850 Dep. Guernsey
(0930)	(1030)	(1045)
0900 Arr. Jersey	1050 Dep. Jersey	1100 Arr. Guernsey
(1100)	(1230)	(1300)
1130 Dep Guernsey	1220 Arr. Heston	1315 Dep. Heston
(1430)	(1445)	(1500)
1425 Arr. Guernsey	1445 Dep. Guernsey	1500 Arr. Jersey
(1530)	(1630)	
1555 Dep. Jersey	1625 Arr. Eastleigh (66)	

Entries in the log-book of Geoffrey R. de Haviland for 20.7.39.

From the D.H. Museum Hatfield by courtesy of British Aerospace

His last flight before handing over to the Airways' pilots took place on July 24, after which the Flamingo carried out an intensive programme of mail, newspaper, and passenger services with just the occasional interruption from "teething" troubles. Favourably impressed Jersey Airways ordered three, said to be at a cost of £25,000 each.

The normal radius of the controlled zone of an aerodrome for QBI weather conditions was 5 miles, but Eastleigh was larger and somewhat elongated to include the flying-boat terminal at Hythe. Towards the end of July with QBI in force the control officer at Eastleigh had a telephone call from a Baddesley resident to say that a plane was circling overhead obviously "lost". Quite a sensible thing to do because, if the plane had radio, they could tell the pilot where he was. Actually it was the Great Western & Southern Rapide waiting to take its "turn for landing" after three machines from the Channel Islands. Later in the month when QBI conditions prevailed again at Eastleigh the *Southern Daily Echo* described the somewhat primitive methods still in vogue when the Jersey Airways' machine flew overhead although invisible from the ground. The control officer stood out on the tarmac and when he heard the engines a message was sent to the aircraft "motors over". In this case the pilot was dead on track, but, if not overhead he would be told "motors north" or as appropriate. The Lorenz equipment at Eastleigh had been tested and was just awaiting Air Ministry acceptance so that Britain now had three aerodromes with this latest device, Croydon and Heston being the other two, although there were alternative systems in use. Over England there was considerable air activity by the R.A.F. and sometimes the French air force, and civil aircraft on charter to the Air Ministry were flying to and fro by day and by night, often without navigation lights, for the benefit of our anti-aircraft defences. As well as Spitfires and Hurricanes the "shadow" factories were turning out Fairey Battles and Bristol Blenheims, and our first batch of conscripts had been called up.

In the middle of August the two huge Imperial Airways biplanes *Scylla* and *Syrinx* arrived at Eastleigh for storage and although the new large hangar had a 30' clearance to the roof these two machines could only be put inside by lowering the radio masts and letting the air out of the tyres. The headlines of the *Guernsey Star* for August 21 read "DO YOU WANT SUNDAY CINEMAS?", but late that night came the announcement of a Russo-German Non-Aggression Pact. German troops were moving towards the Polish border and Parliament was recalled from its Summer Recess. The headlines of the *Southern Daily Echo* for August 24 were "THE PREMIER'S GRAVE WORDS" which included his statement that: ". . . the international situation has steadily deteriorated until to-day we find ourselves confronted with the imminent peril of war." On Friday, 25th the head-lines were "HITLER CONFERS WITH MILITARY CHIEFS" and the last British newspapermen left Berlin for Copenhagen. The British Embassy was "packing" and M. Daladier was about to make a broadcast. The French Government advised those whose presence in Paris was not indispensable to evacuate the capital. In the Channel Islands holiday-makers were taking the advice of the regular Jersey Airways' advert on the front page of the *Evening Post*: "LET'S FLY HOME" and returning in large numbers. On August 26 the head-lines ran "HITLER SENDS PEACE PLAN TO LONDON" and the signing of a mutual assistance pact between the U.K. and Poland was reported. On the 28th the Air France Dinard service ended with the announcement from Paris that: "À partir d'aujourd'hui les lignes aériennes suivant sont suspendues:- Paris-Bucarest, Paris-Berlin, Paris-Le Touquet, Paris-Bordeaux-Biarritz, ainsi que toutes les lignes saisonières . . ." Jersey Airways were limiting their services to Dinard and Southampton with Heston, Brighton, and Exeter passengers having to make their various ways from Southampton as best as they could. The headlines "BRITAIN SENDS HER REPLY TO HITLER" were followed in the ensuing days by "LITTLE CHANGE IN THE SITUATION", "BRITAIN WRITING AGAIN TO HITLER" and "EVACUATION: NO NEED FOR ANY ALARM".

Fig. 6a

On September 1 Germany attacked Poland and the headlines read "GERMAN PUSH IN POLAND" on the 2nd they read "WORLD AWAITING GERMAN REPLY" and on Sunday, September 3 Britain declared war on Germany. The first summer season of the full Channel Island Airways' network had come to a premature end. Figs. 6a, b and c show the complete time-table of Guernsey and Jersey Airways (neglecting Dinard) as given in Bradshaw's International Air Guide for August, 1939. There was no September issue.

Fig. 6b

9C (Jersey)—GUERNSEY—EXETER
GUERNSEY AIRWAYS

Miles	Airports of				Airports of		S	
	Jersey ... ...dep	10 45			EXETER ... ...dep	12 30		
	Guernsey ... ...arr	11 0			GUERNSEY ... ...arr	13 20		
		S			Guernsey ... ...dep	13 30		
0	GUERNSEY ... ...dep	11 10			Jersey ... ...arr	13 45		
96	EXETER ... ...arr	12 0						

S—On Saturdays and Sundays

Distance from Town to Airport—See page 22 Note A respecting Car Conveyance

TOWN	AIRPORT	TOWN TERMINUS	Miles	Minutes
ST. HELIER	St. Peter's	Airway Terminus, St. Helier, by Bus—Fare	5	40
ST. PETER PORT ...	Guernsey	South Esplanade, St. Peter Port—Fare	3½	40
EXETER	Municipal............	⎰ St. David's Railway Station by Coach	6	45
		⎱ Central Railway Station by Coach	5	40

9D GUERNSEY—JERSEY (Inter Island Service)
GUERNSEY AIRWAYS

Miles	Airports of	R	E	S	D	Airports of	R	E	S	D
0	GUERNSEY... ...dep	7 15	8 50	10 15	19 5	JERSEY ... ...dep	7 40	9 15	9 45	19 30
24	JERSEY ... ... arr	7 30	9 5	10 30	19 20	GUERNSEY ... ... arr	7 55	9 30	10 0	19 45

D Daily.   E Daily except Saturdays.   S Saturdays only.
R Sundays, Mondays, Wednesdays, Fridays.

10 LONDON—JERSEY
JERSEY AIRWAYS

Miles	Airports of	R	B	R	B		
0	HESTON ... ...dep	13 0	13 0	17 0	17 0		
172	GUERNSEY ... ... arr	:	14 30	:	18 30		
	,, ...dep	:	14 45	:	18 45		
196	JERSEY ... ... arr	14 30	15 0	18 30	19 0		
	Airports of	B	R	B	R		
	JERSEY ... ...dep	10 30	11 0	14 30	15 0		
	GUERNSEY ... ... arr	10 45	:	14 45	:		
	,, ...dep	11 0	:	15 0	:		
	HESTON ... ... arr	12 30	12 30	16 30	16 30		

B Daily except Saturdays and Sundays.   R Saturdays and Sundays only.

11 — SOUTHAMPTON—JERSEY
JERSEY AIRWAYS

Mls.	Mls.	Airports of	W	S	R	R	E	R	R	D	R	S	F	S
0	0	SOUTHAMPTON ...dep	8 0	9 30	11 0	12 0	12 15	14 0	15 0	17 0	18 0	20 0	20 30	21 0
118	...	GUERNSEY ... ... arr	9 0											
...	...	,, ... dep	9 15											
142	129	JERSEY ... ... arr	9 30	10 35	12 5	13 5	13 20	15 5	16 5	18 5	19 5	21 5	21 35	22 5

Airports of	W	S	R	D	R	R	D	R	E	S	F	N	S
JERSEY ... ... dep	6 0	8 0	9 30	10 30	12 30	13 30	15 30	16 30	18 30	18 30	19 0	19 0	19 30
GUERNSEY ... arr	6 15								18 45				
,, ... dep	6 30								19 0				
SOUTHAMPTON arr	7 30	9 0	10 30	11 30	13 30	14 30	16 30	17 30	20 0	19 30	20 0	20 0	20 30

D Daily. E Daily except Sats. and Suns. F Fris. and Sats. only. N Sundays only.
R Sats. and Suns. only. S Saturdays only. W Weekdays only.

12A — SOUTHAMPTON—GUERNSEY
GUERNSEY AIRWAYS

Miles	Airports of	W	R	B	R	D	S
0	SOUTHAMPTON ... ...dep	8 0	11 0	12 15	14 0	17 0	20 0
118	GUERNSEY ... ...arr	9 0	12 0	13 15	15 0	18 0	21 0

Airports of	W	R	B	R	D	S	E
GUERNSEY ... ...dep	6 30	9 30	10 30	12 30	15 30	18 30	19 0
SOUTHAMPTON ... ...arr	7 30	10 30	11 30	13 30	16 30	19 30	20 0

B Daily except Sats. and Suns. D Daily. E Daily except Sats. R On Sats. and Suns. only.
S Sats. only. W Weekdays only.

12 — LONDON—GUERNSEY
GUERNSEY AIRWAYS

Miles	Airports of	D	D		Airports of	D	D
0	HESTON... ... ...dep	13 0	17 0		GUERNSEY ... ...dep	11 0	15 0
172	GUERNSEY ... ... arr	14 30	18 30		HESTON ... ... arr	12 30	16 30

D Daily

Distance from Town to Airport—See page 22 Note A respecting Car Conveyance

TOWN	AIRPORT	TOWN TERMINUS	Miles	Minutes
LONDON	Heston	Channel Islands, Air Office, Hudson Place, Victoria Station, S.W. 1	12	60
ST. PETER PORT	Guernsey	South Esplanade, St. Peter Port—Fare	3½	40

13 — JERSEY—BRIGHTON
(Service on Fridays and Mondays)
JERSEY AIRWAYS

Miles	Airports of		Airports of	
0	JERSEY ... ...dep	15 0	BRIGHTON ... ...dep	17 15
24	GUERNSEY ... ... arr	15 15	GUERNSEY ... ... arr	18 30
	,, ... dep	15 30	,, ... dep	18 45
164	BRIGHTON ... ... arr	16 45	JERSEY ... ... arr	19 0

14 — JERSEY—EXETER
(Service on Fridays and Mondays)
JERSEY AIRWAYS

Miles	Airports of		Airports of	
0	JERSEY ... ...dep	10 45	EXETER ... ...dep	12 30
24	GUERNSEY ... ... arr	11 0	GUERNSEY ... ... arr	13 20
	,, ... dep	11 10	,, ... dep	13 30
120	EXETER ... ... arr	12 0	JERSEY ... ... arr	13 45

From Bradshaw's International Air Guide – August, 1939

The history of British internal air lines between the wars ends on September 3, 1939, but not the history of Channel Island Airways. Aircraft and personnel were placed at the disposal of the Government, and all the 86's transferred to the National Air Communications scheme for the urgent transport of men and materials wherever required, usually France. The Flamingo was returned to its owners, to go, eventually, to No. 24 Squadron, R.A.F. at Hendon for communications work. However, the value of an air link to the Channel Islands was soon appreciated, and on October 24 permission was given for a limited service from Shoreham to Jersey and Guernsey. During the quiet period sometimes referred to as "the phoney war", more aircraft became available, and over the Easter of 1940 they were able to provide a modest Bank Holiday "rush" to the Islands, and there was even talk of preparations for a summer influx of visitors, but Hitler's drive through the Low Countries, the evacuation of Dunkirk, and the fall of France, altered the situation completely. The limited service was terminated on June 15, and thereafter every attempt was made to carry to the mainland anything or anybody considered to be of value to the war effort. Between dawn on June 19 and noon on June 21 some 320 people were evacuated to Bristol, via Exeter, and the work of the Jersey and Guernsey Airways' pilots was praised in the House of Commons. Only one aircraft was lost, and this was the 86B, G-ADVK, which was in the middle of an overhaul, and had to be left behind, after being made even more unserviceable. The remaining five 86's were taken over by the Fleet Air Arm, as were most of the staff from G. O. Waters down, but by August, 1940, G-ACZP and G-AENR had been released to join the Railway Air Services fleet based at Speke to operate limited civilian services for the Associated Airways Joint Committee on behalf of the Air Ministry. Between June 21, 1940 and June 21, 1945 no services were flown by Channel Island Airways.

For the year ending December 31, 1939 there was a combined profit of about £11,000, thanks to the subsidies, and Channel Island Airways, reported that a net revenue "after taking credit for dividend and bonus proposed by their subsidiary company, Jersey Airways Ltd., and appropriating £1,356 to an Investment Depreciation Reserve in respect of their holding of shares in Guernsey Aero Club Ltd." (14) amounted to £3,056. With a balance of £2,969 carried over from the previous year this made a total of £6,025, of which £1,525 was carried forward to leave £4,500 for distribution as a dividend of 3% (on £150,000), less States of Jersey income tax. As the G.W.R. pointed out, this was the first dividend to be paid since they had acquired an interest in the firm.

See YOU later

Channel Island Airways had purchased 50% of the issued capital of Guernsey Aero Club Ltd. in May, 1939 from British & Foreign Aviation Ltd., the mainly Olley group which had joined with the railways to form

Great Western & Southern Air Lines Ltd. Mr Mansbridge died in December, 1940 and in March, 1941 Mr John Elliott of the S.R. was appointed in his place. At the end of 1942 the Hon. Clive Pearson agreed to sell all the 75,000 shares held by Whitehall Securities to the two railway companies at 23/6d. per £1 ordinary share so that, from December 31, 1942, Channel Island Airways became completely railway owned by the G.W.R. and S.R. as equal partners. W.D.L. Roberts and Morgan-Grenville resigned from the board in consequence, but Mr Roberts was reappointed. The directors were now K. Grand (chairman), J. Elliot and W.D.L. Roberts, with J.A. Perree as president (but not a director).

Subsequent board meetings during the war years must have been largely formalities although they probably tried to make plans for the brave, new, post-war world. With the fighting turning in favour of the Allies, and the invasion of Normandy, the position of the Germans in the Channel Islands became increasingly difficult and eventually the Luftwaffe abandoned their bases at St Peter's and La Villiaze, and the airfields were left in an unusable state with mines and various obstacles scattered about. In May, 1945 the Channel Islands were liberated, and on May 26, a hired Rapide, G-AGLP, was flown to Jersey with a group of Airways' staff led by G.O. Waters, now Commander Waters, to see what the prospects were of restarting services. A regular scheduled service was begun on June 21 using Rapide G-AGPH between Croydon, Guernsey, and Jersey. Further Rapides were soon obtained and by mid-July there were three services daily, with a Jersey-Guernsey inter-island service from July 18. None of the old 86's returned although 'ZP and 'NR survived on the R.A.S. routes from Speke to Croydon, Glasgow, Belfast, and Dublin. The rather cumbersome title of "Jersey and Guernsey Airways" was dropped on September 1, 1945 and "Channel Island Airways" used instead, which was much more convenient. On September 10, by which time 2,000 post-war passengers had been carried, the Southampton service was restarted, and by November 24 10,000 passengers had been carried. By the beginning of 1946 there were three services a day from Croydon, and five from Southampton, and on February 1 Alderney was restored to the time-table. The C.I.A. fleet consisted of six Rapides all painted in the original D.H. 86 colours of silver with orange lettering outlined in black. By the summer of 1946 a Douglas Dakota, on loan from the Air Ministry, was flying on the Croydon route, and on July 1 Bristol Wayfarer, G-AGVB, the first British post-war aircraft to enter air-line service, made its debut on the Croydon-Channel Islands route, with Northolt replacing Croydon later.

Prospects looked good, but the post-war British Government had announced that "public ownership shall be the over-ruling principle in air transport . . ." It had also announced its intention of nationalizing the four main-line railway companies, and as two of these owned Channel Island Airways it looked as though the nationalization of Channel Island Airways would be virtually automatic. But the Channel Islanders did not see it that way; they regarded the Airways as their own, and opposition to nationalization by the British Government was fierce. There were plans for shares to be sold in the Channel Islands, and for Channel Islands directors to sit on the board, but it was of no avail. With a heavy hand the U.K. Government ended the fight by threatening to refuse the entry of Channel Islands Airways aircraft to mainland airports, and on 31.3.47 Channel Island Airways ceased to exist. Its place was taken by British European Airways.

```
                            TABLE   3
                    Time-Table for August, 1938

JERSEY-PORTSMOUTH   60 minutes flying time.          S   Sats & Suns. also
  Dep. St. Peter's    9.30am S,  10.30am M,  3.30pm D        August 1.
  Dep. Portsmouth    11.00am S,  12.15pm M,  5.00pm D    M  Mons. & Fridays,
      D  Fridays, Sats. Sundays, and Mondays                except August 1.
JERSEY-LONDON, VIA PORTSMOUTH 100 minutes overall - Tuesday, Wednesday,Thursday.
  Dep. St. Peter's  10.50am   2.50pm
  Dep. Heston       12.50pm   4.50pm

JERSEY-LONDON, DIRECT  90 minutes      Friday to Monday, incl.
  Dep. St. Peter's  11.00am   3.00pm
  Dep. Heston        1.00pm   5.00pm

JERSEY-SOUTHAMPTON  60-65 minutes.
  Dep. St. Peter's  6.25am W,  9.30am S,  10.30am D,  3.30pm D,  6.30pm R
  Dep. Eastleigh    7.55am W, 11.00am S,  12.15pm D,  5.00pm D,  8.00pm R
 W Weekdays,  S Saturdays & Sundays,  D Daily,  R Saturdays.

JERSEY-EXETER  60 minutes    Saturdays and Mondays
  Dep. St. Peter's  12.30pm         Dep. Clyst Honiton  2.00pm

JERSEY-BRIGHTON  75 minutes  Fridays, Saturdays, Sundays, & Mondays.
  Dep. St. Peter's  2.30pm          Dep. Shoreham  4.15pm

JERSEY-ALDERNEY  20 minutes
  Dep. St. Peter's  12.15pm T,  1.30pm S      S Sundays
  Dep. Alderney      2.00pm S,  2.20pm T      T Tuesdays & Thursdays
```

AIRCRAFT

(A) SUPERMARINE

During the First World War Supermarine built a number of A.D. FLYING BOATS to the design of the Admiralty Air Department. These were pusher biplanes with a crew of two, each in a separate cockpit forward of the wings, and when fitted with the 200 hp Hispano engine had a max. speed of 100 mph and a max. weight of 3,567 lbs. Top wing span was 50' 4" but that of the bottom wing only 39' 7" to give a wing area of 455 sq. ft. The engine was mounted just below the top wing in a narrow centre-section bay fitted with side curtains, and there were two normal wing bays outboard. The wooden hull was of the monocoque design developed by Major Linton Hope, and it could be fitted with jettisonable wheels, for take-off only, from the deck of a carrier. After the War ten A.D. flying-boats were modified by Supermarine to carry three passengers, two side-by-side in a cockpit immediately in front of the pilot, who sat just forward of the wings, and one in a third cockpit in the bow. With a water-rudder for convenience in joy-riding, and a 160 hp Beardmore engine it was called the SUPERMARINE CHANNEL I. Top speed was 80 mph and max. all-up weight 3,400 lbs. A later version with a more powerful engine became the CHANNEL II.

In 1920 Supermarine entered a special machine called the COMMERCIAL AMPHIBIAN for an Air Ministry Competition which was based on the prototype of a deck-landing amphibian they were designing called the SUPERMARINE SEAL. The sole COMMERCIAL AMPHIBIAN (G-EAVE) was to the same basic configuration as the Channel but had a 350 hp Rolls Royce Eagle VIII engine and an all-up weight of 5,700 lbs. The top wing span was 50', almost the same as the Channel, but the bottom wing span was increased to 47' to give a wing area of 600 sq. ft. Two passengers could be carried in a glazed cabin, and the aircraft came second in the Competition. G-EAVE's life was brief, but the lessons of the Competition were incorporated in the building of another deck-landing amphibian called the SUPERMARINE SEAL II which had a 450 hp Napier Lion engine driving a tractor airscrew. The pilot, forward, was separated from his crew, aft, by the fuel tanks! The prototype took the R.A.F. number N146, but after considerable modification in which the span was reduced to 46' it was renamed the SUPERMARINE SEAGULL. Later versions had the fuel tanks in the top wing giving gravity-feed to the engine and removing the barrier between pilot and crew. The SEAGULL II was fitted with the 492 hp Napier Lion IIB whilst the SEAGULL III had the Lion V, and both retained the 46' span with a wing area of 593 sq. ft.

Similar in many ways to the Seagull was the SUPERMARINE SEA EAGLE with wings of 46' span but having a 360 hp Rolls Royce Eagle IX driving a pusher propeller. Fuel was carried in the top wing but the hull, forward of the wings, had the lines of a sea-going cabin cruiser with a stout stem to plough through rough water, and the six passengers sat in a covered cabin, although the pilot was in the open. Max. speed was 93 mph and max. all-up weight 6,050 lbs. They were designed for the cross-Channel services of the B.M.A.N. Co., and the two taken over by Imperial Airways were modified subsequently by the fitting of 450 hp Napier Lion engines and larger top wings. In their final state they had a cruising speed of about 90 mph, and a max. all-up weight of 6,500 lbs. Only three Sea Eagles were built:- G-EBFK registration cancelled 21.5.24: G-EBGR withdrawn from use 1929: and G-EBGS accidentally sunk at her moorings in St Peter Port harbour 14/15.12.26.

It is of interest that the Seagull designs continued through the WALRUS to its final version the SEA OTTER of 10,000 lbs. max. weight with a 965 hp Bristol Mercury engine driving a tractor airscrew to give a max. speed of 163 mph. The wing span was still 46', and the wing area 610 sq. ft. One of the SEAGULL II machines, N9605, was subsequently modified by the addition of Handley Page slots and the fitting of twin fins and rudders. This sole example of a SEAGULL IV was sold to the Tour and Travel Association in 1929 and registered as G-AAIZ for use on the Channel Islands service after modification to a "six seater" with the passengers in a "luxuriously appointed" cabin. G-AAIZ was destroyed by fire at Brooklands in 1933.

In 1924 Supermarine's first twin-engined amphibian appeared. This was the SUPERMARINE SWAN, and it was built to an Air Ministry specification. Initially it was fitted with Rolls Royce Eagle IX engines giving a cruising speed of 83 mph. The wing span was 69' and the wing area 1,265 sq. ft. The undercarriage was raised and lowered by means of a slipstream-driven propeller. Its R.A.F. serial No. was N175 and it was later modified to have 492 hp Napier Lion IIB engines giving a cruising speed of 87 mph. The amphibian undercarriage was removed as well as the wing-folding facility and, after evaluation at Felixstowe, the Air Ministry issued a specification for a slightly larger version which became the very successful SUPERMARINE SOUTHAMPTON. In the summer of 1926 as G-EBJY, the SUPERMARINE SWAN was loaned to Imperial Airways for the Guernsey service after conversion to carry ten passengers, with a max all-up weight of 13,710 lbs. Its first flight to Guernsey was on 30.6.26 and during August and September it made the weekly trip from Woolston to St Peter Port and back, weather and other circumstances permitting, which amounted to about half-a-dozen trips in all. It was not seen again until it reappeared once in Guernsey in February, 1927, after which it was "laid up", and finally scrapped.

(B) SHORT BROTHERS

This old-established firm had considerable experience of building seaplanes and flying-boats; one of their TYPE 184 SEAPLANES was the first aircraft in the world to sink an enemy ship by torpedo; another had been present at the Battle of Jutland. In 1926 they brought out the SHORT SINGAPORE flying-boat which, in its Mark III version, was in full-scale production from 1935 to 1937. Using experience gained with the SINGAPORE I a three-engined biplane flying-boat, the SHORT CALCUTTA, was designed in 1927 for the Mediterranean section of the Imperial Airways' route to India. The wing span was 93', length nearly 67', and the total wing area 1,825 sq. ft. Three 540 hp Bristol Jupiter XIF engines gave a cruising speed of 97 mph, and the all-up weight was   22,500 lb. The first two machines were:-

G-EBVG c. of a. 25.7.28 *City of Alexandria* and
G-EBVH c. of a. 13.9.28 *City of Athens*

and they were used on the Woolston-Guernsey service between 14.8.28 and 20.2.29. Both machines were employed on the Genoa-Rome-Naples-Corfu-Athens-Suda Bay-Tobruk-Alexandria section of the Indian route, and were joined by three more:- G-AADN, G-AASJ, and G-AATZ. Later they were used on the Khartoum-Kisumu section of the South African route. 'VG was scrapped in 1936 and 'VH in 1937.

The SHORT CALCUTTA was Britain's first all-metal commercial flying-boat, mainly duralumin, with a few fittings made from steel. The hull was of monocoque construction and entirely of duralumin. The wing spars and ribs were duralumin but fabric covered. 'VH was distinguished from all the others by having Handley Page slots on the leading edge of the top wing. The Handley Page slot, incidentally, was a small, auxiliary aerofoil mounted snugly along the wing leading edge which lifted upwards and forward as stalling speed was approached and thereby delayed the onset of stalling to a lower speed to give the pilot time to take corrective measures. One machine (G-AATZ) survived until 1939 ending its life at Hamble with Air Service Training. "It was very slow" wrote former Imperial Airways' flying-boat captain Howard Fry "but it handled well on the water and was, above all, very strong. In short it was ideal for sprog flying boat pilots to get used to such mysteries as landing and taking-off in really rough seas and across strong winds . . ." (74)

(C) SAUNDERS-ROE

The first aircraft to be produced by the new combination of Sir Alliott Roe, and S.E. Saunders Ltd. was the SARO CUTTY SARK, a four-seater monoplane flying-boat with two 105 hp Cirrus Hermes I engines mounted above the wooden Fokker-type wing which was bolted on top of a simple boat-shaped hull made from "Alclad", an aluminium-coated alloy. It received its c. of a. on 13.9.29. After conversion to an amphibian it was sold to a Mr Holden, but it changed hands in the spring of 1930 when it was taken over by Kirsten & Mace for their Channel Islands service. According to Mr Mace his aircraft had Gipsy engines, and these may have been fitted to provide more power to compensate for the weight of the landing gear. There was no obvious change in the external appearance of G-AAIP until 1931 when Saunders-Roe took it on a sales tour through Europe with redesigned engine cowlings of an abbreviated close-fitting pattern. In 1932 it went to Tommy Rose and D. Campbell-Shaw for a Liverpool-Isle of Man service but, it was returned to Cowes at the end of the season. Scrapped in 1935. Wing span 45 ft., wing area 320 sq. ft., max. all-up weight 3,850 lbs., and cruising speed 85 mph.

The Cutty Sark: ". . . was quite a jolly little machine and quite easy to

272

land on the fairly calm seas you get in Southampton Water. First of all we had about a couple of hours dual instruction and then we went solo for practice take-offs and landings in calm water into the wind. Then we had to learn the tricks of the trade with landings and take-offs across wind and in the rougher water towards the Isle of Wight. And finally there were the tricky things like mooring up to a buoy and riding up the slipway to be mastered . . ." (74) Howard Fry went on to complete 7,000 hours in flying-boats. On one flight his fellow trainee flying-boat pilot brought his Scotch terrier along for the ride but this creature did not take to flying and coming in to land and trying to keep the dog under control they forgot to raise the undercarriage: ". . . one minute we were doing about 60 mph and the next moment we were stationary and pointing towards the bottom of the sea."

A larger version, the SARO CLOUD, for a crew of two and eight passengers, appeared in 1930. The prototype, G-ABCJ, was fitted with two 300 hp Wright Whirlwind J-6 radial engines. Wing span was 64 ft., wing area 650 sq. ft., and cruising speed 95 mph. This machine went to Canada as CF-ARB but was bought back by Saunders-Roe in 1934 and fitted with two 340 hp Napier Rapier IV engines. Speed was increased to 102 mph and max. all-up weight to 9,700 lbs. In this condition it was loaned to Guernsey Airways in August, 1935 for a very short period. Withdrawn from use at the end of 1936. Another SARO Cloud with Wright Whirlwind engines, G-ABXW, was given its c. of a. on 15.7.32 and went to British Flying Boats, Ltd. for charters and joy-riding in Scotland, North-West England, and the Isle of Man. For one week in August, 1932 it flew a regular service between Greenock and Belfast, but it was returned to Cowes at the end of the 1933 season and British Flying Boats stopped operating. It was used by Spartan Air Lines for various purposes and then sold to Guernsey Airways in 1936 to be lost off the Minquiers on 31.7.36. Other Saro Clouds were used for civilian purposes with various engine arrangements and about 17 went to the R.A.F. The two used by Guernsey Airways could be distinguished from each other by the radial engines of 'XW compared with the in-line "H" form engines of 'CJ, and its small auxiliary aerofoil behind and below the engine nacelles.

The next design was the SARO WINDHOVER of intermediate size for a crew of two and six passengers. The wing span was 54' 4" and the length 41' 4", but only two machines were built. The first went out to Tasmania, and the second was G-ABJP which was fitted with three Gipsy II engines and a small aerofoil above the engines to improve the air flow over the tail. Cruising speed was 90 mph and the max. all-up wight 5,700 lb. It received its c. of a. on 8.7.31 and was sold to Mr F. Francis. On 21.9.31 it opened a twice-daily Gibraltar-Tangier service for Gibraltar Airways, but this service was short-lived and the machine lay in the open until the following year when it was chartered by the Hon. Mrs Victor Bruce for an attempt on the World Endurance Record. In May, 1932 Mrs Bruce, Flight.-Lieut. S.D. Scott, and a mechanic went out to Gibraltar and collected 'JP, but crashed on take-off from Alicante due to corroded carburetters. The damaged aircraft was returned to Gib. by road and shipped to the U.K. On August 9, 1932, after two false starts, Mrs Bruce and Flying Officer Pugh took off from the Solent about noon and landed at Folkestone at 7 pm on August 11 after 54 hours 13 min. aloft. The existing record was 23 days (553 hrs. 41 min. to be exact), and Mrs Bruce had hoped to stay in the air for a month but the starboard engine oil pressure had dropped to zero because of a choked filter. They had intended to service the engines in flight by means of a special cat-walk, but when John Pugh tried to climb out to the starboard engine the interference with the slip-stream made the aircraft too difficult for Mrs Bruce to control. During the flight they were refuelled 18 times from a Bristol Fighter via a 1" hose-pipe. The flight, although a British record, was unofficial because the sealed barograph had been left behind to save weight, together with other non-essentials such as life-belts! The landing gear had been removed also, which meant that the plane had to alight on water. The barograph was needed to provide proof that a landing had not been made somewhere out-of-sight during the record attempt! This SARO WINDHOVER was purchased by Guernsey Airways in 1935 and used on their inter-island service until the summer of 1936. After a period of inactivity it was withdrawn from use in 1938 and the parts sold to the Percival Aircraft Co. Ltd. at Luton.

(D) DE HAVILLAND

When Edward Hillman asked for something bigger than the single-engined Fox Moth for his projected Paris service the DE HAVILLAND DRAGON was on the drawing-board as a light, inexpensive bomber for the Iraqi Air Force and he was offered a civil version. He ordered four, to be ready in time for the opening date of April 1, 1933, and later he ordered two more. This aircraft was a landmark in the history of British internal air-lines and the prototype, G-ACAN, made its first flight on 24.11.32. In Hillman's blue and white colour scheme (blue below the fuselage centre-line and white above) it was regarded as a very smart aeroplane. *Flight* (22.12.32) said that the remarkable ratio of gross weight to tare of 1.825 was an achievement only bettered by the Fox Moth's 1.9. Various other criteria were applied and it was concluded that the D.H. DRAGON was the "nearest approach to an aircraft capable of remunerative operation which has ever come to our notice". Details of the early model were as follows:-

Two 130 hp Gipsy Major I engines, span 47' 4" (25' 4" folded), length 34' 6", wing area 376 sq. ft., tare weight 2,300 lb., all-up weight 4,200 lb., landing speed 50 mph approx., fuel capacity 60 gallons. Price £2,795. At Martlesham Heath, loaded to 4,200 lb. it took off within 456 yards over a 145 ft. screen against a wind of less than 5 mph. The wings and fuselage were made of wood, with metal fittings, the wings were fabric covered, and the fuselage covered with three-ply to form a typical de Havilland box. An intriguing feature was the zip-fastener that ran from nose to tail under the belly of the fuselage. When "un-zipped" the fabric on either side dropped to expose the control wires. With six passengers each weighing 160 lb. and having 45 lb. of luggage a range of about 460 miles was possible. An advertisement in *The Aeroplane* (9.11.33.) for a luxury model to carry four passengers and a steward, with separate luggage and lavatory accommodation, gave the cruising speed as 110 mph, top speed 130 mph, landing run 130 yards, "un-stick" 220 yards, rate of climb 635 ft./min., range 545 miles, and petrol consumption 12 gals/hr. It stated that height could be maintained on one engine at full load and that top-overhauls were not required on the engines, only complete overhauls every 750 hours. In the following week's issue there was an account of an hour's test flight at the controls of G-ACCE by "Pontius" which he described as "air-joy", on the grounds that: ". . . modern advertising is apt to refer to shoes as 'foot-joy', soap as 'bath-joy' . . ." In the cockpit, or "pilot's solarium", he found take-off was short and full control available straight away with no tendency to swing. Landing was "absurdly easy". D.H. DRAGONS still survive and fairly recent experience of flying G-ACIT (now in the Science Museum's collection) is available from Hugh Scanlon: ". . . 'You want to glide in, throttled right back' they said . . . 'and no faster than 65 or you'll never get it down' . . . later . . . I watched a pilot with nine joy-riding passengers . . . 'Aha' I thought 'he's too fast'. Sure enough his airy D.H. 84 floated and floated, and floated for almost the entire length of the grass field until . . . he contrived to settle her to an unwilling stop within feet of the far hedge . . ." An all-up weight of 4,200 lb. gave the Dragon a wing loading of 11 lb/sq. ft. and the ability to operate from small fields on minimal power. "You might think that something so light would blow away in a gale, but the Dragon did not; with quick responses and a powerful aileron for each wing it could be made to ride out the most unpredictable gusts. Many are the recollections by commercial pilots of crabbing in to some island meadow for a load of passengers, kicking it straight at the last moment while eager helpers grabbed hold, then when throttles were opened, lifting again like a gull to the onshore wind. There were no runways then. You aligned the aeroplane with the sock . . . If the shallow glide became limiting, you 'walked' it in with bursts of power just above the stall . . ." (42)

64 D.H. DRAGONS were sold in 1933, and it was continued with improved performance at the reduced price of £2,750 as the "1934 DRAGON". In the later version the continuous window of the passenger compartment was replaced by a series of separate windows, and the two vertical struts of the undercarriage were faired together. Engine performance was improved to give 114 mph cruising and 134 mph max., and the max. permissible load was increased to 4,500 lb. with a tare of 2,336 lb. In later years this version became known as the Dragon 2, and the earlier version the Dragon 1. 62 Dragon 1's were built (works numbers 6000-6061), but one of these was retained by de Havillands and converted into a Dragon 2 which became G-ACMC (No. 6053) and eventually Jersey Airways' *St Brelade's Bay*. 53 Dragon 2's were built (in addition to 'MC), and the first production machine was G-ACMO (No. 6062) *St Ouen's Bay*, although preceded by a specially built luxury model (G-ACKU for Sir Lindsay Everard, M.P.). The first machine to go into service with Jersey Airways was their sole Dragon 1, G-ACMJ (No. 6058) *St Aubin's Bay*. During the war 87 Dragons were built in Australia for use as training machines by the R.A.A.F. The Jersey Airways' fleet comprised:-

G-ACMJ (6058) *St Aubin's Bay* c. of a. 7.12.33 – Sold to Western Airways in 1936. To the R.A.F. as X9396 in April, 1940.

G-ACMC (6053) *St Brelade's Bay* c. of a. 24.11.33. To Australia in 1936 as VH-UXK. Crashed Mundoo, Queensland in 1938.

G-ACMO (6062) *St Ouen's Bay* c. of a. 31.1.34. Transferred to Northern & Scottish in 1935. To Australia in 1938 as VH-ABK.

G-ACMP (6063) *St Clement's Bay* c. of a. 20.2.34. Sold to Western Airways in 1935. Crashed off Cardiff on 23.7.35.

G-ACNG (6069) *Portelet Bay* c. of a. 23.3.34. Transferred to Spartan Air Lines in 1935, British Airways in 1936, Northern & Scottish in 1937, and Scottish Airways in 1938. Crashed Kirkwall 19.4.40.

G-ACNH (6070) *Bouley Bay* c. of a. 26.3.34. Transferred to Northern & Scottish in 1935. Registration cancelled January, 1937.

G-ACNI (6071) *Bonne Nuit Bay* c. of a. 28.3.34. Transferred to British Airways and was used on the Isle of Wight services in 1936. Converted by Airwork Ltd. and sold to the Irish Army Air Corps in 1937.

G-ACNJ (6072) *Rozel Bay* c. of a. 28.3.34. The last Dragon to leave Jersey Airways. Sold to Allied Airways in 1937 and carried the first air mail from Aberdeen to the Shetlands on 23.11.37. Broken up for spares at Dyce in 1946.

The D.H. 86 EXPRESS AIR LINER was a larger version of the Dragon with four engines, designed and built within four months to meet the specification of the Australian Government for an air-liner suitable for the Singapore-Darwin-Cootamundra section of the England-Australia air mail route. One of the conditions of the tender was that the aircraft offered must have obtained a certificate of airworthiness by the closing date of the tender, which was 31.1.34, and the prototype 86, G-ACPL, was first flown on 14.1.34, and received its c. of a. on 30.1.34 after trials at Martlesham. As first built the prototype was arranged to seat ten passengers, with lavatory and baggage accommodation and a crew of two, but dual-control was not provided and the pilot sat in the nose with the second pilot/wireless-operator on the starboard side just behind the pilot. The engines were a newly-developed six cylinder version of the Gipsy Major, and there was another race against time to have four of these engines made and Air Ministry type tested ready for the first flight. The fuselage was the usual wooden box, but the plywood was on the inside of the spruce longerons and stringers, and the intervening space between this and the fabric covering filled with sound-proofing material. The wooden wings were similar to those of the Dragon but heavily tapered over the outer section so that only a single strut was carried at the wing tip. The fixed undercarriage was housed in a streamlined Elektron fairing. Details were as follows:-

Four 200 hp. Gipsy Six engines Cruising speed 145 mph. Max. 170 mph. Span 64' 6", Length 43' 11", Wing area 641 sq. ft. Tare weight 5,520 lbs. All-up weight 9,200 lbs. Stalling speed 66 mph. Fuel capacity 114 gallons.

The prototype was followed by two more of the single-pilot type, G-ACVY *Mercury* and G-ACVZ *Jupiter* for Railway Air Services, but as 'VZ was not available until the end of 1934 'PL shared the R.A.S. Croydon-Belfast-Glasgow service with 'VY until 'VZ arrived. All subsequent 86's were of the dual-control type, with the elongated nose, including those supplied to Jersey Airways in 1935. Perhaps in the rush to meet the various deadlines the choice of a suitable name had not been made by the time the aircraft flew and initially it was called the de Havilland Express air-liner. Names such as the Super-Dragon or the D.H. Express never caught on, nor did the Imperial Airways class name of *Diana"*, and to all and sundry it became just the "86".

G-ACYF (2313) *Giffard Bay* c. of a. 6.2.35. To Wearnes Air Service for the Singapore-Penang route in June, 1938 as VR-SBD. To Australia as VH-ADN.

G-ACYG (2314) *Grouville Bay* c. of a. 8.3.35. To the R.N. July 1940 as AX840. Scrapped 1945.

G-ACZN (2316) *St Catherine's Bay* c. of a. 22.3.35. Crashed Jersey 4.11.38.

G-ACZO (2318) *Ouaine Bay* c. of a. 9.4.35. To the R.N. July 1940 as AX841. Destroyed in an air raid, Lee-on-Solent 16.7.40.

G-ACZP (2321) *Belcroute Bay* c. of a. 11.5.35. To the R.N. July 1940 as AX843 but released to R.A.S. 29.8.40. as G-ACZP. Privately owned at Eastleigh in 1958 but written off in a crash at Madrid on 21.9.58. The last survivor of its type.

G-ACZR (2322) *La Saline Bay* c. of a. 29.5.35. To the R.N. July 1940 as AX844. Written off in a crash at Donibristle, 31.3.43.

Captain Broad, who flew the 86 during all its trials, under all conditions of load, and with all combinations of engines (*Flight* 1.3.34) found it to be: ". . . delightfully light and positive on the controls, straight-forward in landing and, if anything, easier to fly than the Dragon . . ." In *The Aeroplane* of 19.6.35 "Pontius" said: ". . . the aeroplane is delightfully stable in all three senses and can be trimmed to fly by itself; . . . instrument flying is perfectly simple . . . no reason why a pilot should ever go wrong the D.H. 86 even by gross inadvertence, as it is a thoroughly controllable aeroplane in all conditions . . ." However, not everyone was so happy about the 86's flying characteristics, especially in rough weather, and two Australian machines had crashed by the end of 1934. There were more accidents in 1935, and a modified version was produced, the D.H. 86A but with little change to its external appearance, and apparently, its flying characteristics. In August, 1936 British Airways lost D.H. 86 G-ADEB, and on September 15, 1936 they lost D.H. 86A G-ADYF. Although the Accident Report on 'YF suggested that the person sitting in the second pilot's seat may have had his foot in such a position that it jammed the rudder-bar British Airways requested that trials be carried out at Martlesham Heath, and D.H. 86A G-ADYH was supplied for this purpose. At the end of 1936 a highly critical report was published: (45) ". . . extremely difficult to fly in disturbed air conditions . . . Lively in its reaction to bumps, and the lag in response to controls made it impossible to keep it on a straight course in such conditions . . . not satisfactory in flight except in calm air and very gentle manoeuvres . . ." As a result all 86A's on the British register were test flown and put in one of two categories:- Group 1 – unsafe and not to be flown, Group 2 – unsafe for night-flying. Not to be flown by day with passengers by a pilot with less than 50 hours on D.H. 86's. These restrictions caused immediate problems to their owners but, fortunately, other seemingly minor modifications resulted in a great improvement. The most conspicuous was the fitting of an extra fin (or Zulu shield) to the ends of the tailplane, and this version became the D.H. 86B. All new machines were built as 86B's and most, if not all, of the existing 86A's were modified. As Jersey Airways had 86's and not 86A's their machines were not included in the tests, for some reason, but two 86B's were acquired at a later date:-

G-ADVK (2339) c. of a. 21.4.36. Supplied to B.W.C.A.S. as an 86A. It was placed in Group 2 and converted to 86B. Went to I.O.M.A.S. in 1937 and Jersey Airways in December, 1938. Abandoned at Jersey Airport in 1940.

G-AENR (2352) c. of a. 8.2.37. Supplied to B.W.C.A.S. as an 86B. Went to I.O.M.A.S. in 1937 and Jersey Airways in February, 1939. To the R.N. as AX842 in July, 1940 but released to R.A.S. in August, 1940. Scrapped in 1948.

The cruising speed and basic dimensions of the 86B remained as for the 86, but tare weight was 6,140 lb. and all-up weight 10,250 lb.

The D.H. RAPIDE or 89 was an up-to-date version of the DRAGON, incorporating all the improvements of the 86, such as Gipsy-Six engines, tapered wings, and streamlined undercarriage fairings. The wings were similar in construction to those of the 86, but the fuselage had the fabric-covered plywood on the outside of the longerons and sound-proofing material. With seats for six/eight passengers it was first called the D.H. DRAGON-SIX, but this was soon changed to D.H. DRAGON RAPIDE, which, in due course, became just the D.H. RAPIDE. It was test flown by "Pontius" (*The Aeroplane* 20.2.35) who was full of praise but thought that no aeroplane with a wing loading of 14 lb/sq. ft. without flaps could be expected to land particularly slowly and he defined the RAPIDE as being ". . . the class of aeroplane which is rightly intended for reliable pilots . . ." He was not alone in suggesting flaps, and from March, 1937 the flapped version, the D.H. 89A was produced. Many of the existing D.H. RAPIDES were converted to D.H. 89A during overhaul. Jersey Airways bought two D.H. 89's, and it is thought that these would have been converted to D.H. 89A at some stage:-

G-ADBV (6286) *St Ouen's Bay II* c. of a. 6.6.35. Sold to Western Airways in 1937. Taken over by the R.A.F. as X8511 in March, 1940.

G-ADBW (6288) c. of a. 27.6.35. Sold to Airwork, Ltd. in July 1938 for use as a navigational trainer at Airwork's No. 6 Air Observer's Navigational School, Staverton. Taken over by the R.A.F. as Z7265 in July, 1940.

Details are as follows:- (D.H. 89A)

Two 200 hp Gipsy-Six engines, cruising speed 132 mph, max. speed 157 mph, stalling speed 64 mph, Span 48', Length 34' 6". wing area 336 sq. ins. tare weight 3,276 lbs., max. all-up weight 5,500 lb., take-off run 290 yds, landing run 170 yds. (Compared with 220 yds. for the 89). With the final all-up weight of 5,500 lb. the wing loading was nearer to 16 lb/sq. ft. The fuel consumption of the prototype was given as 19 gals/hr. Fuel capacity 76 gals.

The D.H. FLAMINGO was de Havilland's first all-metal stressed-skin aircraft and its performance was quite impressive: ". . . I was fortunate enough to be at Hatfield on that brilliant frosty morning of 28th December, (1938) . . . when young Geoffrey de Havilland stepped into the new FLAMINGO air liner with George Gibbins and flew it for the first time . . . The FLAMINGO had been taxied slowly in the thick snow on 22nd December, and had done a few quick runs on the 23rd when de Havilland had allowed it to leave the ground on three short hops. Next day was Christmas Eve and the weather was bad, and everyone went home to tend the frost-bound water pipes and prepare for festivities . . . But the perfectly cloudless morning of Wednesday was quite irresistible, and a few telephone calls brought a little bunch of people to the aerodrome . . . We expected to see some preliminary runs and hops, but Geoffrey taxied straight from the fuel pumps to the edge of the field, turned into wind, paused only a few seconds, and gave her the gun. I looked at my watch. She left the ground in five seconds and it was just eleven o'clock. What a grand picture! Surely, I thought, five seconds must be wrong. She climbed straight away to the north until she was a speck in the sky and then turned and circled the aerodrome at about 4,000 ft. with undercarriage retracted. Another circuit and she came in to land. Down came the chassis, then the flaps; she glided steeply, flattened out over the club-house, skimmed the snow and settled silently down quite close to us. De Havilland said the new ship handled very pleasantly, the acceleration and take-off had surprised him, and he had landed because he thought the oil pressures were on the high side. He was told they did not require adjustment, and he therefore took off again straight away and flew for over half an hour." (65)

As *Flight* said at the time (16.2.39), there were no intrinsic advantages in all-metal construction as such. Only when orders in quantity could be expected was the all-metal machine an economically reasonable proposition. The Air Ministry was prepared to give some financial assistance with development costs, but to compete in the American market the Flamingo needed to sell at about £17,000, and would be a better buy than the Lockheed 14 at that price. First estimates gave a figure of £17,105, with an extra £1,000 for overseas customers (agent's fees), but there was nothing in this price towards the recovery of initial design and tooling costs, and by mid-1938 a price of £19,000 was thought to be more realistic. In mid-1939 the final market price was given as £22,500 with Sperry automatic pilot and hydromatic airscrews, but U.K. operators would be allowed a 5% discount. (46)

The prototype, G-AFUE, was loaned to Jersey Airways for service trials over their routes, and it performed well despite the inevitable "teething" troubles. The opinion of the pilots was summed up, perhaps, by Captain Jordan when he said: "Lots of snags, but a good aeroplane." A summary of the two months of operation is given below:-

Aircraft mileage		25,915
No. of scheduled services completed		164
Traffic carried:-	Passengers (fare-paying)	1,373
	Freight	40,073 lbs.
	Mail	696 lbs.
Ton Mileage:	Passenger ton miles	17,679
	Freight ton miles	2,532
	Mail ton miles	38
Total carried		20,249
Total available		28,420

Load factor 71.25% (77)

On average this works out at 164 journeys of 158 miles with 8.4 passengers, 244 lb. of freight, and 4.2 lb. of mail, but the high load factor appears to be based on a pay-load of only 2,457 lb. viz:

<u>Total available ton mileage of 28,420</u>
Miles flown 25,915

For subsidy purposes the official capacity of an aircraft (47) assumed that the fuel tanks were ½ full, and the D.H. 86 was rated at 1.32 tons (2,957 lbs.), with the Rapide and the Dragon at .76 and .74 tons respectively. At

282

first the Flamingo was allowed 1.69 tons (3,786 lb.), but this was considered unfair because of its long range, hence large fuel tanks, and the figure was amended to 2 tons (4,480 lb.) *Flight* gave a pay-load of 2,613 lb. with fuel for 1,000 miles, and a crew of three, and 3,505 lb. with fuel for 500 miles, so the Air Ministry's allowance was quite generous.

Details of the earliest version of the Flamingo were:-

Two 890 hp Bristol Perseus XIIc sleeve-valved radial engines,
Span 68', Length 50' 7", Wing area 639 sq. ft.
Tare weight 11,325 lb., All-up weight 17,000 lb.
Cruising speed 184 mph (at sea level), 204 mph (at 10,000 ft.) Max.
243 mph
Landing run (5 mph wind) 275 yards
Take-off run (full load) 250 yards. Max. fuel capacity 410 gals.

G-AFUE was the only Flamingo to see service on the Channel Island routes and was the property of the de Havilland Aircraft Co. Ltd., to whom it was returned on the outbreak of war. In October, 1939 it was taken over by the R.A.F. as T5357 and went to No. 24 Communications Squadron at Hendon, to be written off about twelve months later.

(E)   WESTLAND

The tri-motor high-wing monoplane was a popular transport in the Twenties, and the WESTLAND IV was a small version with three Cirrus engines in its prototype stage for a crew of two and four passengers. It was registered G-EBXK, and made its first flight in 1929. The second machine had Hermes I engines and the rear of the fuselage was made of metal. The third machine, G-ABAJ, was modified to take the 105 hp Armstrong Siddeley Genet Major radial engines and became the prototype WESTLAND WESSEX. Details:- Span 57' 6", length 38', wing area 490 sq. ft., Speed 100 mph cruising, 118 mph max. Weight 3,810 lb. tare, 5,750 lb. max. all-up.

Cobham had four WESTLAND WESSEX:-

G-EBXK (1771) c. of a. 21.3.29 Prototype Westland IV. Retained as a demonstration machine and later converted to WESSEX. Sold to Cobham in 1935 and withdrawn from use in 1936.

G-ABAJ (1897) c. of a. 27.5.30 Built as Westland IV, G-AAJI and intended for Wilson's Airways, Kenya as VP-KAD, but the order was not taken up. Rebuilt as a WESTLAND WESSEX and sold to SABENA as OO-AGC. Sold to Cobham in 1935 for the Guernsey route. Used on the Ryde ferry of P.S.I.O.W.A. but sold to Trafalgar Advertising Co. Ltd., in 1936 to carry illuminated signs at night. A humorous account of a trip over London trying to get all three letters of OXO working simultaneously is given in Robert Chandler's "Off The Beam". Scrapped 1938.

G-ADEW (1899) c. of a. 6.8.30. Sold to SABENA as OO-AGE and bought by Cobham in 1935. Lost in Channel 3.7.35.

G-ADFZ (1900) c. of a. 30.8.30. Sold to SABENA as OO-AGF, and bought by Cobham in 1935 for Cobham Air Routes. The regular partner of 'EW on Guernsey service. Went to the air display and was in collision over Blackpool with an Avro 504N on Sept. 7, 1935, but survived. All three occupants of the Avro were killed. In 1936 it joined 'AJ with Trafalgar Advertising, but was not withdrawn from the register until 1.12.46.

The Wessex was designed to fly on just two engines, if necessary, and during the delivery flight of OO-AGF from Croydon to Brussels the pilot, M. Cocquyt demonstrated this by throttling back the starboard engine, and accidentally stopped it completely. Nothing would get it going again so the flight was continued to Haren on just two.

(F) AIRSPEED

The AIRSPEED ENVOY was a smooth twin-engined low-wing monoplane of wooden construction having a retractable undercarriage. It could carry six to eight passengers and was available with a wide variety of radial engines. Details:- Span 52' 4", Length 34' 6", Wing Area 339 sq. ft., and when fitted with the Armstrong Siddeley Cheetah IX engine of 350 hp had a cruising speed of 170 mph. Tare weight was 4,340 lb. and max. all-up weight 6,600 lb.

Cobham Air Routes had one AIRSPEED ENVOY:

G-ADBA (33) c. of a. 18.4.35. Series 1 AS 6J with Cheetah engine. Passed to Olley Air Service in the summer of 1935 and to North

Eastern Airways early in 1937 for their Croydon-Perth-Aberdeen service, but was sold to the Air Council at the end of 1938 and entered the R.A.F. as P5778. It did not survive the war.

Sales of the AIRSPEED ENVOY to U.K. operators were disappointing to Airspeed but the situation was saved by orders from the Air Ministry for a version suitable for training purposes which, as the AIRSPEED OXFORD, was built in large numbers. It was from an AIRSPEED OXFORD that Amy Johnson baled out over the Thames Estuary in January, 1941 to come down near H.M.S. *Haslemere*, the former Channel Islands cargo boat doing duty as a convoy balloon barrage vessel.

(G)   WIBAULT-PENHOET

Air France is the French national air-line. For many years its only connection with mainland Britain was the service between Paris (Le Bourget) and London (Croydon) which, from 1.1.23 was operated by Air Union, an amalgamation of Compagnie des Messageries Aeriénnes and Grands Express Aeriéns, the two French air-lines which had previously been in competition with each other and the British companies on the London-Paris route. The mainstay of the service was the famous old Farman Goliath but, from 1929, the larger, faster, and more powerful Lioré et Olivier 213 became available, painted in red and gold with the words "RAYON D'OR" on the starboard side of the nose and "GOLDEN RAY" on the port side. They, in their turn, were displaced by faster machines in the spring of 1933, also painted in red and gold but with the words "VOILE D'OR" and "GOLDEN CLIPPER" on their sides. These machines were WIBAULT-PENHOUËT 282T12 low-winged monoplanes with three 350 hp Gnome-Rhône 7kd seven-cylinder radial engines giving a cruising speed of about 125 mph. They could carry a crew of two and ten passengers. The engines on the wings were fitted with cowlings, but not the engine in the nose. On 30.8.33 Air France was formed from Air Union, Air Orient, and other French companies, and their combined fleet included eight Wibault 282's. During 1934 ten more machines of an improved version called the WIBAULT-PENHOËT 283T12 were built for Air France. All three engines were cowled and the undercarriage legs fitted with massive fairings or "tin pants". They had the same overall dimensions as the 282T12's: span 74' 2", length 55' 9", wing area 693 sq. ft. and the same seating capacity, but the cruising speed was increased to 140 mph and the max. all-up weight was 14,000 lb. with a tare of 9,400 lb. The Wibaults remained on the Croydon-Le Bourget service in the blue and silver colours of Air France until 1938 when they were replaced by the Bloch 220, and thus became available for the Paris-Dinard-Jersey service.

The only machines positively identified on the Jersey service were:-

WIBAULT 282 F-AMHM *L'Intrépide*
WIBAULT 283 F-AMYE *L'Intrigant*

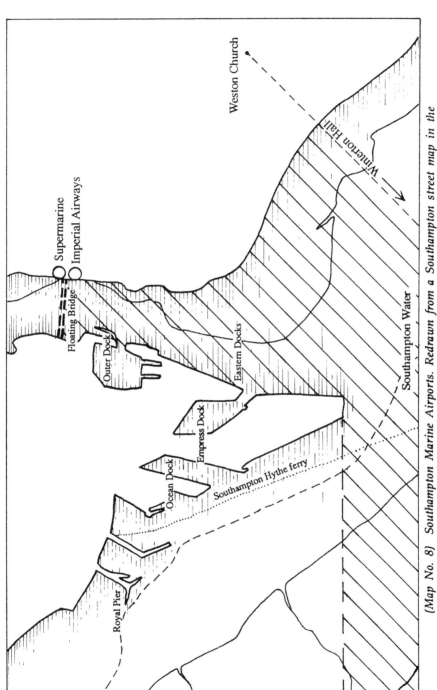

(Map No. 8) Southampton Marine Airports. Redrawn from a Southampton street map in the
Southampton Official Handbook - 1967.

Based upon the Ordnance Survey map with the permission of the Controller of Her Majesty's Stationery Office (c) Crown copyright

Weston Church

Winterton Hall

Southampton Water

Supermarine
Imperial Airways

Floating Bridge

Outer Dock

Eastern Docks

Empress Dock

Ocean Dock

Southampton Hythe ferry

Royal Pier

AERODROMES

Details of the various aerodromes available to aviators in the pre-war years were promulgated in an Air Ministry publication called *The Air Pilot* first issued in 1929. As changes took place the appropriate pages in *The Air Pilot* were replaced by revised sheets so that subscribers were kept up-to-date. Normally there was a small sketch showing the geographical position of the aerodrome, and a larger sketch giving a plan of the airfield itself, as well as one or more pages of useful information.

(A) WOOLSTON (See Map No 8)

The flying-boats of the B.M.A.N. Co. usually landed on Southampton Water and made their way up the River Itchen to the Supermarine Works where there was a slipway, mooring buoys, and other facilities. A passenger terminal was built which was used by B.M.A.N. Co. and Imperial Airways until 1925 when Imperial Airways moved to another site. For their own use the Supermarine facilities were continued as a "Private unlicensed civil seaplane station", but they were not available without permission being previously obtained from the Supermarine Aviation Works Ltd. Its local position was given as "1¼ miles N.N.E. of the S. point of Southampton Docks, on the E. (left) bank of the River Itchen and immediately N. of the steam ferry." The same issue of the *Air Pilot* (1929-34") also gave details of the "SOUTHAMPTON (WOOLSTON) (Imperial Airways') SEAPLANE STATION which was situated "1¼ miles N.N.E. and 200 feet S. of the steam-ferry". By this time there was only a resident caretaker (who was a licensed ground engineer), and there were no hangars, but a mooring buoy was available and a slip-way, although the winch was disconnected from the power mains. "The alighting area available for use by seaplanes requiring customs examination is as follows:- The whole portion of the River Itchen, S. of the Itchen Steam-Ferry, and that portion of Southampton Water contained within a line joining Weston Church and Winterton Hall, Hythe on the S., and a line running due W. of the S. extremity of the Southampton Docks on the N." It was a licensed civil customs seaplane station available for public use, although 24 hours notice was required for refuelling.

(B)   ST PETER PORT, GUERNSEY (See Map No 9)

In Guernsey the flying-boats of the B.M.A.N. Co. and Imperial Airways used the main harbour of the island at St Peter Port. According to *The Air Pilot* it was a seaport with facilities for the customs examination of seaplanes under the controlling authority of the Harbour Master and was available for public use. The area for use by seaplanes requiring customs clearance was within St Peter Port Harbour, excluding Albert Dock, the Old Harbour, and the Careening Hard, and the alighting area available at low water was approximately 300 yards, North – South, 300 yards North East – South West, 450 yards East – West, and 330 yards South East – North West, but an ample expanse of water was available outside the harbour. "The coast to the N. and S. of St Peter Port is rocky and dangerous. The water immediately outside the entrance to St Peter Port Harbour is sheltered from all winds between S.S.W. through W., and N., but those from between N.N.E. and S.E., if strong, cause much sea. Winds from between S.S.W. and S.E., also send in much swell and sea, especially on the ebb tide . . ." (70)

(C)   ST HELIER, JERSEY (See Map No 10)

As at Guernsey, the flying boats used the main harbour of the island, in this case St Helier, a seaport with facilities for the customs examination of seaplanes under the controlling authority of the Harbour Master, and available for public use. The area available was "within a radius of ¼ mile of Elizabeth Castle. This area includes the main portion of St Helier Harbour . . . There is normally a sufficient expanse of water for alighting and taking-off in any wind, except, perhaps, in S.W. gales . . ." (70) The Air Ministry at this time was very correct and flying-boats never "landed" on the sea as, presumably, a contradiction in terms, they always "alighted"! The harbour dimensions were not given and although the "alightings" were probably expected to be outside the harbour walls there was no prohibition on a direct landing inside the harbour area subject to the fact that "a certain amount of marine traffic" was in the vicinity at all times. From the shape of the harbour it would appear that a North – South alighting between the Albert and North piers was quite feasible.

From a 1930's guide book (Map No 9)

(Ward, Lock Ltd)

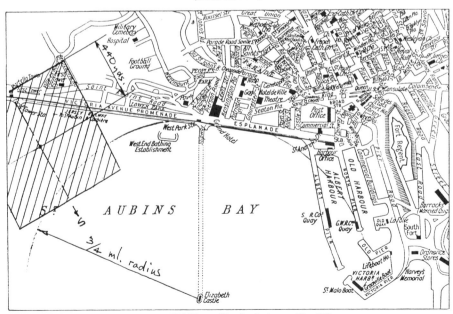

From a 1930's guide book (map No 10)

(Ward, Lock Ltd)

"St. Aubin's Bay is sheltered from all winds except those from the south east through south to west, and partially even from them. S.W. gales send in a heavy rolling sea between half-flood and high water, but as the water falls the sea subsides . . . A stretch of sand and rocks, ½ to 1 mile wide, exposed at low-water, extends around the bay. Elizabeth Castle, the centre of the seaplane customs area, stands on craggy rocks fronting St Helier Harbour, on the east side of the bay . . . Note . . . Numerous rocks, sunken or exposed, exist within the seaplane customs area . . ." (70)

In Supplement No. 3 of December, 1934 the following note appears: ". . . For landplanes at St Helier – Special Authorization Only – An area of foreshore ½ mile square having its centre at a point 440 yards due south of the second tower in St Aubin's Bay." (70) It was pointed out by the editor of the *Jersey Evening Post* that this second tower was actually the tower known locally as the "First Tower" and there was a station of that name on the former Jersey Railway. However, there are three Martello towers around St Aubin's Bay, and, by any direction of counting, the second tower is always the one in the middle. Also, a point 440 yards due south of this tower (adjacent to the former Bel Royal railway station) is in the centre of a half mile square of sand, unlike a point 440 yards south of the "First Tower" which includes a large section of the promenade and the built-up area behind, so that some 15% of the half mile square is definitely not sand. Furthermore, the high-water mark is lower down the beach in the area of the "Second" tower. Hence it is reasonable to suppose that the responsible authorities did mean the second tower from St Helier, (as numbered on the contemporary O.S. maps), but Jersey Airways had chosen to use the area nearest to St Helier (for convenience, presumably) and as this was only just outside the ¼ mile radius the editor's interpretation was not opposed.

(D) PORTSMOUTH (See Map No 11)

Opened on July 2, 1932 by Sir Phillip Sassoon, the Under Secretary of State for Air, the Portsmouth Municipal aerodrome was 2½ miles north east of the city centre and one mile from the boundary of the Portsmouth Dockyard prohibited area. The dimensions of the landing area were:- 780 yards, North – South; 700 yards North East – South West; 980 yards East – West; and 1,325 yards South East – North West, but by 1935 these figures had become 800, 820, 980, and 1,100 yards respectively. The extreme W. portion of the landing area was used as a sports ground and when games were in progress red and white boundary markers indicated the western limit of the landing area!

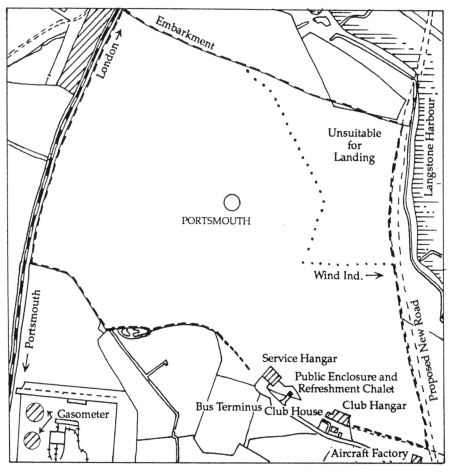

(Map No 11)   Portsmouth airport   (Redrawn from 'The Air Pilot')

Reproduced from a contemporary edition of the Ordnance Survey map

To the north there was a 30 ft. embankment, to the west a railway with 30 ft. telegraph wires, and to the south the hangars and aerodrome buildings together with two gasometers 140 ft. high within a distance of 350 yards from the aerodrome boundary. A mobile radio set was provided by the Air Ministry late in 1934, but a more permanent arrangement followed and by the end of 1935 there were two 70 ft. radio masts amongst the airport hangar 45' x 49', but a new factory was built for the Airspeed company, which moved down from York in March, 1933 to accept the favourable terms offered by the Portsmouth Corporation. Such was Airspeed's financial situation the Corporation stipulated that the factory must be suitable for use as a hangar in the event of the company failing! By 1939 there were four hangars. The first Airspeed machine to be assembled and test flown at Portsmouth was the prototype Courier, a single-engined low-wing monoplane with a retractable undercarriage. In 1936 a production machine was stolen by two employees, neither with any piloting experience, who attempted to take off for a flight to Spain where they hoped to sell the Courier. The plane stalled and crashed into a ditch on the airport boundary. Map No. 11 shows Portsmouth airport as given in *The Air Pilot* of 1934. The last aircraft to land here did so on 31.12.1973.

(E) HESTON (See Map No 12)

11¾ miles West by South from Charing Cross and continuously developed under the progressive management of Airwork Ltd. from 1929 until taken over by the Air Ministry towards the end of 1937. The landing area dimensions in 1934 were:- 700 yards N.-S.; 700 yards N.E.-S.W.; 575 yards E.-W.; and 650 yards S.E.-N.W., but these had been increased to 900, 1,170, 1,200, and 1,150 yards respectively by 1939. By the end of 1935 there were eight hangars, the smallest measuring 130 ft. x 41 ft., and the shadow-bar floodlight in front of the control tower had been replaced by three floodlights in fixed positions on the eastern and southern boundaries, and the north-west corner. See Map No. 12 for details of Heston in 1935. There was a red neon beacon flashing the morse numeral 4 (. . . . -) every eight seconds, the form of the beacon appearing from north and south as a monogram composed of the letters AW (Airwork). There were the normal boundary and obstruction lights, but, under the heading "Obstructions Requiring Special Caution" in *The Air Pilot* was the warning of a "Large gasometer, 307 ft. high, about 1 mile distant" on the North side, and "Four radio masts, two 75 feet high, and two 85 feet high" on the South side (Supplement No. 29, Feb. 1937). The notorious Southall gasometer was left unlit for many years despite considerable agitation on the part of regular Heston users. In March, 1932 Captain Balfour had asked the Under Secretary of State for Air, Sir Phillip Sassoon, whether his Right Honourable Friend was "aware of the disastrous consequences that would

Honourable Friend was "aware of the disastrous consequences that would follow to a neighbourhood such as Southall, if the Gasometer were hit by an aeroplane"? (71) The airport owners disclaimed responsibility and although the Gas Co. were willing to have lights on the gasometer they would not pay for the electricity. The powers of the Air Ministry were limited to a zone within 500 yards of the airport perimeter until increased to 1,000 yards in March, 1936 but the gasometer was over a mile away. In reply to a question from Oliver Simmonds in February, 1936 Sir Phillip announced that the case would "be treated exceptionally, and on its merits . . ." (71), and in August, 1936 the *G.A.P.A.N. Journal* reported that the gasholder was to be lit by eleven lights, and a central light on the ventilator.

The closure of Heston was proclaimed by the Air Ministry in March, 1946 and to-day it is better known as a stop on the motorway, as it is traversed from east to west by the M4 and is the site of the first service station west of London. Some of the hangars still survive, performing other functions, although the control tower block has been demolished.

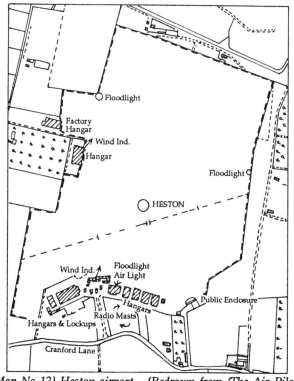

(Map No 12) Heston airport   (Redrawn from 'The Air Pilot')
Reproduced from a contemporary edition of the Ordnance Survey map

(F) SOUTHAMPTON (Eastleigh) (See Map No 13)

The former Atlantic Park U.S. Naval air station was reopened in 1932 as a private civil aerodrome and was not available without the permission of the controlling authority, Southampton Corporation. It was used by the Hampshire Aero Club and Supermarine Vickers. Its local position was 3 miles N.N.E. of Southampton, 1½ miles S. by W. of Eastleigh railway station, and 2/3 mile N.E. of Swaythling railway station. There were two brick, two bay hangars 172 ft. x 204 ft. and one brick, four bay hangar 152 ft. x 244 ft., and the dimensions of the landing area were:- 600 yards N.-S., 700 yards N.E.-S.W., 620 yards E.-W., and 700 yards S.E.-N.W.

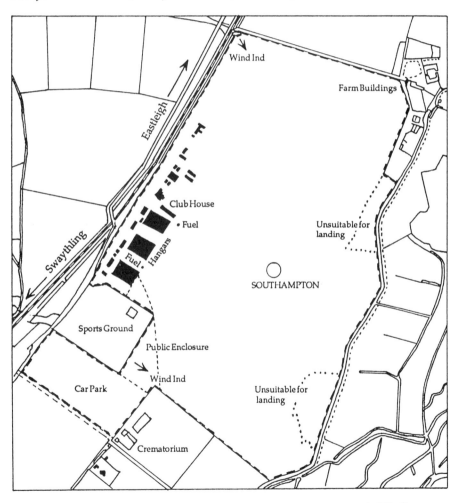

(Map No 13)   Eastleigh Airport   (Redrawn from 'The Air Pilot')

Reproduced from a contemporary edition of the Ordnance Survey map

By 1934 it had been licensed for public use and the landing area then measured:- 1,450 yards N.-S., 600 yards N.E.-S.W., 700 yards E.-W., and 800 yards S.E.-N.W. which, by 1935, had become 1,450, 1,100, 800, and 850 yards respectively. By January, 1936 there were three fixed floodlights, the usual orange boundary lights, and red obstruction lights, and there was a red neon beacon flashing the morse letters SN (. . . - .) every 9.9 seconds. By 1939 there was a fourth hangar 150 ft. x 175 ft. In 1937 radio with D/F became available to assist aircraft approach only, and there were press reports of additional D/F facilities in the Summer of 1939. The manager (from August, 1935) was Mr L.F. Payne, ex. R.A.F., who had been with Redwing Aircraft, Ltd.

Southampton, of course, was the birthplace of the Spitfire, and the prototype, K 5054, (the forerunner of 20,000 plus) was flown for the first time at Eastleigh in March, 1936. Happily, Eastleigh continues in use as a civil airport and has its regular services to the Channel Islands. Map No. 13 shows Eastleigh as given in *The Air Pilot* of 1934.

(G) LE BOURGET (PARIS) (See Map No 14)

This aerodrome was the French equivalent to Croydon and the main airport of Paris from 1919 until 1939. It was first used by a British air-line on July 15, 1919 for the well-known flight of Captain Jerry Shaw of Aircraft Transport & Travel Ltd. who wrote that: ". . . Le Bourget in those days consisted of several canvas hangars, some wooden sheds and a lot of mud. Of course nobody took the slightest interest in our arrival, so I taxied over to the French Air Force Officers' Mess, where I had many friends . . . I had not yet acquired a passport. That deficiency was easily overcome by the simple expedient of boarding a tramcar in the village and alighting once we were through the barrier at the Octroi . . ." (56) Some airport buildings were erected in 1920-24, but were soon found to be inadequate. They remained inadequate for some time and Mr Strachan former Air France Traffic Manager (U.K.) writes: "I wonder whether you knew the old Terminal Building of the 1929/30 era when there was just the one crude building with rough Customs benches, nor any other amenities. The Airlines operated from wooden sheds . . ." (15) Map 14 show Le Bourget as it was at the time of the Jersey Airways service in 1934, but great changes took place before the start of the Paris-Dinard service in 1938. The new terminal buildings were opened on November 12, 1937 and covered 11,000 sq. yds. said *The Times*. The aerodrome was enlarged from 500 to 800 acres and the principal landing line extended from 1,300 to 2,750 yards. As the airport was said to be equipped with optical apparatus, searchlights, and blind-landing apparatus the report was obviously translated from the French! A later *Times* report (10.12.37) said: ". . . the spacious airport building is merely a token of a wider project – One may feel that too much space has been allowed in that incredibly long and lofty building, yet it is perhaps appropriate to an aerodrome which will measure nearly two miles from north to south and a mile and a quarter from east to west. The building is a vast hall fringed on the side near the aerodrome with a narrow band of offices rising in three stories to the flat roof, which may be used as a grandstand . . . More than half of the hall is for the use of travellers and the rest belongs to the Customs service and the staff which handles air freight; the control, wireless, weather, and administrative offices are, or will be housed in the four tiers of the central tower . . . A great restaurant is set on an upper floor . . . Landing Facilities . . . Its size alone is a great comfort . . . but the clearness of its bad weather approach from the north is an additional blessing . . . The approaching aeroplane will come in on a wireless beam, over wireless beacons, and when it reaches the aerodrome it will be helped by white lines set in the surface of the field along the direction of approach, the principal line lit by sodium lights sunk in the ground . . ."

Le Bourget is still an operational aerodrome, but no longer the principal airport of Paris, and the magnificent halls and hangars now house the equally magnificent collection of the Musée de l'Air et de l'Espace.

(H)   ST JACQUES DE LA LANDE (RENNES) (See Map No 15)

This private aerodrome was operated by the Rennes Chamber of Commerce. Although Rennes was the scene of some aviation activity in the early days this may not have been on the site of the present airport, and before the arrival of Jersey Airways flying was probably limited to the activities of the local aero club, Aero-Club d'Ille-et-Vilaine, and there are no records of any other regular air-lines being operated. Map No. 15 shows Rennes as it was in 1935. It is still in use to-day but very much larger and busier.

PARIS - LE BOURGET - DUGNY (Seine)
Aérodrome d'Etat
Port aérien douanier de l'Aéronautique Civile
et Terrain de l'Armée de l'Air

Position :

6 km NE de Paris et 12 km de Notre-Dame, 0 km 200 N du Bourget. — Lat. : 48° 57' N, Long. : 2° 26' E. — Alt. : 44 m.

Description : Aire d'atterrissage : 1.800 m × 1.200 m.

Nature du terrain : gazonné, utilisable en toute saison, mauvais dans sa partie N aux environs de la Morée.

Caractères des environs : S et W, banlieue parisienne impropre aux atterrissages; N et E, région plate.

Reperes :

De jour : à Asnières, sur le toit de l'usine Ford,

lettre B en blanc sur fond noir, avec flèche indiquant la direction de l'aérodrome.

A Goussainville, sur le toit de la gare, lettre B en blanc sur fond rouge avec flèche indiquant la direction de l'aérodrome.

De nuit : Le Bourget, voie ferrée et gare des marchandises.

Ne pas compter sur la lueur de Paris, souvent invisible à quelques kilomètres de distance.

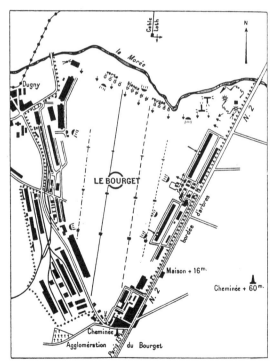

Le Bourget from the "Guide Aérien" of 1935-36 . . (Map No 14)

Reproduced by permission of Michelin, Tourism Department, Paris

298

RENNES

Position : 6 km 500 SW de Rennes,
1 km 500 W de St-Jacques-de-la-
Lande. — Lat. : 48° 04' N, Long. :
1° 45' W. — Alt. : 26 m.

Description : Aire d'atterrissage :
1.100 m × 1.200 m.

    Nature du terrain : ferme, par-
faitement drainé.

    Caractères des environs : région
vallonnée, boisée et coupée de talus,
se prêtant mal aux atterrissages
accidentels.

Installations : 2 hangars : 20 m
× 28 m et 20 m × 30 m. — 🚐
Stations-service : Caudron-Re-
nault, Club. — ☏ 1 Aéroport. (Les
télégrammes peuvent être téléphonés.) — Poste de secours F. A. F.

Ravitaillement : ⛽, ⓗ, ⓔ distributeurs.

Renseignements : M. Gillet, chef pilote, ou à la Chambre de Commerce
de Rennes, ☏ 27.69.

Consignes spéciales : Interdiction de survoler l'arsenal au N-NE du
terrain à 5 km.

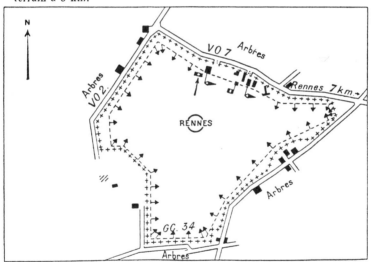

Rennes from the "Guide Aérien" of 1935-36 (Map No 15)

Reproduced by permission of Michelin, Tourism Department, Paris

(J) L'ERÉE (GUERNSEY) (See Map No 16)

About five miles due east of St Peter Port. This aerodrome was below the
general level of the surrounding area. It was separated from L'Erée Bay by
a stone dyke and a road, Rue de la Roque, which was well above the
surface of the aerodrome. In fact the northern part of the airfield was less

than 11 ft. above ordnance datum, whereas the height of a normal spring tide was 13.7 ft. above ordnance datum, and the highest recorded spring tide (up to 1935) was 19.7 ft. above datum.

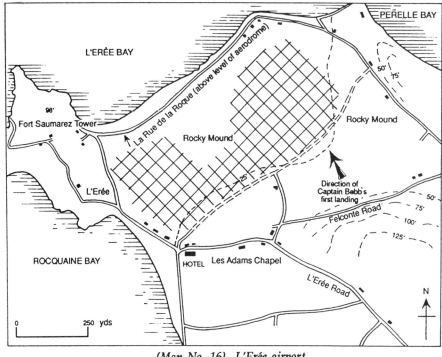

(Map No. 16) L'Erée airport

Based on a sketch in the Guernsey Evening Press of 18.10.35

To the west the Fort Saumarez Martello tower rose to 98 ft., and there was ground rising to 75 ft. on the N.E. and to 125 ft. just south of the Felconte Road. It was granted a temporary licence for commercial operation by aircraft of the Westland Wessex type only, and this lapsed with the departure of Cobham Air Routes. Few details were published at the time, and it never appeared in the pages of *The Air Pilot*, but the min. length of run was less than 300 yards (in the N.W.-S.E. direction) with a max. of about 450 yards (in the N.E.-S.W. direction). Despite Olley's attempt to make improvements it was never re-licensed and very much out of the running once La Villiaze was authorized. It has now reverted to agricultural purposes. See Map No. 16 for the approx. position of the landing area, indicated by the cross-hatching.

There were few facilities, and refuelling was by means of a fuel tank man-handled into position, and the offices and waiting rooms were in a near-by house called "Les Sablons".

(K)   CROYDON (See Map No 17)

Situated 10½ miles S. of London (Charing Cross), 2 miles S.W. of Croydon, and 1¼ miles N.N.W. of Purley, Croydon was Britain's premier airport and the Heathrow of pre-war years. It was the main airport for international traffic and our equivalent of Paris's Le Bourget and Berlin's Tempelhof.

When used in 1935 for just nine weeks by Cobham Air Routes the fortunate few arriving from Guernsey and Bournemouth with Captain Bebb in the Envoy G-ADBA saw Croydon in its hey day. On the concrete apron surrounding the control tower and admin. block they could have seen the Handley Page Heracles and Short Scylla types of Imperial Airways, the Wibaults of Air France, the Junkers 52's of Luft Hansa, the Fokker F XII's of K.L.M. and much else besides. Croydon was controlled by the Air Ministry and in 1935 the landing area dimensions were:- 900 yards N.-S., 1,000 yards N.E.-S.W., 700 yards E.-W., and 900 yards S.E.-N.W. There were two hangars 303 ft. x 152 ft., and one 720 ft. x 150 ft., all of steel and concrete, the first two having two bays, and the third six bays. It had the usual boundary and obstruction lights, a neon beacon at the south end of the hangars, and for night-landings there was a mobile 1,000,000 candle-power floodlight with a beam of 180 degrees divergence which was directed up wind. A conspicuous land-mark 5 miles N.N.E. was Crystal Palace and although burned down on 1.12.36 the two tall towers remained. Nearer the airport boundary obstructions included tramway wires 30 ft. high on the N. side, and a few years earlier (1931) an Air Union Farman Goliath was nearly in collision with a tram when it over-shot and went through the fence into Stafford Road. Croydon was a controlled zone in QBI conditions (visibility less than 1,000 yds.) which meant that aircraft could only enter the zone with permission, whilst others waited their turn, and aircraft without radio were prohibited. It was responsible for the Radio Area Zone known as the London-Continental Airway which was bounded approximately on the north by the north bank of the Thames from Kingston to Westminster and then by straight lines joining Stapleford aerodrome (Essex), Clacton, and the North Hinder Light Vessel; on the south-east by a straight line from the N. Hinder light to Ostend and then the coast to Dieppe; and on the west by straight lines joining Dieppe,

Newhaven, Dorking, and Kingston. The control tower could obtain bearings of, and communicate with, aircraft by R/T on 825 m, and by W/T on 900 m (receiving) and 893 m (transmitting). Also, there was a short-range system for incoming machines only in bad weather, which received on 923 m and transmitted on 932 m, and this was equipped with a D/F loop. In conjunction with the radio stations at Lympne and Pulham, Croydon was capable of giving a pilot his correct position (within about 2 miles) in less than two minutes from the time of the request. Other wavelengths were in use for communication with various ground stations, and for met. purposes.

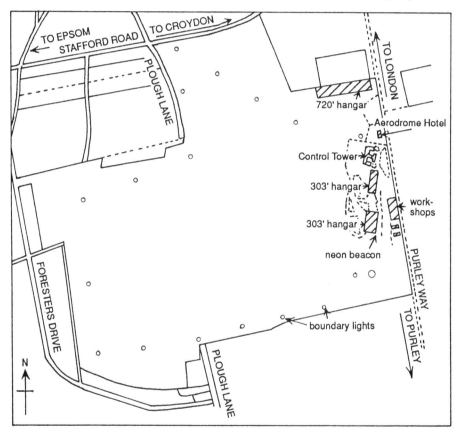

(Map No 17) Croydon Airport Redrawn from the 1929 London airport Guide
Reproduced from a contemporary edition of the Ordnance Survey map

The Croydon boundaries in 1935 were Purley Way on the east, Stafford Road on the north, and Foresters Drive on the west (See Map No. 17), but it started life as two separate aerodromes divided by Plough Lane running due south from Stafford Road, and the two ends of Plough Lane still exist.

To the west of Plough Lane was Beddington, one of a ring of airfields built round London for protection against Zeppelins, which began its R.F.C. career in January, 1916 with the arrival of two B.E.2c's. The first operational sortie from Beddington took place on January 31, 1916 when Zeppelins were reported crossing the coast. To the east of Plough Lane was the Waddon National Aircraft factory which started production in January, 1918 and test flew the aircraft on its own Waddon aerodrome. In 1920 the two airfields were combined together as Croydon and replaced Hounslow as the Customs Air Port for London. Aircraft landed on the Waddon side and the control and the temporary wooden buildings used by the operating companies, such as Handley Page and Instone, were on the east side of Plough Lane, but there was a level crossing so that aircraft could be moved across the lane to the hangars on the west side of Plough Lane. In 1928 new control buildings and hangars were built on the opposite side of the Waddon field adjacent to Purley Way and the old buildings, and much of Plough Lane itself, removed to make a single large aerodrome. Croydon airport became one of the "sights" of London and had its own official guide book, but it was closed down on 30.9.59. Happily the famous old control tower and terminal buildings survive intact, and the Aerodrome Hotel still performs its original function.

(L)   BOURNEMOUTH (Christchurch) (See Map No 18)

Situated about one mile E. of Christchurch the eastern boundary was formed by the River Mude which runs into Christchurch Harbour near Mudeford. On the N.W. its boundary was about 200 yards from the London-Christchurch road behind the main frontage on the S. side of this road, since replaced by the modern A35 about ½ mile farther N. On the S.W. the boundary was about 300 yards from the nearest houses of the estates being developed paralled to the road to Mudeford from Christchurch (Purewell). The dimensions of the grass landing area were:- 860 yards N.-S., 800 yards N.E.-S.W., 650 yards E.-W., and 750 yards S.E.-N.W., and the controlling authority was Bournemouth Air Port, Ltd. Nothing came of the great plans of 1935 and by 1938 there were just three wooden hangars measuring 12' x 26' and very little else. The only obstructions in the vicinity were trees, 35' high, on the eastern boundary, and given sufficient warning before sunset, a flare path could be laid out for a night landing. Map No. 18 shows Christchurch in 1938. During the war a new aerodrome was built at Hurn, 4 mls. N.N.E. of Bournemouth and this eventually replaced Christchurch which is now an industrial estate.

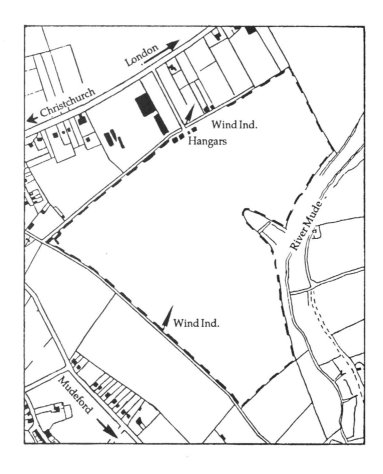

(Map No 18)   Christchurch airport   (Redrawn from the 'The Air Pilot')
Reproduced from a contemporary edition of the Ordnance Survey map

(M) ALDERNEY

The isle of Alderney is about 3½ miles long and one mile wide, with its axis running approximately W.S.W. to E.N.E. At the southern end of the island the rugged coast line runs due east from Telegraph Bay and not very far inland from the top of the cliffs was the southern boundary of the aerodrome which lay on the western side of a plateau called La Grande Blaye. It was 1 ml. S.W. of St Anne.

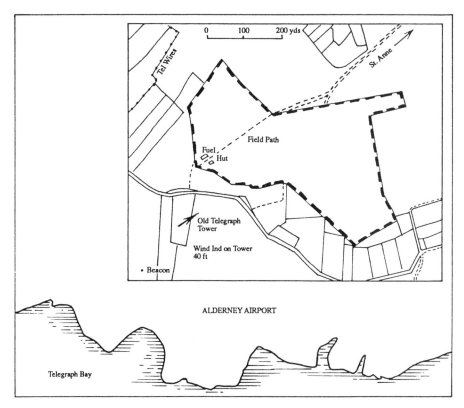

(Map No 19) Alderney Airport (Redrawn from the 'The Air Pilot')
Reproduced from a contemporary edition of the Ordnance Survey map

In 1939 the landing area dimensions were:- 365 yards, N.-S.; 330 yards N.E.-S.W.; 570 yards E.-W.; and 600 yards S.E.-N.W. at an altitude of 292 feet above mean sea level. The controlling authority was Channel Island Airways, and as a private aerodrome it could not be used without their consent. To the S.W. 187 yards from the airport perimeter was the old Telegraph Tower, 40 ft. high, surmounted by a wind-sock, and on the other side of the roadway, almost opposite the pathway leading to the tower was the entrance to the airfield, and the tiny office used by Miss Le Cocq when dealing with the aircraft. Customs were available with prior warning and Channel Island Airways had a hand-pump for refuelling.

Alderney airport is still in use, considerably enlarged, and the control tower and terminal buildings, of modest size, are now on the St Anne side of the field giving more convenient access. Map No. 19 shows the aerodrome as first published in *The Air Pilot* (supplement of May, 1939) super-imposed on a very approximate outline of the adjacent coast.

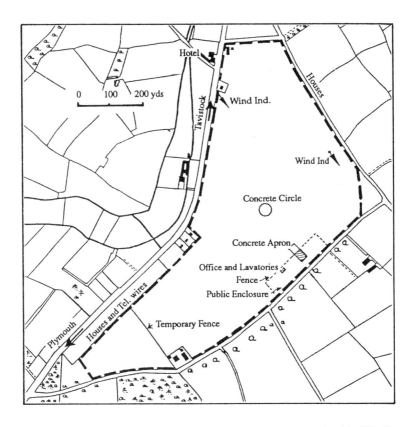

(Map No 20)   Plymouth Airport   (Redrawn from the 'The Air Pilot')
Reproduced from a contemporary edition of the Ordnance Survey map

(N)   PLYMOUTH (Roborough) (See Map No 20)

Situated about four miles N.N.E. of Plymouth on the east side of the main
Plymouth-Tavistock road (A386) Roborough was officially opened in 1931,
but was used by Jersey Airways for regular services in the summer of 1936
only. At this time the controlling authority was Plymouth Airport, Ltd., a
subsidiary of the Straight Corporation, and the landing area dimensions
were:- 775 yds. N.-S.; 750 yds. N.E.-S.W.; 500 yds. E.-W.; and 550 yds.
S.E.-N.W. Altitude 460 ft. There were no lights and no radio, but there
was a control officer, to whom pilots were asked to report, and a Customs
officer was available given the usual notice. There was one steel and
asbestos hangar, 82 ft. x 90 ft. surmounted by the control tower, a
restaurant, and a club-house and the grass covered landing area was
"slightly dome-shaped". Fuel, oil, and fresh water were available which

306

may or may not have been an improvement on the earlier situation when the "George Hotel", adjoining the N.W. corner of the landing ground, was given as the source of fuel, oil, fresh water, and accommodation. Map No. 20 shows Roborough as it was in 1936. (*The Air Pilot*)

(P) JERSEY (St Peter's) (See Map No 21)

Approx. 4 mls, W.N.W. from St Helier, between St Peter and St Ouen's Bay, under the controlling authority of the States of Jersey, the St Peter's airport was opened for public use on 10.3.37. The landing area dimensions were:- 528 yds. N.-S.; 720 yds. N.E.-S.W.; 980 yds. E.-W.; and 720 yds. S.E.-N.W. at an altitude of 273 ft. It was a typical grass airfield of the time and the above figures give the max. length of run in the given directions, but there were no concrete runways as on modern aerodromes and the pilot could use any part of the landing area. As an aid to taking off in bad visibility there was a 980 yard white concrete fog-line in the direction 083 to 263 degrees (True) corresponding to the max. length of run available in the E.-W. direction. Wind velocity is normally low in fog conditions. There was one hangar 220' x 100' and one 110' x 100', both of steel and concrete construction, and Map No. 21 shows the situation when published in the *Air Pilot* supplement No. 43 of April, 1938. There were four fixed flood-lights of 6,000 watts each giving an output of one and a quarter million candle-power, and the usual orange boundary lights and red obstruction lights. Mounted on a tower 1,900 yds. south of the aerodrome (at Red Houses, about a ¼ of a mile north of St Brelade's church) was a beacon flashing one white light for 0.1 sec. after an eclipse of 3.9 secs. visible 30 mls., and above this was a red neon beacon flashing the letter J in morse (. - - -) ever four seconds during the eclipse of the white light. It was in operation daily for 1½ hrs. after sunset, or on request. During the daylight hours the airfield could be identified by a white circle 100' in diameter and the word JERSEY in white letters.

The temporary radio station which had been in use for over two years was moved to permanent accommodation and four 100' radio masts were erected 400 yds. S.E. of the admin. building. The station was equipped with sets capable of transmitting and received R/T or W/T on the 20-200 and 750-1500 m wave-bands, and there was an Adcock D/F apparatus. From October, 1937 the airport and the surrounding area became a "controlled zone" in QBI (i.e. bad weather conditions), and from December, 1938 it was the Area Station for the air space bounded by the Portsmouth, Exeter, Tours, and Le Bourget areas. Enlarged and improved it is still very much in use to-day.

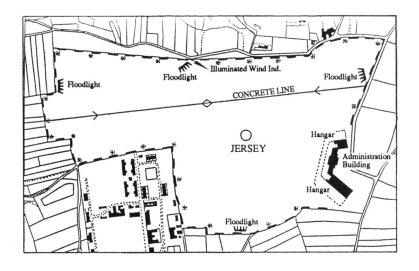

(Map No 21) Jersey Airport   (Redrawn from the 'The Air Pilot')
Reproduced from a contemporary edition of the Ordnance Survey map

(Q) BRIGHTON (Shoreham) (Map No 22)

On the west bank of the Adur and immediately north of the railway line the controlling authority was Olley Air Service Ltd. on behalf of the municipal authorities of Brighton, Hove, and Worthing. In 1937 the landing area dimensions were:- 800 yds. N.-S.; 750 yds. N.E.-S.W.; 730 yds. E.-W.; and 760 yds. S.E.-N.W., but by 1939 these figures had been increased to 1,000, 760, 760, and 1.050 yards respectively. Its altitude was 10 ft. above mean sea level. The airport was completed in September, 1935 and officially opened in 1936, and Map No. 22 (from *The Air Pilot*) shows it as it was in 1937 with two steel and asbestos hangars, each 106' x 100'. By 1939 there were two more hangars each measuring 175' x 95'. There were the usual orange boundary lights and red obstruction lights and a mobile floodlight could be located in any of the four corners of the airfield. Mounted on a hangar 48 ft. above the ground was a red beacon, visible 12 mls. flashing the letters BT in morse (- . . . . -). These lights had not been provided by February, 1937, but were available in March, 1939, on request. Obstructions in the vicinity were the electric power cables running east-west on pylons 40-80 ft. high, 800 yds. distant, and the chapel of Lancing College, 225' above sea level and 1,100 yds. distant. Shoreham remains in use and in appearance has changed very little since it was first built in 1935.

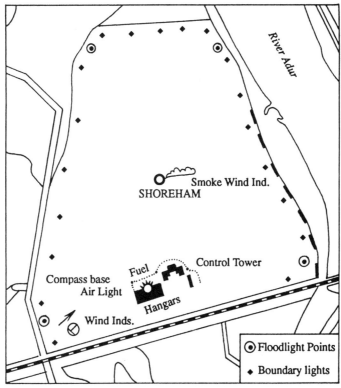

(Map No 22) Brighton Airport   (Redrawn from the 'The Air Pilot')
Reproduced from a contemporary edition of the Ordnance Survey map

(R)   EXETER (Clyst Honiton) (See Map No 23)

Situated about 4½ mls. due east from Exeter city centre and about ½ ml. from Clyst Honiton along the road leading to Aylesbeare. Clyst Honiton is on the main London road (A30). The controlling authority was Exeter Airport, Ltd., a branch of the Straight Corporation. Whitney Straight's idea was to run a number of aerodromes in order to cut costs, and to make them social centres with restaurants, squash courts, and so forth. By 1939 the Straight Corporation was responsible for Ramsgate, Ipswich, Clacton, Exeter, Haldon, Plymouth, Weston-Super-Mare, Swansea, and Inverness. The landing area dimensions were:- 700 yds. N.-S.; 870 yds N.E.-S.W.; 750 yds. E.-W.; and 780 yds. S.E.-N.W. and the altitude 100' above mean sea level. Although in use since May, 1937 the official opening was not until 1938 when the terminal block was completed, and Map No. 23 (from *The Air Pilot*) shows the aerodrome as it was in 1937 with one steel and asbestos hangar measuring 90' x 65'.

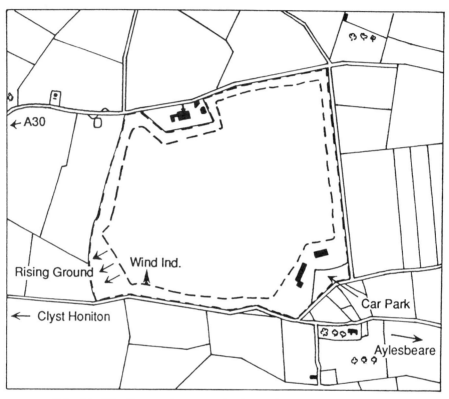

(Map No 23) Exeter Airport   (Redrawn from the 'The Air Pilot')
Reproduced from a contemporary edition of the Ordnance Survey map

A ground engineer was available and fuel, oil, and water could be obtained, but there was no lighting for night landings, and no radio. By 1939 there was a licensed restaurant, and work was proceeding on a radio station, as Exeter had been designated the Area Station for the South-West, bordering the area stations of Jersey, Portsmouth, and Bristol. The only obstructions were trees 55' high on the south-east side. Clyst Honiton continues to function as a civil aerodrome.

(S) DINARD-PLEURTUIT (See Map No 24)

About 5 km. S.S.W. of Dinard and 2 km. N.W. of Pleurtuit this aerodrome, named after Brindejonc des Moulinais, a local First World War pilot of note, lies to the south of the Route Nationale 168 (D 168) in the vicinity of the Bois de Ponthual and to the west of the railway line from Dinan to Dinard.

Originally it was the Dinard Race Course (Hippodrome), but from 1927 on attempts were made to permit its use by aircraft. By 1930 it was suitable for commercial operation by a company called STAR (Société des Transports Aériens Rapides) which offered flights to Cherbourg, Deauville and Paris for 275f, 350f, and 600f respectively, but this company did not survive for long and aviation at the Hippodrome appears to have lapsed until 1 April, 1936 when it was officially opened as Dinard Airport. In 1938 it was taken over by the French Air Ministry and the landing area increased to give a run of 1,400 metres.

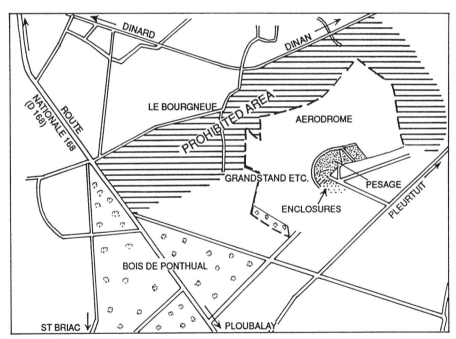

(Map No 24)   Dinard-Pleurtuit airport

Map No. 24 is based on the aerodrome plan provided at the back of the official programme issued for the "Fêtes Aériennes de Dinard" which took place on 28 August, 1938 with evidence of horse-racing very prominent in its lay-out. The sinister-looking "zone interdite" probably indicated the part of the aerodrome where enlargement, levelling, and other work was in progress rather than highly-secret military installations, and as the object of the plan was to help spectators find their way to the correct enclosure no information was given regarding the facilities available for aviators. Probably not a great deal, although the Dinard Aero Club was active, and in 1938 and 1939 the airport was used by Jersey Airways, Air France, and Wrightways Ltd.

(T) GUERNSEY (La Villiaze) (See Map No 25)

Located some 3 miles W.S.W. of St Peter Port on the highest part of the island (345 ft.) La Villiaze was opened on May 5, 1939 just four months before the outbreak of war and too late to appear in *The Air Pilot*, but the following details have been obtained from the brochure published by the States of Guernsey for the official opening:- The approximately L-shaped landing area gives a max. run of 1,020 yards with a minimum of 680 yards and there is a 950 yard concrete fog-line. Also in concrete is a 100 ft. dia. circle and the name GUERNSEY in letters 20 ft. long. No gradient is steeper than 1 in 50, and the perimeter is marked by 26 orange boundary lights. Any obstructions in the immediate vicinity are marked by twin red lights and four 6,000 watt floodlights are available for night landings together with an illuminated wind-tee. From a distance the aerodrome can be identified by a 200,000 candle-power beacon sending out a red flash once in every four seconds. The terminal building is on the south side with access from Forest Road and, according to *Flight* it is of a "somewhat familiar layout – since the design work . . . has been in the hands of Norman and Dawbarn – and has two floors with an observation centre above the control room. A large hangar is now in process of erection . . ."

That they had gone one better than their neighbours was admitted by the *Jersey Evening Post* of 25.4.39 when comparing the new airport's dimensions with "The Jersey flightways" and saying "it will be seen that Guernsey has a decided advantage over this island in that respect . . ."

The landing fees complied with Air Ministry recommendations and were similar to those of Jersey at this time:- For every passenger landed or embarked 1/9d. reduced to 1/- if landed from or embarked for another Channel Island, also 1/- for every passenger from Guernsey landed at

Guernsey (i.e. joy flights). For excess baggage, mail, or freight 1/- per lb. (6d. min.), or 9d. and 3d. respectively if to or from other Channel Islands. Per aircraft landing 4½d. per 1,000 lbs. of max. authorised weight of aircraft (if from outside the Channel Islands). Night landings 7/6d.

Larger and busier La Villiaze continues in use as Guernsey's airport and recently celebrated its 50th anniversary.

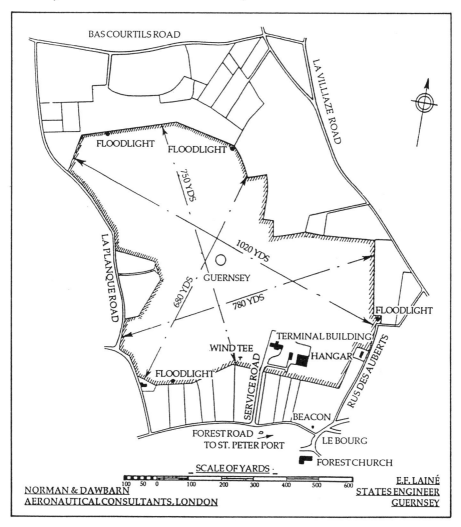

(Map 25) From States of Guernsey Official Opening Programme 5.5.39
(By kind permission of the Airport Director)

REFERENCES

1. *"De Havilland Gazette"*, April 1954
2. *"The Pioneer Days of Aviation in Jersey"*, J. Edouard Slade, 1965/1966.
3. *"The Aeroplane"*, contemporary with event described.
4. *"The Aeroplane"*, 23.12.36.
5. Crown copyright – AVIA 2/666. P.R.O., Kew
6. *"Jersey Evening Post"*.
7. Jersey Official Leisure Map, 1:25000, Ordnance Survey.
8. *"Jersey Almanac"*, 1934
9. *"Air and Airways"*, August, 1932.
10 *"Aeroplane Monthly"*, December, 1979.
11. Jersey Airway's time-tables, 1934
12. Crown copyright – RAIL 258/510, P.R.O., Kew.
13. Crown copyright – RAIL 258/513, P.R.O., Kew.
14. Crown copyright – RAIL 258/512, P.R.O., Kew.
15. Mr Leslie Strachan, Correspondence.
16. *"Pathfinder"*, Air Vice-Marshal D.C.T. Bennett, C.B., C.B.E., D.S.O., Muller. 1958.
17. *"Aerial A.B.C."*, May-July, 1929.
18. *"Architect of Air Power"*, W.J. Reader, Collins. 1968.
19. *"Nottingham Evening Post"*, 20.8.34.
20. *"Flight"*, contemporary with event described.
21. *"A Time to Fly"*, Sir Alan Cobham, Shepheard-Walwyn. 1978.
22. *"Guernsey Evening Press"*.
23. *"Guernsey Star"*.
24. *"Popular Flying"*, November, 1935.
25. *"Flight"*, 24.10.35.
26. *"Jersey Morning News"*.
27. Pearson Archives, Science Museum Library, Kensington.
28. *"Weather Flying"*, R.N. Buck, Black. 1977.
29. *"Channel Islands Pilot"*, Admiralty.
30. *"The Mary Deare"*, Hammond Innes, Collins.
31. *"Jersey Evening Post"*, 15.2.37.
32. Crown copyright – AVIA 5/18, P.R.O., Kew.
33. *"Wings Over Westminster"*, Lord Balfour of Inchrye, P.C., M.C., Hutchinson. 1973.
34. Mr. J.W. Beuzeval, Correspondence and conversation.
35 Senator the Rev. Peter Manton, Correspondence.
36. *"Early Birds"*, Alfred Instone, *Western Mail & Echo* 1938.
37. *"Flight"*, 6.4.22.
38. *"From Many Angles"*, Major-General Sir F. Sykes, G.C.S.I., C.G.I.E., G.B.E., K.C.B., C.M.G., Harrap 1942.
39. *"The Aeroplane"*, 30.6.20.

40. *"The Aeroplane"*, 6.11.35

41. *"Channel T.V,Times"*, 9.3.85

42. *"Aeroplane Monthly"*, February, 1981.

43. *Journal of the Guild of Air Pilots and Navigators.* April, 1936.

44. *"Popular Flying"*, February, 1939.

45. Crown copyright – AVIA 2/1059, P.R.O., Kew.

46. Crown copyright – AVIA 2/2025, P.R.O., Kew.

47. Crown copyright – AVIA 2/2171, P.R.O., Kew.

48. British Airways Archives.

49. *"Bournemouth Echo"*.

50. *"Southern Daily Echo"*.

51. Crown copyright – AVIA 2/1705, P.R.O., Kew.

52. *"Wings"*, Henri Biard, Hurst & Blackett 1934.

53. *"Popular Flying"*, September, 1935.

54. Air Ministry Agreement made with the British, Foreign, and Colonial Corporation, Ltd. providing for the formation of a Heavier-than-Air Transport Company . . . H.M.S.O., Kingsway.

55. *"Recollections of an Airman"*, Lt.-Col. L.A. Strange, D.S.O., M.C., D.F.C. John Hamilton 1933,

56. *"The Seven Skies"*, John Pudney, Putnam 1959.

57. Journal of the Royal Aeronautical Society, January, 1966.

58. *"Empire of the Air"*, Viscount Templewood, Collins 1957.

59. *"The Forging of a Family"*, Lord Geddes, G.C.M.G., K.C.B.(Mil.), M.D. Faber & Faber 1952.

60. *"Croissants at Croydon"*, J.M. Bamford, Sutton Libraries & Arts 1986.

61. *"Air"*, January, 1929.

62. *"Air"*, February, 1929.

63. *"Nine Lives Plus"*, The Hon. Mrs. Victor Bruce, F.R.G.S. Pelham 1977.

64. *"The Great Crash 1929"*, Professor J.K. Galbraith, Ph.D. Hamish Hamilton 1954.

65. *"Meccano Magazine"*, March, 1939.

66. The Log Book of Geoffrey R. de Havilland, D.H. Museum, Hatfield.

67. *"Airways"*, June, 1926.

68. *"Twenty Thousands Miles in a Flying Boat"* Sir Alan Cobham, Harrap 1930.

69. *"Jersey Morning News"*, 10.3.37.

70. *"The Air Pilot"*, Air Ministry, 1929-39.

71. *"The Daily News"*.

72. *"L'Ouest Éclair"*.

73. *"Guide Aérien"* 1935-36 Michelin.

74. Journal of the Croydon Airport Society, Issue 6, 1983.

75. Bradshaw's International Air Guide, August, 1939.

76. Captain Cecil Bebb, Correspondence.

77. *"Wings over the Channel."* M. Romain, Jersey Morning News.

BIBLIOGRAPHY

Air Ministry, Annual Reports on the Progress of Civil Aviation. 1923–39.

Air Ministry, *"The Cloud Aeroplane (Amphibian)"* Air Publication 1462 H.M.S.O.

Aldcroft, D.H., *"Studies in British Transport History, 1870–1970"* David & Charles, 1974.

Baldwin, N.C. *"Catalogue of Internal Air Mails, 1910–41"* F.J. Field, 1941.

Brackley, Frida, *"Brackles"*, Putnam, 1952.

Collier, Basil, *"Heavenly Adventurer"*, Secker & Warburg, 1939.

Grey, C.G., *"A History of the Air Ministry"*, Allen & Unwin, 1940.

Hatchard, David, *"Southampton/Eastleigh Airport"*, Kingfisher, 1990.

Higham, Robin, *"Britain's Imperial Air Routes 1918–1939"* Foulis, 1960.

Imperial Airways, Ltd. *"Pilot's Handbook & General Instructions, 1924."* (Reprint), Ducimus Books, 1974.

Jackson, A.J., *"British Civil Aircraft, 1919–59"*, Putnam , 1959.

Jones, T. Merton, *"A.A.J.C."*, Propliner, July-September, 1981.

Lake, Chris, *"Jersey Airport, The First 50 Years"*, Stephen, 1987.

Layzell, Alastair, *"Announcing The Arrival"* CTV, 1987.

Learmouth, Nash, and Cluett, *"Croydon Airport – The Great Days, 1928–39"*, Sutton Libraries and Arts Services, 1977.

London, Peter, *"Saunders and Saro Aircraft Since 1917"* Putnam , 1988.

Middlemas, R.K., *"The Master Builders"*, Hutchinson, 1963.

Morgan & Andrews, *"Supermarine Aircraft Since 1914"*, 1981.

Moss, P.W., *"The de Havilland 84 Dragon"* Aircraft Illustrated, July, 1969.

Penrose, Harald, *"Widening Horizons, 1930–34"*, H.M.S.O., 1979.

Penrose Harald, *"Ominous Skies 1935–39"*, H.M.S.O., 1980.

Rance, A.B., *"Sea Planes and Flying Boats of the Solent"*, Southampton University & City Museums. 1981.

Riding, R. *"De Havilland, The Golden Years 1919–39"*, IPC Transport Press, 1981.

Spender, J.A., *"Weetman Pearson, First Viscount Cowdray"* Cassell, 1930.

States of Guernsey, Billets D'Etat – Appendices – Passengers Arrivals 1924–30.

Thetford, Owen, *"Aircraft of the Royal Air Force 1918–58"* Putnam, 1958.

Thetford, Owen, *"British Naval Aircraft Since 1912"*, Putnam, 1962.

Worrall, Geoff. *"Exeter Airport in Peace and War"*, Devon Books, 1988.

INDEX